Guides to Wines & Top Vi

C000127790

Burgundy: Complete

2022 Edition

Benjamin Lewin MW

ISBN 9798496832939

Vendange Press

www.vendangepress.com

Preface

This Guide combines the guides to the Côte d'Or, Côte Chalonnaise, Mâcon, and Chablis to present a complete view of all Burgundy. In the first part, I address the nature of the wines made today and ask how this has changed, how it's driven by tradition or competition, and how styles may evolve in the future. I show how the wines are related to the terroir and to the types of grape varieties that are grown, and I explain the classification system. For each region, I suggest reference wines that illustrate the character and variety of the area.

In the second part, there's no single definition for what constitutes a top producer. Leading producers range from those who are so prominent as to represent the common public face of an appellation to those who demonstrate an unexpected potential on a tiny scale. The producers profiled in the guide represent the best of both tradition and innovation in wine in the region. In each profile, I have tried to give a sense of the producer's aims for his wines, of the personality and philosophy behind them—to meet the person who makes the wine, as it were, as much as to review the wines themselves.

Each profile gives contact information and details of production, followed by a description of the producer and the range of wines. For major producers (rated from 1 to 4 stars), I suggest reference wines that are a good starting point for understanding the style. Most of the producers welcome visits, although some require appointments: details are in the profiles. Profiles are organized geographically, and each group of profiles is preceded by maps showing the locations of producers to help plan itineraries.

The guide is based on many visits to France over recent years. I owe an enormous debt to the many producers who cooperated in this venture by engaging in discussion and opening innumerable bottles for tasting. This guide would not have been possible without them.

Benjamin Lewin

Contents

Profiles of Producers

Tables

Appellation Maps

Producer Maps

Overview of Burgundy

Burgundy is nonpareil for two of the world's most grape varieties. At its peak, the Pinot Noir of Burgundy has a sublime, sensuous quality that no other wine in the world can match. And while Burgundy remains unchallenged as the pinnacle for Pinot Noir, the greatest Chardonnays in the world also come from here.

No one knows exactly when wine production started in Burgundy, but there was a vineyard in Gevrey Chambertin by the first century. Vines were well distributed in Burgundy by 312, when Emperor Constantin visited Autun and discussed the economic difficulties of producing wine in the region. Burgundy originated as a distinct region in the fifth century.

With Dijon as their capital from the ninth to fifteenth centuries, the Dukes of Burgundy ruled from the eastern end of the Loire (around Sancerre) to Auxerre in the north (the present area of Chablis), across to the Dijon-Mâcon axis. Aside from Sancerre, which was split off in the fifteenth century, the old Duchy more or less coincides with the limits of Burgundy today.

During the thousand years following the fall of the Roman Empire, the Church became the driving force for viticulture. Many of today's top vineyards were established in the first millennium. Founded near Mâcon in 910, the Benedictine abbey of Cluny was a major influence, until it declined and was replaced by the Cistercian abbey of Cîteaux. The monks kept busy, and the region from Auxerre to Beaune was described as "a sea of vines."

The notion that Burgundy should be devoted to producing wine of high quality goes back at least to the end of the fourteenth century, when Philip the Bold issued his famous edict requiring "bad and disloyal" Gamay grapes to be uprooted, and to be replaced by Pinot. (The basic objection to Gamay was that it was too productive).

Burgundy's focus on Pinot Noir and Chardonnay dates from the replanting that was forced by the phylloxera epidemic at the end of the nineteenth century. Today Burgundy produces 65% white wine and 26% red wine: another 9% is Crémant (sparkling wine). The heart of Burgundy, where the greatest wines are produced, is the Côte d'Or, a narrow strip of vineyards running south from Dijon through Beaune to Chagny. It is divided into two parts: in the north, the Côte de Nuits produces almost exclusively red wine; in the south, the Côte de Beaune is split between red and white. There's a trend to move from black to white grapes when vineyards are replanted.

Chablis is an outpost well to the north and west, where the cooler climate supports only white wine. To the south, the Côte Chalonnaise follows the Côte d'Or in style, but with less concentration and complexity. Then farther south the Mâconnais is devoted almost exclusively to Chardonnay. Over the border from the Mâconnais lies Beaujolais, almost entirely producing red wine, but with a switch to Gamay as the sole black grape (see *Guide to Southern Burgundy and Beaujolais*).

The Appellation Hierarchy

The view that every vineyard has a different potential is the basis for Burgundy's highly hierarchical appellation system. The classification system is organized into a relatively steep pyramid, steadily narrowing from the base of two thirds of regional AOPs, to a quarter in village appellations, with 11% of premier crus and 1.4% of grand crus at the peak.

At the base of the pyramid, generic Bourgogne AOPs can come from anywhere in the entire region of Burgundy. This includes a very wide range of wines, extending from those including Gamay and Aligoté to those coming from Pinot Noir or Chardonnay from just outside the borders of famous vil-

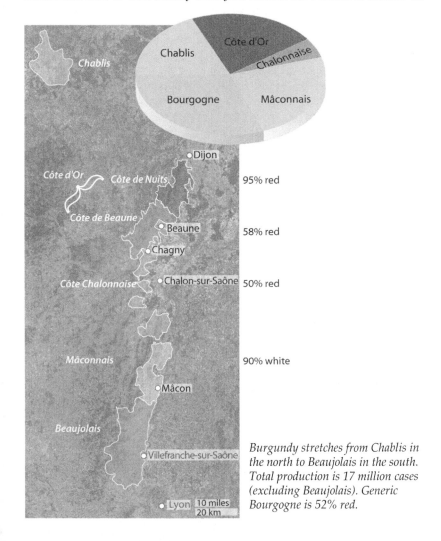

95% red

58% red

50% red

90% white

Burgundy stretches from Chablis in the north to Beaujolais in the south. Total production is 17 million cases (excluding Beaujolais). Generic Bourgogne is 52% red.

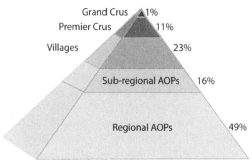

Grand crus and premier crus (in the Côte d'Or and Chablis) are only a small part of production.

lages. It's now allowed to put the name of the grape variety on the label. The name of the producer is the only guide to the potential quality of Bourgogne AOP.

The next level up is sub-regional, indicated by Bourgogne followed by the name of a region. such as Bourgogne Côte Chalonnaise or Bourgogne Hautes Côtes de Nuits. (Officially they are called regional appellations with geographical denomination.)

Smaller areas identified simply by their name, such as Chablis or Mâcon or Côtes de Nuits, are higher in the hierarchy. Within these areas, the next level consists of individual villages. The communes of the Côte d'Or and Côte Chalonnaise, and also some of the Mâconnais, are the most important village AOPs. Of course, they vary significantly in quality. Within each area there's a gradation of quality from the lesser to the best regarded villages. A village wine is identified by the name of the village followed by AOP. But the villages are only the start of detailed classification in Burgundy: within each village, the best plots are assigned to premier or grand crus. The definition of Crus is at its most detailed in the Côte d'Or, where it originated.

The Scale of Burgundy

"I have 10 ha and I make 10 different wines," really tells the story of Burgundy: when you ask a producer how many hectares he has and how many different appellation wines he makes, the answers are often pretty much the same. So the typical wine is made in quite small quantities—around 15-20 barrels or 5,000 bottles. Sometimes amounts of premier crus are so small that it's not worth maturing them separately, in which case a label may simply say premier cru, without an individual name, meaning that the wine comes from a blend of from premier crus within a village.

Usually a producer's range starts with Bourgogne, continues with a village wine, and then has several individual premier or sometimes grand crus. Bourgogne from a small producer usually comes from vines just outside his village, and may therefore be at a completely different level from Bourgogne sourced from lesser areas of Burgundy. A new sub-regional AOP was introduced for the Côte d'Or in 2017, and may now be used for vineyards outside the famous communes that previously were only Bourgogne. It had much limited impact at first, because, at this level, the producer's name (and the price) has more significance. "Bourgogne Côte d'Or doesn't mean much for us. Our clients know where our wines come from, it may have more significance for larger negociants," says winemaker Thomas Pascal at Domaine François Carillon.

Before the French Revolution in 1789, most vineyards were owned by the Church or large landowners. Afterwards they were confiscated as "biens nationaux" and subdivided. Now most premier and grand crus are divided between multiple owners, and the situation is exacerbated by the requirement of French inheritance law that an estate must be split equally between all the heirs. Once a single vineyard, today Clos Vougeot's 50 hectares are distributed among 80 growers; the largest has only 5.5 ha, and the smallest has only a few rows of vines. In Chambertin, the holdings of the smallest proprietors are measured in ares (a hundredth of a hectare or 100 square meters), producing at most a few hundred bottles.

The price of land has become a major issue. The sea change is indicated by Marie-Andrée Mugneret's recollection that, "A Clos Vougeot was the first parcel my father (Georges Mugneret) bought in 1953 when he was a medical student. But I doubt that a medical student could afford to buy in Clos Vougeot now!" A single hectare in Vosne Romanée now runs for more than $2 million, premier crus achieve a multiple of that, and the peak, at Le Montrachet, commands around $20 million. This is a driving force for family estates to sell out to larger organizations. "Burgundy is the most authentic region. This is a family domain, I work with my brother, my parents live here—but we may be the last generation," says Fabrice Amiot at Domaine Guy Amiot in Chassagne Montrachet.

Growers and Negociants

The major part of production in Burgundy as a whole comes from negociants, followed by cooperatives, with independent growers as the smallest category. On the Côte d'Or, the cooperatives are much less important, and the proportion of independent producers is higher. The boundaries between growers and negociants are less fixed than the numbers might suggest. Negociants in Burgundy are not usually mere traders in finished wine: as *negociant-éleveurs*, they buy grapes, juice, or wine, and are responsible for the major production decisions.

There's a split between the fragmented nature of the holdings of small growers and the increasing holdings of the large negociants. Today the major negociants usually also own vineyards and produce wines from their own estate as well as from grapes bought from outside growers. And at the other end of the scale, many growers who formerly produced only estate wine have small negociant businesses in which they extend their range by buying grapes. But even this is becoming more difficult. "The négoce has been a bit challenging in recent years," says Jean-Nicolas Méo of Méo-Camuzet. "Prices in the bulk market have increased and make it more difficult for people like us to purchase grapes."

The Grape Varieties

Chardonnay is the only variety for almost all white wines. It can make good wine at all levels, with its style greatly influenced by winemaking, and in particular the extent of exposure to new oak. It can be soft, nutty, and opulent (the old stereotype of Meursault) or more linear and mineral, even with a whiff of gunflint, as in Puligny Montrachet.

Aligoté is an old variety that is now mostly restricted to two AOPs: Bourgogne Aligoté (a regional AOP) and Bouzeron (on Côte Chalonnaise). Its major characteristic is very high acidity. There are two variants: Vert (which can be over-productive); and Doré (higher quality). There is one very high-end Aligoté: Domaine Ponsot's Clos des Monts Luisants from Morey St. Denis. It's allowed to be a premier cru because the vines were planted in 1911, before the AOC was created. However, there may be other odd patches of old vines. "You'd be surprised how much old Aligoté there is in Corton Charle-magne," one producer says darkly. There's an association of producers, Les Aligoteurs, committed to preserving Aligoté.

There are vanishingly small amounts of *Pinot Blanc* and *Pinot Gris*. The best known example of Pinot Blanc is the spontaneous mutant of Pinot Noir that appeared Henri Gouge's vineyards; having lost its color, it is used to make a white wine. Pinot Gris (known locally as Pinot Beurot) is now illegal in Burgundy, but there is the occasional producer who still has some.

Pinot Noir is the only black variety for village wines and crus, but Gamay can be in-cluded in a blend with Pinot Noir in Bourgogne Passe-Tout-Grains. Pinot Noir can be bright and cherry-like from regional AOPs, but is not really a variety for entry-level wines; it becomes interesting at village level, where it can be precise from Volnay, broader from Pommard, softer from Beaune, generous from Clos Vougeot, powerful from Vosne Romanée, elegant from Chambolle Musigny, or forceful from Gevrey Chambertin.

The latest trend in Burgundy is the micro-negociant, so named not just because of their small size, but because they tend to make many different cu-vées in very small amounts. One factor is that grapes from top appellations may be scarce. "Many (of my wines) are made in small quantities, sometimes only 1-3 barrels. If we were anywhere else it would be a total nonsense, but that's how it is in Burgundy," says Pascal Marchand in Nuits St. Georges. In some ways, because they are not committed to estate vineyards, micro-negociants have a freer hand.

Even if you don't have the capital to buy land, you can buy grapes. New negociants come from a variety of sources: winemakers at established estates who strike out on their own; people from winemaking families who left the family firm; and outsiders whose passion is to make wine in Burgundy. Some of the new negociants really don't like the term. "We are at the border of the domain and the micro-negociants. I don't like the word negociant, because we are doing the same work as the domain," says Olivier Bernstein, a micro-negociant in Beaune.

"I make the wine, from the beginning of vinification to bottling, I view myself as a winemaker, even though there's no word for it in French, not as a

Red Winemaking

There's consensus on winemaking on some issues, and differences on others. The biggest differences come before and after fermentation.

Grapes are harvested as bunches in the vineyard. Until the modern era, the whole bunches were used for fermentation. Including the stems increases the extraction of tannins (and also reduces alcohol slightly as the stems have water but no sugar). Destemming the crop before fermentation, so that only grapes go into the vat, became fashionable due to the influence of Henri Jayer in the 1970s-1980s. This makes for softer, richer wines. While some producers today are committed either to using whole bunches or to destemming completely, many use a combination, with more whole bunches for stronger wines or more powerful vintages.

Some producers use cold maceration, in which grapes are kept at low temperature for a few days before fermentation is allowed to start, to increase extraction of softer tannins. During fermentation, pigeage (punch-down) is usually used to immerse the cap of skins in the wine, as pump-over is considered too strong for Pinot Noir. Maceration after fermentation, when the wine is kept in contact with the skins, extracts more powerful tannins than cold maceration, due to the presence of alcohol.

Virtually all Burgundy above the generic level is aged in oak barriques (see p. 11) with a capacity of 228 liters, about 300 bottles. Barriques can be used for several years, and the main determinant of the effect of oak is what proportion is new and how the long wine stays in the barriques. The tendency in recent years has been to reduce the proportion of new oak.

negociant," says Olivier Leflaive. Alex Gambal, who started as a negociant but now owns vineyards that provide a third of his supply, says that, "The lines between the traditional domains and the négoce have become blurred."

The label may indicate whether a wine comes from a domain or negociant, as the word "Domaine" can be used only for estate-grown grapes, whereas "Maison" indicates that they come from a negociant activity. Some producers who undertake both activities distinguish between them by different labels; others don't use either Domaine or Maison, and make no distinction. The blurring of the boundaries means you can no longer make the traditional assumption that estate-bottled wines will be superior.

One of the common criticisms of the large negociants is that house style may be more evident than nuances of place. But Olivier Masmondet of Maison Jadot explains, "The style of the house does show beyond terroir, but this is just as true of small producers as the large negociants." It's just that when a producer only has a few wines, the differences between them may be more evident than the similarities.

Indeed, you could find half a dozen "minimalist" producers in, say, Chambolle Musigny, all claiming to allow the grapes to speak clearly in the wine, and yet every one of their village wines will be different. The key thing is not so much whether styles are distinct from producer to producer as whether a producer's wines show relative differences reflecting each individual terroir.

The Côte d'Or

The Côte d'Or is the heart of Burgundy. Its spine consists of 5,000 hectares (12,000 acres), divided into 27 communes, mostly between 100 and 300 ha each. It accounts for 10% of the production of all Burgundy.

The villages include 470 premier crus and 32 grand crus, mostly less than 10 ha. The Crus give Burgundy its great complexity. Almost all the villages have premier crus, but of course their significance is relative to the village. A premier cru in the Côte Chalonnaise will not be as interesting as (say) a village Vosne Romanée.

Wide variation in quality among premier crus is due partly to the intrinsic difficulties in classification on such a scale, and partly to political compromises. The definition of the crus goes back to the nineteenth century, when an official map of 1860 coded the vineyards with pink for first class vineyards, yellow for second class, and green for third. Only minor changes have occurred in the classification since then, although price differences have widened enormously.

When the AOCs were defined in 1935, the grand crus became appellations in their own right. Standing at the very top of the hierarchy, they are considered so grand that they do not need to include the village name: I suppose this is a way of saying that each is unique. In fact, there is a reversal here. The greatest grand cru of Gevrey Chambertin, Le Chambertin, had its name when the village was simply called Gevrey. Later the village became Gevrey Chambertin to reflect the glory of the grand cru.

Premier crus were created later, when Burgundy was part of occupied France during the second world war. Classification as premier crus allowed wines to be protected from requisition by the occupying forces. Introduced rather hastily, the system basically followed the old map. Premier crus were regarded as part of each village, so the system requires both the village name and the premier cru to be stated on the label.

An extract from the map of the Côte d'Or prepared in 1860 could be used as a guide to the appellations today.

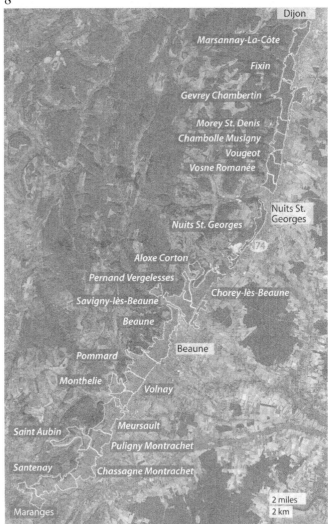

The Côte d'Or consists of the Côte de Nuits (running north from Nuits St. Georges) and the Côte de Beaune (running south from Aloxe Corton). The Côte de Nuits produces red wine. On the Côte de Beaune, Aloxe Corton and Beaune produce more red than white, Pommard and Volnay are exclusively red, while Meursault, Puligny Montrachet, and Chassagne Montrachet are white. The AOPs of the Hautes Côtes and Côtes de Beaune and Nuits lie on either side of the narrow line of communes.

The names of *lieu-dits* (individually named vineyards) may be used on the label when the wine comes from the specific vineyard, even if it is only classified at village level. (But it must appear in smaller type than the name of the AOP.) Some lieu-dits are well respected and considered to be better than a communal AOP as such.

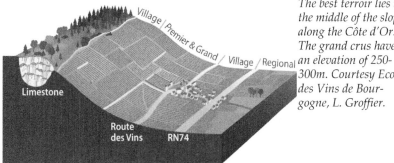

The best terroir lies in the middle of the slope along the Côte d'Or. The grand crus have an elevation of 250-300m. Courtesy Ecole des Vins de Bourgogne, L. Groffier.

But beware: casual brand descriptions for cuvées are also used, and no distinction is made between them and the authentic lieu-dits. So when you see a name on the label under the communal AOP, you have no means of knowing whether it really represents wine from a special vineyard or is merely a fantasy name.

Sometimes individual sites are identified within a cru. Burgundy has always had a focus on identifying particular sites—the word *climat* has become very fashionable—but has the trend gone too far? "The press is forcing us to identify every *climat*, and it's very difficult to work with such small quantities," says Fabrice Latour at Maison Louis Latour. "When I hear people are making one barrel of Montrachet—how can you do that? We've gone too far into the terroir concept, there is too small as well as too big."

Appellations are an accurate guide insofar as a producer's premier cru will be better than his village wine, and any grand crus will be better than premier crus. The hierarchy is only a relative guide, however, as it's certainly true that a top producer's village wine may be better than another producer's premier cru. We had better not get into the issue of whether one producer's generic Bourgogne can be better than another producer's village wine...

The principle is that the appellation system identifies the *potential* of the land. As Beaune negociant Alex Gambal says: "It's a totally confusing system. You automatically think just because you've got a grand cru or a premier cru you've got a good wine—but it is just a ranking of the potential of the land.

Gevrey Chambertin village wine (left) has the name of the village; premier cru Cazetiers has the name of the Cru in smaller letters than the village name, and states Appellation Gevrey Chambertin Premier Cru (center); and the grand cru (right) has the name of the Cru without any village name.

The Côte de Nuits is a narrow band of vineyards stretching up the slope from the N74 to the woods at the top.

The quality of wine produced from a similar piece of land will vary greatly according to who has made it."

The areas for red and white wines are more or less segregated. Most villages of the Côte de Nuits are basically red, with only occasional plots of white grapevines. The most northern parts of the Côte de Beaune, Aloxe Corton and Beaune, produce both red and white wines. South of Beaune, Pommard and Volnay turn back to red, but when you reach the Montrachets and Meursault, there is very little red wine.

Within the appellation hierarchy, differences between village, premier cru, and grand cru wines are intricately connected with yields. The principle is that vineyards classified at higher levels are restricted to lower yields. In Burgundy, the nominal limits for red wines are 55 hl/ha for generic or regional Bourgogne, 40 hl/ha for village wines and premier crus, and 35-37 hl/ha for grand crus. (Values are slightly higher for white wines.) Curiously, village wines have the same yield limits as premier crus. Yet for my money, the sharpest increase in quality level when I taste Burgundy is going from village wine to premier cru.

The key to Burgundy is understanding that apparently imperceptible differences in vineyards consistently produce significant differences in the wines. How differences in soils and micro-climates determine the characters of the wines is not at all obvious, but over and over again there are examples of adjacent vineyards seeming all but identical, but producing consistently different wines. This is the mystery of terroir.

Each village has its own character. Of course, this is only an approximation, as each producer also has his own style, and the relative characters of villages, or premier or grand crus within them, are interpreted through the prism of the producers' styles.

Oak

Barriques are characterized by the age of the barrel, as new (never used for aging wine previously), to 1-year (used in one previous year) 2-year (used in two previous years), and so on. New barriques will convey the strongest impression of oak to the wine, and the effect of the oak then diminishes with the age of the barrel, until after about 4 years, the barrique is basically a neutral container. Oak offers more exposure to oxygen than vats of concrete or stainless steel, and this does not depend on the age of the oak.

Except for wines that are aged in 100% new oak, a mix of barriques of different ages is often used. Oak exposure is often characterized simply in terms of the per cent of new barriques, but this can be a bit misleading as large proportions of 1-year or 2-year barriques still have a strong effect.

The most common approach in Burgundy is to assume that the stronger the wine, the more it benefits from oak exposure, and to increase the proportion of new oak going from regional to communal wine to premier crus and then to grand crus, and also to increase the length of time in aging (élevage). At the extremes, a communal wine might spend 12 months in older barriques, while a grand cru might spend 24 months all in new barriques. There's a minority view that it's more interesting to compare different terroirs when the oak regime is the same for all cuvées.

Barriques are not used in the form of raw oak, but are "toasted" first. In some regions, the extent of toasting (light, medium, or strong) is an issue, but in Burgundy there's more a less a consensus on a medium level.

Oak can be an obvious presence in a young wine, but should integrate and become imperceptible with time. One of the arguments for using more new oak with stronger wines is that they are expected to age longer.

Côte de Nuits

Côte d'Or might perfectly well mean "hillside of gold" judging from the price of Burgundy today, but for all its fame, the exact derivation is unknown. The name originated after the Revolution, but it is unclear whether it was an abbreviation for Côte d'Orient, meaning a slope facing east, or was a reference to the fame of the vineyards. The Côte is an escarpment running roughly south to north, with hills sharply defining its western boundary, and a plain opening out to the east.

The Côte de Nuits is quite narrow, at some points only a couple of hundred meters deep; even at its widest it is not much more than a kilometer. The common features giving the region its general character are the gentle slope and southeast exposure. A myriad of small faults cause the underlying structure to change rapidly, but the major defining feature is the Saône fault, a large break running along the side of the Côte d'Or. The N74 (Route Nationale 74) is the dividing line. To the north of Nuits St. Georges, the Saône fault is just to the east of the road, and to the south it is just to the west. (Farther south, the road crosses back over the fault around Beaune.)

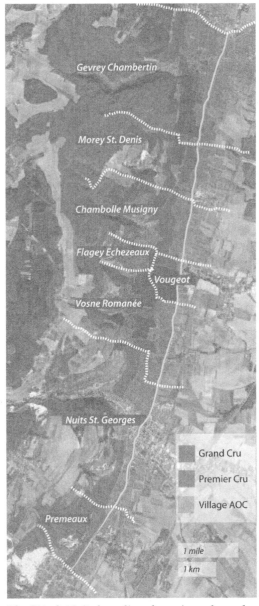

The Côte de Nuits has a line of premier and grand crus along the middle of the slope. Village AOPs are on either side.

To the west of the fault, the terroir has variations of limestone, ranging from white limestone at the top of the slope to ochre-colored limestone at the bottom. There is also some marl (a mixture of clay and shale). Chardonnay tends to be planted on the soils that are richer in marl, Pinot Noir on the most active limestone. To the east of the fault, the soils are deeper and richer, having filled in when the fault collapsed, and the water table is higher (increasing fertility of the vines).

Two geographical axes impact the wine. Going up the N74 from the Côte de Beaune to the Côte de Nuits, the wines become firmer, less earthy, perhaps even a touch more austere, although each commune is different. Going up the slope from the N74 at the bottom to the woods at the top, the highest quality is found in the middle. Position on the slope is the main determinant of level in the classification hierarchy, with premier and grand crus occupying the center of the slope. Vineyards at the top and bottom are classified for village wines (those across the fault on the other side of the N74 are classified as regional).

The slope gives good drainage and the best exposure to the sun. The climate historically has been marginal for ripening Pinot Noir, making the key to quality which sites ripen best. When the relationships between village vineyards, premier crus, and grand crus were defined, those in mid-slope had an advantage and became the premier and grand crus. Will this remain true if global warming continues?

Almost all the wines from the Côte de Nuits are red, although in the early nineteenth century, white wines from Clos Vougeot and Le Chambertin were regarded on a par with Le Montrachet. There are only a few whites now. De Vogüé makes a famous Musigny Blanc, and Domaine de la Vougeraie make a white premier cru from the Clos Blanc de Vougeot. There is also a little white Morey St. Denis. Moving away from Chardonnay, Ponsot's Mont St. Luisants stands out as an Aligoté of unusual quality; and Gouges makes a Pinot Blanc from Nuits St. Georges Les Perrières (from a mutant of Pinot Noir that occurred spontaneously in the vineyard).

The emphasis on nuances of terroir sharpens on the Côte de Nuits, where there are 135 premier crus and 24 grand crus. The grand crus start with La Tâche in Vosne Romanée and extend in a line all the way up to Chambertin and Clos de Bèze. (Corton is the only grand cru for red wine south of Vosne Romanée.) This is where you will find the ultimate expression of Pinot Noir in Burgundy; and this is the place to try to define the quality that lifts a wine from premier to grand cru.

Nuits St. Georges

Nuits St. Georges
297 ha
  97% red
41 premier crus
  136 ha
Top Crus
Les St. Georges
Les Boudots
126 producers

Nuits St. Georges is the largest town between Beaune and Dijon and is in the center of the appellation.

At the southern end of the Côte de Nuits, size and variability make it difficult to draw a clear bead on Nuits St. Georges. It used to be said that Nuits St. Georges had a certain four-square quality, a lack of the refinement that you see farther north. The two major parts of the commune are separated by the town, which is now quite gentrified. The appellation has something of a split

Vosne Romanée

Damodes
Boudots
Au Cras
La Richemone
Murgers
Chaignots
Vignerondes
Bousselots
Argillas

N74

Nuits St. Georges

Rue de Chaux
Le Procès
Pruliers

Roncière

Poirets

Perrières

Cailles

Les St. Georges

Didiers

Forêts

Corvées

Argilières   Premaux

Clos Arlot

Clos de la Maréchale

AOP

Premier Cru

500m

Nuits St. Georges AOP is divided into two parts by the town. The 37 premier crus form a band along the middle of the slope, except at the very narrow southern end where they fill the whole width. Premeaux is the start of the Côte de Nuits.

personality between heavier wines north of the town and lighter wines to its south.

The best premier cru in the northern part, Les Boudots, is adjacent to Vosne Romanée. The main sweep of premier crus in the southern half runs down to Les St. Georges, the best premier cru in Nuits St. Georges, and often mentioned as a possible candidate for promotion. (When grand crus were defined, Pierre Gouges refused to have Les St. Georges considered, on the grounds that this would "create inequalities.") The mixture of clay and limestone along this stretch makes this the best part of Nuits St. Georges. The wines can be rich and structured, but even here they rarely achieve the finesse and silkiness of Vosne Romanée. Perhaps there is too much clay in the soil. At the very southern end in Premeaux, the wines are lighter. Two monopoles, Clos de la Maréchale and Clos de l'Arlot, stand out as the most elegant.

A new generation of winemakers is steadily changing the view of Nuits St. Georges. "The reputation of Nuits St. Georges for rusticity is largely undeserved," says Jean-Nicolas Méo of Méo-Camuzet, although he admits that perhaps the classification is a little too generous with some of the premier crus that still show traditional robustness. A revealing comment about traditional attitudes comes from Domaine Arnoux-Lachaux, where Pascal Lachaux comments on his premier cru Clos des Corvées Pagets, "This is not typical Nuits St. Georges, it is too elegant." The old generalizations of village character don't always apply any more.

Vosne Romanée

Vosne Romanée
152 ha
  100% red
  6 grand crus
14 premier crus
  85 ha
Top Premier Crus
Les Suchots
Beaux Monts
87 producers

The premier and grand crus of Vosne Romanée are directly above the village.

Immediately to the north of Nuits St. Georges, Vosne Romanée is by general acclamation the best village on the Côte de Nuits. It's usually considered together with Flagey-Echézeaux, because, with the exception of the grand crus Echézeaux and Grands Echézeaux, the wines of Flagey-Echézeaux are labeled as Vosne Romanée premier crus. (There is no separate appellation for Flagey-Echézeaux.) The quality of Vosne Romanée is indicated by the fact that grand and premier crus account for more than half of the appellation.

Vosne Romanée is the epitome of refinement. "There are no ordinary wines in Vosne," said a French historian dryly in the eighteenth century. Four of the grand crus are monopoles, most famously Romanée Conti and La Tâche, owned by the Domaine de la Romanée Conti; the others are La Romanée (owned by Liger-Belair) and La Grande Rue (owned by François Lamarche, and unusually having been promoted from premier to grand cru in 1992). The other grand crus are divided among many producers.

Richebourg and Romanée St. Vivant are widely acknowledged to be the best crus after the monopoles. Their reputations are not hurt by the fact that their largest proprietors are the Domaine de la Romanée Conti and Domaine Leroy (generally acknowledged as the best producers in Burgundy). Richebourg is more powerful, Romanée St. Vivant is more elegant. Grands Echézeaux is in third place.

The most fabled wine of all, Romanée Conti comes from the middle of the slope, and has the most homogeneous terroir. The measure of greatness is not power, but subtlety and variety, with endless, seamless, layers of flavor. Second by reputation, and somewhat larger, with more variation going up

16

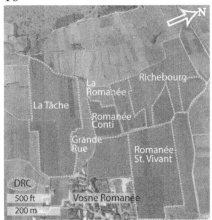

The great grand crus of Vosne Romanée are immediately outside the village. La Tâche and Romanée Conti are monopoles of DRC, which also owns about half of Richebourg and Romanée St. Vivant.

the slope, La Tâche has more body. To the north is Richebourg, with its relatively full style, and below comes the delicate Romanée St. Vivant. From the hill above the town, you see a panorama of grand crus, but their differences are not at all obvious to the eye.

At the north of Vosne Romanée, Echézeaux and Clos Vougeot are the two largest, and most dubious, grand crus. Echézeaux is rather variable, and many people believe that much of it does not live up to grand cru status. (Echézeaux should not be confused with Grands Echézeaux, a much smaller area of 9 ha, which lies between Echézeaux and Clos Vougeot, and is undoubtedly grand cru.)

Clos Vougeot

Vougeot
65 ha
  95% red
  5% white
1 grand cru
  50 ha
4 premier crus
  11 ha
70 producers

The walled clos surrounding the château is now broken up into many holdings. The château belongs to the Confrérie du Tastevin.

Clos Vougeot symbolizes the monastic history of Burgundy and was at the center of winemaking in Burgundy until it was confiscated during the French Revolution. It is a single grand cru only because it was physically enclosed by a wall when the monks created the vineyard. In fact, the monks were well aware of differences within the clos, and a sixteenth century map identifies 16 individual *climats* within it. The monks were said to make three cuvées:

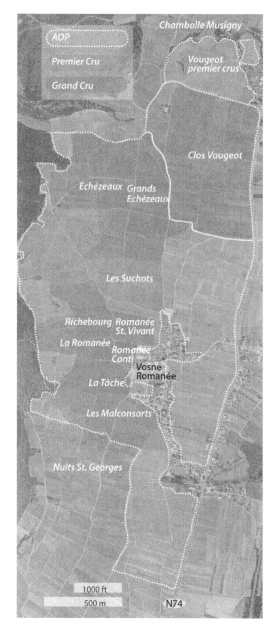

Romanée Conti, La Tâche, Richebourg, and Romanée St. Vivant are the top grand crus, but Clos Vougeot and Echézeaux are questionable.

the best came from the top of the slope and was kept for crowned heads and princes. The second, from the middle, was almost as good and was sold at high price. The third, from the bottom, was somewhat cheaper.

Clos Vougeot extends across the Saône fault, so only the upper half has the characteristic limestone base of the Côte d'Or; the lower part is more like the land that usually lies on the other side of the N74. Attempts to distinguish parts of the Clos during classification were beaten off, so in due course it became the biggest discrepancy in the AOC. At its best, Clos Vougeot makes the most overtly generous and fleshy wine of the Côte de Nuits, rich and round. Yet while the quality is certainly variable, it is not always easy to distinguish wines by their position on the slope in blind tasting.

Clos Vougeot and Echézeaux together total 86 ha, almost a fifth of the 471 total hectares of grand crus on the Côte d'Or. Couple this with the 160 ha of Corton (on the Côte de Beaune), a rather sprawling grand cru with a variety of *climats* of varying quality, and this is not a very impressive start to viewing classification as a guide to the quality of terroir. But it's fair to say that the rest of the grand crus, ranging in size from under 1 ha to almost 20 ha, consistently produce the very finest Burgundy (with the addition of a couple of under-classified premier crus).

Chambolle Musigny and Morey St. Denis

Chambolle Musigny
153 ha
  100% red
  2 grand crus
  24 premier crus
  55 ha
Top Crus
Bonnes Mares
Le Musigny
Les Amoureuses
98 producers

Chambolle Musigny is a tiny village on the Côte de Nuits. Le Musigny is immediately to the south, Bonnes Mares is immediately to the north, and leads directly into the line of grand crus in Morey. St. Denis.

To the north of Clos Vougeot come Chambolle Musigny and Morey St. Denis, the lightest wines of the Côte de Nuits. Chambolle Musigny produces the most elegant wines, with a delicate floral edge, sometimes described as feminine. The pebbly soils are marked by a high proportion of active limestone (which decreases acidity) and a low proportion of clay, making for lightness in the wine. At premier cru level, the wines can be ethereal.

At the south end of Chambolle Musigny, the grand cru Le Musigny is just west of Clos Vougeot. Les Amoureuses, the best premier cru in Chambolle, just below Le Musigny, is often judged to be of grand cru quality; often more expensive than most grand crus, it would very likely be promoted in the

Morey St. Denis
96 ha
  99% red
  5 grand crus
  40 ha
  20 premier crus
  39 ha
Top Premier Cru
La Riotte
Clos des Ormes

The grand crus are on the slope immediately above the village

unlikely event of a reclassification. All these crus show silky elegance with a sense of precision more than power. At the north end, the major part of Bonnes Mares is in Chambolle, with a small part over the border in Morey.

Morey St. Denis is harder to pin down. The village wines and premier crus are really overshadowed by the grand crus here. Many of the premier crus are so small that they are often merged to be labeled simply as Morey Premier Cru. Clos de la Bussière (a monopole of Roumier), Clos des Ormes, Les Ruchots, La Riotte, and Clos Sorbès are the largest, and mostly likely to be found as individual cuvées.

Bonnes Mares lies adjacent to the grand crus in Morey St. Denis, which form a solid line through the center of the appellation. Clos de Tart and Clos des Lambrays are both monopoles, then comes Clos St. Denis, followed by Clos de la Roche at the northern end, which usually has the edge, showing more of the richness and longevity of adjacent Gevrey Chambertin.

Gevrey Chambertin

Gevrey Chambertin
495 ha
  100% red
9 grand crus
  86 ha
29 premier crus
  80 ha
Top Premier Crus
Clos St. Jacques
Les Cazetiers
140 producers

Gevrey Chambertin's most important grand crus and premier crus are just under the woods at the top of the slope. Clos St. Jacques (in photo) is a premier cru, but is often considered equivalent to the grand crus.

With vineyards extending from village level to premier and grand crus, Gevrey Chambertin is the largest commune on the Côte d'Or. As a rarity, it includes some vineyards on the "wrong" side of the N74, among which Clos de la Justice is an exception that can offer wines above the village level.

Premier and grand crus fall into two stretches. The lineup of grand crus runs almost uninterrupted from the town south to the boundary with Morey St. Denis. At the center, Chambertin and Clos de Bèze occupy the upper edge of the slope. They are flanked by other grand crus both to north and south, and just below on the slope. Some premier crus are adjacent. Then beyond the town itself, running around the edge of the hill to the west, is a sweep of premier crus, including Lavaux St. Jacques, Estournelles St. Jacques, and Clos St. Jacques, with Les Cazetiers and Combe aux Moines to their north.

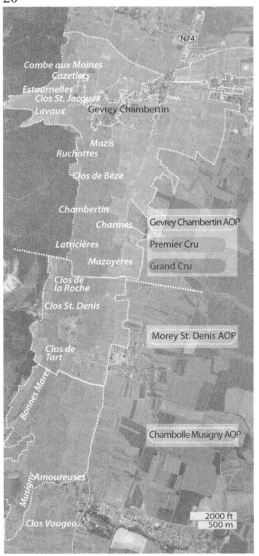

The northernmost part of the Côte de Nuits stretches from Chambolle Musigny to Gevrey Chambertin.

Differences in exposure may be more important than soils here. A comparison between Combe aux Moines and Les Cazetiers is compelling because the plots are contiguous. "The tractor doesn't stop," says Jérôme Flous of Maison Faiveley. Combe aux Moines has a cooler exposure because it angles more to the north than Cazetiers, which extends farther down the slope and so has slightly lower average elevation. Ripening is slightly slower in Combe aux Moines, which harvests two days later than Cazetiers. The difference is due to sunlight exposure; phenolic ripeness doesn't quite catch up in Combe aux Moines. Yet the impression is not simply that Cazetiers is riper than Combe aux Moines; Cazetiers always has a finer impression, Combe aux Moines seems more four-square.

Clos St. Jacques, the top premier cru of Gevrey Chambertin, provides an unusually clear demonstration of the impact of producers. Often considered to be at the level of the grand crus, it was a rated as a premier cru because its owner at the time refused to comply with the classification procedure. It has a good slope with perfect southeast exposure, and was a monopole until 1956, when the present five owners

Chambertin and Clos de Bèze are intimately connected. Wine made in Clos de Bèze can also be labeled as Chambertin, which has been known by its present name since 1276; Clos de Bèze takes its name from the Abbaye de Bèze, which was given the vineyard by the Duke of Burgundy in 630.

purchased it. Unusually for Burgundy, instead of being subdivided higgledy-piggledy, each owner has a strip running from top to bottom of the Clos.

There's quite a bit of variation in soil from top to bottom, but not much from side to side, so each owner has the same diversity of soils. Since their plots are exactly parallel, it's reasonable to associate differences in the wines with differences in viticulture or vinification. The wines range from Fourrier's elegance, Rousseau's earthiness, Jadot's roundness, Bruno Clair's sturdiness, to Esmonin's sometimes stern representation. Differences result from factors such as harvest dates to the amount of destemming. Here is a powerful demonstration of the effect of the producer on style.

At the very top of the hierarchy, only the grand crus of Gevrey Chambertin, notably Le Chambertin itself and Clos de Bèze, challenge those of Vosne Romanée for leadership. Until the start of the twentieth century, the reputation of Le Chambertin was more or less level pegging with Romanée Conti. One reason why Romanée Conti and La Tâche are now far ahead may be their status as monopoles; under the aegis of Domaine de la Romanée Conti, their quality has been consistently at the top. Divided among many growers, by contrast, Chambertin's quality is far more variable.

Chambertin and Clos de Bèze have historically been set apart from all the other crus of Gevrey Chambertin, but the distinction between them has not always been clear. Clos de Bèze can be sold under its own name, as Chambertin, or as Chambertin-Clos de Bèze. The name of Chambertin became better known, and few wines were labeled as Clos de Bèze during the eighteenth or nineteenth centuries; almost all were simply described as Chambertin. (Chambertin is supposed to have been Napoleon's favorite wine.)

In terms of climate, there's a slight difference between Chambertin and Clos de Bèze, because Chambertin is more exposed to the small valley that divides Gevrey Chambertin from Chambolle Musigny. Cold winds that slide across the upper part may make Le Chambertin cooler than Clos de Bèze, which is more protected. No one has actually measured any physical difference, but a telling measure is that Eric Rousseau says that Domaine Rousseau always harvests Clos de Bèze earlier than Chambertin.

Comparing vintages, my impression is that Chambertin has the advantage in warmer vintages, when its fruits take on a delicious ripeness, but in cooler vintages the best balance is obtained by Clos de Bèze. I am inclined to the view that there is a continuum of differences all along the length of the two appellations, and that intrinsic variations in the wines depend on the individual microplots. Terroir and climate are crucial determinants, but they are not defined by an arbitrary line between the two appellations.

Marsannay

This is not the end of the Côte de Nuits: beyond Gevrey Chambertin come Fixin and Marsannay, running into the outskirts of Dijon. Marsannay has the only appellation in Burgundy for rosé. "Back in the fifties and sixties, people knew Marsannay for the rosé, and although the image of rosé was poor at the time, people thought of Marsannay rosé as being made more like a red wine. In the last 25 years, Marsannay has gone from rosé into making good red wines. When you taste blind, Marsannay is better than Fixin," says Bruno Clair, whose grandfather was instrumental in creating the AOC for rosé.

Marsannay became a village AOC in 1987; previously the wines were Bourgogne. Vineyards are classified according to color. Those to the west are mostly able to produce all colors; those on the east are mostly classified for rosé, and if they produce red it is labeled as simple Bourgogne. "The problem with Marsannay is that Dijon is expanding. We are resisting as best we can, the best way is to make top wines," Bruno declares.

There are no premier crus. Marsannay has had a dossier at INAO since 2002 requesting the definition of premier crus, and producers are hopeful of some action in the near future. Anticipating approval, they already distinguish between village wines and the lieu-dits, much as though they were premier crus. The best are Clos du Roy (well regarded in the nineteenth century) and Longeroies.

Marsannay is allowed to include Pinot Gris in its rosé, and the law of unintended consequences means that in fact there is sometimes Pinot Gris in the white wines. The style of Marsannay, both red and white, has a relatively light sense of extraction for the Côte de Nuits, tending to freshness rather than power, but similar in flavor to the great communes to its south.

Reference Wines for Côte de Nuits	
Nuits St. Georges	Henri Gouges
Vosne Romanée	Arnoux-Lachaux
Chambolle Musigny	Mongeard-Mugneret
Morey St. Denis	Lucien Le Moine
Gevrey Chambertin	Jean-Marie Fourrier
Fixin	Domaine Ponsot
Marsannay	Armand Rousseau
Top Premier Crus	
Chambolle Musigny, Les Amoureuses	Robert Groffier
Nuits St. Georges, Les St. Georges	Henri Gouges
Nuits S. Georges, Les Boudots	Méo-Camuzet
Vosne Romanée, Les Suchots	Arnoux-Lachaux
Vosne Romanée, Beaux Monts	Jean Grivot
Morey St. Denis, La Riotte	Henri Perrot-Minot
Gevrey Chambertin, Les Cazetiers	Domaine Faiveley
Gevrey Chambertin, Clos St. Jacques	Bruno Clair
Grand Crus	
Chambertin	Armand Rousseau
Clos de Bèze	Bruno Clair
Chapelle Chambertin	Domaine Trapet Père
Charmes Chambertin	Louis Jadot
Griotte Chambertin	Joseph Drouhin
Mazis Chambertin	Maison Faiveley
Ruchottes Chambertin	Georges Roumier
Clos St. Denis	Domaine Dujac
Clos de la Roche	Domaine Ponsot
Bonnes Mares	Jacques Frédéric Mugnier
Le Musigny	Comte de Vogüé
Echézeaux	Georges Mugneret-Gibourg
Clos Vougeot	Méo-Camuzet

Côte de Nuits versus Côte de Beaune

The classification of grand and premier crus does not completely correspond with current reputation. The Côte de Nuit's dominance of red wines is shown by ranking appellations on the basis of price. The grand crus of Vosne Romanée and Gevrey Chambertin fill most of the top twenty places, rounded out by entries from Chambolle Musigny and Morey St. Denis. Two premier crus, Les Amoureuses (Chambolle Musigny) and Clos St. Jacques (Gevrey Chambertin) place among the grand crus. The next group is dominated by premier crus of Vosne Romanée. The top entries from the Côte de Beaune are the best *climats* of Corton, whose varying reputations intersperse them among the premier crus. Several premier crus make Volnay the only other village to be well represented in the top hundred.

The distinction between the Côte de Nuits and Côte de Beaune is not completely consistent, but as a general rule the Côte de Nuits provides sterner red wines, as much inclined to black fruits as to red fruits, somewhat more generous and rounded, often forceful at premier and grand cru level. Gevrey Chambertin is perhaps the sternest, sometimes with a hard edge when young. Nuits St. Georges ranges from sturdy, almost rustic wines to elegance. Clos Vougeot at its best can be the most generous. There is absolutely no gainsaying Vosne Romanée's unique combination of power and smoothness, whereas Chambolle Musigny and Morey St. Denis can verge on delicate.

This compares with the soft roundness of Corton at its best, the sheen of Aloxe-Corton, the very varied range of Beaune from soft fruits to relatively thin wines, the rustic sturdiness of Pommard, and the crystalline purity of Volnay. With the exception of that taut precision in Volnay, the Côte de Beaune is more likely to offer earthy strawberries than black fruits.

Côte de Beaune

Beaune is the center of the wine trade. Most of the old negociants have their headquarters here, although they have been moving steadily out of the old town to more practical, purpose built, locations on the outskirts. In the center of the old town is the Hospice de Dieu, established as a hospital in the Middle Ages, and funded by wine produced from its own vineyards.

One of the highlights of the year in Beaune is an auction at which the latest vintage from the Hospice is sold to local negociants, who then mature the barrels in their own particular styles. At one time these wines were well regarded for their quality, but today the auction is more an occasion to kick off sales of the current vintage than a supply of top-flight wine.

To the west, the city of Beaune is surrounded by the semicircle of the appellation of Beaune. To the south, vineyards extend to the Côte Chalonnaise.

Corton and Corton Charlemagne

Aloxe Corton
242 ha
 98% red
Grand crus
Corton (95% red)
 95 ha
Corton Charlemagne
(white)   48 ha
14 premier crus

The hill of Corton dominates Aloxe Corton.

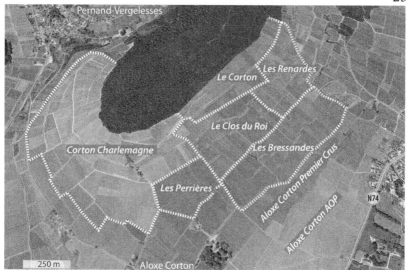

Vineyards wind around the hill of Corton. Corton Charlemagne is on the southwest slopes. Corton runs down the eastern flank; the most important climats are indicated. Aloxe-Corton premier crus are below, and village wines are at the bottom.

To the north of Beaune, Corton is the largest grand cru in Burgundy. "Everything seems so easy to understand in Burgundy. There are village wines, premier crus, and grand crus. But in Corton you have all the different *climats* inside the grand cru," says Philippe Prost at Bouchard Père.

Occupying 160 ha, Corton is somewhat of an anomaly: nominally a single grand cru, occupying the upper slopes going up the hill of Corton to the forest at the top, it is divided into many separate *climats,* and it's really their individual names that carry weight. The best, at the top, are worthy of grand cru status: the rest are more doubtful. Clos du Roi is the best.

Below Corton, the premier crus of Aloxe-Corton are on the lower slopes of the hill, and the village appellation is just below. The best reds of Aloxe-Corton have a glossy sheen, with more body than, say, Beaune, but not approaching the structure of the Côte de Nuits.

Corton is famous for the white wine of Corton Charlemagne, from southwest end of the hill. Its name reflects Emperor Charlemagne's ownership of vineyards on the hill; the story goes that the wine originated when he demanded white wine to avoid staining his beard with red. The proportions of red and white wine from Corton have changed dramatically with time. In the nineteenth century, most Corton was red. The focus changed to white during the twentieth century, and today 72 ha are classified for the white Corton Charlemagne. Corton Blanc describes white wine produced elsewhere in Corton. Some of the Charlemagne area can also be used for red; for example, the *climat* of Corton-Pougets is contained entirely within Corton Charlemagne.

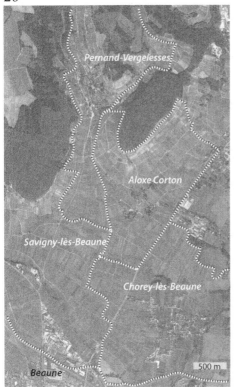

Aloxe Corton has the best exposure, with Pernand-Vergelesses facing more to the west, and Savigny-lès-Beaune and Chorey-lès-Beaune at lower elevations.

The hill is based on a substratum of limestone, but the topsoil changes going up the slope, from more iron and pebbles lower down (better suited to Pinot Noir) to higher clay content at the top. But here as elsewhere, market forces push growers to replant with Chardonnay when vineyards come up for renewal. Going round the hill from Aloxe-Corton towards Pernand Vergelesses, there is more flint in the soil, giving more austerity to the white wine (and creating difficulties for black grapes in ripening.)

The two poles of Corton Charlemagne are expressed by the largest two owners, with opulence from Louis Latour, and restrained minerality from Bonneau du Martray. At its best, Corton Charlemagne can be generous, with a touch of citrus cutting the stone fruits. But given the variety of terroirs, there is no single character. Bonneau du Martray's block extends from Pernand Vergelesses to Aloxe Corton. "The styles provided by each block are quite distinct," said former owner Jean-Charles le Bault de la Morinière, and of course you see that variety in the wines by other producers from smaller holdings. Overall, I would say Corton Charlemagne has a sense of linearity, and sometimes a sense of austerity that recalls the white wines of the Côte de Nuits, contrasted with more open character of the whites from south of Beaune.

The Environs of Beaune

Around Corton are satellite appellations—Pernand-Vergelesses to the north, Savigny-lès-Beaune to the south, and Chorey-lès-Beaune to the east. They produce both red and white wines, with the best vineyards marked out as premier crus. Less well known than the major appellations along the Côte d'Or, the wines are more straightforward, and can offer good value.

Île-des-Vergelesses, at the border with Savigny-lès-Beaune, is generally considered the best of the premier crus of Pernand-Vergelesses. Adjacent to it, Les Vergelesses is one of the best premier crus of Savigny-lès-Beaune, so this is a favored patch, extending in fact to Les Lavières just beyond. Vineyards are in the valley of Bouilland on either side of the Le Rhoin stream: on the south-facing side, Guettes, Clous, Gravains and Serpentières have richer soils and produce more powerful wines; on the opposite side, Les Narbantons and La Dominode have more gravel and sand and produce lighter wines.

Immediately to the east, most of the vineyards of Chorey-lès-Beaune are on the relatively flat land on the other side of the N74; the greater content of clay means that the wines here are not so fine, and there are no premier crus. Before Chorey was granted its appellation in 1970, the wines were sold as Côte de Beaune Villages, and some still are.

Beaune

Beaune
410 ha
  90% red
  10% white
42 premier crus
  317 ha
Top Crus
Clos des Mouches
Les Grèves
Les Bressandes
177 producers

Vineyards extend from the town of Beaune, but reflecting the large size of the appellation, are the most variable on the Côte de Beaune. Clos des Mouches is one of the premier crus in Beaune that has both red and white plantings.

The largest appellation on the Côte d'Or, Beaune is hard to pin down. Vineyards stretch from Savigny-lès-Beaune to Pommard. The large size, high number of premier crus, and the fact that they represent three quarters of the appellation, makes for what might kindly be described as variability in quality. (Personally I would demote several of the premier crus, and judging from the low prices they fetch, the market agrees with me.)

There is more Pinot Noir than Chardonnay in Beaune, but the whites can be finely structured, sometimes a little tight. The best whites, from premier crus, can tend towards an earthy or stony character, compared with the more mineral character of, say, Puligny Montrachet. The reds are somewhere between the elegance of Volnay and the firmness of Pommard, and generally not as tight as the reds of the Côte de Nuits.

The effects of terroir are shown by the different characters of two of the top premier crus. At the southern boundary of Beaune with Pommard, Clos des Mouches is calcareous. Terraces face from east to southeast and are relatively breezy. Two kilometers to the north, the steep slope of Grèves angles

28

Reference Wines for Red Côte de Beaune	
Chorey-lès-Beaune	Tollot-Beaut
Savigny-lès-Beaune	Benjamin Leroux
Pernand Vergelesses	Rapet Père et Fils
Aloxe-Corton	Comte Senard
Beaune	Remoissenet
Pommard	Comte Armand
Volnay	Marquis d'Angerville
Blagny	Robert Ampeau
Saint-Romain	Alain Gras
Auxey-Duresses	Comte Armand
Santenay	Anne-Marie & Jean-Marc Vincent
Top Premier Crus	
Beaune, Clos des Mouches	Joseph Drouhin
Beaune, Grèves	Domaine les Croix
Volnay, Clos des Ducs	Marquis d'Angerville
Volnay, Taillepieds	Hubert de Montille
Pommard, Clos des Epeneaux	Comte Armand
Pommard, Les Rugiens	Domaine de Courcel
Pernand-Vergelesses, Île des Vergelesses	Rapet Père et Fils
Grand Cru	
Corton, Clos du Roi	Comte Senard
Corton	Louis Latour, Château Corton Grancey

more east; the soil is clay and limestone, shallow with lots of stones and there is often a water deficit. (Grèves is local dialect for stony.) There is a lot of iron in the soil. Clos des Mouches is lighter with more aromatics and finesse, Grèves is sturdier with firmer tannins and structure.

Volnay and Pommard

Volnay
220 ha
  100% red
29 premier crus
  135 ha
Top Crus
Caillerets
Taillepieds
Clos des 60 Ou-
vrées
116 producers

Volnay produces the most refined red wines on the Cote de Beaune. Vineyards run right up to the village.

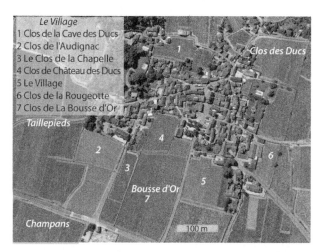

Le Village
1 Clos de la Cave des Ducs
2 Clos de l'Audignac
3 Le Clos de la Chapelle
4 Clos de Château des Ducs
5 Le Village
6 Clos de la Rougeotte
7 Clos de La Bousse d'Or
Taillepieds
Clos des Ducs
Bousse d'Or
Champans
100 m

The best premier crus in Volnay are close to the village. Numbers indicate monopoles in Le Village. Clos des Ducs, Taillepieds, and Champans are other top premier crus.

Volnay and Pommard are the southernmost regions for the top red wines, but although they are adjacent, the communes have different styles. Volnay is the epitome of elegance, with precisely delineated red fruit flavors that at their best have a remarkable crystalline quality. Pommard has softer, lusher fruits, sometimes considered to be a touch rustic.

Volnay is one of the smaller communes; perhaps that is why there is more consistency to style and quality. It sits on a limestone base, with some variety in the types of limestone, but the base is generally light in color and relatively crumbly. The best plots in Volnay are close to the village. In fact, a premier cru called simply *Le Village* consists of various plots surrounding the village, but you rarely see Le Village on the label because most of these plots are monopoles whose proprietors use their individual names. Other top premier crus are Taillepieds, Champans, Clos des Chênes, and Caillerets.

Pommard
322 ha
  100% red
28 premier crus
  116 ha
Top Crus
Les Epenots
Les Rugiens
205 producers

Pommard produces firm red wines.

At the northern boundary, Volnay joins Pommard, where the limestone-based soils have more clay. This is said to give the wines of Pommard their sturdier character. There's also more iron in Pommard, due to ferrous oxide in the soil. Nicholas Rossignol says that the difference in the structure of the wine is because Pommard is slightly cooler, on what used to be a riverbed, while Volnay is on a slope facing the sun. Volnay has finer tannins compared to Pommard. "The tannins of Volnay are riper and integrated in the wine, the tannins of Pommard are more foursquare and show on the finish."

White Burgundy

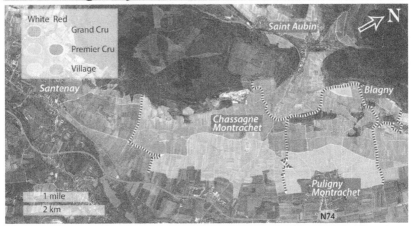

The top white wine appellations lie in a group to the south of Beaune. The line of premier and grand crus runs along the middle and upper slope.

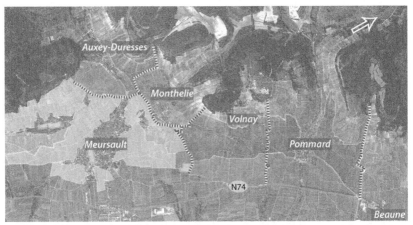

Meursault is almost all white wine, but Volnay and Pommard are exclusively red.

South of Volnay, the tip of the Côte de Beaune is white wine territory. Characterizing the differences between Meursault, Chassagne Montrachet, and Puligny Montrachet is complicated by the variety of producer styles in each appellation. Conventional wisdom identifies Meursault as soft, nutty, and buttery, while Chassagne Montrachet has a bit more of a citrus edge, and Puligny Montrachet is taut, precise, and mineral.

Changes over the past decade or so, especially in Meursault, show that these styles are due only in part to the intrinsic character of each appellation, but "Puligny has more acidity, Meursault is broader," says Philippe Prost at Bouchard Père. "Puligny you have to keep the freshness, Meursault you have to give it energy." Puligny is the most linear, and has the most tension of the three appellations, Chassagne is always a touch broader and softer, and Meursault varies from traditionally broad to a modern impression of minerality, but is richer.

Meursault

Meursault
396 ha
  96% white
   4% red
19 premier crus
 107 ha
Top Crus
Les Charmes
Les Perrières
Les Genevrières
Porusot
192 producers

Meursault is the largest village on the Côte de Beaune.

Meursault is the largest of the three appellations. Although it has no grand crus, its top premier crus are excellent, with Les Perrières sometimes approaching grand cru quality. Les Genevrières is also very fine: "for me, it is the little brother of Chevalier Montrachet," says Philippe Prost.

The whites used to be rich rather than mineral, although those of the top producer, Coche-Dury, tend towards a savory minerality. Others have now followed Coche-Dury in a more mineral direction, most notably Arnaud Ente and Antoine Jobard. Comtes Lafon makes some of the longest-lived wines of the appellation, halfway in style between minerality and nuttiness, and Jean-Marc Roulot at Domaine Guy Roulot makes elegant wines.

The New Meursault, as I think of it, is as mineral as rich. Is the change to a more mineral focus now the typicity of Meursault, I asked Dominique Lafon. "I think it is typical for the good producers," he holds. At the southwest edge of Meursault is the village of Blagny, whose name appears on Meursault-Blagny premier cru and also in the Hameau de Blagny premier cru of Puligny Montrachet.

Some red wine is produced in Meursault, but the best is a premier cru that is actually labeled as Volnay Santenots. There's also Blagny premier cru red.

Puligny Montrachet

Puligny Montrachet
211 ha
  100% white
  4 grand crus
  17 premier crus
  98 ha
Top Premier Crus
Les Pucelles
Les Demoiselles
Les Folatières
Les Combettes
127 producers

Puligny Montrachet can be seen through the gateway into Les Pucelles, its most important premier cru.

Puligny Montrachet is for me the quintessence of white Burgundy: its steely minerality, the precision in the fruits, the sense of backbone—the combination is unique. Some of the premier crus are within a hair's breadth of grand cru quality, with Les Pucelles and Le Cailleret sometimes crossing the line. The hierarchy of Puligny is captured at Domaine Leflaive, where the classic style shows in the village wine, intensifies through the premier crus, and then with Les Pucelles or the grand crus, adds a Rolls Royce sense of power to that steely finesse.

Le Montrachet is in the middle of the white grand crus, with Chevalier above it, and Bâtard and Bienvenues-Bâtard below it.

Of course, the epitome of white wine is the grand cru Le Montrachet: I am in the camp of those who consider it potentially the greatest white wine in the world (depending of course on the producer). Chevalier Montrachet is usually considered second, followed by Bâtard-Montrachet and Bienvenues-Bâtard-Montrachet. Le Montrachet and Bâtard-Montrachet actually are only partly in Puligny Montrachet, with some of each vineyard across the border in Chassagne Montrachet. Criots-Bâtard-Montrachet is solely in Chassagne.

The unique quality of these grand crus is that subtly shifting balance of power with finesse. Chardonnays from elsewhere may have one or the other, but I have yet to experience any other wine with both. In terms of the villages, Puligny is the closest in style to the grand crus, especially its top premier crus. The trend to increasing ripeness at most producers means that many premier crus now show richness before minerality, but there should always be tension in Puligny. In fact, village character may show most clearly at the premier cru level, as the grand crus can be so powerful as to subdue that steely minerality.

Chassagne Montrachet

Chassagne Montrachet
313 ha
  63% white
  37% red
55 premier crus
  149 ha
Top Crus
Morgeot
Les Champs Gain
105 producers

Chassagne Montrachet's most important premier cru is Morgeot, with the derelict Abbaye de Morgeot at the center. Including various climats (sometimes used instead of Morgeot), it is by far the largest premier cru.

"Sometimes people ask us what we think is the difference between Chassagne and Puligny, and it's a really difficult question, because there are so many different areas in Chassagne—Morgeot is rich, but other areas are more mineral," says Hubert Lestime at Domaine Jean-Noël Gagnard. It is fair to say that Chassagne is more heterogeneous than Puligny.

The typicity of Chassagne Montrachet is usually considered to lie between Meursault and Puligny Montrachet: not as rich as Meursault but not as linear as Puligny. "Chassagne is always rounder, I've never had a vintage where Puligny is rounder," says Laurent Pillot. "When you plough our vineyards you can see there's more clay in Chassagne." It is fair to say that on average Puligny is more precise, whereas Chassagne has more breadth.

The top premier crus in Chassagne are Morgeot (very large, including some others), Caillerets, Champs Gains, Ruchottes, Chaumées, and La Boudriotte. There is more red wine in Chassagne Montrachet than either of the other two appellations; indeed, white wine took over here more recently, as a result of market pressure. This is not always a good thing, because some parts of Chassagne Montrachet might be more suited to black grapes.

Today, Pinot Noir vineyards tend to be replaced with Chardonnay when it's time to replant. "We think it's a pity the area at the bottom of the village has been replanted; it reduces the reputation of the village because those soils give less minerality. It's a problem to plant white there," says Jean-Marc Blain Gagnard.

Limits of the Côte de Beaune

Adjacent to the great white wine appellations are the satellite appellations at the southern tip of the Côte de Beaune: Saint-Romain, Auxey-Duresses, and Saint-Aubin to the west, and Santenay just south of Chassagne Montrachet. These can be good sources for wines in similar style, albeit less concentrated and complex, but at considerably lower prices than the more famous communes.

The whites of Saint-Aubin are the best known, while Auxey-Duresses and Saint-Romain have become more popular as Saint-Aubin has increased in price. "The vines in Saint-Aubin are relatively young because it used to be Pinot Noir, and much was replanted with Chardonnay thirty years ago. The appellation may have the opportunity to improve as the vines get older," says Damien Colin of Domaine Marc Colin. Now with a clear focus on white, Saint-Aubin is 80% Chardonnay. The terroir is similar to Puligny Montrachet, but the climate is cooler.

If Saint Aubin is a less expensive alternative to Puligny, Santenay may be a poor man's Chassagne. Indeed, Chassagne runs almost imperceptibly into Santenay, where vineyards lie along a valley with slopes at all angles. If a producer has vines in both, the Chassagne is usually more intense. However, less than a quarter of Santenay is white, and the reds of Santenay are the best known of the satellite appellations, representing a somewhat softer version of Chassagne reds.

Auxey Duresses is about two thirds red, and the style of both reds and whites is a bit on the austere side compared, for example, with Meursault just to its south.

Saint Romain is somewhat different from the other satellites, as it essentially a closed valley, running north-south, with vineyards on the slopes on both sides. Relatively protected by the hills at the end, it tends to be cooler than the other satellites due to higher elevations of 100-400m.

Reference Wines for White Côte de Beaune	
Pernand-Vergelesses	Rapet Père et Fils
Savigny-lès-Beaune	Simon Bize
Beaune	Bouchard Père et Fils
Meursault	Guy Roulot
Chassagne Montrachet	Pierre-Yves Colin-Morey
Puligny Montrachet	Domaine Leflaive
Saint-Romain	Henri et Gilles Buisson
Auxey-Duresses	Benjamin Leroux
Saint-Aubin	Hubert Lamy
Santenay	Jean-Marc Vincent
Bourgogne Aligoté	Pierre Morey
Top Premier Crus	
Beaune, Clos des Mouches	Joseph Drouhin
Puligny Montrachet, Les Pucelles	Domaine Leflaive
Puligny Montrachet, Les Folatières	Etienne Sauzet
Chassagne Montrachet, Morgeot	Joseph Drouhin, Marquis de Laguiche
Chassagne Montrachet	Louis Jadot, Clos de la Chapelle (Duc de Magenta)
Chassagne Montrachet, Champs Gain	Pierre-Yves Colin-Morey
Meursault, Clos de la Perrière	Albert Grivot
Meursault, Charmes	Comtes Lafon
Grand Crus	
Corton Charlemagne	Bonneau du Martray Louis Latour
Chevalier Montrachet	Etienne Sauzet
Bâtard Montrachet	Paul Pernot
Bienvenues Bâtard Montrachet	Domaine Leflaive

All of the satellite appellations produce white wines that are credible alternative to their more expensive counterparts in the great appellations, albeit less complex, but the reds tend to be less successful. It's really a matter of ripeness, because the reds often fail to reach the roundness that comes from the top communes, leaving them with an austere impression. Of course, that could change with global warming.

Premature Oxidation

The great issue of the day in white Burgundy crosses all appellation boundaries. This is premature oxidation, so prevalent today that it has become known by the abbreviation of premox. Before premox became an issue, a village white Burgundy would probably last for six years or so, a premier cru would not be ready to start for, say, 4-6 years, and would last for more than a decade beyond the vintage, and grand crus would start even more slowly and last even longer. The problem with premature oxidation first became apparent with the 1996 vintage, when soon after 2000, many wines, even at premier cru level, began to show signs of oxidation: deepening color, madeirized nose, and drying out on the palate.

Given significant variability between individual bottles, the immediate reaction was that this was due to a problem with the corks (possibly due to changes in the sterilization procedure). It soon became clear that the answer was not so straightforward, and a variety of causes was proposed, ranging from changes in viticulture, pressing the juice too clean (because this removes anti-oxidants), too much battonage (stirring up the lees while the wine is in barrique), or reduced use of sulfur at bottling.

More than a decade on, however, no one has pinpointed any single cause, so no white Burgundy of more than three or four years old can be considered safe. This greatly shortens the period for drinking: you have to steer between the Scylla of new oak and the Charybdis of premox. Many wines, especially at the premier or grand cru level, have somewhat evident oak on release, and it takes two or three years for this to calm down; sometimes longer, as premier crus with 100% new oak may still display obvious oak after, say, 6 years. So not much time is left before premox might set in. And not only is the window for enjoying wines at their optimum much shortened, but it seems to be different for every bottle.

White Burgundy has become a wine that must be enjoyed young. Even though there is a tendency to reduce new oak, levels are still often appropriate for wines that are expected to last for ten or more years. If the wine needs to be consumed sooner, it follows that new oak should be dialed back more. Too high a proportion of new oak means that many wines now slide straight from showing too much oak into being too tired and old.

Dominique Lafon, who has been at the forefront of efforts to fix the problem, believes that premox is a perfect storm of many factors. "What puzzled us was that it was very random. The first thing we thought was that we had cork failures—I think we did—but it was showing the fragility of the wine," he says. He's changed a variety of procedures to make vinification more reductive, and believes the issue has finally been resolved.

The underlying problem was that the wines did not have enough resistance to oxidation, so the slightest problem with the cork would allow oxidation. This explains the random occurrence. "Even in the cellars here, one in four bottles of white Beaune from 1999 is oxidized, but the others are absolutely fine," Philippe Drouhin told me in 2010, "so what can it be but the cork?" Since producers are unwilling to change to screwcaps, the important thing is to ensure that the wines are more resistant to oxidation.

Is the problem over? "No one really knows where premox is coming from, so no one can really claim they've solved the problem," says Brice de la

Morandière at Domaine Leflaive. While it's fair to say that premox is no longer as severe a problem as before, I find that the wines do not age as long as they used to: they seem to tire sooner, even if not showing premox.

Côte Chalonnaise

The Côte Chalonnaise extends more or less from Chagny (just south of Chassagne Montrachet) to Chalon-sur-Saône, and produces both red and white; the style is lighter for the whites and not so generous for the reds as the Côte d'Or.

The five villages of the Côte Chalonnaise extend for about twenty miles to the immediate south of the Côte d'Or. Unlike the monoculture of the Côte d'Or, viticulture is interspersed with other sorts of agriculture. The wines fol-

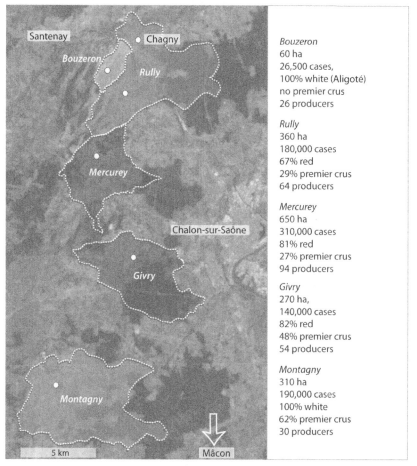

Bouzeron
60 ha
26,500 cases,
100% white (Aligoté)
no premier crus
26 producers

Rully
360 ha
180,000 cases
67% red
29% premier crus
64 producers

Mercurey
650 ha
310,000 cases
81% red
27% premier crus
94 producers

Givry
270 ha,
140,000 cases
82% red
48% premier crus
54 producers

Montagny
310 ha
190,000 cases
100% white
62% premier crus
30 producers

The Côte Chalonnaise has five AOPs.

low the style of the Côte de Beaune, but the fruits achieve less concentration. There is less use of new oak, and the wines are tighter. For the most part, Côte Chalonnaise has its own producers, although some appellations have negociants who have come from the Côte d'Or, the two leading examples being Faiveley in Mercurey and Louis Latour in Montagny.

The Bouzeron AOP is a rare source for Aligoté (the other being the more generic Bourgogne Aligoté). Growers have to decide whether to label their wines as Bouzeron (without mentioning the grape variety, which might therefore come as a surprise to the uninitiated) or whether to admit the variety but to use the lower-level appellation label of AOP Bourgogne Aligoté.

Aside from Bouzeron, the objective here is to achieve a level of reliability for Pinot Noir or Chardonnay in a mainstream style. With Côte Chalonnaise you don't get the fat, the richness, the uplift of the Côte d'Or, and this is more of a problem for the reds than the whites. The difference from the Côte d'Or is clear if you compare wines directly from those producers who have vineyards in both areas. Both reds and whites are generally best drunk young while still fresh and charming; it's a bit doubtful how much extra complexity is gained by long aging. The limit for whites is usually about five years after release. Reds are best after three or four years, but will last another three or four.

Mercurey is more than 90% red, and makes the firmest wines, although they sometimes reveal a slightly hard edge. There is a counterpoise between a superficial, rich glycerinic sheen to the fruits, and that touch of hardness on the finish. Givry produces mostly red wines in much the same style, perhaps not quite as firm. The reds of Rully are lighter. "For me, Rully always has more elegance, finesse; Mercurey has more depth, it's more robust," says Marie Jacqueson in Rully. Similarly, the relatively rare whites of Mercurey or Givry tend to have less overt fruit compared with Rully.

With 600 ha, Mercurey is the largest appellation. About a quarter of Mercurey is classified as premier cru, with just under 150 ha classified for red and less than 15 ha for white. The Faiveley negociant from Nuits St. Georges is a dominant force in Mercurey, having bought 60 ha in 1964, and owning

The most common premier crus of Montagny		
Les Vignes Longues		Northeast corner, facing north to northeast, cooler because not protected from north winds
Les Burnins	11 ha	In center of AOP, clay-limestone soils, facing south
Les Beaux Champs		Part of a valley in west of appellation with more clay
Montcuchot	12 ha	In center of AOP, plantings face east at tops of steep slopes of limestone and blue clay
Les Coères	34 ha	Southeast part of AOP, just above Chaniots, facing north and southeast, various types of clay, and some limestone
Les Chaniots	12 ha	Southeast corner, facing south and southeast, shallow soils, pebbles with lots of clay

several monopoles, including premier cru Les Myglands and lieu-dit Framboisières. Aside from Faiveley, the big name in Mercurey is the Château de Chamirey, where a policy of late picking gives unusually ripe wines for the appellation.

Almost half of Givry is classified into 38 premier crus, somewhat reducing their distinction. The line of premier crus essentially forms the center of the appellation, on an axis from southwest to northeast, with the village plots (including 29 named *climats*) lying on either side. The best vineyards are immediately west of the village of Givry, on soils with limestone terroir facing south. Altitude varies from 150-300m.

Rully is dominated by Vincent Dureuil-Janthial, whose wide range of cuvées from premier crus show unusual refinement for Côte Chalonnaise, and an interesting comparison with his wines from the Côte d'Or. The domain of Paul and Marie Jacqueson is a growing concern that offers an opportunity to compare Rully with Mercurey and Bouzeron.

Montagny is an appellation for white wines only. It has the distinction that all its vineyards were classified as premier cru in 1943, although they were reduced to two thirds of the area when the appellation was extended in 1989. But this still means that premier cru is a less reliable description in Montagny than elsewhere, although only about half the names are used anyway.

Many of the 51 premier crus are so small, only 2-3 ha, that it's impractical to bottle them alone, and most Montagny is simply bottled as generic premier cru. One way to handle the situation would be to imitate Chablis, and label minor premier crus under the name of an overlapping, more important cru. By this measure, the names of about 17 premier crus would be used.

Montagny also stands out for the loss of independent domains and the rise of the cooperative at Buxy, which together with the coop at Bissey-sous-Cruchaud now accounts for almost three quarters of production. The most

Some important premier crus in Givry		
Clos Jus	8 ha	Red clay and limestone, facing east, high up at north end of appellation, abandoned after phylloxera and replanted more recently, known for its black fruit character
Cellier aux Moins	4.5 ha	Another demonstration that the monks knew how to pick the best sites, south-facing on limestone
Clos de la Servoisine	6.6 ha	Adjacent to Cellier aux Moines, with rocky soils based on limestone
Clos Salomon	7 ha	A monopole of Domaine du Clos Salomon, facing east and south, with silty-clay soils on a limestone base of steep (8-30%) slopes.
Les Grands Prétans	5 ha	In the center of the appellation with clay-limestone soils
Les Grand Vignes	2.5 ha	At the south end of the appellation with clay-limestone soils

Reference wines for Côte Chalonnaise	
Bouzeron	Domaine A. & P. Villaine Guy Amiot
Givry (red)	François Lumpp, Petit Marole
Mercurey (red)	Paul & Marie Jacqueson, Les Naugues
Mercurey (white)	Château de Chamirey, La Mission
Montagny	Stéphane Aladame, Les Maroques
Rully (red)	Vincent Dureuil-Janthial, Chapitre
Rully (white)	Vincent Dureuil-Janthial, Les Meix Cadot

interesting wines in Montagny come from Stéphane Aladame's series of premier crus.

The whites are the strongest point of Côte Chalonnaise. At their best they can approach the flavor spectrum of the Côte d'Or, although they rarely achieve the same depth or flavor variety. Reds tend more to show the limitations of the Chalonnaise, but there are definite terroir differences between the appellations.

The Mâconnais

Mâcon stretches from just south of the Côte Chalonnaise to the border with Beaujolais, but very little wine is bottled as Mâcon plain and simple. About 60% of the area is classified as Mâcon Villages, and about 40% of that consists of individual villages whose names can be added after Mâcon. Almost all the wine is white, exclusively from Chardonnay, with just a little red and rosé (from Gamay) in the Mâcon appellation and from some of the individual villages.

Twenty seven villages can attach their names to Mâcon, and most of them are clustered in the southern half of the appellation, where the town of Mâcon itself is situated. Mâcon-Lugny is probably the best known example, and provides a major part of the individual village wines. (The cooperative in Lugny accounts for around a quarter.)

While there are differences in soil types between the villages that potentially affect the character of the wine, they are not as pronounced as in the more famous appellations of the Côte d'Or, and the major importance of the individual village name is that it indicates a higher quality level than simple Mâcon Villages. Differences between producers are more important than differences between the villages here.

There are also some individual appellations within the Mâconnais. Viré-Clessé, which was created in 1999 by merging the former village AOCs of Mâcon-Viré and Mâcon-Clessé, is in the center, but the others are located at

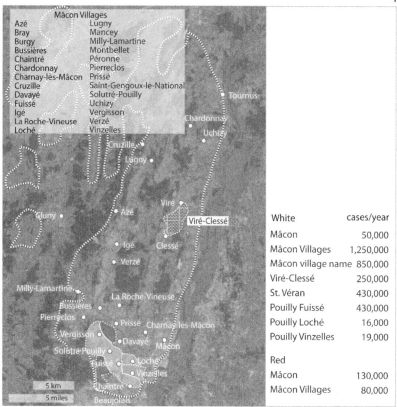

Mâcon Villages

Azé	Lugny
Bray	Mancey
Burgy	Milly-Lamartine
Bussières	Montbellet
Chaintré	Péronne
Chardonnay	Pierreclos
Charnay-lès-Mâcon	Prissé
Cruzille	Saint-Gengoux-le-National
Davayé	Solutré-Pouilly
Fuissé	Uchizy
Igé	Vergisson
La Roche-Vineuse	Verzé
Loché	Vinzelles

White	cases/year
Mâcon	50,000
Mâcon Villages	1,250,000
Mâcon village name	850,000
Viré-Clessé	250,000
St. Véran	430,000
Pouilly Fuissé	430,000
Pouilly Loché	16,000
Pouilly Vinzelles	19,000
Red	
Mâcon	130,000
Mâcon Villages	80,000

The best-known appellations and villages are clustered in the southern part of the Mâconnais.

the southern tip. By far the best known is Pouilly-Fuissé, accompanied by the much smaller satellites of Pouilly-Loché and Pouilly-Vinzelles. Split into two parts, the appellation of St. Véran straddles Pouilly-Fuissé and presents wines that used to be labeled as white Beaujolais.

Mâcon is usually a relatively straightforward wine, vinified and matured in stainless steel. The main difference between the named villages and the general Mâcon Villages appellation is a requirement for slightly greater ripeness (a named village must achieve at least 11% natural alcohol, compared with 10.5% for Mâcon Villages), but there is no great change in style, and it would be overly ambitious to try to define differences between individual villages. The general style is for light citrus fruits, without oak influence, with fruit intensity and aromatics depending on the producer and vintage. By and large, the most detailed specification on the label is a village, but there are occasional cuvées from single vineyards.

Viré-Clessé is a step up, making dry wines that also are mostly vinified in stainless steel. I specifically mention dry wines, because since 2018, producers have been allowed to make wines with some residual sugar, using the descriptions Demi-Sec (4-8 g/l) and Levrouté (8-18 g/l). (Levrouté is an old Mâconnais word meaning slightly sweet.) Sometimes there are botrytized cuvées with more residual sugar.

St. Véran makes only dry wines. It is close enough to Pouilly-Fuissé that some of the climat names overlap (and to add to the confusion, some of the names are used also in Mâcon). The difference between the two parts is that the western half is based on slopes of gray marl facing south and west, while the eastern half has slopes of marly limestone facing east. It's a step up from Viré-Clessé, but it's a much bigger step up to Pouilly-Fuissé.

There's a feeling that local interests aren't best served by the predominance of negociants who almost all come from the north. Most Mâcon—around three quarters—is made by negociants; four big negociants from Beaune have around 80% of the negociant market. The largest local negociant is Georges Duboeuf, but his focus is mostly on reds from Beaujolais. Yet there has been significant improvement in the quality of Mâcon at all levels in the past couple of decades, partly driven by growers from the Côte d'Or. Comtes Lafon of Meursault came to Milly-Lamartine in 1999, and Domaine Leflaive purchased vineyards in Mâcon-Verzé in 2003. Undoubtedly the most distinctive local negociant is Maison Verget, established by Jean-Marie Guffens in 1990, following the establishment of Guffens-Heynen as a small grower in 1979.

The wines from Guffens-Heynen mark the full potential of the region, and those of Verget show what can be done within practical limitations. "They are completely different," says Jean-Marie. "When you purchase grapes at Verget, you buy an appellation. When you buy Guffens, you buy a spirit. At Verget I work with pre-printed words but at the domain I have a blank page. We have a philosophy at Verget, but at the domain we don't have a philosophy. At the domain there is no leading idea. At Verget the philosophy is to make good wine within appellation rules at a decent price. We try to make wines as personal as possible, admitting the grapes are not grown as I would grow them. The cost price of picking at the domain is higher than the price I pay for the grapes for Verget."

Part of Jean-Marie's success in redefining the region comes from a difference in perspective. "People say no wood for Mâcon, but a lot for Bâtard Montrachet because it's a great wine. It's stupid, of course. My view is that all wines have to have the same treatment in order to show the terroir. I change my barrels every five years so there will be no difference between Corton Charlemagne and Mâcon-Vergisson." The Guffens-Heynen wines, from Mâcon-Pierreclos, St. Véran, and Pouilly-Fuissé, convey a textured impression of coming from grander appellations. With a very wide range of cuvées from Mâcon Villages to Pouilly-Fuissé, Verget's wines offer an unusual op-

Reference Wines for Mâconnais	
Mâcon Villages	Maison Verget
Mâcon-Milly Lamartine	Héritiers de Comtes Lafon
Mâcon-Pierreclos	Guffens-Heynen, Le Chavigne
Mâcon-Verzé	Domaine Leflaive
Viré-Clessé	André Bonhomme, Cuvée Spéciale
St. Véran	Guffens-Heynen, Cuvée Unique
Pouilly-Loché	Bret Brothers
Pouilly-Vinzelles	Domaine la Soufrandière, Les Quarts

portunity to see what difference terroir makes in the Mâconnais. (Verget also produces many cuvées of Chablis and some of Côte d'Or.) Moving from Mâcon to St. Véran to Pouilly-Fuissé, the Verget wines show increasing fruit concentration and a more subtle range of flavors, rather than changing in style. It's as clear a view of variations in the region as can be found.

Pouilly-Fuissé

The great name in the region is Pouilly-Fuissé. "Pouilly-Fuissé used to be a big brand name in the U.S., and visitors were very upset to come here and find only a small village," says Frédéric-Marc Burrier of Château de Beauregard. In fact, there are multiple Pouilly's, and in the nineteenth century all the wine was known simply as Pouilly. When the appellation contrôlée was formed, four of the villages decided to join Pouilly-Fuissé, but Loché and Vinzelles stayed out, becoming separate appellations. This may not have been so clever, as Pouilly-Loché and Pouilly-Vinzelles tend to be regarded now as distinctly second rank compared to Pouilly-Fuissé.

The general distinction between the Pouilly's and the surrounding appellations is that the Pouilly vineyards are on the slopes, and at the bottom the AOP changes to Mâcon. So Mâcon-Vinzelles comes from vineyards just below those of Pouilly-Vinzelles. (Similarly, when Viré-Clessé was created from the best parcels on the slopes above the villages in the old Mâcon-Viré and Mâcon-Clessé appellations, the rest became Mâcon Villages.) Pouilly-Fuissé is usually aged in oak, and although the tendency to new oak has been reduced (in the old days it often used to cover up the fruits), the style is lighter (and less complex) than the Côte d'Or, but more interesting than Mâcon.

The northern part of the appellation is marked by two calcareous cliff-faces, the Rock of Vergisson and the Rock of Solutré. Vineyards run up to the rocks, but lose the appellation at high elevations. This may be a consequence of history rather than a reflection of current reality. "The committee of INAO

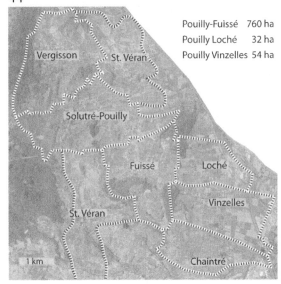

Pouilly-Fuissé	760 ha
Pouilly Loché	32 ha
Pouilly Vinzelles	54 ha

Pouilly-Fuissé consists of four communes; Pouilly-Loché and Pouilly-Vinzelles are separate appellations. St. Véran consists of two separate areas, one northeast of the Pouillys, the other southwest.

is blind like a horse," says Christine Saumaize-Michelin, whose vineyards are all around the rock of Vergisson. "They won't classify the *climat* above the rock because the elevation is too high, but in the time of global warming, this is completely ridiculous, a north-facing vineyard today is very good."

Pouilly-Fuissé is far from homogeneous. "There is no typicity in Pouilly-Fuissé; it all depends on the villages. Chaintré is always fruity, Vergisson is more mineral," says Jean-Philippe Bret at La Soufrandière in Fuissé. The big question then becomes whether to blend across the villages or to show them as separate cuvées. The trend today is towards defining individual vineyards.

A tasting at Château de Beauregard illustrates the range of terroir differences in Pouilly-Fuissé. Around ten cuvées from different climats range from precise and elegant to full bodied. Each is distinctive. And a vertical tasting going back four decades gives a stunning impression of the capacity of Pouilly-Fuissé to age. In a blind tasting, I would place the wines from seventies in the eighties, and the wines from the eighties in the nineties. These are terrific examples of the potential for aging, achieving a complexity more like what you expect from Meursault than Pouilly-Fuissé.

A move to precision is a common trend at top producers. "What we have at Domaine Ferret is the modern Pouilly-Fuissé, wines that let the grapes speak, and they vary significantly with the terroir. It might be hard to recognize these wines for some who have a stereotypical view of Pouilly-Fuissé with oak covering up the fruits. We are seeing a transparency now that gives a new view of the appellation and the wines," says Audrey Braccini, who took over winemaking at Ferret after Jadot bought the estate.

Until 2020 there was only a single appellation for Pouilly-Fuissé, although producers might distinguish cuvées from top vineyards by including the

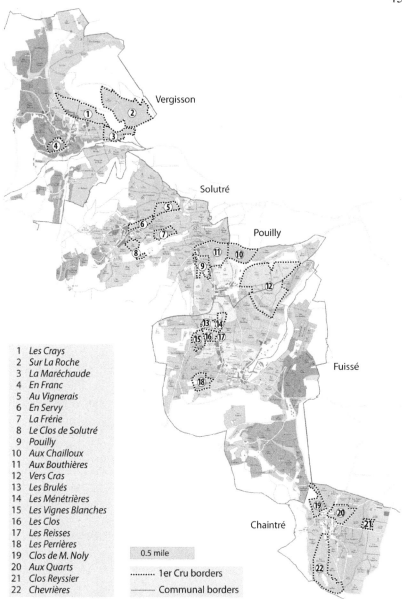

1. Les Crays
2. Sur La Roche
3. La Maréchaude
4. En Franc
5. Au Vignerais
6. En Servy
7. La Frérie
8. Le Clos de Solutré
9. Pouilly
10. Aux Chailloux
11. Aux Bouthières
12. Vers Cras
13. Les Brulés
14. Les Ménétrières
15. Les Vignes Blanches
16. Les Clos
17. Les Reisses
18. Les Perrières
19. Clos de M. Noly
20. Aux Quarts
21. Clos Reyssier
22. Chevrières

0.5 mile

.... 1er Cru borders

————— Communal borders

Pouilly-Fuissé has 22 premier crus, with the almost half (10) in Fuissé.

name of the climat on the label. The official map divides the appellation into 217 sites, and 10-20 of these are well-known enough to add some weight to the label. A process started in 2007 to get approval from INAO to promote the best to premier crus.

The village of Fuissé is in the heart of the Pouilly appellations, surrounded by vineyards on slopes.

"We are working hard to define premier crus. We think it has been really damaging for Mâcon to be the only area in Burgundy without a hierarchy of appellations," says Frédéric-Marc Burrier, in his capacity as president of the growers association in Pouilly-Fuissé, when the proposal was submitted. "We were using our best *climats* with an additional indication on the label before the war in exactly the same way as the Côte d'Or," he says ruefully, "but when Burgundy introduced the premier cru system, here they had a letter asking them to classify premier crus, but the president of the time did nothing about it. So Mâcon became the only part of Burgundy not to have premier crus and we have been paying for that ever since."

Finally INAO approved 22 premier crus, which cover 24% of the appellation area. They range about 10-fold in size, from the tiny 0.5 ha monopole of Les Reisses to the 50 ha cru of Les Cras, which straddles the border between Pouilly and Fuissé.

Terroirs have been much better defined as part of the preparation for premier crus. Frédéric-Marc maintains that, "The reputation of Pouilly-Fuissé for opulent, rich wines is quite wrong, we have wonderful variety of terroirs, we have all those levels mixed up from different geological periods, we have identified fifty different types of soil and geology. There's a million years' difference between the soils. We can find mineral Pouilly-Fuissé and we can find rich Pouilly-Fuissé from clay all over the appellation."

After tasting through the cuvées of Les Combettes, Le Clos, and Les Brûlées at Château Fuissé, winemaker Antoine Vincent says, "You were asking if there was a single style for Pouilly-Fuissé, here you have all three!" The

The famous rock formation of Solutré looms over the vineyards in the northern part of Pouilly-Fuissé.

lightest, Les Combettes, comes from deep soils on limestone, and is aged in old barriques. Just behind the winery, the slope of Le Clos has enough variation to justify older oak for the plots at the top and younger oak for the bottom. Les Brulées comes from the most powerful soils of the domain and uses 100% new oak. So here is a completely Burgundian view: "As I go to more powerful soils I use more oak and more new oak."

Although premier crus have more restrictive regulations, these are well below the standard set by top producers anyway. The importance of the definition is to formalize the existence of the best sites, which will make things easier for the consumer. The crus meet the criterion that that there is a difference in character and increase in complexity, not merely an increase in reliable ripeness. The introduction of a hierarchy will also have the effect of encouraging growers to bottle their own wines, which is perhaps another (unstated) intention. The main effect may be not so much to increase recognition (and prices) for the crus, as to counteract the idea of Pouilly-Fuissé as a relatively homogeneous lower-priced alternative to the Côte d'Or, and to place it on its own pedestal.

Reference Wines for Pouilly-Fuissé Crus	
Le Clos	Château Fuissé Domaine J.-A. Ferret
Les Brulés	Château Fuissé
Les Crays	Daniel et Martine Barraud
Les Ménétrières	Domaine J.-A. Ferret Château de Beauregard
Les Reisses	Robert-Denogent
Vers Cras	Château de Beauregard
Vignes Blanches	Domaine Saumaize-Michelin

Overview of Chablis

About 80 miles northwest of Beaune (and only 50 miles from Sancerre), Chablis is an outpost of Burgundy. Because of its cooler climate, Chablis today is thought of as a crisper, more mineral wine than Côte d'Or, but historically the difference was not so obvious. In the fourteenth century, wine from Auxerre (just to the west of Chablis) sold at a higher price than wine from Beaune. Before phylloxera, in fact, Auxerre was close to a monoculture of vines, but it never recovered from the loss of the vineyards. Chablis is essentially what remains.

Just to the southwest, the tiny AOP of Sauvignon St. Bris is the one place in Burgundy where Sauvignon Blanc is allowed, and adjacent to it lies Irancy AOP, where Pinot Noir is grown. Some Chablis producers also have small vineyards in these appellations. Chablis was very much a minor region until recently, but with around 5,000 ha today, it's comparable to the Côte de Beaune.

Chablis has a similar hierarchy of vineyards to the Côte d'Or, but not so detailed since Chablis is a single commune. In ascending order, the levels are Petit Chablis, Chablis, Premier Cru, and Grand Cru. The only grape grown in Chablis is Chardonnay. Chablis accounts for 20% of production in Burgundy.

Like the rest of Burgundy, individual vineyard holdings are quite small. Most producers have a range of wines, from Petit Chablis and Chablis to premier and grand crus. A typical producer probably makes 6-10 different wines. Some Chablis producers make a little red wine under the Bourgogne Epineuil or Irancy AOPs or a little Sauvignon Blanc under the Sauvignon St. Bris AOP.

As in the rest of Burgundy, most premier and grand crus are divided between multiple owners. Chablis has just over 100 ha of grand cru vineyards, but they are divided among (probably) around a hundred growers, with more than 60 producers making grand cru Chablis.

There was a great fuss in 2019 when INAO (the organization controlling appellations in France) proposed to remove the Chablis area from the regions allowed to make generic Bourgogne. This led to headlines asking, "Is Chablis part of Burgundy?" Chablis is distinct in its northern location, but its attitude remains distinctly Burgundian. The proposal was withdrawn after protests, so it remains technically possible for Chablis to be declassified to Bourgogne Blanc, although this is rare. (It's a more important issue for the surrounding areas immediately outside the Chablis AOP.)

Chablis has 23 negociants and 353 individual growers. Many growers belong to a cooperative; cooperatives account for a quarter of production. Most Chablis producers are entirely local, but some of the important negociants in Burgundy own estates in Chablis; Joseph Drouhin owns Drouhin-Vaudon, Louis Latour owns Simonnet-Febvre, and Faiveley owns Billaud-Simon.

Chablis and Limestone

Chablis stands alone from the rest of Burgundy, both geographically and climatically. Well to the north, it has the most marginal climate; ripening has traditionally been a problem. It's been the epitome of minerality in white wine, traditionally very different from the fleshiness of the Côte d'Or. Its distinctive geology is based on the famous Kimmeridgian limestone, a soft mixture of clay and limestone, generally gray in color. This was laid down when the sea retreated in the Jurassic period, leaving a bed of fossils that give the soil its calcareous nature. (Several producers have large fossils, retrieved from their vineyards, on show in their tasting rooms.)

A stretch of limestone, the Kimmeridgian chain, runs from Sancerre, through Chablis, to the southernmost part of Champagne. It is history and climate that focus on Sauvignon Blanc in Sancerre, Chardonnay in Chablis, and sparkling wine in Champagne. (Premier Cru Mont de Milieu in Chablis supposedly takes its name for being halfway between Champagne and Burgundy.)

Kimmeridgian limestone occupies about half of the Chablis region; the rest consists of Portlandian limestone, harder in structure and browner in color. When the AOC was defined, the area for Chablis and its premier and grand crus was restricted to vineyards on Kimmeridgian soil. There was not much doubt that the quality dropped on leaving Kimmeridgian terroir. Portlandian limestone was restricted to the lowest level, Petit Chablis.

Kimmeridgian soil is based on a slightly crumbly mixture of limestone and clay with fossilised shells. Courtesy BIVB.

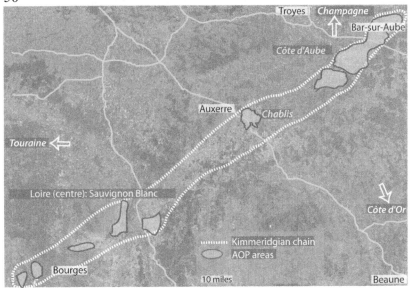

The vineyards of Chablis are in the middle of the Kimmeridgian chain. Chardonnay is also grown to the northeast for the Aube area of Champagne. Sauvignon Blanc is grown to the southwest in the Loire.

Was the superiority of Kimmeridgian limestone due only to the soil? The Kimmeridgian soil is located on the south and east-facing slopes, where good exposure helps to compensate for the cool climate, whereas the harder Portlandian soil occupies the plateaus at higher elevations (where the grapes are slower to ripen). The original distinction was not ill-founded, but it had more to do with aspect and slope than with the underlying geology.

When the Chablis AOC was defined in 1938, the total vineyard area was only 400 ha. Restricting Chablis and its premier and grand crus to Kimmeridgian limestone continued to be the case as the AOC expanded to include vineyards in communes around Chablis. But in 1978, when a further expansion occurred, the restriction was dropped. It's hard to better producer William Fèvre's protest at the time: "These areas of woodland and scrub have never had Chardonnay vines in the past. When these bounds are passed, there are no longer any limits."

The Chablis AOP

Chablis comes from both banks of the river Serein, extending away from the town. Petit Chablis comes from outlying areas (the best Petit Chablis tend to come from the plateau above the grand crus). The most important vineyards are near the town. The premier crus are not quite as numerous as they might seem from the variety of labels—there are 40 different names alto-

Lighting candles at night to warm the vineyard at ground level is a common means of fighting frost, which is frequent in Chablis given its Northern location.

gether—because many have separate names for different climats within them. Just opposite the town on the right bank, a long curve of vineyards is divided into seven Grand Cru climats.

Coming from a cool climate (often marginal until the recent warming trend), Chablis traditionally has crisp acidity. Petit Chablis has greatly benefited from warmer vintages, and the best Petit Chablis today is close to the quality of Chablis twenty or so years ago. There is always good acidity, but the wine can be quite fruity and very agreeable for drinking immediately.

The main difference in going to Chablis AOP is a sense of greater fruit density on the palate, with more texture and flavor variety. Chablis AOP is intended for drinking soon after release; it is a rare cuvée that benefits from being held for more than three years.

Premier crus show the greatest range of quality, from those that are barely distinguishable from a top communal wine in a good year, to those that skirt the quality of the grand crus. Alcohol is more moderate than on the Côte d'Or, usually 12.5% for communal Chablis, often 13% for the premier crus and usually 13% for the grand crus, but rarely more than 13%. "If you harvest at more than 13% alcohol you make Chardonnay not Chablis. If we harvested by the same criteria as 20-30 years ago, we would have a great increase in alcohol, but now we harvest 2-3 weeks earlier to keep freshness and avoid it," says Benoît Droin.

Once you leave the grand crus and top premier crus behind, Chablis is a good deal less interesting. It's certainly worth paying the (relatively) modest premium for a premier cru compared to communal Chablis.

Like all Burgundy, the producer's name is of paramount importance, and negociants have generally been well in second place behind individual growers. There are some important exceptions. Verget (based in Mâcon) was

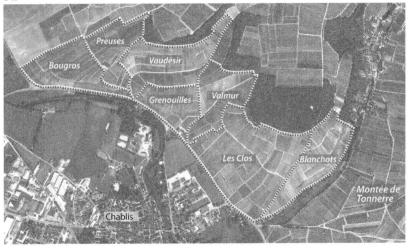

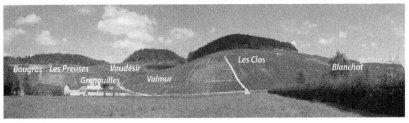

The grand crus form a single continuous line of vineyards with varying slopes and exposures. (Premier Cru Montée de Tonnerre lies across a gully at the eastern end.)

viewed with suspicion for producing Chablis in a richer style twenty years ago. More recently, Patrick Piuze and Benjamin Laroche (La Manufacture) have adopted a micro-negociant model, being involved in grape-growing of specific plots, and making wine to their own specifications.

The major cooperative in Chablis, La Chablisienne, is unusually important, one of the most respected in the country; and because it represents many small growers, offers the widest range of wines (in fact, probably the only opportunity to compare the entire range of crus).

Grand Crus

The grand crus occupy a continuous slope, but the land folds and turns so there are changes in exposure and slope, with significant variation in character. Technically there is one Chablis grand cru, with seven *climats*, but in practice these are regarded as though there were seven different grand crus.

The grand crus extend all the way from the road just on the edge of the town to the woods at the top of the hill. With the much slighter slope along the Côte de Nuits, for example, everything depends on position on the slope, but no distinction is made within Chablis grand crus, even though there are differences in soil types as well as exposure to the sun. As a general rule, the grand crus tend to be more directly south-facing than the premier crus—this is part of their advantage—but there are sufficient twists and turns in the land that it's not a hard and fast rule.

Les Clos, the largest grand cru, always makes the most powerful wine, irrespective of whether the plot is in a protected position under the trees at the top or exposed in the middle or at the bottom. The minerality of Chablis reaches its peak in Les Clos. Whenever a producer has more than one grand cru, the Les Clos stands out for its reserve when young, which translates into greater longevity. Les Clos can be austere when young: wines from top growers, such as Vincent Dauvissat or Raveneau, may take a decade to come out.

Next to Les Clos, Valmur is usually richer and less mineral. Between Valmur and Preuses on the upper part of the slope, Vaudésir is elegant and more aromatic, with an intensity that can border on spicy. Les Preuses is the most delicate of the grand crus, with something of a sense of perfume. Blanchots can be delicate also, and is sometimes described as the most feminine of the grand crus. Grenouilles, at the foot of the slope, is the smallest of the grand crus (with most owned by the cooperative La Chablisienne); it is firm but accessible. Bougros, at the northwestern end of the range, is considered to be the slightest of the grand crus.

Premier Crus

There are three premier crus on the right bank. Fourchaume is just to the north of the grand crus; the largest of the premier crus, its size is roughly equivalent to all the grand crus. Of course, this makes for some variability, the Vaulorent part of Fourchaume is the best. Montée de Tonnerre is across a deep gully just to the south of Les Clos, and is the premier cru that most often approaches the grand crus in quality. Mont de Milieu is parallel to Montée de Tonnerre, but farther south.

On the left bank, Chablis is really a series of valleys, fanning out from the town. As there are vineyards on both sides of the valleys, they face in all directions. Usually the premier crus are the most south facing. Montmains and Vaillons, which are the best premier crus on the left bank, have similar southeast exposures on parallel hillsides in adjacent valleys, as does Côte de Léchet. Montmains tends to be more powerful and more complex than Vaillons.

Usually in Burgundy there's a fine line between premier crus and grand crus, with some premier crus standing out above the others and occasioning argument as to whether they should be promoted to grand cru. In Chablis the argument is more at the other end: there is doubt whether some of the premier crus created in 1978 merit the description.

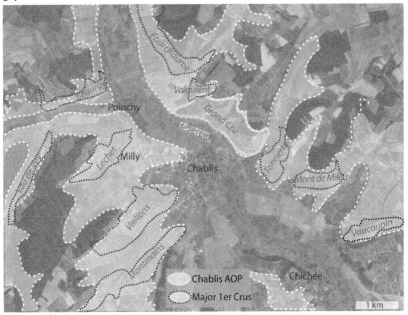

The best premier crus are in line with the grand crus or immediately across the river.

There are certainly far too many premier crus, or to be more precise, too many overlapping names within the premier crus. This can make it more difficult for a premier cru to establish a clear impression. A handful of the *climats* within the premier crus are well known, mostly because they used by top producers, such as Vaulorent (in Fourchaume), Chapelot (in Montée de Tonnerre), La Fôret and Butteaux (in Montmains) or Séchets (in Vaillons), but for the most part they are more like brand names than useful descriptions of origin.

It is not straightforward to find a defining difference between the premier crus of the left and right banks. There's a tendency for the left bank to have less marne (clay and limestone) and shallower soils, and perhaps it is fair to say that the left bank crus tend to be more linear, more mineral, and to show more salinity; while the right bank crus are is broader and denser. Mont de Milieu, Montée de Tonnerre, and especially Fourchaume, have more fat, more weight on the palate. In the hands of top producers, Montée de Tonnerre and Fourchaume are the premier crus that come closest to the style of the grand crus.

It is also true that the right bank premier crus are all long established as adjuncts to the grand crus, but the impression of left bank premier crus is somewhat diluted by the "new" premier crus (created in 1978), which vary from approaching the quality of the original premier crus to barely above appellation standard.

Premier Cru	Climats
Chablis has 17 premier crus but a total of 89 individual climats	
Right Bank	
Fourchaume	Côte de Fontenay, L'Homme Mort, Vaulorent, Vaupulent
Vaucoupin	
Montée de Tonnerre	Chapelot, Pied d'Aloup, Côte de Bréchain
Mont de Milieu	
Left Bank	
Beauroy	Côte de Savant, Troesmes
Berdiot	
Les Beauregards	Côte de Cuisy
Chaume de Talvat	
Côte de Jouan	
Côte de Léchet	
Côte de Vaubarousse	
Les Fourneaux	Morein, Côte des Près Girots
Montmains	Forêts, Butteaux
Vaillons	Beugnons, Chatains, les Épinottes, Les Lys, Mélinots, Roncières, Séchets
Vaudevey	Vaux Ragons
Vauligneau	Vau de Longue, Vau Girault, La Forêt, Sur la Forêt
Vosgros	Vaugiraut

The most important premier crus are shown in bold. The most commonly found climats for each premier cru are shown on the right.

Styles of Chablis

"They were all so bad in Chablis twenty years ago. For me, concentration is important, lower yields and riper. But everyone said, we are making Chablis, it's never ripe, the typical Chablis is green. People said, when you make ripe Chablis, it loses its character. But you can't make wine from unripe grapes—all green wines taste the same," says negociant Jean-Marie Guffens, who makes a wide range of Chablis at Verget. Today the rest of Chablis has caught up, and that increase in ripeness is typical of the entire appellation. If effects of global warming on white wine are evident anywhere in Burgundy, it's in Chablis.

The first time I tasted a Chablis from Verget, I was certainly surprised: its density and fatness of structure were quite unusual. It seemed of Domaine François Raveneau. Didier Seguier at William Fèvre thinks global warming is a great opportunity, giving better wines that retain acidity and balance, but without losing character. "The typicity of our wine comes from the Kimmeridgian terroir, it's very different (from the Côte d'Or). Warming gives a very interesting maturity today but not sur-maturity."

At one of the domains that has stayed true to the traditions of Chablis right through the era of global warming, Bernard Raveneau expressed an interesting view of the difference between Chablis and the Côte d'Or when I asked why Chablis does not seem to have had the same problems with premox (premature oxidation) as white Burgundy. "We haven't been following some of the trends of the Côte d'Or such as excessive battonage or reduction of sulfur. On the Côte d'Or they are very traditional, here in Chablis we are more modern, oenological techniques are more evident, it's a different mentality. People in Chablis pay more attention to winemaking; on Cote d'Or, if malo doesn't start, they'll shrug and wait until the Spring when it warms up, here people will do something about it, to get the process finished. Chablis is the New World of Burgundy. In the 1960s, Chablis was 700 ha, today it's 5,500 ha—so it's a very new vineyard and people are more modern, they like investing in technology, where in Côte d'Or it's very ancestral."

When I ask producers how they see Chablis today, the answers are pretty uniform: it should retain freshness and minerality. Following up by asking how its character has changed, the answer is generally dismissive: it hasn't really changed at all, they say. Global warming has been beneficial; chaptalization has become rare, difficult vintages have turned out much better than they used to, but that essential tension between fruit and acidity, perhaps what the French call nervosité, hasn't changed at all. I don't agree on this last, crucial point about character.

I remember when most Chablis was thin and acid, where the fruits (if you could detect them) were bitter lemon or grapefruit. Granted that citrus remains the dominant flavor in the Chablis spectrum, often enough today it moves from fresh citrus to stewed fruits, rounder and softer, and often enough there are notes of stone fruits running in the direction of peaches or even apricots. Minerality is hard to describe, but like pornography you know it when you taste it, and it's fair in my opinion to say that in some cases it has now become subservient to the fruits.

Climate change has certainly had a significant effect in Chablis. While the effects have mostly been beneficial, there has also been collateral damage in the form of more erratic weather patterns, especially in the crucial period of the Spring. The historic problem in Chablis has always been frost in the Spring, at any time from the end of March to middle of May. This has not stopped, in fact recently it has been worse than ever. Freezing weather in April dramatically reduced the crop in 2016 and 2017, even hitting areas that usually have been exempt. Hailstorms have become more of an occupational hazard, to the point at which INAO finally relented and allowed hail nets to be used as of 2018. But the general drift of these problems is that they reduce quantity, and the wine that is made is good quality. Like other marginal wine regions, the balance has shifted from a minority of really good vintages each decade to a minority of poor vintages.

Oak in Chablis

The big divide in Chablis used to be between producers who do or do not use oak. "In the eighties there were two big schools, cuve and oak; my father was always stainless steel; he used to say, I'm not in the timber business. But he has changed his mind," says Fabien Moreau at Christian Moreau. "William Fèvre always used some new oak, but that stopped as soon as Henriot took over in 1998. We didn't want to *boisé* the vin, to the contrary we wanted to keep freshness," says Didier Seguier, who came to Fèvre from Bouchard at the time. Here you see the convergence in Chablis: protagonists for stainless steel have taken up oak, while protagonists for oak have backed off.

Richer vintages may be partly responsible for the convergence of style. Many producers now use a mixture of maturation in cuve and barrique. Where partial oak is used, the wine may spend only six months in oak before assemblage with the wine from cuve, after which it spends another six months in cuve only.

Two producers stand out in the oak camp: François Raveneau and Vincent Dauvissat are generally recognized as the best in Chablis. But neither uses any new oak. Each house is notable for the subtlety of its style. Is global warming a threat to that subtlety? "No, personally I think the place will adjust. I harvest early, the terroir resets the balance, it's the backbone of the wine," says Vincent Dauvissat.

Minerality is always there as a thread running from nose through palate to finish, fruits tend to the citrus spectrum but with hints of stone fruits more evident in warmer vintages, and there's a delicious overtone of anise or liquorice on the finish. Les Clos is the epitome of the style for both producers, always showing a more evident streak of structure, with Valmur placing second for Raveneau, and Les Preuses second for Dauvissat. Montée de Tonnerre is the best of the premier crus for both.

Other producers in the oak camp have their own styles. At Jean-Paul and Benoît Droin, the style is richer, and the various crus have different maturation regimes. Stainless steel is used for Chablis AOP, some premier crus, and Blanchots, but Mont de Milieu and Montée de Tonnerre have 25% oak, which increases to 35% for Vaudésir, 40% for Montmains and Valmur, and 50% for Fourchaume and Les Clos. The interesting feature is that there isn't a straight

Reference Wines for Chablis	
Petit Chablis	L. C. Poitout Domaine Vrignaud
Chablis	Jean-Claude Bessin Samuel Billaud Gilbert Picq (Vieilles Vignes)
Premier Crus	
Fourchaume	William Fèvre Nathalie & Gilles Fèvre
L'Homme Mort	Domaine de Chantermerle (Francis Boudin)
Mont de Milieu	Louis Pinson Jean Collet et Fils
Montmains	Domaine Laroche Laurent Tribut
Montée de Tonnerre	Jean-Paul et Benoît Droin Louis Michel
Vaillons	Christian Moreau Louis Moreau La Manufacture
Grand Crus	
Blanchots	Domaine Laroche
Bougros	William Fèvre
Grenouilles	La Chablisienne
Preuses	Vincent Dauvissat William Fèvre
Vaudésir	Billaud Simon Louis Michel
Valmur	François Raveneau Jean-Paul et Benoît Droin
Les Clos	François Raveneau Vincent Dauvissat

increase going from premier crus to grand crus, as would be usual in the Côte d'Or, but a view that different terroirs have different potentials for handling oak. There is a little new oak here, but less than there used to be, now limited to no more than 10% in the grand crus.

The arch exponent of the unoaked style is Louis Michel, whose premier and grand crus often achieve a complexity creating the impression in blind tasting that they must have been matured in oak. But the use of barriques stopped forty years ago; since then the wines have been vinified exclusively

François Raveneau
Vincent Dauvissat
Laurent Tribut
Pattes Loup
Jean-Claude Bessin
Louis Michel
Domaine Pinson
Samuel Billaud
William Fèvre
Christian Moreau
Billaud-Simon
Domaine Droin
Gilbert Picq
Patrick Piuze
Maison Verget
Jean Collet
Daniel Dampt
Jean Dauvissat
Drouhin-Vaudon
La Chablisienne
Nathalie et Gilles Fèvre
La Manufacture
Domaine des Malandes
Denis Race
Jean-Marc Brocard
Simonnet-Febvre
Domain Grossot
Domaine Laroche
Domaine Servin
Long-Depaquit
Verget
Garnier

SAVORY

FRUITY

A classification of producers on a scale from savory to fruity.

in stainless steel. In fact, the texture and structure are due to slow fermentation followed by time on the lees (typically 6 months for Chablis, 12 months for premier cru, and 18 months for grand cru).

The top wines have an almost granular texture supporting what is perhaps more a sense of steel and stone than overt minerality. They are great wines, although I don't think they have quite the same longevity as the oaked style.

Each producer has his own view on how best to express terroir differences in Chablis. Is this done by vinifying all wines in the same way, so that the only significant difference is the terroir? This is the view of both Dauvissat and Raveneau (with only oak) and Louis Michel (with only steel), and Jean-Claude Bessin (all premier and grand crus with 60% oak). Or should vinification be adjusted to the Cru, as it is at William Fèvre, Droin, Laroche, Long-Depaquit, Christian Moreau, and La Manufacture, with a general policy of increasing oak proportion going up a hierarchy of premier and grand crus. Somewhere in between are Pinson and the Chablisienne cooperative, where all premier crus get the same treatment, but grand crus get more oak.

Unlike the Côte d'Or, where all wines age in oak, and the progression from communal wine to premier cru to grand cru usually involves increasing the proportion of new oak, in Chablis the progress is more a matter of adjusting the mix of stainless steel to old oak. While many producers are committed to stainless steel and a few are committed to barriques, most of those producers who use barriques use them only partially. Lots matured in stainless steel are blended with lots matured in barrique, and there is a rough correlation between the quality of the terroir and the proportion matured in barrique, increasing through the premier crus to the grand crus.

Producers who age in oak do not necessarily ferment in the barrel, but may transfer to barrique after fermenting in stainless steel. Fermentation in concrete is rare in Chablis, but occasional producers are now trying concrete eggs for aging. There are also some experiments with amphora. But for the most part, Chablis is stainless steel or oak or a mix of the two.

As a rough measure, it seems to me that producers can be classified on savory/fruity balance. The most savory would be Raveneau and Dauvissat, both committed to oak, and perhaps for that reason my favorites. But there is no exact correlation between use of oak and tendency to savory. The balance changes with every cuvée and vintage, of course, but perhaps this is a useful guide to thinking about how producers fit into changing styles. The differences are not as violent as the arguments in some other locations between modernists and traditionalists, but the fruity style may be more modern, at least in the sense that wines like this would have been difficult or impossible to produce until recent times.

The Longevity of Chablis

Chablis suffers less than whites from the Côte d'Or from the premature oxidation (premox) that has been spoiling white wines since the 1996 vintage. I wonder whether a difference is battonage is a contributing factor to the occurrence of premature oxidation on the Côte d'Or and its relative absence in Chablis. Named for the wooden baton that used to be used, battonage stirs up the lees periodically to increase richness in the wine. Although maturation on the lees is common, typically for around 12 months for premier cru and around 18 months for grand cru, battonage is unusual in Chablis. "We don't have the same body and strength as the Cote de Beaune, if we go too far with battonage the wine will be good at first but will tire quickly," says Sandrine Audegond at Domaine Laroche.

Premox is not a problem with Petit Chablis or Chablis anyway, as they are intended to be enjoyed young: I would drink Petit Chablis immediately and would not keep a Chablis AOP for more than a couple of years. The best premier crus—Montée de Tonnerre, Fourchaume, Mont de Milieu, Vaillons, Montmains—from a good producer should improve over four or five years; premier crus from Raveneau or Dauvissat will last for around a decade. Grand Crus really should not really be started until five or six years after the vintage and should last for a decade. Les Clos is the longest lived of all; it can even be on the austere side when young.

Vintages

The most common problem historically in Burgundy has been cool or wet weather, especially at time of harvest, but more recently there have also been problems with heat. The increasingly erratic nature of weather conditions is summarized by Marie-Andrée Mugneret's comment that, "In 2016 we lost 80% of the harvest to frost, in 2017 we needed to do a green harvest to reduce yields." "The first half of the decade through 2014 was cool—2013 was the coolest vintage I've ever made—but since then the years have all been warm," says Jean-Nicolas Méo. 2018 was a large, ripe vintage. "There was no need to sort in 2018," says Jean-Nicolas.

Climate change has increased alcohol levels. "The last four vintages—2015, 2016, 2017, 2018—we had to fight for freshness. Some of my colleagues got 15% alcohol. Years ago they would have been happy to get 11%," says Michel Mallard at Domaine d'Eugenie. Yet chaptalization still occurs in weaker vintages.

While there are distinctions between areas, with local conditions giving different results in the Côte de Beaune and Côte de Nuits, the most important distinction is between red and white wines. Sometimes the best vintages for red wines result in white wines with less acidity and aging potential (a concern increased by the occurrence of premox).

Some pairs of vintages, such as 2015/2016, 2009/2010, or 2005/2006, have a first year with superb red wines, but a second year where whites are crisper and likely to age better. However, uncertainty about the premature oxidation problem means that any white Burgundy more than, say, five years old for village, and eight years for premier or grand cru, is suspect, so notes for older vintages are now really of historical interest only.

"With climate change, the wines of Chablis have really changed, the situation is completely different from the eighties," says Vincent Dampt at Domaine Daniel Dampt. Global warming has brought the style of Chablis more into line with the rest of Burgundy, and vintages today tend to be divided into those that are characterized as classic, because the predominant

Climate Change in Burgundy

Like everywhere in Northern France, Burgundy has had problems with frost killing the crop in the Spring because bud break was advanced by mild temperatures, significant increases in temperatures during the growing season, and hang times becoming shorter because of early harvests. Alcohol has increased to up to 14%, which is problematic in terms of maintaining style, especially for Pinot Noir.

Burgundy is a mix of vineyards propagated by selection massale (taking cuttings from existing vines) or using clones. There are 47 officially approved clones of Pinot Noir, but the best-known are the series known as the Dijon clones; indeed, they have spread beyond Burgundy and are used worldwide. Selected in Domaine Ponsot's vineyard in Morey St. Denis in the 1970s, they originated in a cooler period when the concern was to reach sufficient ripeness. There is growing realization that they may not be the best choice in the era of global warming.

"To moderate effect of climate change on the style of the wines of Burgundy, we can seek clones that accumulate less sugar and ripen later," says Laurent Audeguin at the French Vine and Wine Institute (IFV)." The house of Louis Latour has a project to identify cultivars that produce less sugar and more acidity; they are also looking at rootstocks that slow growth and delay ripening. The authorities are considering adding some old grape varieties to the approved list, but all the precedents suggest this will have no effect against the predominance of Pinot Noir and Chardonnay.

influence is that fresh, lively acidity, as opposed to warmer vintages where there is palpably more richness. In warmer vintages such as 2005 and 2009, the wines have been lovely at first, but have not had their usual longevity. In 2015 the wines were attractive on release, but give the impression of retaining enough freshness to last well. "Our experience in 2009 has helped us to do better in 2015," says Vincent Dampt. "2015 is a very straightforward vintage, very facile, but Chablisiens prefer 2014 or 2016 to 2015," says Samuel Billaud. However, "in 50 years of making Chablis, I have never known such difficult conditions (as in 2016)," says Michel Laroche. There was frost in April, hail in May, virtually no Spring, and rain until the end of June, followed by mildew. This is the other side of climate change.

2020		The early start on August 12 was a record. The vintage was 2 weeks ahead of the average for the past 25 years. Harvest finished the second week of September. Yields were reduced by the low rainfall during the season.
2019	***	Following a hot, dry summer, there is small volume (substantially less than 2018, especially in more exposed sites), equally good for reds and whites, and wines are concentrated with strong structure.
2018	***	Hailed by producers as a great vintage, possibly a rival to 1947 (which was very hot, rich, and alcoholic). Another large vintage (although not a large as 2017), with harvest starting very early in August, and grapes reaching high levels of ripeness, so alcohol may be high, sometimes 14% for grand crus. Acidification was common. Reds will be rich, whites could have problems with freshness.
2017	**	Largest crop since 2009, some differences depending on whether producers picked before or after rain was forecast for first week of September. Quality is good, although not as concentrated as 2016 or 2015 for reds, and whites range from very good to outstanding. Both reds and whites often show a tang of acidity on the finish. Early drinking, this is a lovely restaurant vintage.
2016	**	A very small vintage because crop size was reduced by frost and hail; some producers have made only a quarter of normal production. A warm September gave good harvest conditions, and the wines are of excellent quality, lively for the whites and rich for the reds. However, they will be in short supply. Considered a more "classic" vintage in terms of structure, more linear than 2015. Reds are well structured, and may last longer than those of 2015. Whites have appealing freshness and precision, and should age well if premox does not set in.
2015	***	A rich vintage. Reds have good structure as well as richness, deep and round, and should age well. They are superficially more opulent than the 2016 vintage. Whites are immediately appealing, but seem to have enough freshness to last better than the 2009 vintage.

2014	*	Storms with hail during growing season reduced crop greatly in many communes, but weather improved after very difficult August. Whites started out fruity and easy, but now seem leaner and more acid. Reds are not as rich as 2009, 2012, or 2015, but should be good for short to mid term.
2013		Cold growing season was difficult, but some improvement in September allowed decent harvest for wines that will be good rather than great.
2012	*	Erratic conditions led to low yields of both reds and whites, but quality is quite good, although some whites are developing herbaceous overtones which suggest grapes may not have been completely ripe. It is not a graceful vintage.
2011		Difficulties in getting to ripeness make this the least successful vintage of the decade to date.
2010	***	Reds are tighter than the opulent 2009s, with an elegant balance, and potential for good aging. Whites show good acidity, a crisper, leaner style than 2009, but with greater potential for longevity.
2009	***	A great year for reds, rich, ripe and opulent, but a lingering question is whether they will have the tannic structure for extended longevity. Whites were opulent at first, but unlikely to age long as richness is well ahead of acidity. Most have reached their peaks.
2008		Difficult vintage with problems of rain and humidity. Reds show high acidity, whites are on the fresh side.
2007	***	Growing season was too wet, reds suffered from problems with humidity, the whites are better but on the acid side.
2006	*	Reds have a tendency towards austerity resulting from cool conditions leading to high acidity.
2005	***	Reds are on the opulent side but with good tannic structure for long-term development. Whites show classic opulence for a warm year, impression of fat when young, but by now the tendency to earlier aging is making most questionable.
2004	*	Both reds and whites are on the lighter, more acid side, and there are not many of interest today.
2003		Reds tended to be cooked from the outset, and almost all were short-lived. The heat was too much for the whites, which tended to be flabby.
2002	***	Reds are quite rich but well structured, and the best are à point. Whites tended to show opulence but the premature aging of white Burgundy means most are now too old.
2001	*	Not a bad vintage at the time, although a bit tannic for reds and acid for whites, but not of serious interest today.
2000	*	Nice enough wines for early drinking, but few survived to the end of the decade.

1999	***	Generous vintage for reds with good supporting structure; the best are still at their peak. Whites showed nice combination of generosity and minerality, but are now too old.
1998	*	Not very interesting at the time and no longer of interest.
1997	*	Pleasant wines for short term drinking at the time.
1996	***	A frustrating year for reds. Billed as vins de garde, they started with strong tannins, but have never come around. The problem is a punishing bitter medicinal acidity that tarnishes the finish. Some grand crus are rare exceptions where concentration of fruits compensates. This was a lovely vintage for whites at the outset: crisp, mineral, and precise, but it was the first vintage where premox became a major problem, cutting short longevity.
1995	**	Reds seemed a little tight at first but in retrospect were generous compared with the following vintage in 1996. They developed in a charming, lighter style, rather than opulent. Whites showed good concentration and weight, but are too old now.
1994		Autumn rains spoiled the harvest, but whites were better than reds.
1993	*	Reds gave quite a charming vintage in a lighter style for mid-term consumption, but the whites were less successful due to lack of concentration.
1992		The best wines were picked before rain spoiled the harvest.
1991		A rare vintage where the whites were quite successful, tending to elegance on Côte d'Or, but the reds never quite made it.
1990	***	A great vintage with good balance of fruit to structure; long-lived for reds. A great vintage for the opulent style of white Burgundy.

Visiting the Region

The Côte d'Or is compact, but even so it can take a while to go up and down the N74 (now the D974), so it is a good idea to group visits into villages or adjacent villages. The two bottlenecks in driving around are Beaune and Nuits St. Georges. The best way is to divide producers into three groups: south of Beaune; Beaune to Nuits St. Georges; and north of Nuits St. Georges.

Be prepared for it to take time negotiating the larger towns (Beaune, Nuits St. Georges, Gevrey Chambertin) to find producers, especially the rabbit warren of small streets in Beaune.

To get a good perspective on the region, it is useful to visit both larger negociants (mostly located in or around Beaune) and smaller producers (spread around the villages). The N74 is lined with producers who can be visited without an appointment, but these are not usually the most interesting. It is a much better experience to make an appointment.

The Hospices de Beaune is the major tourist attraction in the town

At the large negociants, a visit and tasting is likely to be conducted by a guide, but at the smaller producers in the villages it will very likely be the owner/ winemaker (more properly the vigneron) who shows you around. (This makes it important to have an appointment: it is a good idea to make this a few weeks in advance.) Seeing winery facilities is common, but you do not usually get taken into the vineyards. Larger negociants have English speaking guides, but some smaller producers may not speak English.

There's a long tradition of selling wines directly to consumers in Burgundy—people used to come down from Paris and fill up containers in the past—so most large producers and many family concerns will sell to visitors, but the more important domains whose wines are in high demand, often on allocation, will not.

Beaune is the gastronomic center, with restaurants at all levels from bistros to Michelin stars. Le Beneton is the most innovative of the one stars. Jardin des Remparts has recovered its form and has a lovely garden. Loiseau des Vignes has excellent food, and a vast number of wines by the glass, but is spoiled by over-priced wines. Prices at Le Carmin reflect its expensive location in Place Carnot. Among bistros, Ma Cuisine is a hangout for wine people with a very long wine list, L'Ecrit Vin has a good atmosphere, but the Bistro de l'Hôtel de Beaune is terribly overpriced.

To the north, the center of Nuits St. Georges has been gentrified with a pedestrian precinct. There are several casual eating places in Nuits St. Georges, but otherwise there are mostly formal restaurants to the north

The center of Nuits St. Georges is a pedestrian precinct with shops and cafes.

With the Château at its center, Meursault is the largest and liveliest of the villages south of Beaune.

of Beaune. Gevrey Chambertin is the only other village of any size until you get to Dijon. There are wine shops in Nuits St. Georges, including Cavon de Bacchus, which has a good display from local and other sources, and the Caveau des Vignerons in Gevrey Chambertin, where the wines of 32 producers who do not sell direct can be tasted. There is not much of interest for the tourist between Gevrey Chambertin and Dijon, but Marsannay plans to introduce a Caveau des Vignerons.

Gentrification is less extensive in the villages south of Beaune. The only village where signs to the Centre Ville have much significance is Meursault, which sprawls out around the old Château de Citeaux, which is surrounded by shops and restaurants. Pommard has a grand church dominating its square, but restaurants are off to the side by the N74. Volnay and Chassagne Montrachet are each really little more than a church and few houses. Puligny Montrachet, perhaps the best known, is the most chic, perhaps a bit stultified by gentrification. The Place des Marroniers at its core has been reworked and turned into a chic square—alas there are no longer any Marroniers (chestnut trees)—but there isn't otherwise very much in the center. Farther south, Santenay has the liveliest village center, with some cafés in the main square.

Côte Chalonnaise

This is quite an accessible region, with the main road running straight down from the southernmost part of the Côte d'Or. It would be easy to visit producers in all the appellations in the same day in one day. Mercurey is the main town. Like the Côte d'Or, larger producers have tasting rooms that are open with no appointment required, but it is a good idea to call ahead to smaller producers, where the owner may be the only person available to show visitors around. The producers' organization has a tasting room with wines from many producers:

- La Maison Des Vins De La Côte Chalonnaise
  2 promenade Sainte Marie, 71100 Chalon Sur Saône
  (+33 3 85 41 64 00) contact@maisondesvins-chalon.com
  www.maisondesvins-chalon.com

There's also a tasting room for the appellation of Mercurey at:

- Caveau Divin Mercurey
  Place Genappe, 101 Grande Rue, 71640 Mercurey
  (+33 3 85 45 22 96) caveau@mercurey.com
  www.mercurey.com/fr/le-caveau

Mâcon

The most interesting producers in Mâcon are in its southern part (and the most interesting producers in Beaujolais are in its northern part, so it is possible to combine visits to the two regions). Mâcon is the largest town in the area, but 30-45 minutes away from the producers. The producers of Pouilly-Fuissé have a tasting room and boutique that represents more than 80 producers at:

- Atrium du Pouilly-Fuissé
  Route de la Roche, 71960 Solutré-Pouilly
  (+33 3 85 35 83 83) contact@pouilly-fuisse.net
  www.pouilly-fuisse.net/atrium

There's a tasting room for the producers of Mâcon at:

- Maison Mâconnaise Des Vins
  484 Av. Maréchal de Lattre de Tassigny 71000 Mâcon
  (+33 3 85 22 91 11) contact@maison-des-vins.com
  maison-des-vins.com

Chablis

Chablis is a tiny area. Many producers are located in the town itself, and it's possible to walk from one to the next. Many whose addresses are in Chablis are actually in small villages on the outskirts, 5-10 minutes drive away. Staying in the town means you can easily walk to about half of the producers. Some can be visited without an appointment, but you may get a more comprehensive tasting if you make an appointment a few days or a week or so ahead.

The town of Chablis used to be something of a wasteland for tourists, but with producers moving more towards an interest in oenotourism, some now run restaurants and small hotels in the town, so the scene for tourists is much improved.

There are not many large negociants or producers, and at the smaller producers in the villages it will very likely be the owner/ winemaker (more properly the vigneron) who shows you around. (This makes it a very good idea to have an appointment.) Seeing winery facilities is common, but you do not usually get taken into the vineyards. Some of the smaller producers may not speak English.

Chablis is a compact town with an increased interest in tourism. Many producers are within a five minute walk of the entrance.

Only the larger negociants or producers have dedicated tasting rooms. At smaller producers, often enough the winery is basically an extension of the family residence. Tastings are often in the cave (take a sweater), and sometimes from barrels if bottles are considered too precious to open for visitors. Be prepared to taste samples taken from the barrel with a pipette (sometimes involving shared glasses. Most visits last around an hour, but the more enthusiastic producers may take you out to see the vineyards if there is time. Most producers sell wine at the cellar.

The etiquette of tasting assumes you will spit. A producer will be surprised if you drink the wine. Usually a tasting room or cellar is equipped with spittoons, but ask if you do not see one (crachoir in French).

Profiles of Producers

Ratings	
****	Sui generis, standing out above everything else in the appellation
***	Excellent producers defining the very best of the appellation
**	Top producers whose wines typify the appellation
*	Very good producers making wines of character that rarely disappoint

Symbols for Producers	
Ⓞ *Address*	☺ *Tasting room with especially warm welcome*
📞 *Phone*	🉑 *Tastings/visits possible*
👤 *Owner/winemaker/contact*	📅 *By appointment only*
@ *Email*	Ⓝ *No visits*
🌐 *Website*	⛏ *Sales directly at producer*
▣ *Principal AOP or IGP*	▨ *No direct sales*
🍾 *Red* 🍾 *White Reference wines*	☒ *Winery with restaurant*
🍇 *Grower-producer*	🛏 *Winery with accommodation*
🛢 *Negociant (or purchases grapes)*	
▬ *Cooperative*	
🚜 *Conventional viticulture*	
✆ *Sustainable viticulture*	
🌿 *Organic*	
◎ *Biodynamic*	
🍓 *Natural Wine*	
∅ *Wine with No Sulfur*	
◉ *Vegan Wine*	
ha=estate vineyards	
bottles=annual production	

Côte de Nuits

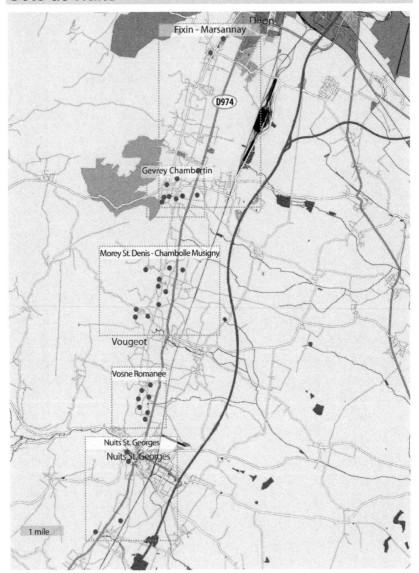

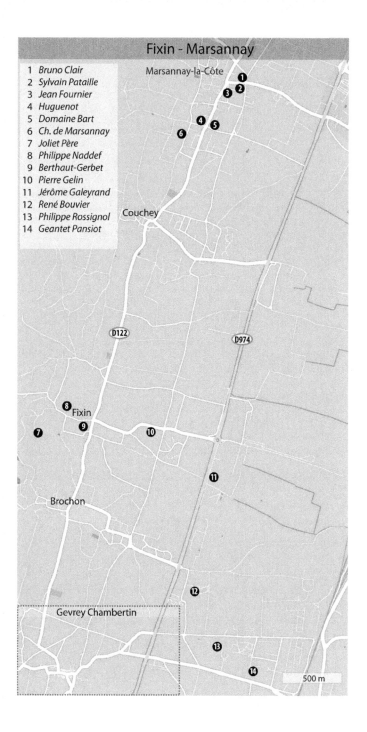

Fixin - Marsannay

1 Bruno Clair
2 Sylvain Pataille
3 Jean Fournier
4 Huguenot
5 Domaine Bart
6 Ch. de Marsannay
7 Joliet Père
8 Philippe Naddef
9 Berthaut-Gerbet
10 Pierre Gelin
11 Jérôme Galeyrand
12 René Bouvier
13 Philippe Rossignol
14 Geantet Pansiot

Marsannay-la-Côte

Couchey

Fixin

Brochon

Gevrey Chambertin

500 m

Profiles of Leading Estates

Domaine Bruno Clair ★★

5 rue du Vieux-Collège,21160 Marsannay-la-Côte	📞 +33 3 80 52 28 95
@ domaine@brunoclair.com	👤 Bruno Clair
🌐 www.bruno-clair.com	📷 Marsannay-la-Côte [map]
📅 🏭 🍇 🥃	🍾 Chambolle Musigny, Verouilles
25 ha; 100,000 btl	🍷 Morey St. Denis

"The history of the domain is very complicated, it would take hours," says Bruno Clair with a sigh when you ask how it came to be. "My grandfather created the Clair-Daü domain in 1914, but I started all by myself in 1979 by creating my own domain." It's evident that Bruno greatly respects his grandfather, who was clearly a formative influence, but when he died, the vineyards were divided. One daughter sold all her vines to Jadot, the other kept hers, and Bruno's father gave him his third. That's where the grand crus come from. The other vineyards have since been added by Bruno.

The domain is located in buildings around a charming courtyard in a back street of Marsannay, but vineyard holdings extend south through Gevrey Chambertin, Morey St. Denis, Chambolle Musigny, Vosne Romanée, Aloxe Corton, and Savigny-lès-Beaune. There are five premier crus, mostly in Gevrey, as well as two grand crus (Chambertin Clos de Bèze and Bonnes Mares). Vinification is traditional (with no more than 10-20% whole bunches), and new oak is restrained. "I hate to taste new wood, you won't smell it in my wines, it's up to 50% depending on the cuvée."

The style is always smooth and elegant. Fruits show precision, usually more red than black; tannins never stick out. Appellations show their best side; the Morey St. Denis has a silky elegance approaching Chambolle, and the Marsannay has a weight approaching Gevrey. There is refinement right across the range.

Domaine Jean Fournier ★

29 rue du Château, 21160 Marsannay-La-Côte	📞 +33 3 80 52 24 38
@ domaine.jean.fournier@orange.fr	👤 Laurent Fournier
	📷 Marsannay-la-Côte [map]
😊 🏭 🍇 🥃 🥃	🍾 Marsannay, Clos du Roy
23 ha; 130,000 btl	🍷 Bourgogne Aligoté, Champ Forey

The Fournier family has been growing grapes in Marsannay for generations, but turned exclusively to viticulture when Jean Fournier created the domain in the 1960s. His son Laurent took over in 2003. The old cellars are just off the main road through Marsannay, and now there's a stylish tasting room. Vineyards are mostly in Marsannay, with some small plots in other appellations. Most (80%) are for red wine, but there's also white and a little rosé.

Laurent is committed both to Marsannay and to old varieties. The whites are distinctive in including some unusual blends for

Burgundy. The Bourgogne Blanc is two thirds Pinot Blanc and a third Pinot Gris. More aromatic than Chardonnay, it is a lovely aperitif wine. Marsannay Clos St. Urbain is 80% Chardonnay and 20% Pinot Blanc. Laurent is a moving spirit in the association of Aligoteurs—producers who are trying to preserve and improve Aligoté—and he produces three cuvées of Aligoté. Champ Forey Vieilles Vignes is a little tight but with real depth to the fruits. The lieu-dits from Marsannay are 100% Chardonnay, with Les Longeroies rounder and deeper than Clos du Roi.

The rosé is unusually characterful, with a tang of saline minerality. "We make the same aging for whites and rosés, because I want to change the image of the rosé. We age for 18 months for white and rosé—it's expensive for Marsannay but I think it's important." So the rosé is a more "serious" wine than you usually find in Burgundy. "I don't produce rosé for the summer, it's for gastronomy."

In reds, the Saint Urban blend from about six plots shows fresh cherry fruits. In the lieu-dits, Cloy du Roy, from 40-year-old vines, inclines towards minerality—"the salty character is a feature of Cloy du Roy," Laurent says—while Longeroies, from 40- to 80-year-old vines, is rounder and deeper. The biggest red comes from Ez Chezots (the locals are amused that it is pronounced just like Echézeaux), where the limestone is darker and the plots is windier. The 30-40-year-old vines give a reserved wine that shows its structure more obviously and needs some time. Black grapes are usually 50% destemmed, and the wine ages in a mix of barriques and demi-muids (with a small proportion of new wood) in Austrian oak to limit oak influence.

Domaine Sylvain Pataille   *

14 Rue Neuf, 21160 Marsannay-La-Côte	📞 +33 3 80 51 17 35
@ *domaine.sylvain.pataille@wanadoo.fr*	👤 *Sylvain Pataille*
	🔘 *Marsannay-la-Côte [map]*
📅 🏭 🍇 ⚙️ *13 ha; 50,000 btl*	🍷 *Marsannay, Clos du Roy*

After studying in Bordeaux, Sylvain Pataille returned to Burgundy and became a consulting oenologist in 1997 (including Roumier and Groffier among his clients); he still consults for several domains, but in 2001 he established his own domain, starting out with a hectare. The domain focuses on Marsannay and its environs, producing red, white, and rosé. In addition to Marsannay, there's AOP Bourgogne from vineyards just to the north in Chenôve (which Sylvain comments had a higher reputation when it used to be known as part of the Côte de Dijon). Most of the vineyards are rented on long term contracts.

Altogether there are 8 reds, 5 whites, and 2 rosés. In addition to communal Marsannay cuvées of all three colors, there are several red cuvées from individual lieu-dits of Marsannay (there are presently no premier crus in the Marsannay appellation, but perhaps Sylvain's efforts will result in some lieu-dits being promoted). Sylvain is a modernist in the context of Marsannay. Vinification is in stainless steel and fiberglass tanks, and élevage usually uses a maximum of 30-35% new oak for 12-18 months. The reds are round, the whites are crisp, and the rosés have unusual character. Sylvain is actually a fan of Aligoté, and his largest vineyard is 3 ha of Bourgogne Aligoté. The best of the lieu-dits in Marsannay are Les Longeroies and Clos du Roy, but the top wine of the domain is L'Ancestrale, a cuvée from a 1 ha plot of vines planted in 1946.

Profiles of Important Estates

Domaine Bart

23, Rue Moreau, 21160 Marsannay-La-Côte	📞 *+33 3 80 51 49 76*
@ *domaine.bart@wanadoo.fr*	👤 *Martin Bart*
📅 🏭 🍇 🌾 *22 ha; 100,000 btl*	◉ *Marsannay-la-Côte [map]*

The origins of this domain go back to André Bart's 6 ha holding. The domain grew substantially when the Clair-Daü domain was broken up among members of the family in 1985, as André's wife came from Clair-Daü. In fact, because of shared inheritance, many of the holdings of Domaine Bart are the same as those of Bruno Clair (see profile), who is a cousin of the Barts. There is a familial resemblance in the same seriousness of approach. Andre's children, Martin and Odile, took over the domain in 1982, and work today with Odile's son, Pierre. "We don't produce big extracted wines. We try to respect the fruit," Pierre says. Holdings are mostly (85%) red. Marsannay is treated in terms of separate terroirs, with individual cuvées from ten different lieu-dits. New oak is used in moderation. The entry-level Marsannay, Finottes, ages a third in used barriques, a third in demi-muids, and a third in tank. The top Marsannay lieu-dits, such as Longeroies, age in barriques with 30% new oak. There are also Fixin and Chambolle Musigny, but the top wines come from the old Clair-Daü holdings in Bonnes Mares and Clos de Bèze, which see 60% new oak. Marsannay is mostly destemmed, but the two grand crus use 50% whole bunches. Because the vines in Bonnes Mares are older than in Clos de Bèze, the usual relationship of the grand crus is reversed, and Bonnes Mares tends to be the more concentrated.

Domaine Berthaut-Gerbet

9 rue Noisot, 21220 Fixin	📞 *+33 3 80 52 45 48*
@ *contact@berthaut-gerbet.com*	👤 *Amélie Berthaut*
⊕ *www.berthaut-gerbet.com*	◉ *Fixin [map]*
🧍 🏭 🍇 🌾	*18 ha; 80,000 btl*

The domain comes from the merger of two domains run independently by Amélie Berthaut's parents: Domaine Denis Berthaut in Fixin, run by her father; and Domaine Françoise Gerbet in Vosne Romanée, in her mother's family. Amélie has worked in Napa Valley and New Zealand, and took over in 2013 when her father decided it was time for a change of generations. The combined domain has all the Berthaut holdings in Fixin and her mother's share of the Gerbet holdings, including plots in Hautes-Côtes de Nuits, Gevrey Chambertin, Chambolle-Musigny, Clos Vougeot, and Vosne Romanée. The majority of vineyards are in Fixin, where the Berthauts go back at least to the eighteenth century; Amélie is the seventh generation. The vineyards are managed by Amélie's partner, Nicolas Fauré (who also manages his own, tiny 1 ha domain on the Hautes-Côtes de Nuits). Fixin has become the least well-regarded appellation of the Côtes de Nuits: there are hopes that Berthaut-Gerbet may become a flagship domain that will revive it. There has been a period of change. Extraction has been reduced with the Fixin cuvées to make the tannins less rustic. Denis used to destem everything, but now whole bunches vary from 20-80% depending on the year and cuvée. The cellars are cold, so fermentation and malolactic are slow; wines ferment in concrete and then since 2015 have moved to barriques for malolactic. Denis Berthaut used to age in foudres, but Amélie has switched to barriques, and has been slowly reducing new oak until reaching an equilibrium with 20-50% depending on the cuvée. Production is almost all red, but Chardonnay was planted in a plot in Fixin in 2010, with the first vintage in 2014. There's a consensus that this is a domain to watch to see whether it changes the view of Fixin.

Domaine Pierre Gelin

2, rue de la Croix Blanche , 21220 Fixin	📞 +33 3 80 52 45 24
@ *info@domaine-pierregelin.fr*	👤 *Pierre-Emmanuel Gelin*
🌐 *www.domaine-pierregelin.fr*	🔘 *Fixin [map]*
🗓 🏭 🍇 🥄	*13 ha; 44,000 btl*

Pierre Gelin founded the estate in 1925. His son Stéphane took over in 1969, and his grandson, Pierre-Emmanuel, is in charge today. Fixin is a small AOP, only 109 ha for the village and another 21 ha for premier crus, so the domain's holdings of village plots plus premier cru, including a monopole, Clos Napoléon, make it a leading producer. The village Fixin red is the largest production, about a quarter of total; Clos Napoléon is the next most important cuvée. The domain added some vineyards in Gevrey Chambertin in 1961, including a lieu-dit monopole, Clos de Meixvelle, premier cru Clos Prieur, and grand cru Clos de Bèze. The winery was renovated in 2011. Grapes are destemmed, and wines age for 20-24 months in used barriques for village wine, 25% new oak for premier crus, and up to 80% new oak for the grand cru.

Domaine Huguenot Père et fils

5 Rue des Carrières , 21160 Marsannay-La-Côte	📞 +33 3 80 52 11 56
@ *contact@domainehuguenot.com*	👤 *Philippe Huguenot*
🌐 *www.domainehuguenot.com*	🔘 *Marsannay-la-Côte [map]*
🗓 🏭 🍇 🥄	*23 ha; 120,000 btl*

The family has traced its winemaking activities back to the Revolution (1790). The domaine was just 2-3 ha two generations ago. Jean-Louis Huguenot, who took over in 1968, expanded it to 17 ha by 1993, when his son Philippe took over and expanded further. More than half the plots are in Marsannay, with 6 ha in Fixin, and 4 ha in Gevrey Chambertin. The largest parcel for a lieu-dit is 2.5 ha in Marsannay Champs Perdrix. In whites, there are village wines from Marsannay and Fixin and a Bourgogne Côte d'Or; they ferment and age mostly in 500-liter barrels for around 8 months. In reds, there are three cuvées from specific lieu-dits in Marsannay, and Fixin, and Gevrey Chambertin. The top cuvées are from premier cru Les Fontenys in Gevrey Chambertin and grand cru Charmes Chambertin. There are some cuvées from old vines, especially lieu-dit Les Champs in Gevrey Chambertin (80 years old), and Les Fontenys and Charmes Chambertin (40 years old).

Domaine Joliet Père et Fils

Rue de la Perrière, 21220 Fixin	📞 +33 3 80 52 47 85
@ *benigne@wanadoo.fr*	👤 *Bénigne Joliet*
🌐 *www.domainejoliet.fr*	🔘 *Fixin [map]*
🗓 🏭 🍇 🚜	*5 ha; 17,000 btl*

The Manoir de la Perrière in the center of Fixin premier cru Clos de la Perrière was constructed by the monks of Cîteaux around 1132. The monks were forced to sell the property in 1622 during the religious wars, and it changed hands several times until the Joliet family purchased it in 1853. Bénigne Joliet started making wine in 1994, but did not really have a free hand until he bought out the other members of the family in 2004. The domain's only vineyard, Clos de la Perrière is a monopole and had a high reputation in the nineteenth century. Bénigne aims to restore it. The first sign was an increase in price from €20 in 2004 to €70 in 2005. Production of the *clos* dropped from 23,000 bottles to 15,000 bottles. The wine is now made by complete destemming, one month for cuvaison, and aging for 12-18 months in 70% new barriques. The 2005 actually aged for 25 months because malolactic fermentation was very slow to complete in the cold twelfth century cellar, although there is now a new cuverie. The red is the major part of production, but 0.5 ha is planted with Chardonnay.

Domaine du Château de Marsannay

Route Des Grands Crus, Bp78, 21160 Marsannay-La-Côte	📞 *+33 3 80 51 71 11*
@ *chateau.marsannay@kriter.com*	👤 *Catherine Thevenard*
🌐 *www.chateau-marsannay.com*	🔴 *Marsannay-la-Côte [map]*
🧍🏭🚚🍷	*40 ha; 200,000 btl*

Something of a tourist site, the domain is based in a faux château, perhaps really more of a grand manor house, just outside Dijon, which actually was built in the ancient style in 1990 by the Boisseaux family, owners of major negociant Patriarche and the Kriter sparkling wine company. The domain was purchased in 2012, together with the Château de Meursault (see profile) by Olivier Halley, an owner of the Carrefour supermarket chain, who also owns other wineries. The major part of the estate, 28 ha, is in various lieu-dits of Marsannay, but the rest includes some significant premier and grand crus on the Côte de Nuits. Stéphane Follin-Arbelet makes the wines at both the Château de Marsannay and Château de Meursault.

Domaine Philippe Naddef

30, Route Des Grands Crus, 21220 Fixin	📞 *+33 3 80 51 45 99*
@ *contact@bourgogne-naddef.com*	👤 *Michel Naddef*
🌐 *www.bourgogne-naddef.com*	🔴 *Fixin [map]*
🧍🏭🚚🍷	*6 ha; 30,000 btl*

Philippe Naddef founded the domain when he inherited 2 ha in Gevrey Chambertin from his grandfather in 1983. His son Michel joined him in 2008 and has made the reds since 2014; Philippe continues to make the whites. The domain presently owns its vineyards in Gevrey Chambertin, which total a hectare of village plots (including some old vines), and less than 0.5 ha each of premier crus Les Cazetiers and Les Champeaux and grand cru Mazis Chambertin. Les Champeaux and Mazis Chambertin have the domain's oldest vines, 80 years of age. Vineyards in Fixin and Marsannay are rented. Altogether there are 33 plots and all but 0.7 ha is Pinot Noir. Reds are mostly destemmed, but Michel is tending to keep more stems, there is cold maceration for 8-10 days, and wines age with no new oak for Bourgogne, 20% for village appellations, and 100% new oak for the premier and grand crus.

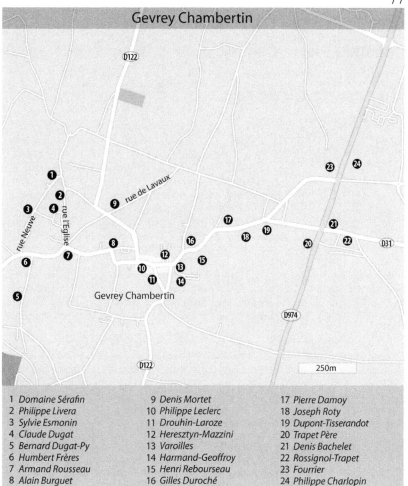

Gevrey Chambertin

1 Domaine Sérafin	9 Denis Mortet	17 Pierre Damoy
2 Philippe Livera	10 Philippe Leclerc	18 Joseph Roty
3 Sylvie Esmonin	11 Drouhin-Laroze	19 Dupont-Tisserandot
4 Claude Dugat	12 Heresztyn-Mazzini	20 Trapet Père
5 Bernard Dugat-Py	13 Varoilles	21 Denis Bachelet
6 Humbert Frères	14 Harmand-Geoffroy	22 Rossignol-Trapet
7 Armand Rousseau	15 Henri Rebourseau	23 Fourrier
8 Alain Burguet	16 Gilles Duroché	24 Philippe Charlopin

Profiles of Leading Estates

Domaine Pierre Damoy ★★

11, Rue du Maréchal-de-Lattre-de-Tassigny, 21220	📞 +33 3 80 34 30 47
@ info@domaine-pierre-damoy.com	👤 Pierre Damoy
	🟢 Gevrey Chambertin [map]
🚫🔪🍇🍶 ☞ 13 ha; 45,000 btl	🍷 Gevrey Chambertin, Clos Tamisot

The majority of the domain's holdings are in three important grand crus, Chambertin, Clos de Bèze, and Chapelle Chambertin, but the domain was a significant under-achiever until the current Pierre Damoy took over in 1992. The domain is the largest owner in Clos de Bèze, but sells most of the grapes. Its Clos de Bèze is made from an assemblage of berries from parcels at both ends of the appellation; the vines in the northern parcel are younger; the southern parcel, and the adjacent parcel over the border in Chambertin, were mostly planted in 1973-1974.

Pierre Damoy harvests late. "I like ripe berries," he says, although he points out that the late harvest partly reflects the fact that almost all his vineyards are in grand crus. Sometimes there has been a Vieilles Vignes cuvée from a small part of Clos de Bèze. There may also be a Reserve bottling (just two barrels), which is not usually commercialized.

The domain actually started with the purchase of the Clos Tamisot vineyard, which is a village Gevrey Chambertin, and is the most affordable representation of the domain. In addition to the wines from Gevrey Chambertin, there's an unusually refined Marsannay, and a generic Bourgogne that comes from a mix of estate and purchased grapes, and is labeled simply Pierre Damoy (not Domaine). The style tends to be rich and powerful, with quite a bit of new oak usage, ranging from 30% in the Bourgogne, to 50% in Gevrey Chambertin, and 80% or more in the grand crus.

Domaine Claude Dugat ★★

1 place de la Cure, 21220 Gevrey-Chambertin	📞 +33 3 80 34 36 18
@ claude.dugat@wanadoo.fr	👤 Laetitia, Bertrand, or Jeanne Dugat
	🟢 Gevrey Chambertin [map]
🚫🔪🍇☞ 7 ha; 35,000 btl	🍷 Gevrey Chambertin

It is not often that a mere communal wine from a great vintage is still unready after a decade, but Claude Dugat's Gevrey Chambertin can take years to come around, although promising to showcase a characteristic smooth sheen of black fruits as it develops over its second decade. This small domain, which has something of a cult following in the Anglo-Saxon world, owns 3 ha and rents another 3 ha, and has been managed entirely by Claude and his family. Claude has now retired, and his son Bertrand makes the wine.

The estate is housed in the Cellier des Dimes, a thirteenth century building in the heart of Gevrey Chambertin, just by the church, purchased and restored by Claude's father in

1955. A new cave was constructed in 1976. All the wines come from or near Gevrey Chambertin, extending from a Bourgogne Rouge, through the village wine, two premier crus and three grand crus.

The key to the style here is the low yield, usually below 18 hl/ha, which is a consequence more of small berries than of the number of grape clusters (aided by a proportion of very old vines). The wines have a strong sense of structure resembling the results of whole cluster fermentation, although here everything is in fact destemmed. After fermentation in concrete for about two weeks, the village wine goes into 40-50% new oak, and the premier and grand crus into 100% new oak. When asked about vinification, Bertrand is dismissive. "For me the vines are more important. There are no great winemakers, only great growers," but he adds, "I think Burgundy today makes wines that are too ripe and powerful, I like freshness."

Full of smooth, dense black fruits, the Bourgogne would put many communal wines to shame. The Gevrey Chambertin village wine has the same style, but shows more aromatic lift. Moving to premier crus, the wines become blacker and deeper. At the top of the range, "my three grand crus are like three different people. Charmes Chambertin is jovial and easy, Chapelle Chambertin is larger, more muscular, and Griotte Chambertin is timid and very calm."

All the wines are true vins de garde; they are not for the faint of heart, but definitely require patience. The family's activities are extended by a negociant label, La Gibryotte, which also is confined exclusively to Gevrey Chambertin.

Domaine Bernard Dugat-Py   **

Rue De Planteligone, B.P. 31, 21220 Gevrey-	📞 +33 3 80 51 82 46
@ contact@dugat-py.fr	👤 Bernard & Loïc Dugat
🌐 www.dugat-py.fr	📍 Gevrey Chambertin [map]
🚫🌿🍇🍷 11 ha; 35,000 btl	🍷 Gevrey Chambertin, Coeur du Roy

This domain is much praised by critics in the U.S. for the density and power of its wine, but sometimes criticized in Europe for over-extraction. Bernard Dugat, a cousin of Claude Dugat, has been making wine since 1975, but bottling his own wine only since 1989. The cuverie is located at the foot of the Combe de Lavaux in Gevrey Chambertin, in the remains of the Aumônerie that was constructed in the twelfth century. The winery was renovated in 2004.

Until recently the domain was tightly focused on Gevrey Chambertin, where there are three cuvées of village wine, all rather small: Vieilles Vignes, Coeur du Roy (very old vines of 65-90 years), and the parcel Les Evocelles. There are three premier crus and four grand crus, with the peak being a single barrel of Chambertin. The first white wine of the domain came from a parcel of Morgeots in Chassagne Montrachet purchased in 2004, and Corton Charlemagne was added in 2011. There are other small plots in Vosne Romanée and the Côte de Beaune.

There's always a high proportion of whole clusters, new oak runs 60% or more, and élevage lasts 18 to 24 months. If the wines didn't have so much fruit, they would be quite stern, but as it is, Bernard says a minimum of 6-8 years is required before opening. The huge sense of power comes from low yields rather than extraction during vinification, but certainly the style is enormously rich, with dense black fruits hiding the strong structure. Vin de garde is an under statement.

Domaine Sylvie Esmonin ⁂

**

1 Rue Neuve, 21220 Gevrey-Chambertin	☎ *+33 3 80 34 36 44*
@ *sylvie-esmonin@orange.fr*	👤 *Sylvie Esmonin*
	🌐 *Gevrey Chambertin [map]*
◯ ▨ 🍇 🍷 *8 ha; 35,000 btl*	🍾 *Gevrey Chambertin Vieilles Vignes*

Sylvie Esmonin was all but born in Clos St. Jacques—when she was a baby she was left in her cot at the end of the row while her parents worked the vines. "It's full of sentiment for me," she says. The domain is on the road along the base of the Clos St. Jacques, with Sylvie's house right at the end of the clos. This is a very hands-on domain: my visit was set for the end of the day because Sylvie was working in the vines during the day. "Working in the vines is my real métier," she says.

The domain is mostly in Gevrey Chambertin, but includes Bourgogne, Côte de Nuits Villages, and some Meursault and Volnay Santenots. "It's a little family domain started by my great grandfather," Sylvie explains. The caves below go deep into the rock and are always cool, so the wines develop slowly: when I visited at the start of July, the previous vintage was just at the start of malolactic fermentation. There's an emphasis on whole cluster fermentation, which is around 30% for communal wines with 5-10% new oak, increasing to 50% for the Vieilles Vignes cuvée of Gevrey Chambertin with a third new oak, and then almost complete for Clos St. Jacques with 100% new oak.

These are very traditional wines. "I don't want to make wines by technique, I work in the same way as my grandparents," Sylvie says. The style is quite dense, increasing in intensity from Gevrey Chambertin to the Vieilles Vignes to the peak of Clos St. Jacques.

Domaine Fourrier ⁂

***

7 Route Dijon, 21220 Gevrey-Chambertin	☎ *+33 3 80 34 33 99*
@ *contact@domainefourrier.com*	👤 *Jean-Marie or Vicki Fourrier*
	🌐 *Gevrey Chambertin [map]*
🗓 ▨ 🍇 🛢 ⏱ *10 ha; 50,000 btl*	🍾 *Gevrey Chambertin, Champeaux*

Founded by Fernand Pernot in the 1930s, the domain became known as Pernot-Fourrier when his nephew Jean-Claude Fourrier joined, and then Domaine Fourrier when Jean-Marie Fourrier took over in 1984. The focus is on Gevrey Chambertin, with five premier crus as well as village and grand cru wine. Jean-Marie does not believe in manipulation in the vineyard or winemaking, but says he would call himself more a biologist than a minimalist. He harvests at 100 days after flowering plus or minus five days, and believes that people who harvest very early in warm years or very late in cool years do not necessarily get full ripeness.

His philosophy is also a little different from the usual Burgundian approach. "In Burgundy many producers make a difference in how they handle village, premier cru, and grand cru wines, but this does not make any sense, the difference should rest on the terroir," he says. Jean-Marie uses 20% new oak for all cuvées, more to renew the barrels than to add flavor. All of his vines are old, typically around 50 years.

Grapes are destemmed, there are five days of cold maceration before fermentation, and during aging there is no racking, which keeps a high level of CO_2 and minimizes the requirement for sulfur. The style is fine and precise for Gevrey Chambertin, and there's a clear gradation going from the village wines, which have that slightly hard edge to the palate that's typical of Gevrey, to premier crus such as Goulots, which is more mineral, Champeaux which is earthier, and Clos St. Jacques whose ripe opulence reinforces the impression that it should have been a grand cru. The impression is modern, but continuing to respect Gevrey's typicity.

Domaine Geantet-Pansiot   ★★

3 Route de Beaune, 21220 Gevrey-Chambertin	📞 +33 3 80 34 32 37
@ domaine.geantet@wanadoo.fr	👤 Vincent Geantet
	◎ Gevrey Chambertin [map]
📅 🏭 🍇 ❄ 24 ha; 120,000 btl	⚲ Gevrey Chambertin, Vieilles Vignes

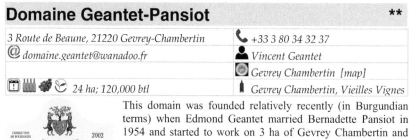

This domain was founded relatively recently (in Burgundian terms) when Edmond Geantet married Bernadette Pansiot in 1954 and started to work on 3 ha of Gevrey Chambertin and Bourgogne. The domain increased to 7 ha by 1977 when their son Vincent joined. Vincent has been running the domain since 1989, and Fabien, the third generation, joined in 2006. Vineyard holdings have continued to increase, remaining focused on Gevrey Chambertin, where there are six cuvées extending from village to grand cru, and Chambolle Musigny, where there are two premier crus and a vieilles vignes cuvée. There's still a building with the domain's name on the side on the N74, but production moved in 2013 to a spacious new winery in the quasi-industrial area across the main road to the east of the town.

After destemming and sorting, uncrushed berries go directly into open-topped wooden fermentation vats for a period of cold maceration. Following fermentation, "élevage is the same for all wines in order to show the terroir," Vincent says. There is a third each of new, one-year, and two-year oak barriques. There are 24 cuvées, extending from Bourgogne, Côte de Nuits, Ladoix, and Marsannay, but the focus is on Gevrey Chambertin. The only white is a Bourgogne Blanc, and there's also a rosé.

The Gevrey Chambertin and premier crus are on the lighter side for the appellation, with that typical tightness of the commune when they are young. In classical manner they require a little time to come around, a couple of years for a light vintage, longer for a strong one. Moving from village wine to premier cru, there is greater elegance rather than more power, with tannins becoming increasingly silky, giving a really fine texture to the black fruits. En Champs is finer than the village wine, Poissenot is finer and also rounder than En Champs, and then grand cru Charmes Chambertin has an aromatic lift showcasing the purity of fruits. "We're looking for fruits and fine tannins, giving finesse," is how Vincent describes his style.

Vincent's daughter has a small negociant business under the name of Emilie Geantet, for which she makes wine in conjunction with her father, with winemaking following the same principles as at Geantet-Pansiot.

Domaine Philippe Leclerc   ★

9 rue-des-Halles, 21220 Gevrey-Chambertin	📞 +33 3 80 34 30 72
@ philippe.leclerc60@wanadoo.fr	👤 Stephanie & Philippe Leclerc
🌐 www.philippe-leclerc.com	◎ Gevrey Chambertin [map]
☺ 🏭 🍇 ❄ 8 ha; 45,000 btl	⚲ Gevrey Chambertin, en Champs

Philippe Leclerc has adopted an economic model that would be familiar in the New World, but is quite rare in France. When Philippe took over the family domain in the 1970s, he bought a building right in the center of Gevrey Chambertin, and since then has expanded into neighboring buildings. The building has a tasting room and shop above old caves that are used for stockage and display. The tasting room is almost always open (even on Sundays), and a tasting of 6 wines is offered for a nominal fee. The wines are produced in a cuverie across the street. There's a village wine, a lieu-dit, and four premier crus, all in Gevrey Chambertin, and also a Chambolle Musigny and Bourgogne.

"We are producing wines mostly to sell here in the tasting room, but we are not making wines to drink very young. The goal is that we sell a lot here, almost three quarters is sold here, perhaps one day we will sell it all here. When people make wines (exclusively) to export, they have to make wines that sell very young, but we want to keep the taste of the real Gevrey Chambertin. If you make a very light Gevrey that you could drink immediately, it is not a real Gevrey." All the same, the style has been evolving. "Ten or twenty years ago you had to wait 10 or 15 years to open our wines, now it's 4 or 5 years. The wines are smoother and rounder at an earlier age." The change was fairly abrupt, as indicated by a comment that, "We have a Chambolle from 2005, but it is typical of the old style, it is rather full bodied"—so we tasted a Combe aux Moines from 2006 instead.

The Gevrey Chambertin shows a light style for the village wine, and the en Champs lieu-dit (just below the premier crus) is a touch smoother and silkier in the same style. The first impression of roundness to the hard edge of Gevrey comes with the Champeaux premier cru. The real jump in quality comes with Les Cazetiers, where the house style shows as elegant, pure, and precise. Combe aux Moines is more structured and requires longer, not really opening out until around eight years after the vintage. More clay in the soil gives a richer wine at Champonnets.

Domaine Denis Mortet ★★

Rue de Lavaux, 21220 Gevrey-Chambertin	📞 +33 3 80 34 10 05
@ *contact@domaine-denis-mortet.fr*	👤 Arnaud Mortet
🌐 *www.domaine-denis-mortet.com*	Gevrey Chambertin [map]
🚫🛇🍇🕓 *13 ha; 70,000 btl*	Gevrey Chambertin, Les Champeaux

There's a sad history to this domain, which has continued to develop its style in recent years. The domain was founded by Denis Mortet in 1991, with vines he obtained when his father retired. (The other half of the family inheritance became Domaine Thierry Mortet.) The domain more or less doubled in size when Denis took over the Guyot estate in 1993. His focus was on working the vineyards to reduce yields and obtain ripe berries, and the result was that wines tended to be somewhat ripe and powerful in what was often regarded as the new wave style. He was known for bringing as much care and attention to his communal vines as to the grand crus. His well known description was that the wines should be "a pleasure to drink young or old." Denis died young in 2006 after taking his own life as the result of depression.

The wines now are made by his son Arnaud. Holdings include 14 different appellations; the most important are in Gevrey Chambertin, extending from Le Chambertin, several premier crus, and a variety of communal plots (which may be bottled as one or more cuvées). There's a strong use of new barriques, with most of the premier and grand crus seeing 100% new oak; communal wines see about 60% new oak, and even the Bourgogne has 30-40%. Whether because the vineyards are maturing, the work in the vineyards is more detailed, or vinification is more precise, there is general agreement that the wines show increasing finesse.

Domaine Rossignol-Trapet ★★

4, Rue De La Petite Issue, 21220 Gevrey-Chambertin	📞 +33 3 80 51 87 26
@ info@rossignol-trapet.com	👤 Nicolas Rossignol
🌐 www.rossignol-trapet.com	🔴 Gevrey Chambertin [map]
📅 🏭 🍇 🍷 13 ha; 55,000 btl	🍷 Gevrey Chambertin, Clos Prieur

Jacques Rossignol created the domain in 1990 when the original Trapet domain was divided (the other half is Trapet Père et Fils, in the original building, a couple of hundred yards up the N74 from the Rossignol-Trapet domain, which occupies a building constructed in 1994). The domain is run today by Jacques's two sons, Nicolas (the winemaker) and David (viticulturalist). The winery was renovated in 2002 and extended to have more space. There are vast caves underneath.

There are 13 cuvées of exclusively red wine. Most of the vineyards are in Gevrey Chambertin, extending from Bourgogne to grand cru. There are 2 ha in Beaune. Vineyards have changed only slightly since the domain was established. Winemaking is traditional, usually with one third whole bunches, no new oak of Bourgogne, 10-15% for village Gevrey Chambertin and Beaune premier cru, 25% for Gevrey premier crus, and 40-50% for grand crus. Élevage extends from 12 months for Beaune and village Gevrey to 18 months for grand crus.

House style is very much in the tradition of Gevrey Chambertin. The Beaune premier cru Teurons is lighter and purer, the village Gevrey has more direct fruits, and then moving through the series of premier crus, first there is a sense of the fruits becoming brighter, and then the wines become more overtly structured; usually they need a few years after the vintage to come around. Clos Prieur is on the verge of austere, more clay in the soil gives more weight on the palate to La Petite Chapelle.

Moving to the grand crus, the sense of structure becomes more finely textured: Latricières Chambertin is very fine with an earthy palate and sense of minerality, Chapelle Chambertin is more intense and slightly earthier with blacker fruits, while Le Chambertin is on another level, making a different impression, rounder and more supple, and moving in a savory direction. The wines give an impression of no compromise.

Domaine Armand Rousseau ★★★

1, Rue De L'Aumonerie, 21220 Gevrey-Chambertin	📞 +33 3 80 34 30 55
@ contact@domaine-rousseau.com	👤 Éric Rousseau
🌐 www.domaine-rousseau.com	🔴 Gevrey Chambertin [map]
🚫 🏭 🍇 🍷 16 ha; 65,000 btl	🍷 Gevrey Chambertin

Armand Rousseau is the doyen of Chambertin, widely acknowledged to set the standard with his premier and grand crus. The domain is the largest single owner of Le Chambertin and has a substantial parcel in Clos de Bèze, as well as holdings in three other grand crus and three premier crus in Gevrey

Chambertin. The eponymous Armand Rousseau was involved in the drive to domain bottling in the 1930s; today his grandson Eric is in charge of the domain. Its increasing success in rising into the stratosphere with DRC and Leroy was indicated by the throes of construction when I visited, with the small courtyard being excavated in order to construct a new cave underground. With better capacity for storage, Rousseau won't have to sell all the wine at the vintage.

As is evident from the generally soft style, there is usually at least 90% destemming. Vinification is the same for all wines; the only difference is in the use of new oak. Both Chambertin and Clos de Bèze have their élevage in 100% new oak; Clos St. Jacques is 60-70%. All wines spend 20 months in barrique. "I am completely against over-extraction of color and material. I prefer Pinot Noir with elegance. If you go too far, you eliminate the effects of terroir," Eric Rousseau says. The style here is consistent across the range, with increasing concentration as you go from the village wine to Clos St. Jacques, and then up to Chambertin or Clos de Bèze.

Domaine Sérafin Père et Fils ★★

Place du Château, 21220 Gevrey-Chambertin	📞 +33 3 80 34 35 40
@ domaine.serafin@orange.fr	👤 Karine Sérafin
	🅖 Gevrey Chambertin [map]
🚫 🔪 🍇 ⌖ 6 ha; 26,000 btl	⚑ Gevrey Chambertin, Vieilles Vignes

"The domain mostly consists of the vineyards my grandfather bought," says Karine Sérafin. "He came to France from Poland in 1936, was taken prisoner in the war, and then was employed in the vineyards here after the war. There were lots of abandoned vineyards as a result of the war, and he was able to buy his own vines. Almost all our vineyards date from then, and were planted just after the war. My father turned more to export, and his move to quality was driven by Robert Kacher (the American importer). He purchased two more parcels of premier crus in Morey St. Denis and Chambolle Musigny." Karine's father, Christian, is still making the wines, now assisted by his niece Frédérique Bachotet. The domain is located at the top of Gevrey Chambertin, just below the northeast group of premier crus, opposite the church on the edge of the Place du Château, in buildings that look new but actually date back to the beginning. Most of the 9 cuvées come from Gevrey Chambertin. The domain produces only red wine.

Usage of new oak is high, extending from 50% for the Bourgogne Rouge to 100% for the Cazetiers premier cru and Charmes Chambertin grand cru. In terms of new oak and length of élevage, the wines are divided into Bourgogne, Gevrey Chambertin, Gevrey Chambertin Vieilles Vignes, the premier crus, and then Cazetiers and Charmes Chambertin. The wines are firmly structured, well-rounded with concentrated fruits that may hide the tannins when they are young, but they require time, typically a few years, to develop flavor variety. The purity of the cherry fruits makes a modern impression. Powerful but restrained might be a fair description of the young wines.

Although a big distinction is drawn between the village wine and the Vieilles Vignes—the average age is 70 years, but some are as old as 90 years—there are really no young wines in the domain. The Gevrey Chambertin village wine is the youngest, with vines that are 35-years-old. Les Cazetiers and Charmes Chambertin are close in age to the Vieilles Vignes, which comes from several of the original parcels near the winery. The age of the vines, and perhaps the locations of the parcels close to the premier crus, makes the Vieilles Vignes close in quality to the premier crus.

Domaine Trapet Père et Fils   **

53, Route de Beaune, 21220 Gevrey-Chambertin	📞 +33 3 80 34 30 40
@ *message@trapet.fr*	👤 *Famille Trapet*
🌐 *www.domaine-trapet.com*	◉ *Gevrey Chambertin [map]*
📅 🏭 ✖ 🍇 ◖ *19 ha; 60,000 btl*	⚲ *Gevrey Chambertin*

Located right on the N74 in Gevrey Chambertin, Domain Louis Trapet was established in 1870, and was one of the major suppliers to negociants until estate bottling started in the 1960s. Its extensive holdings made it the most important domain in Gevrey Chambertin, but it was divided in 1993 as the result of inheritance issues. One half was renamed as Domaine Trapet Père et Fils. (The other part gave rise to what is now Domaine Rossignol-Trapet: it can be interesting to compare the styles of the two domains since the holdings are so parallel.)

Trapet Père et Fils is presently run by Jean-Louis Trapet, and has holdings in some of the best terroirs of Gevrey Chambertin, including almost 2 ha of Le Chambertin, with vines going back to 1919. The other grand crus are Latricières Chambertin and Chapelle Chambertin, and there are three premier crus, as well of course as the communal Gevrey Chambertin, which is the largest production of the house. There are also Marsannay and Bourgogne.

Vinification uses partial (typically 70%) destemming, cold maceration before fermentation in open top vats, with 30-70% new oak used for élevage of 15-18 months depending on the appellation. The style is structured, but not especially powerful. At its best, it may be very smooth, but it can be austere when young. There is also a Domaine Trapet in Alsace, as Jean-Louis's wife, Andrée, comes from Alsace and took over her parents' vineyards in 2002.

There is now a small restaurant facility in Gevrey Chambertin, where tastings are held.

Profiles of Important Estates

Domaine Bachelet

3, rue de la Petite Issue, 21220 Gevrey-Chambertin	📞 +33 6 23 05 22 83
	👤 *Denis Bachelet*
🚫 🍾 🍇 ◔ *4 ha*	◉ *Gevrey Chambertin [map]*

Bachelet is something of a cult, enhanced by the small size of the domain, which can make it difficult to find the wines. When Denis took over the domain it was just 1.8 ha of vines with no cellar or equipment, as his grandparents had retired in 1973. The vineyards consisted of Charmes Chambertin, village and premier cru Gevrey Chambertin, and a parcel of Bourgogne. Denis has bought further vineyards when he has had the chance, but the domain remains very small. His son Nicolas joined him in 2008. Much of the domain consists of plots of old vines, which are maintained by replacing individual vines as they die. The approach is traditional, but there have been some changes. The cooper was changed in 2014 to get barriques bringing out the fruit more, and extraction has become gentler by reducing the number of punch-downs. Winemaking starts with 3-5 days cold maceration. All grapes go through a crusher-destemmer (as opposed to the modern fashion for destemming only) before fermentation, which takes place in concrete or stainless steel. After fermentation, the wine goes into barriques, and is cooled to 13°C to ensure that malolactic fermentation does not start until the following Spring.

Denis says that making the malo as late as possible keeps a high level of carbon dioxide in the wine that preserves freshness. The wines spend 16 months in barrique. The Bourgogne Rouge comes from two plots totaling just over a half hectare, planted in 1977 and 1986; it ages in used barriques. Côte de Nuits Villages is three parcels totaling almost a hectare and has 25% new oak. The Gevrey Chambertin, premier crus, and Charmes Chambertin are all labeled as Vieilles Vignes. Gevrey Chambertin is the largest cuvée, from over a hectare of multiple parcels planted in 1932 and 1937, aged with 20% new oak. Premier Cru Les Evocelles is only 0.17 ha, planted in 1960 at the top of the slope, and sees 60% new oak. Les Corbeaux is just under a half hectare from three parcels, adjacent to Mazis Chambertin, planted in 1920 and 1961, and ages with 50% new oak. From a couple of parcels with about the same total area, Charmes Chambertin comes from the oldest vines of the domain, planted between 1907-1917; it uses 30-60% new oak depending on vintage.

Pierre Bourée Fils

11-13, Route de Beaune, 21220 Gevrey-Chambertin	☎ +33 3 80 34 30 25
@ contact@pierre-bouree-fils.com	👤 Jean-Christophe Vallet
🌐 www.pierre-bouree-fils.com	🔘 Gevrey Chambertin
📅 🏭 🍇 🛢 🚜	9 ha; 150,000 btl

This is a traditional, one might even say old-fashioned, producer, founded in 1864. Pierre Bourée's son Bernard took over in 1922, than passed the baton to his nephew Louis Vallet in 1945; Jean-Christophe Vallet is in charge today. There are old cellars in Gevrey Chambertin, but the main winery is in Chambolle Musigny. The firm has always been a negociant, then bought its best-known vineyard in 1901. This is a monopole, in lieu-dit La Justice, on the 'wrong' side of the D974 in Gevrey Chambertin. It's a 2 ha clos, so the wine was called Clos de la Justice. Indeed, the label said only Clos de la Justice, until 1936, when INAO demanded that Gevrey Chambertin should be added because this is not a grand cru. Although only village AOP, it's often reckoned to be at a level closer to the premier crus. The other old holding in the estate is Charmes Chambertin. The traditional approach to winemaking means fermentation of whole bunches, no temperature control to cool the must, mostly punch-down rather than pump-over, and élevage for 18-20 months before bottling. Most cuvées come from purchased grapes, with a wide range of about 60 wines. The style is somewhat sturdy.

Domaine René Bouvier

Chemin De Saule, Brochon, 21220 Gevrey-Chambertin	☎ +33 3 80 52 21 37
@ domaine@renebouvier.com	👤 Bernard Bouvier
🌐 www.renebouvier.com	🔘 Gevrey Chambertin [map]
🚫 ▨ 🍇 🍷 🌿	30 ha; 100,000 btl

Henri Bouvier founded the estate in 1910 in Marsannay, René took over in 1950 and expanded the estate, and Bernard took over in 1992 and expanded further. A new winery on the road north out of Gevrey was built in 2006. Bernard's brother Régis had a separate domain in Marsannay until Bernard took over his vineuards in 2019. The balance remains with Marsannay, although vineyards now extend from Marsannay to Gevrey. Focused on terroir, Bernard aims to produce a cuvée from each plot. The domain is known especially for its Marsannay, where there are four cuvées, both red and white; Bernard was president of the grower's syndicate in Marsannay. Aging is 18 months; new oak is 20-30%, but only premier and grand crus spend the full period in barrique, other cuvées spend the last 6 months in cuve.

Domaine Alain Burguet

18 rue de l'Église, 21220 Gevrey-Chambertin	☎ +33 3 80 34 36 35
@ contact@domainealainburguet.fr	👤 Jean-Luc & Eric Burguet
📅 🏭 🍇 🛢 🍷 🌿 10 ha; 50,000 btl	🔘 Gevrey Chambertin [map]

Alain Burguet comes from a family of growers, but decided to start his own domain, at first renting, and then buying his first 2 ha in Gevrey Chambertin in 1974. (Alain's brother, Gilles, started a separate small domain in his own name.) At first, Alain produced only two wines: Gevrey Chambertin and Gevrey Chambertin Vieilles Vignes. Most of his plots were rented until he was able to afford some purchases. He added Les Chalumeaux premier cru in Gevrey Chambertin in 1985, and inherited some small plots from his father in 1991. His top plot is 0.27 ha in Chambertin Clos de Beze, planted in 1955. Other cuvees include Vosne Romanée Les Rouges du Dessus and Chambolle Musigny Les Echézeaux. His sons Jean-Luc and Eric joined him in 1997 and 1999, and Alain retired officially in 2011. The domain is one of the last to harvest, grapes are destemmed, punch-down and pump-over have been reduced to keep extraction on the lighter side, there is little use of new oak (the maximum is 30% for Clos de Bèze), and wines age on average for 20 months in barrique.

Domaine Camus Père et Fils

21, Rue Mar de Lattre De Tassigny, 21220 Gevrey-Chambertin	📞 +33 3 80 34 30 64
@ domaine.camus.gevrey@orange.fr	👤 Hubert Camus
🌐 camusscea.site-solocal.com	🔵 Gevrey Chambertin
🈁 🏭 🚜	18 ha; 80,000 btl

The distinction of this domain is its ownership of grand crus, with two thirds of its plots in grand crus in Gevrey Chambertin. The domain dates from 1732, and Hubert Camus took over from his father in 1974. Grand crus include Mazoyères Chambertin, Mazis Chambertin, Latricières Chambertin, Charmes Chambertin, and Le Chambertin. Winemaking is traditional, wines age in barrique for 14-18 months, but there is general agreement than the wines do not live up to the potential of the sites.

Domaine Philippe Charlopin-Parizot

18 Route de Dijon, 21220 Gevrey-Chambertin	📞 +33 3 80 58 50 46
@ charlopin.philippe21@orange.fr	👤 Philippe Charlopin
🌐 domaine-charlopin-parizot.com	🔵 Gevrey Chambertin [map]
🧍 🏭 🚜	25 ha; 150,000 btl

Philippe Charlopin purchased his first hectare of vines in 1978 in Gevrey and then continued to build up his domain, now located on the main road to the north out of Gevrey. His son Yann joined in 2004, and in order to make white wines they purchased new plots in Pernand and Corton, and even in Chablis. Most of the wine remains red, with a concentration around Gevrey Chambertin. The seven grand crus include three in Gevrey Chambertin. The wines can be tasted at the wine bar Caveau des Vignerons in Gevrey Chambertin. Grapes are destemmed, and new oak is around a third.

Domaine des Chézeaux

4, Avenue de La Gare, 21220 Gevrey-Chambertin	📞 +33 1 47 50 40 14
@ cnemes@wanadoo.fr	
🌐 www.domaine-des-chezeaux.com	🔵 Gevrey Chambertin
🚫 ✒ 🚜	4 ha

The Mercier family have owned vines in Gevrey Chambertin since 1928, and organized their holdings into the Domaine des Chézeaux in 1982. However, they do not make wine themselves but lease out the vineyards in a 'métayage' arrangement in which other domains work the vineyards, make the wine, and then keep two thirds for themselves with one third going to the vineyard owner. In effect, this means that wines labeled as Domaine des Chézeaux are made by a variety of producers. Half of the holdings are in grand crus, and the domain is notable for holding the largest share of the grand cru Griotte Chambertin (1.57 ha of the total 2.6 ha). The holding is in two plots, one rented to Domaine Ponsot (since 1982), the other to René Leclerc (since it was acquired in 1992), so if you buy a Domaine Des Chézeaux Griotte Chambertin, you may get either the Ponsot or the Leclerc bottling. Other holdings are Le Chambertin, Clos St. Denis, and Chambolle Musigny Les Charmes (also leased to Domaine Ponsot), and Gevrey Chambertin village and premier crus Lavaux St. Jacques and Cazetiers, leased to Domaine Berthaut.

Domaine Drouhin-Laroze

20 Rue Du Gaizot, 21220 Gevrey-Chambertin	📞 +33 3 80 34 31 49
@ domaine@drouhin-laroze.com	👤 Philippe Drouhin
🌐 www.drouhin-laroze.com	🗺 Gevrey Chambertin [map]
📅 🏭 🍇 🛢 ☘	12 ha; 60,000 btl

Jean-Baptiste Laroze created the domain in 1850, when his granddaughter married Alexandre Drouin the estate was renamed as Drouhin-Laroze, and it is still in the hands of the family. Philippe has now handed over to his children Caroline and Nicolas, who have lightened the approach. New oak has been reduced to 50% for premeir crus, and grand crus get 70% insyead of 100%. The holdings are top heavy with premier and grand crus, four premier crus in Gevrey Chambertin, and six grand crus. The range is extended under the negociant label of Maison Drouhin-Laroze, which adds two premier and two grand crus. and village wines, altogether providing a quarter of production.

Domaine Dupont-Tisserandot

2 Place Marronniers, 21220 Gevrey-Chambertin	📞 +33 3 80 34 10 50
@ contact@duponttisserandot.com	👤 Didier Chevillon
🌐 www.duponttisserandot.com	🗺 Gevrey Chambertin [map]
🚫 🖊 🍇 🏭	20 ha; 50,000 btl

The domain has important holdings in Gevrey Chambertin, including grand crus. Marie-Françoise Guillard and Patricia Chevillon took over from their father in 1990. The domain was an important source of wine for top negocants until Didier Chevillon took over as winemaker in 1999. The domain was purchased by Faiveley (see profile) in 2014, who already have significant holdings in Gevrey Chambertin. Dupont-Tisserandot continues to be run independently by the same team, but the style is expected to converge more with Faiveley, especially when winemaking is moved to a new facility, possibly in Nuits St. Georges with Faiveley's. The policy until now has been to destem completely, and to use 1-3-year oak for village wines and 100% new oak for premier and grand crus, with 16-18 months élevage.

Domaine Gilles Duroché

7, Place Du Monument, 21220 Gevrey-Chambertin	📞 +33 3 80 51 82 77
	👤 Pierre Duroché
🌐 domaine-duroche.com	🗺 Gevrey Chambertin [map]
🚫 🖊 🍇 ☘	9 ha; 40,000 btl

Philippe Duroché started the domain as such with 3 ha in 1954. His son Gilles sold most of his production to negociants until his son Pierre joined him in 2005. Pierre took over in 2008, and now all production is bottled by the estate. Parcels are in Gevrey and its crus. Vineyards include many old vines and are maintained by selection massale from the domain's own vineyards. After complete destemming, winemaking is artisanal: long élevage (13-15 months) without racking, no fining, and rarely any filtration. The 14 cuvées come from highly fragmented parcels, mostly a quarter to a third hectare each. The red Bourgogne comes from two plots in the vicinity, and the sole white is Bourgogne from an unusual parcel of Chardonnay in Gevrey. The Gevrey Chambertin as such is a blend from several parcels, and there are also several cuvées from lieu-dits with different terroirs. There are three premier crus and four grand crus, including Clos de Bèze, which comes from the oldest vines, planted in 1920. There are two cuvées from Lavaux St. Jacques: the normal cuvée comes from vines around 40 years old, and Lavaut St Jacques Vignes 23 comes from a plot adjacent to Clos St. Jacques where the vines were planted in 1923. Village wines age in 10-20% new oak, premier crus in 30-50%, and grand crus get 50-75% new oak.

Domaine Jérôme Galeyrand

2 route nationale 74, 21220 Brochon, France	📞 +33 6 61 83 39 69
@ jerome@jerome-galeyrand.fr	👤 Jérôme Galeyrand
🌐 www.jerome-galeyrand.fr	🔵 Gevrey Chambertin [map]
🗓️ ◻/ 🐝 🍷	5 ha; 24,000 btl

Jérôme Galeyrand started out in cheese and got the wine bug while working at Alain Burguet in Gevrey Chambertin. After qualifying in oenology, he bought his first plot, only 5% of a hectare, and made his first wine in 2002 in his house. He's expanded by finding plots of old vines, extending from Comblanchien to Marsannay. A small negociant activity increases the range a little. Côtes de Nuits Villages is his largest appellation, starting as a blend between a plot of vines planted in 1925 and 1932 at the south and a plot planted in 1947 at the north. Since 2016 they've been bottled separately as Les Retraits (from Comblanchien) and Vieilles Vignes (from Brochon). Fixin comes from lieu-dit Champs des Charmes and premier cru Les Hervelets. There are several cuvees from Gevrey Chambertin, including La Justice (the most powerful) where the vines were planted in 1947. The domaine does not sell its wines directly, but they can be found at the caveau des vignerons, La Halle Chambertin, in Gevrey Chambertin.

Domaine Le Guellec-Ducouet

8, chemin de Saule, 21220 Brochon	📞 +33 6 77 76 91 78
@ domaine@leguellec-ducouet.com	👤 Arnaud Ducouet & Michaël Le Guellec
🌐 leguellec-ducouet.com	🔵 Gevrey Chambertin
🗓️ ⛏️ 🐝 ☘️	4 ha

Michaël Le Guellec joined with his ex-brother-in-law Arnaud Ducouet to change career from banking in 2018 and resurrect a 3.5 ha domain at Brochon abandoned by his grandfather thirty years ago. They built a new winery in 2020. The wine is Gevrey Chambertin, which they describe as 'typical of the Côte de Brochon, basically from the northern part of the appellation, near Fixin.

Domaine Harmand-Geoffroy

1, Place Des Lois, 21220 Gevrey-Chambertin	📞 +33 3 80 34 10 65
@ harmand-geoffroy@wanadoo.fr	👤 Philippe Harmand
🌐 www.harmand-geoffroy.com	🔵 Gevrey Chambertin [map]
🗓️ ⛏️ 🐝 ☘️	9 ha; 50,000 btl

The strength of this old-line domain is its extensive range of Gevrey Chambertin, from village wine and lieu-dits to four premier crus and grand cru Mazis Chambertin. The family has been in Gevrey since the late nineteenth century. Gérard Harmand started as an electrician with a few plots, but moved to winemaking after his marriage, which brought vineyards from his wine's side (previously known as the Lucien Geoffroy domain). He expanded the domain by acquiring 3 ha in 1986. Philippe, the next generation, started making the wine with his father in 2007. The vineyards are well established, spread across 30 small parcels, with vines varying from 30 to 90-years old. One of the youngest plots is the monopole of premier cru La Boissière, which had to be replanted following frost in 1985. Some of the older vines are in lieudits En Jouise and Le Prieur, which are bottled as separate cuvées. Winemaking is traditional. Following destemming, there is cold maceration, and after fermentation the wine is racked into barriques for malolactic, with the traditional usage of more new oak going up the appellation hierarchy, with 20% for village wines, 40% for premier crus, and 90% for grand cru. Aging lasts 12-26 months. The wines are well-structured, in the classic character of Gevrey.

Domaine Heresztyn-Mazzini

27 Rue Richebourg, 21220 Gevrey-Chambertin	☎ *+33 3 80 33 62 71*
@ *info@heresztyn-mazzini.com*	👤 *Florence Heresztyn-mazzini & Simon Mazzini*
⊕ *www.heresztyn-mazzini.com*	🅶 *Gevrey Chambertin [map]*
📅 🏭 🍇 ◯	*6 ha; 30,000 btl*

The Heresztyns arrived from Poland in 1932, and after years of working at Domaine Trapet and growing onions on the side, Jan Heresztyn created his own domain in 1959. His granddaughter Florence took over in 2012 together with her husband Simon Mazzini, who also has vineyards in Champagne, and the domain changed its name from Heresztyn. The focus is on Gevrey Chambertin, with a Vieilles Vignes cuvée (the largest production with 500 cases), three lieu-dits, and three premier crus. Florence has introduced the use of whole bunches for fermentation, varying from 50-100%, with new oak ranging from 30-40%.

Domaine Humbert Frères

Rue De Planteligone, 21220 Gevrey-Chambertin	☎ *+33 3 80 51 84 23*
@ *dom.humbert@wanadoo.fr*	👤 *Frédéric & Emmanuel Humbert*
📅 🏭 🍇 🌳 *7 ha; 30,000 btl*	🅶 *Gevrey Chambertin [map]*

Brothers Emmanuel and Frédéric Humbert took over the domain from their parents in 1989. Vineyards in Gevrey Chambertin extend from village wine to four premier crus and Charmes Chambertin, and contain 80-year-old vines planted by their grandfather Fernand Dugat, who had a nursery. (The domain is sometimes known as the third Dugat, after Domaines Dugat and Dugat-Py, also run by grandchildren of Fernand.) There is cold maceration before fermentation, and village wines age in 40% new oak, with 100% new oak for premier and grand crus. The wines are known for their intensity and structure.

Domaine Philippe Livera

7 rue du Château, 21220 Gevrey-Chambertin	☎ *+33 6 18 07 83 53*
@ *philippe.livera@orange.fr*	👤 *Hélène Livera*
📅 🏭 🍇 🌳 *9 ha; 39,000 btl*	🅶 *Gevrey Chambertin [map]*

Also known as the Domaine des Tilleuls, the winery is housed in an old stables. The domain was founded around 1920. Philippe Livera began estate bottling when he took over from his parents in 1986, and his son Damien took charge in 2007. Vineyards extend from the Hautes Côtes de Nuits to Fixin and Gevrey Chambertin, with Chapelle Chambertin at the top (although it makes only 3 barriques). (The domain has half of the Livera inheritance of the grand cru, because some went to the Ponsot domain in a marriage in 1970.) The wine from the home vineyard, as it were, is Clos Village, from the lieu-dit immediately in front of the building. New oak increases from 20% for Hautes Côtes or Fixin, to 30-40% for village wines, and 100% for the grand cru.

Domaine Henri Rebourseau

10, Place Du Monument, 21220 Gevrey-Chambertin	📞 *+33 3 80 51 88 94*
@ *domaine@rebourseau.com*	👤 *Louis de Surrel*
🌐 *www.rebourseau.com*	⚫ *Gevrey Chambertin [map]*
📅 ✏🍇🌑	*14 ha; 50,000 btl*

Founded in 1782, the domain is located in a gracious eighteenth century building set in 3 ha of gardens in the center of Gevrey Chambertin. Henri Rebourseau bought the property in 1919 to be the center of the family's holdings. His son Pierre made the wine until 1980 when his son Jean de Surrel took over. Jean's sons Louis and Bénigne took over from their father in 2018, when there was a major change as the Bouygues brothers, owners of Château Montrose in Bordeaux and Clos Rougeard in the Loire, bought a controlling share (reputedly for €45 million). The domain has impressive holdings, with half in grand crus, including 0.5 ha in Chambertin, more than 1 ha in Charmes Chambertin, 0.3 ha in Clos de Bèze, 1 ha in Mazis Chambertin, and 2 ha in Clos Vougeot. The 7 ha of village Gevrey is unusually mostly in large blocks, including one very large plot extending directly from the house. They include some very old vines. Unusually for a top domain, harvesting is mechanical. The policy has been for complete destemming, and aging for 6 months before racking out of the new barriques. They are bottled after 18 months.

René Leclerc

29 Route de Dijon, 21220 Gevrey-Chambertin	📞 *+33 6 31 05 68 50*
@ *contact@domainereneleclerc.com*	👤 *François Leclerc*
🌐 *www.domaine-reneleclerc.com*	⚫ *Gevrey Chambertin*
📅 🍇🚜	*12 ha*

The family has been growing vines in Gevrey Chambertin since 1897. René Leclerc established the domain in 1962 and has now handed over to his son, François, who worked in Oregon before taking over. The domain is known for its policy of keeping pressing time short, 3 hours instead of the more usual 10 hours, in order to keep extraction light. Use of new oak is limited in order to focus on the fruits. Cuvées include Bourgogone, village Gevrey Chambertin and a lieu-dit, three premier crus, and Griotte Chambertin (which comes from the holding of Domaine de Chézeaux; see profile). The labels now say Domaine François Leclerc.

Domaine Philippe Rossignol

59 Avenue de la Gare, 21220 Gevrey-Chambertin	📞 *+33 3 80 51 81 17*
@ *sceaphilipperossignol@hotmail.fr*	👤 *Philippe Rossignol*
📅 🏭 🍇 🚜 *6 ha; 20,000 btl*	⚫ *Gevrey Chambertin [map]*

Philippe Rossignol took over the family vineyards in 1975, and his son Sylvain joined the domain in 2005. His brother-in-law is Joseph Roty (see profile). The focus is on Gevrey Chambertin, with a Fixin from a small plot of old vines called en Tabellion near the premier crus. New oak is a third for the village Gevrey, and increases for the premier crus; Estournelles St. Jacques is the top wine.

Domaine Joseph Roty

24 rue du Mal de Lattre de Tassigny, 21220 Gevrey-Chambertin	📞 *+33 3 80 34 38 97*
@ *domainejosephroty@orange.fr*	👤 *Françoise Roty*
📅 🍇 🌙 *15 ha; 50,000 btl*	⚫ *Gevrey Chambertin [map]*

Joseph Roty had a reputation for being reticent if not inaccessible, refusing to discuss his winemaking techniques. The family has been in Gevrey since the eighteenth century, and Joseph created the domain with family vineyards in the 1960s. Many of the plots have old vines, with an average age over 60 years; the oldest plot goes into the Charmes Chambertin Très Vieilles Vignes, from the first planting after phylloxera, in 1881. Since Joseph's death in 2008, his sons Philippe and Pierre-Jean have been running the domain. Philippe made some Marsannay under his own name as well as the wines from Gevrey, but died prematurely in 2015. Pierre-Jean, who had been looking after the vineyards, now makes the wine as well. The style is powerful, structured, and rich.

Domaine des Varoilles

rue de La Croix-des-Champs, 21220 Gevrey-Chambertin	📞 *+33 3 80 34 30 30*
@ *contact@domaine-des-varoilles.com*	👤 *Gilbert Hammel*
🌐 *www.domaine-des-varoilles.com*	🔘 *Gevrey Chambertin [map]*
🏠 ⛏ 🍇 ☘	*10 ha*

Dating from the twelfth century, this is an old domain whose name is the same as one of the monopoles it owns in Gevrey Chambertin, premier cru Clos des Varoilles, the other being premier cru La Romanée. Other holdings include premier cru Champonnets and lieu-dits Clos de Meix and Clos du Couvent. It also owns grand crus Charmes Chambertin, Bonnes Mares, and Clos Vougeot. It was owned by a partnership between Domain Paul Misset and negociant Naigeon-Chauveau, until a new era started in 1990 when it was sold to Gilbert Hammel, who owns eight domains in his native Switzerland. Winemaking starts with destemming, then there is 5-6 days cold maceration before fermentation, followed by aging in barriques for 12-14 months, with new oak ranging from 10-15% for village wines, 20% for premier cru, and 60% for grand cru. Gilbert Hammel sold the Clos des Varoilles in 2021 to Domaine Prieuré-Roch in Nuits St. Georges.

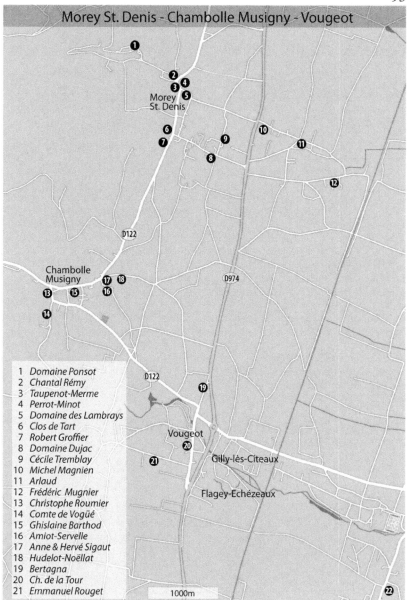

1   Domaine Ponsot
2   Chantal Rémy
3   Taupenot-Merme
4   Perrot-Minot
5   Domaine des Lambrays
6   Clos de Tart
7   Robert Groffier
8   Domaine Dujac
9   Cécile Tremblay
10 Michel Magnien
11 Arlaud
12 Frédéric Mugnier
13 Christophe Roumier
14 Comte de Vogüé
15 Ghislaine Barthod
16 Amiot-Servelle
17 Anne & Hervé Sigaut
18 Hudelot-Noëllat
19 Bertagna
20 Ch. de la Tour
21 Emmanuel Rouget

Profiles of Leading Estates

Domaine Dujac ✸✸

7 Rue De La Bussière, 21220 Morey St. Denis	📞 +33 3 80 34 01 00
@ *dujac@dujac.com*	👤 *Rosalind Seysses*
🌐 *www.dujac.com*	🔵 *Morey St. Denis [map]*
📅 🗡 🍇 🛢 🧀 🅲 *17 ha; 70,000 btl*	🏛 *Morey St. Denis*

MOREY SAINT-DENIS
1ᵉʳ CRU MONTS LUISANTS
2008
DOMAINE DUJAC

"Starting in Burgundy I had the disadvantage of not having many generations before me. But I had the advantage of not having three to ten generations before me," says Jacques Seysses, ironically pointing out that being an outsider was balanced by not being overly bound by precedents. He started in 1968 by purchasing a small run-down domain, only 4.5 ha, in Morey St. Denis, which had sold off its grapes. Everything had to be developed from scratch, but the domain has been expanding steadily ever since. After purchasing half of the old Charles Thomas domain in 2005, the winery had to be expanded.

The range now extends from Bourgogne to Grand Cru. Three quarters of the holdings are in premier or grand crus. Jacques's general policy was to use whole bunches for vinification, close to 100% new oak. Belief in tradition extends to cooling the cellar to delay malolactic fermentation until the Spring. After his son Jeremy became involved in 1999, the style softened, with some destemming, and reduced usage of new oak (40-100% today, depending on the cuvée). The general feeling is that terroir shows better as a result of backing off from using complete stems and new oak, but even so, the style can still be a little severe, coming off best with the grand crus where there is the greatest fruit concentration, but the Morey St. Denis can show a lovely balance between crystalline precision and femininity. In addition to the domain wines, the family has a negociant activity, Dujac Père et Fils.

Domaine Robert Groffier Père Et Fils ✸✸

3 Route Grands Crus, 21220 Morey St. Denis	📞 +33 3 80 34 31 53
@ *domaine.groffier@gmail.com*	👤 *Nicolas Groffier*
	🔵 *Morey St. Denis [map]*
🚫 🗡 🍇 🛢 *8 ha; 40,000 btl*	🏛 *Gevrey Chambertin*

Chambertin Clos de Bèze
"Grand Cru"

APPELLATION CHAMBERTIN CLOS DE BÈZE CONTRÔLÉE

RED BURGUNDY WINE
Mis en Bouteille au Domaine
Robert GROFFIER Père & Fils
Propriétaire Récoltant à Morey-Saint-Denis - Côte d'Or - France

"Most of our vineyards are in Chambolle Musigny and most are premier or grand cru. We try to represent the appellation elegance, that's sure, but each cru is different. Sentiers is strong, Haut Doix is more feminine, we try to get the best out of each," says Nicolas Groffier. The domain is located on the main road through Morey St. Denis, but its vineyards are to the south (in Chambolle Musigny) or to the north (in Gevrey Chambertin). It dates back to the nineteenth century, but most of the vineyard holdings were acquired by Jules Groffier in the 1930s; it was his son Robert who started domain bottling after 1973. Nicolas is Robert's grandson.

There's a hectare of Gevrey Chambertin and half hectare of Clos de Bèze, but the main holdings are in three premier crus of Chambolle Musigny, including Les Amoureuses (where Groffier has the single largest holding, with three parcels that total 20% of the cru), and also grand cru Bonnes Mares. Vines are trained in the Cordon Royale instead of the more usual Guyot, in order to reduce yields; the objective is "to seek concentration in the berries and not in the cave."

The Groffiers are late pickers, so the style tends to be full and powerful. Policy on destemming has gone to and fro, and now varies with the vintage; usually there are some whole clusters. Cold maceration is followed by fermentation at unusually high temperature. Since the late 1990s, new oak has been moderate, 20-25% for premier crus, up to 50% for grand crus.

Bourgogne Rouge comes from just on the other side of the N74 from Clos Vougeot, and ages in old barriques. "I could put it in new oak, but that wouldn't serve the purpose, It should drink in 3 years, 5 years maximum, but it's a serious wine, it's well-placed, the separation from Bourgogne to Clos Vougeot is a bit brutal."

Gevrey Chambertin has 30% whole bunches and a little new oak. Fruits are more obvious than the Bourgogne, with the stern character of the appellation showing faintly in the background. The vines in premier cru Haut Doix are 60-years old, and the wine is a beautiful demonstration of the elegance of Chambolle Musigny. "This is the wine that's the most open and easiest to approach that I make." You can see a direct lineage from the Chambolle premier crus to grand cru Bonnes Mares, which is smooth, deep, and seamless, but showing the sense of firmness that characterizes the house style. The rising reputation of the domain has been accompanied by a commensurate increase in prices.

Domaine des Lambrays ***

31 Rue Basse, 21220 Morey St. Denis	+33 3 80 51 84 33
clos@lambrays.com	Jacques Devauges
www.lambrays.com	Morey St. Denis [map]
11 ha; 40,000 btl	Clos des Lambrays

The domain is effectively synonymous with the Clos des Lambrays, a 9 ha vineyard in Morey St. Denis. References to Cloux des Lambrey go back to 1365. It was divided between 74 owners after the Revolution, but reunited in 1868. The domain owns all but a tiny parcel at the bottom (Domaine Taupenot-Merme owns a tiny plot of 420 square meters, which they planted in 1974. It makes less than a barrel, but despite repeated efforts they have refused to sell it to Domaine des Lambrays). Clos des Lambrays was classified as premier cru in 1936 because its owner did not submit the paperwork to become a grand cru. The estate was somewhat neglected until a change of ownership in 1979, when Thierry Brouin came as winemaker. He is generally credited with restoring the estate to its former glory; he retired in 2015.

The clos was promoted to grand cru in 1981. The domain also produces two other red cuvées: Les Loups is a blend from young vines of the clos together with plots in two premier crus, and there is a communal Morey St. Denis. There are also two Puligny Montrachets from tiny plots in Caillerets and Folatières. Occasionally there is a rosé (from less ripe grapes selected out during sorting; it is superb, with the quality of the grand cru evident).

Winemaking is traditional, with fermentation of whole bunches irrespective of vintage. I would describe the style as upright. Younger vintages can seem tight, and older vintages soften slowly, with fruits moving from cherries towards strawberries, but not evolving in a savory or tertiary direction in the first couple of decades. The focus is on purity and precision of fruit. Running counter to the modern trend, these are definitely not wines for instant gratification: it remains to be seen how that will play under the aegis of LVMH, who purchased the estate in 2014 for €101 million.

Domaine Michel Magnien   *

4 rue Ribordot, 21220 Morey St. Denis	📞 *+33 3 80 51 82 98*
@ *domaine@michel-magnien.com*	🚶 *Frédéric Magnien*
🌐 *www.domaine-magnien.com*	🟢 *Morey St. Denis* [map]
📅 🏭 🍇 🍷 📷	*18 ha; 160,000 btl*

There are two Magniens. Michel and Frédéric are father and son, but their names on the label have different meanings. Domaine Michel Magnien means the wines come from the estate, which includes 23 cuvées from the Côte de Nuits. Maison Frédéric Magnien refers to the negociant, with grapes coming from around 20 growers, and production a little greater than the domain. The negociant is a bit broader in scope, still more focused on the Côte de Nuits, but including some whites from the Côte de Beaune. Frédéric joined his father in 1993, and started Maison Frédéric Magnien in 1995; Michel has now retired and Frédéric makes all the wines at the cuverie on the N74 at Morey St. Denis. Black labels are used for Domaine Michel Magnien, and white labels for Frédéric Magnien. The tasting room was renovated and opened to the public in 2016, but unusually does not sell the latest vintages, and mostly offers vintages from 5 to 10 years old.

Winemaking is identical whether for black or white label. Frédéric does not like the taste of oak in the wine—"we want to taste the typicity of the terroir." Only old barriques are used, and in 2015 terracotta amphora were introduced for maturation. More than a hundred amphora were purchased in 2016. Each amphora holds 160 liters (about three quarters of a barrique). "We think the clay jars make the wine more accessible. We get more oxygenation and finer tannins." A couple of grand crus have been vinified exclusively in clay jars, but most of the premier and grand crus are vinified in a roughly equal mix of old barriques and clay jars.

The house style is light, never highly extracted. Whites show as fresh rather than powerful. For reds, this plays well for Chambolle Musigny and Morey St. Denis, but the wines are lighter than expected for, say, Vosne Romanée. Even the Vosne Romanée is ready to drink by, say, four years after the vintage. In a generous vintage such as 2015, Chambolle and Morey St. Denis may be virtually ready to drink on release.

Domaine Henri Perrot-Minot   ***

54 Route-des-Grands Crus, 21220 Morey St. Denis	📞 *+33 3 80 34 32 51*
@ *gfa.perrot-minot@wanadoo.fr*	🚶 *Christophe Perrot-Minot*
🌐 *www.perrot-minot.com*	🟢 *Morey St. Denis* [map]
📅 ✒ 🍇 🛢 📷 *10 ha; 45,000 btl*	⚑ *Morey St. Denis, La Riotte*

I started off on the wrong foot when I visited Perrot-Minot by mistakenly going to the new winery across the N74, but Christophe Perrot-Minot was typically charming about it, and the next day we had a splendid tasting in the cellars of the old domain in the center of Morey St. Denis. Christophe is the fourth generation, and worked as a wine broker before making his first vintage in 1993. The domain originated with Domaine

Maume Morizot, which was formed by his great grandfather, but the estate was subsequently divided into four parts in 1973. Christophe is quite hands on, spending his mornings in the vineyards; when I arrived, he had just returned from the green pruning.

The key here is a combination of old vines and low yields, 20-30 hl/ha for everything, even the Bourgogne. Everything is destemmed except for four cuvées: grapes are cut one by one from the central stem—Christophe calls this destructuration. The house style is faintly spicy and nutty with perfumed hints. Smooth palates show round fruits with silky tannins, never any rough edges; the overall impression is ultra-modern, with a silky approachability even in Gevrey Chambertin or Vosne Romanée, but there's structure behind. Yet when I asked Christophe if he regards himself as a modernist, he was a bit indignant. "For me this is traditional, not modern. It's not that I'm looking for drinking young, I'm looking for elegance, balance, and concentration, but it must be natural, it must come from the berries."

Domaine Ponsot ***

17 à 21 rue de La Montagne, BP 11, 21220 Morey St. Denis	+33 3 80 34 32 46
info@domaine-ponsot.com	Alexandre Abel
www.domaine-ponsot.com	Morey St. Denis [map]
	Morey St. Denis, Premier Cru
10 ha; 50,000 btl	Morey St. Denis, Monts Luisants

William Ponsot established the domain in 1870 with the vineyards that are still at its heart: premier cru Monts Luisants and grand cru Clos de La Roche. Jean-Marie Ponsot took over in 1957, expanding the domain by marriage, and becoming mayor of Morey St. Denis. Laurent Ponsot took over in 1981, and expanded north into Gevrey Chambertin and south into Chambolle Musigny. Ponsot's vineyard in Clos de la Roche was the origin for the now-famous Dijon clones of Pinot Noir. An impressive gravity-feed winery at the top of the hill in the town extends several storeys underground. The range extends from communal Morey St. Denis and Gevrey Chambertin to grand crus.

Owned by Laurent together with his three sisters, the domain encountered an unexpected turn of events when Laurent announced in 2017 that he was leaving after 36 years with his son Clément to form his own negociant (see profile). His sister Rose-Marie is now in charge, and Alexandre Abel was appointed as winemaker in time to make the 2017 vintage. Some of the vines are owned by Laurent personally, so the domain no longer produces Clos St. Denis, for example.

Winemaking policy has not changed. Ponsot harvests late in order to get maximum ripeness, and usually is the last in the village. Regarded as a fashion, there is no new oak, the wines are not filtered, and there is minimum use of sulfur (for reds a little sulfur is added only at bottling).One of the rare white wines produced in the Côte de Nuits, Mont Luisants is unique in consisting of Aligoté. The vines go back to 1911. "It's not always easy to distinguish as Aligoté from Chardonnay, it's really premier cru white Burgundy," Alexandre says. This wine usually is delicious for its first couple of years and then closes up; Laurent Ponsot said it takes a decade to emerge from its shell. About the only change in winemaking is that Mont Luisants moved to whole cluster pressing in 2017. The other top white is Corton Charlemagne, which can be quite stern when young.

The communal reds are relatively bright in style. In grand crus, Griotte Chambertin is exceedingly elegant, and Chapelle Chambertin has just a touch more weight. The top red is Clos de la Roche Vieilles Vignes, coming from two plots, the largest from the historic parcel of 1872, the rest from a smaller plot lower down. Most of the vines were planted in 1954, but about 15% date from 1938 and another 15% from the 1990s. The style is smooth and velvety, chocolaty in a warm vintage, and brighter in a cool vintage.

Domaine du Clos de Tart   ★★★

7 Route des Grands Crus, 21220 Morey St. Denis	📞 +33 3 80 34 30 91
@ contact@clos-de-tart.com	👤 Alessandro Noli
🌐 www.clos-de-tart.com	🗺 Morey St. Denis [map]
🚫🍷🍇◐ 8 ha; 23,000 btl	🍷 Clos de Tart

This splendid domain is synonymous with the largest grand cru monopole in Burgundy, occupying a single plot on the slope running up behind the Maison. It has had only three owners since it was created by nuns in 1141. After the Revolution in 1789 it was acquired by Marey-Monge, and then it was sold to the Mommessin family in 1932. The Mommessins also owned a negociant business (since sold to Jean-Claude Boisset). Clos de Tart went through a difficult period until Sylvain Pitiot became the winemaker in 1996; he retired in 2015. The vineyard unusually is planted with rows in north-south orientation across the slope, and Clos de Tart has its own nursery for selecting vines for propagation by selection massale.

There are two cuvées. Until vines are 25 years old, production is declassified into La Forge des Tarts (labeled as premier cru). In addition, lots may be assigned to La Forge on the basis of blind tasting. Usually La Forge is about a quarter of production, but there have been extreme vintages where there has been much less La Forge or no Clos de Tart. Although this is a genuine clos (entirely surrounded by walls), soils vary extensively, and it is divided into 23 plots, which are vinified separately. Vinification matches the plot, in some cases with complete destemming, in others with partial or entire whole clusters. Only new oak is used. There is no difference in winemaking between La Forge and Clos de Tart, but La Forge is less structured and ready to drink sooner.

Clos de Tart has never been divided in its history, which is a remarkable contrast with the fate of most properties in Burgundy. But it is following a more common path with its sale in 2017 for more than €210 million to François Pinault, one of the richest men in France, who owns Château Latour and other wine properties, including Domaine d'Eugénie in Vosne-Romanée. There is speculation that the style will now change, as it has at Domaine d'Eugénie.

Domaine Cécile Tremblay   ★★

8 rue de Très Girard, 21220 Morey St. Denis	📞 +33 3 45 83 60 08
@ domainetremblay@yahoo.fr	👤 Cécile Tremblay
🌐 www.domaine-ceciletremblay.com	🗺 Morey St. Denis [map]
🚫🍷🍇🌿 5 ha; 30,000 btl	🍷 Bourgogne Grande Ordinaire

This is essentially a new domain. The family lives in Vosne Romanée, but has always rented out its vineyards. When some of the rental agreements ended in 2003, Cécile was able to take back 3 ha of vineyards. In 2009, she purchased vineyards in Bourgogne AOP and Chambolle Musigny, bringing the domain to its present size. In 2021, rental agreements expire on another 3 ha, so the domain will come to about 7 ha. Cécile started by

making wine in borrowed facilities at other producers, but constructed a cuverie in a quiet residential street in Morey St. Denis in 2012, just behind the hotel Castel Très Girard. Although the domain is small—"we have two and a half people working here, we do everything"—there are 11 cuvées.

Depending on the vintage, usually there is some whole bunch, about 15% for Bourgogne, a third for village wine, up to 75% for premier or grand crus. Cécile tries to ensure the stems are ripe, but cuts out the biggest stems from whole bunches to avoid astringency. There is no general rule for new oak; generally there's about 50% for grand cru and less for others. Élevage is 15-18 months with no racking, but the small cellar forces them to roll the barrels to move, so the lees get stirred up anyway.

The Bourgogne Grande Ordinaire is a blend of two plots, one in Vosne Romanée, one the other side of the N74 in Chambolle. "It's rare to have Bourgogne in Vosne, so we are lucky to have it." The wine follows the imperatives of Vosne intensity rather than Chambolle delicacy, showing unusual breed and class for Bourgogne AOP. The Chambolle Musigny and Morey St. Denis have less weight but greater refinement than the Bourgogne, with more of a sheen on the Chambolle. The Morey St. Denis comes from a tiny holding. "It's an example of how Burgundy works: three rows and it's already a plot." Vosne Romanée and the premier crus are tighter and more structured, and the structure becomes more obvious moving from the premier crus to Echézeaux. The wines are classic representations of their appellations with a common thread of refinement.

Profiles of Important Estates

Domaine Arlaud

41 Rue D'epernay, 21220 Morey St. Denis	📞 *+33 3 80 34 32 65*
@ *contact@domainearlaud.com*	👤 *Cyprien Arlaud*
🌐 *www.domainearlaud.com*	🔵 *Morey St. Denis [map]*
📅 🖌 🍇 🛢 🍶	*15 ha; 60,000 btl*

Joseph Arlaud founded the domain in 1942 with vineyards from his wife's family, and he and his son Hervé expanded with further purchases. The label shows the historic building in Nuits St. Georges that the domain purchased for its winery in 1966; this is still used for events, but since 2003 production has been at a modern gravity-feed facility in Morey St. Denis. Joseph's grandson, Cyprien Arlaud, has been making the wine since 2004. Vineyards are concentrated in Chambolle Musigny (including three premier crus) and Morey St. Denis (including four premier crus); there are also four grand crus. The domain also makes Gevrey Chambertin and a Bourgogne Aligoté (the only white). Under his own name, Cyprien also has a negociant activity that extends the range to Vosne Romanée (also biodynamic). There's some use of whole clusters for the top wines, and new oak varies from 25-30% for villages and premier crus, more for grand crus.

Domaine Castagnier

20, Rue Des Jardins, 21220 Morey St. Denis	📞 *+33 3 80 34 31 62*
@ *jeromecastagnier@yahoo.fr*	👤 *Jérôme Castagnier*
📅 🍶 🍇 ⏳ *5 ha; 45,000 btl*	🔵 *Morey St. Denis [map]*

The domaine is in its fifth generation, but because it has been passed through the female line, it has changed its name several times. It became Domaine Castagnier in 2004 when Jérôme returned home to take over, having been a professional trumpeter. It's a very small domain, but half is in grand cru, including Clos de la Roche and Clos Saint Denis (it's unusual to have both grand crus of Morey in the same domain), and Charmes Chambertin and Clos Vougeot (only 27 rows). His smallest holding is actually 2 rows of vines in Morey St. Denis village; this is too little to vinify separately, so it goes into the Bourgogne Rouge, where it comprises 25%. Domaine wines are about three quarters of production, with the rest coming from a small negociant activity started in 2007. Destemming depends on the year, and was 60% in 2015, but 100% in 2016 and 2017. Fermentation starts of 4-6 days maceration, and the wine ages in barriques for 14-16 months, with up to 40% new oak for the grand crus.

Domaine Georges Lignier et Fils

41, Grande Rue, 21220 Morey St. Denis	📞 *+33 3 80 34 32 55*
📠 *+33 3 80 34 13 74*	👤 *Benoit Stehly*
🚜 *16 ha; 40,000 btl*	🍷 *Morey St. Denis*

Georges Lignier founded the estate at the start of the twentieth century with some vines he inherited from his father, His son Bernard took over in 1949, Bernard's son Georges took over in 1970, and then George's nephew Benoit Stehly joined the domain in 2002 and took over in 2008. Vines are distributed among 50 parcels, with an average age of 50 years. The domain's 1.5 ha in Clos St. Denis make it the largest holder in the grand cru. Other grand crus are Clos de la Roche (1 ha), Bonnes Mares, and Charmes Chambertin. The domain also has Clos des Ormes premier cru in Morey St. Denis (the holding is 2 ha, just aboiut half the Cru), and village wines from Morey St. Denis and Chambolle Musigny. Harvest tends to be a little on the later side, grapes are 80% destemmed, there is 3-4 day cold soak before fermentation, village wines age in used barriques, premier crus get 30% new oak, and grand crus have 50% new oak, with aging for around 18-20 months. Wines are all red except for a Bourgogne Aligoté (from 1.8 ha within Morey St. Denis) and a Morey St. Denis Blanc (just a couple of barrels from a few rows in the Clos Solon lieu-dit). The style tends more to elegance than power, compared with Domaine Hubert Lignier (the Ligniers at each domain are cousins).

Domaine Hubert Lignier

45 Grande Rue, 21220 Morey St. Denis	📞 *+33 3 80 51 87 40*
@ *chateau.lacoste.a.roques@wanadoo.fr*	👤 *Laurent Lignier*
🌐 *hubert-lignier.com*	🍷 *Morey St. Denis*
🍇 🍷 🍂	*9 ha; 70,000 btl*

Founded in 1880, the domain is now in its fifth generation. Hubert Lignier established the domain, his son Romain and daughter-in-law Kellen took over in 1992, but Romain sadly died in 2004. Then in 2006 Hubert returned to the domain to work with his other son, Laurent. There was a disagreement with Kellen, which led to a division of the domain. Hubert recovered most of the vineyards in 2013. (During this period, Kellen started Domaine Lucie et Auguste Lignier; named for her children, at first bottling some of the wines from Hubert Lignier, and then making her own in the former cellars of the local cooperative, under the hotel Castel Très Girard. The wines showed a somewhat light style. After 2013, production ceased.). Laurent bought some new plots to extend the domain, and buys grapes from about another 4 ha to increase the range, which now extends to about 24 cuvées. Élevage is relatively long, at 20-22 months, but use of new oak is quite light, only 20-30%. The official address is in the village of Morey St. Denis, but the winery is actually on the D974. Holdings in Morey St. Denis are fairly similar to those of Hubert's cousin, Domaine Georges Lignier, and the style at Hubert Lignier is a little more powerful.

Domaine Chantal Rémy

1 place du Monument, 21220 Morey St. Denis	📞 +33 3 80 34 32 59
@ domaine.chantal.remy@orange.fr	👤 Chantal Rémy
🌐 www.domaine-chantal-remy.com	🔘 Morey St. Denis [map]
🏃🏭🍇🍶 🍃	3 ha; 13,000 btl

The Louis Rémy domain was founded in 1820 and is still located in the same building in the center of the village. Louis died in 1982, his wife took over, and then his daughter Chantal returned to take over in 1988. The domain name changed to Chantal Rémy in 1992. When her mother died in 2008, Chantal split the vineyards with her two brothers, so the domain was reduced to only 1.5 ha, although it retained all the grand crus. Chantal's son Florian has been making the wine since 2013; the style has become fresher. The flagship wine is a monopole, Clos des Rosiers, just behind the house, and adjacent to both Clos des Lambrays and Clos de Tart. This was once classified as premier cru, but it became a rose garden, before being replanted with vines. There are some negociant wines under the label Héritiers Louis Rémy.

Domaine Taupenot-Merme

33 Route Des Grands Crus, 21220 Morey St. Denis	📞 +33 3 80 34 35 24
@ domaine.taupenot-merme@wanadoo.fr	👤 Romain Taupenot
🏃🍂🍇🍃 19 ha	🔘 Morey St. Denis [map]

The domain has vineyards from two sides of the family. the Taupenot vineyards are in Saint Romain and Auxey-Duresses; the Merme vineyards run from Nuits St. Georges to Gevrey Chambertin, and originated when the Maume Morizot estate was divided. One part became Perrot-Minot (see profile); another part, immediately across the street, became Taupenot-Merme. Romain Taupenot has been in charge since 1998. The holdings on the Côte de Nuits are impressive, but somehow the estate does not quite seem to fulfill their potential. The attitude here is somewhat commercial.

Chambolle Musigny

Profiles of Leading Estates

Domaine Amiot-Servelle ★★

34 Rue Caroline Aigle, 21220 Chambolle Musigny	📞 *+33 3 80 62 80 39*
@ *domaine@amiot-servelle.com*	👤 *Prune & Antoine Amiot*
🌐 *www.amiot-servelle.com*	🖥 *Chambolle Musigny [map]*
📅 🏭 🍇 🍷 *8 ha; 40,000 btl*	🍾 *Chambolle Musigny*

The activity of the family in Chambolle Musigny started in the 1920s, and Domaine Servelle-Tachot was created in the 1950s. The name changed to Amiot-Servelle when Christian Amiot and his wife Elisabeth (née Servelle) took over in 1989. Their daughter Prune, who has a degree in oenology, joined the domain in 2011. Tastings take place in a small cave just below the family residence in the center of Chambolle Musigny.

This is very much a domain of the village, with most of the vineyards in Chambolle Musigny coming from the Servelle side, including five premier crus, culminating in Les Amoureuses. There are also wines from the Amiot side, including Morey St. Denis and grand cru Clos St. Denis from the neighboring village, as well as Charmes Chambertin. There are both red and white Bourgogne, coming from the other side of the N74. The Bourgogne is almost the only white; sometimes there is an exchange of berries with a producer in Puligny Montrachet.

The approach to vinification is conventional, with increasing use of new oak going up the appellation hierarchy: Bourgogne is 10% new oak, village is 20%, premier cru is 30%, Amoureuses is 50%, grand cru is 75%. Élevage is 15-18 months. "There is no rule about whole bunches," Prune says. "We look at the grapes, if they are really ripe it could be 100%."

The style here is very expressive of the two villages, with a great sense of purity of fruits, showing as a mixture of red and black cherries. The difference going from Bourgogne to village to premier cru is a greater sense of black fruits and more texture. The tannins are always silky but they are so fine that the village Morey St. Denis and Chambolle Musigny can be started soon after the vintage; the Chambolle is finer than Morey St. Denis. The premier crus have more structure, with a sense of silky tannins on the finish, which needs more time to resolve. Les Plantes gives a finer sense of Chambolle compared to the village wine, and Les Charmes adds weight.

Domaine Ghislaine Barthod ★★

4 Rue du Lavoir, 21220 Chambolle Musigny	📞 *+33 3 80 62 80 16*
@ *domaine.ghislaine.barthod@orange.fr*	👤 *Ghislaine Barthod*
	🖥 *Chambolle Musigny [map]*
📅 🔪 🍇 ☕ *7 ha; 30,000 btl*	🍾 *Chambolle Musigny, Les Charmes*

This small domain is tightly focused on Chambolle Musigny, where there are nine premier crus as well as the communal wine. The domain started with Marcel Noëllat in the 1920s, became known as Barthod-Noëllat after the union of the Barthod and Noëllat families, and then changed to Barthod after Gaston Barthod took over in the 1960s; his

daughter Ghislaine started making the wines in the early 1990s, and has been fully in charge since 1999. The domain has remained the same, except for the recent addition of the Gruenchers premier cru.

Ghislaine's husband is Louis Boillot, who left his family domain, started to make wine independently in Gevrey Chambertin, and now makes wine in Chambolle Musigny in the Barthod cellars (see profile). The Barthod domain is located in the heart of Chambolle Musigny, with the winery backing right onto the vineyards. Ghislaine and Louis share the same team for managing the vineyards, but winemaking has been independent. Since 2019, their son, Clément Boillot, has taken charge of winemaking for both estates.

All grapes are destemmed at Ghislaine Barthod, then there's a period of maceration before fermentation starts naturally in open-topped wood cuves, with aging following in barriques with up to about 30% new oak for 12-18 months. The regime is the same for all the premier crus. The wines are considered to showcase the characteristic finesse of the commune, with Les Charmes and Les Cras usually at the top of the hierarchy. There is also a Bourgogne Rouge from a vineyard just outside of Chambolle Musigny in Gilly. The wines are definitely taut and elegant, but can be tight when young: even from rich vintages, the communal Chambolle Musigny can still be quite closed several years later.

Domaine Hudelot-Noëllat   **

5 Ancienne Route Nationale 74, 221220 Chambolle Musigny	📞 +33 3 80 62 85 17
@ contact@domaine-hudelot-noellat.com	👤 Charles Van Caneyt
🌐 www.domaine-hudelot-noellat.com	🗺 Chambolle Musigny [map]
📋 🚜 🍇 🍷 11 ha; 60,000 btl	Vouvray Moelleux, Plan de Jean

Alain Hudelot formed the domain in 1964, then changed the name to Hudelot-Noëllat in 1978 when he married Odile Noëllat, the granddaughter of Charles Noëllat (whose domain was purchased by Lalou Bize-Leroy in 1998). Alain retired in 2008, and his grandson Charles van Canneyt took over.

There are 15 appellations in the domain, in Chambolle Musigny, Vosne Romanée, and Vougeot. Vineyards include some top premier crus—Vosne Romanée les Malconsorts, Les Beaumonts and Les Suchots—and grand crus Richebourg and Romanée St. Vivant. Many of the vines are close to a hundred years old. Winemaking is traditional, with 15% new oak for village wines, 30% for premier crus, and a maximum of 50% for Romanée St. Vivant.

As you would expect from the focus on Vosne Romanée, the style tends to opulence, but is very refined. Richebourg shows characteristic breadth while Romanée St. Vivant shows typical precision. Tasting a vertical of Romanée St. Vivant identifies that characteristic line of purity, even in lesser vintages. Even in the grand crus, the wines are never heavy. "We are looking for freshness and elegance. The difficulty in 2015 was to keep the balance between richness and acidity. Personally I don't want to do heavy wines."

Charles decided also to add a negociant activity under his own name, beginning with only 7 barrels. Now there are 25 barrels at the negociant, mostly grand crus, premier crus, and some villages, and sometimes Bourgogne. "I try to produce appellations we don't have at the domain." The wines for the negociant are made at separate facilities in Beaune.

Domaine Jacques Frédéric Mugnier   ***

Château De Chambolle-Musigny, 21220 Chambolle Musigny	📞 *+33 3 80 62 85 39*
@ *info@mugnier.fr*	👤 *Frédéric Mugnier*
🌐 *mugnier.fr*	🔵 *Chambolle Musigny [map]*
🚫 ⁄ 🍇 🚜 *14 ha; 45,000 btl*	🍶 *Chambolle Musigny*

In the early nineteenth century the Mugniers developed a successful business in liqueurs in Dijon. In 1863 they purchased the Château de Chambolle Musigny, an imposing Château at the foot of the hill, and they acquired the vineyards that form the basis of the domain. All the vineyards were in Chambolle Musigny until their last purchase, the Clos de la Maréchale in Nuits St. Georges, in 1902. This vineyard was leased to Faiveley and reverted to Mugnier only in 2004; now it is their largest single property. The vineyards are not formally organic, but there is no use of fertilizers, herbicides, or pesticides. All the wines are red, except for a white that was introduced at the Clos de la Maréchale.

Frédéric Mugnier was an airline pilot until he started to run the domain full time in 2000. Soon he was forced to expand, building a new cuverie under the courtyard of the Château, when the domain was tripled by the reversion of the Clos de la Maréchale. The Chambolle Musigny and the two premier crus, Les Fuées and Les Amoureuses, are the quintessence of elegance, textbook examples of the "femininity" of Chambolle. The Clos de la Maréchale follows the same style but is more obviously structured. "It took me years to realize that the best way to vinify the different terroirs was to make all the wine exactly the same," says Frédéric, and today all the wines get the same 15-20% new oak. Freddy says he would be happy to be described as a minimalist but would prefer "essentialist."

Domaine Georges Roumier   ***

4, Rue De Vergy, 21220 Chambolle Musigny	📞 *+33 3 80 62 86 37*
@ *domaine@roumier.com*	👤 *Christophe Roumier*
🌐 *www.roumier.com*	🔵 *Chambolle Musigny [map]*
📅 ⁄ 🍇 🌿 *14 ha; 50,000 btl*	🍶 *Morey St. Denis, Les Bussières*

The domain originated in 1924 when Georges Roumier obtained vineyards in Chambolle Musigny by marriage. The wines have been estate bottled since 1945. His son, Jean-Marie, took over in 1961, and the domain is now run by Christophe, who joined his father in 1981 and took over in 1990. Expanded from the original holdings, the heart of the estate still lies in Chambolle Musigny, and includes vineyards in the two grand crus, Bonnes Mares and Le Musigny (a really tiny holding, giving only 300 bottles), and in three important premier crus, Les Amoureuses, Les Cras, and Les Combottes. The average age of vines is around forty years. There is a little white wine in the form of Corton Charlemagne (only a hundred cases).

The style is on the sturdy side for Chambolle Musigny, and the wines usually require some time to open up: the monopole of Clos de la Bussières from Morey St. Denis, for example, can be positively hard when first released, but give it a decade and it acquires a silky sheen. Some of that initial hardness may be due to the practice of not necessarily destemming—only the village wine is always destemmed, otherwise each vintage is judged separately. A short cold maceration is followed by fermentation under 30 °C and warm post-fermentation maceration. New oak is usually around 25% (perhaps 30% for the grand crus). The corollary of making wines in traditional style requiring time to open out is that they are correspondingly long-lived.

Domaine Comte Georges de Vogüé   ***

7 Rue Ste. Barbe, 21220 Chambolle Musigny	📞 +33 3 80 62 86 25
📠 +33 3 80 62 82 38	🧑 Jean-Luc Pepin
	🖥 Chambolle Musigny [map]
🚫🏷🍇🌿	🍷 Chambolle Musigny
13 ha; 36,000 btl	📋 Musigny Blanc

One look at the fifteenth century entrance, and you can see this is a really old domain: ownership has not changed since 1450. Comte de Vogüé is by far the most important holder of Musigny, with 7 of the 11 ha. A small part (0.65 ha) makes the Musigny Blanc, one of (perhaps the) top white wine of the Côte de Nuits, but after 1994, when the vineyard was re-planted, it was declassified to Bourgogne Blanc. "It seems a bit brutal to declassify grand cru to Bourgogne, but we didn't have any choice," says François Millet, who has made the wine here from 1986 until handing over to Jean Lupatelli in 2021. Production as Musigny Blanc resumed in 2015. There's a stringent policy of de-classification. "We declassify young vines (everything under 25 years) from (red) Musigny into Chambolle Musigny premier cru," he explains, adding, "I don't consider this to be a second wine, it's a younger Musigny." The domain also has a large holding in Bonnes Mares, and some Chambolle Amoureuses and village Chambolle Musigny.

François has strong views on winemaking. "Grapes are destemmed and used as whole berries. I've never used whole bunches. The question I ask is, if we have whole berries, why should I use whole bunches?" And as for oak, "I have chosen to be a winemaker not a forester." There is 15% new oak in Chambolle Musigny, 25% in premier crus, and 35% in grand crus. The best single word to describe the de Vogüé wines is soignée: they give a silky impression of infinite smoothness, ranging from the precision of Chambolle Musigny, to the sheer elegance of the firmer premier cru, the classic seamless Amoureuses, and the weight of Musigny.

Profiles of Important Estates

Domaine Louis Boillot et Fils

21220 4 rue du Lavoir, Chambolle Musigny	📞 +33 3 80 62 80 16
@ domaine.louis.boillot@orange.fr	🧑 Louis Boillot
📅 🏭 🍇 🌿 11 ha; 45,000 btl	🖥 Chambolle Musigny

Louis Boillot has half the vineyards of his father's domain, Lucien Boillot (now run by his brother Pierre from the original cellars in Gevrey Chambertin). Louis set up his own domain in 2003, and is married to Ghislaine Barthod (see profile); the wines are made in the same cellar. Since 2019, their son Clément Boillet has made the wines for both estates. (Although all the Boillots are related the Louis Boillot domain in Volnay was completely different, but in any case was renamed as Domaine Clos de la Chapelle after it changed owners in 2011.) Louis's vineyards are mostly in Gevrey Chambertin and Volnay, making him an unusual family estate with holdings on both Côte de Nuits and Côte de Beaune. Grapes are destalked and new wood is usually 20-30%.

Domaine Anne et Hervé Sigaut

12 rue-des-Champs, 21220 Chambolle Musigny	📞 +33 3 80 62 80 28
@ herve.sigaut@wanadoo.fr	👤 Anne Sigaut
🌐 www.domaine-sigaut.com	Chambolle Musigny [map]
📅 ⛏ 🍇 🍷	7 ha; 30,000 btl

This small family domain is totally focused on Chambolle Musigny, with village wine (coming from ten plots), lieu-dit Les Bussières (a plot of 50-year old vines) and four premier crus. The only exception is a small plot of Morey St. Denis premier cru. Anne and Hervé took over from Maurice Sigaut in 1990. The cellar was renovated in 2004. The domain is not officially organic, but Hervé follows the lunar calendar for winemaking. There's cold maceration before fermentation, and aging in around a third new oak. The style showcases the elegance of Chambolle Musigny, and Les Bussières is a top example at village level.

Vougeot

Profiles of Important Estates

Domaine Bertagna

Rue Du Vieux Château, 21640 Vougeot	📞 *+33 3 80 62 86 04*
@ *contact@domainebertagna.com*	👤 *Eva Reh*
⊕ *www.domainebertagna.com*	🔵 *Vougeot [map]*
🔲 📊 ✖ 🍇 🔥	*17 ha; 55,000 btl*

The domain was created by Claude Bertagna when he returned from Algeria in 1950. The Gunther-Reh family, of von Kesselstatt in the Mosel in Germany, purchased the state in 1982. Holdings are dominated by Vougeot (6 of the 18 cuvées), including one white cuvée. The only other white is Corton Charlemagne. Altogether the holdings include 12 premier and grand crus. There's also a large vineyard on the Hautes Côtes de Nuits. The flagship wine is the monopole of the Clos de la Perrière premier cru. Use of oak is traditional, with 1-year and 2-year barriques for village wines, 20-30% new for premier crus, and 30-50% for grand crus.

Domaine du Château de la Tour

Clos de Vougeot, 21640 Vougeot	📞 *+33 3 80 62 86 13*
@ *contact@chateaudelatour.com*	👤 *Edouard Labet*
⊕ *www.chateaudelatour.com*	🔵 *Vougeot [map]*
🔲 📊 🍇 🔥	*6 ha; 26,000 btl*

The domain owns the largest single holding in Clos Vougeot and has the distinction of being the only producer allowed to make its wines within the clos. It has been owned by the same family since M. Beaudet purchased it in 1899. François Labet, who is the son of M. Beaudet's granddaughter, has been in charge since 1984, and also runs his father's family estate, Pierre Labet, in Beaune (slightly larger with 10 ha). Today he works with his son Edouard Labet. The wines for both estates are vinified at Clos Vougeot. Although there is only the one holding in Clos Vougeot, there are usually two cuvées: Clos Vougeot tout court, and a Vieilles Vignes from a 1 ha plot near the center of the clos, planted in 1910. Sometimes there is also a Cuvée Hommage Jean Morin from this plot. A white (from a tiny plot of Pinot Gris, known locally as Pinot Beurot), planted in 1990, was introduced with the 2020 vintage, and is labeled as Vin de France.

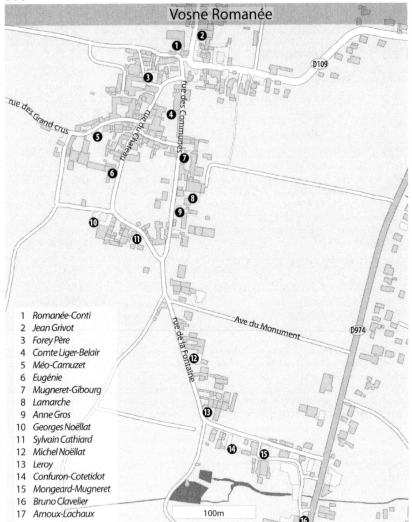

Vosne Romanée

1 Romanée-Conti
2 Jean Grivot
3 Forey Père
4 Comte Liger-Belair
5 Méo-Camuzet
6 Eugénie
7 Mugneret-Gibourg
8 Lamarche
9 Anne Gros
10 Georges Noëllat
11 Sylvain Cathiard
12 Michel Noëllat
13 Leroy
14 Confuron-Cotetidot
15 Mongeard-Mugneret
16 Bruno Clavelier
17 Arnoux-Lachaux

rue des Grand crus

rue des Communes

rue du Château

rue de la Fontaine

Ave du Monument

D109

D974

100m

Profiles of Leading Estates

Domaine Arnoux-Lachaux ★★

3, Route Nationale 74, 21700 Vosne Romanée	📞 *+33 3 80 61 08 41*
@ *info@arnoux-lachaux.com*	👤 *Florence Arnoux-Lachaux*
🌐 *www.arnoux-lachaux.com*	🔘 *Vosne Romanée [map]*
📅 🏭 🍇 🗐 *14 ha; 50,000 btl*	🍷 *Nuits St. Georges, Clos de Corvées Pagets*

This started as Domaine Robert Arnoux, in 1858, and was considered to be a typical domain of Vosne Romanée, with strong wines, well structured and concentrated: robust was a common description. Pascal Lachaux, Robert Arnoux's son-in-law, has been running the estate since 1993, and in 2007 changed the name of the domain to Arnoux-Lachaux. There are grand cru holdings in Romanée St Vivant, Echézeaux, Latricières Chambertin, and Clos Vougeot, and some top premier crus, including Suchots, Reignots and Chaumes in Vosne Romanée, and others in Nuits St Georges.

Pascal states his objective as being to make elegant wines, and made a revealing comment when we tasted a 2009 Nuits St. Georges, "This is not typical Nuits St. Georges, it is too elegant." That's the direction of the domain these days. This is aided by the new cuverie, right on the N74, with a stylish tasting room and shop open to visitors. Extending the estate holdings, since 2002 there has been a small negociant activity.

Everything is destemmed, there's cold maceration, and then slow fermentation; part of the change in style here may be due to the fact that fermentation now is slower than it used to be. Wines are aged for 16 months in barriques, with 30% new oak for the village wines, 40-60% for premier crus, and 100% for grand crus. There is no fining or filtration. The leading wines are Romanée St. Vivant and Vosne Romanée Les Suchots.

Domaine d'Eugénie ★★

14 rue de la Gaoillotte, 21700 Vosne Romanée	📞 *+33 3 80 61 10 54*
@ *contact@domaine-eugenie.com*	👤 *Michel Mallard*
🌐 *www.domaine-eugenie.com*	🔘 *Vosne Romanée [map]*
◐ 🍾 🍇 🗐 *7 ha; 20,000 btl*	🍷 *Vosne Romanée*

The old René Engel domain produced some of the most elegant wines of Vosne Romanée during the 1990s, with village wines as well as the premier cru Brûlées, and holdings also in Clos Vougeot, Echézeaux, and Grands Echézeaux. Created in the early twentieth century by René Engel, who was an oenologist at the university in Dijon, the domain fell into some neglect under his son in the 1970s, and then revived under his grandson Philippe in the 1980s. After the death of Philippe Engel in 2005, the domain was purchased by François Pinault, owner of Château Latour, and the name was changed to Domaine d'Eugénie.

In 2009 the domain moved out of its old house in Vosne Romanée into the Clos Frantin property, which was purchased from Albert Bichot and has been undergoing more or less continuous renovation ever since. There was a change in vineyards. "When we bought this building we swapped some vineyards to get the *clos* outside, which is village AOP, but just next to La Tache," says winemaker Michel Mallard, who came in 2006, and has been stamping his own style on the domain.

Vinification is conventional: a few days cold maceration is followed by fermentation, and then wines go into oak depending on appellation: 40-60% new oak for the village wines, two thirds for the premier crus, and 80% for the grand crus. Regarded as a rising new domain, Domaine d'Eugénie is more a demonstration of the reincarnation of an old domain resulting from unlimited investment. The high price paid to purchase the domain, reportedly €25 million, has been reflected in increased price for the wines.

"The Vosne Romanée village wine is the only blend of the domain," Michel says. It includes younger vines and two specific plots. Its sense of Rolls Royce power epitomizes Vosne Romanée. Clos Eugenie is the new name for the plot outside the winery, and it's a little fuller and rounder, with less obvious fruits and more structure. Premier cru Aux Brulées is more powerful, but smooth and silky in the unique style of Vosne Romanée. Echézeaux comes from a north-facing plot, which explains its sense of restraint and greater structure. Grands Echézeaux is more refined, with real grip from firm tannins. Clos Vougeot comes from an upper plot, and is more opulent with a livelier impression; it's the most precise wine of the domain.

Domaine Jean Grivot **

6 rue de La Croix Rameau, 21700 Vosne Romanée	📞 *+33 3 80 61 05 95*
@ *domaine.grivot@domainegrivot.fr*	👤 *Mathilde Grivot*
🌐 *www.domainegrivot.fr*	🔵 *Vosne Romanée [map]*
📅 🏭 🍇 *15 ha; 72,000 btl*	🍾 *Vosne Romanée, Bossières*

The Grivots have an interesting record of buying and selling vineyards advantageously. Coming from the Jura in the seventeenth century, they purchased vineyards at Arcenant (over the mountain from Nuits St. Georges). Just before the Revolution, Joseph Grivot sold these vineyards in order to purchase in Vosne Romanée. In 1919 his son Gaston sold the lesser holdings in order to buy part of Clos Vougeot, running up from the N74 where a splendid entrance gate with a view of the château was built. More recently Jean Grivot purchased a tiny holding in Richebourg. Since 1987, the domain has been run by his son, Etienne.

At almost 2 ha, Clos Vougeot is the largest parcel; parcels in five premier crus of Vosne Romanée and three premier crus of Nuits St. Georges, as well as communal plots, are all under a hectare, sometimes much less. Altogether there are around twenty different cuvées. Vines are replaced individually as necessary, and the average age is around 40 years. Vinification starts with complete destemming, followed by 5 days cold maceration, with fermentation lasting just over two weeks. Elevage lasts 18 months, with 25% new oak for communal wine, 30-60% for premier crus, and 40-70% for grand crus. The style has seemed relatively light in the past, with a spectrum of red rather than black fruits, which can pay off by bringing elegance rather than power to grand crus such as Clos Vougeot, but I find more overt fruits in the young wines of more recent vintages.

Domaine Anne Gros **

11, Rue Des Communes, 21700 Vosne Romanée	📞 *+33 3 80 61 07 95*
@ *domaine-annegros@orange.fr*	👤 *Anne Gros*
🌐 *www.anne-gros.com*	🔵 *Vosne Romanée [map]*
📅 🏭 🍇 *7 ha; 30,000 btl*	🍾 *Vosne Romanée, Les Barreaux*

The old Louis Gros domain produced some splendid wines in the fifties and sixties, but in the way of French inheritance, the domain became divided into several parts, today represented by Gros Frère et Soeur, Jean Gros, Michel Gros, A. F. Gros, and Anne Gros. After a decade during which production was sold to negociants, Anne Gros and her father François effectively restarted his part of the domain in 1988 (as Anne et François Gros, not to be confused with A. F. Gros!), and then changed the name to Anne Gros in 1998. The best plots are the village parcels and grand crus from Louis Gros. The only whites are Hautes Côtes de Nuits and Bourgogne.

The domain is located around a gracious courtyard in the center of Vosne Romanée, but extends well back into a practical building on the edge of the vineyards. All vinification is in stainless steel and there is 100% destemming. "Je deteste vendange entière (using whole bunches)", Anne says. "I am looking for aromatic precision, and the grapes are uncrushed, so we get the advantages of whole berries without the stems. You need to focus on finesse, if you push too much, the wine becomes square. I want as much extraction as I can, but without getting to the point where tannins become rustic." Village wines usually get 30% new oak, going up to a limit of 60% for grand crus.

The wines are precise and well-structured at all levels. Hautes Côtes de Nuits comes from vineyards at 400m just above Vosne Romanée, and is fresh but well-rounded for the AOP. The Bourgogne Rouge comes from just the other side of the N74, and gets extra roundness from 50-year-old vines. The delicacy of the Chambolle Musigny is a bit of an exception from the line of intense black fruit purity, but Vosne Romanée is classic for the appellation and the domain. The domain passes straight from village wines to grand crus, with Echézeaux round and intense, Clos Vougeot balanced between intrinsic fleshiness and the structure of Côtes de Nuits, and Richebourg remarkable for its finesse and purity.

Anne is married to Jean Paul Tollot (of Tollot-Beaune in Savigny-lès-Beaune) and in 2008 they extended their winemaking into a domain in Minervois. "We wanted to work together, so we decided to have a joint enterprise. And we have three children, so there are family reasons as well as the passion for wine," Anne says.

Domaine François Lamarche ★★★

9 Rue Des Communes, 21700 Vosne Romanée	📞 +33 3 80 61 07 94
@ *vins@domaine-lamarche.fr*	👤 *Nathalie Lamarche*
🌐 *www.domaine-lamarche.com*	⬤ *Vosne Romanée [map]*
😊 🏭 🍇 🍂 *11 ha; 60,000 btl*	⚑ *Vosne Romanée*

"This has been a family domain for five generations," says Nathalie Lamarche. "Today we are a feminine domain. My cousin Nicole is the winemaker and viticulturalist; I deal with the commercial part." The domain took its present form under Henri Lamarche in the early twentieth century. His grandson, François, was the winemaker until Nicole took over in 2007. Aside from the Bourgogne and a Nuits St. Georges premier cru and Clos Vougeot, all the wines come from Vosne Romanée, mostly premier crus and grand crus. The only white wine is a Bourgogne Aligoté. The vineyards have old vines, and the average age (now around 60 years) is maintained by replacing vines one by one as necessary. The domain is appropriately located in a rather grand house in Vosne Romanée.

The wines have improved steadily since a new cellar was constructed in 1990. New oak is moderate, usually around 30%, but with a maximum of 50% for the grand crus.

Élevage is usually 12-15 months. After racking off, wine stays in stainless steel for a few months before bottling. There is no fining and no filtration.

With important holdings in Vosne Romanée and its premier and grand crus, all Lamarche wines are at a high level. The Rolls Royce combination of silkiness and power reaches its peak in the monopole La Grand Rue, which was a wedding present to Henri Lamarche, and has the rare distinction of having been promoted from premier cru to grand cru (with effect from 1991), but a ripe, round style, with fruits supported by supple tannins, runs through the whole range. They do require some time to develop: Nathalie recommends waiting at least five years after the vintage.

The Vosne Romanée village wine is classic: rich, round, ripe with great grip and a touch of aromatics. Malconsorts is not so much deeper than the village wine as more precise, with greater flavor variety as it develops. Suchots is always the top premier cru. Echézeaux has a marginally deeper expression than the Vosne Romanée premier crus. Clos Vougeot is a blend of plots from the upper and lower parts, showing classic opulence in a rich expression of black fruits. Grands Echézeaux is finer and more linear. The seamless quality of La Grande Rue is very much in line with La Tache and Romanée St. Vivant.

Domaine Leroy   ****

15 Rue De La Fontaine, 21700 Vosne Romanée	📞 +33 3 80 21 21 10
@ domaine.leroy@wanadoo.fr	👤 Lalou Bize Leroy or Frédéric Roemer
🌐 www.domaineleroy.com	Vosne Romanée [map]
🚫🔪🍇◐	Nuits St. Georges
22 ha; 40,000 btl	Meursault-Blagny, Premier Cru

Maison Leroy was a negociant, but Henri Leroy also acquired a half share in Domaine de la Romanée Conti. Henri's daughter, Lalou Bize-Leroy, ran Maison Leroy and distributed DRC wines until a disagreement caused her to leave DRC in 1992. Domaine Leroy was founded in 1988 by purchasing the vineyards of Charles Noëllat in Vosne Romanée; Takayashima of Japan is a sleeping partner.

Located in an unassuming house in Vosne Romanée, the domain has a small winemaking facility, with open-topped wood fermenters. All wines go into new barriques, as they have the character to stand up to, and indeed, require, new oak. Yields are minuscule here: "25hl/ha is, for me, the absolute maximum for a grand cru," Lalou says. The domain has been biodynamic since its creation: Lalou is a fervent believer to the point of following the lunar cycle to apply the preparations.

Vinification is traditional. "Jamais, jamais, jamais" was the response when I asked if destemming is used. The wines show an intensity and concentration across the range that would put most producers to shame; the character of each appellation is magnified by sheer purity of expression. There was a look of surprise when I asked whether Lalou would call her wines "vins de garde" as though the question was simply too obvious to be worth answering. She also owns Domaine d'Auvenay in Saint Romain, a small domain inherited from her father, which is run on the same principles.

Domaine du Comte Liger-Belair   **

Château De Vosne Romanée, 21700 Vosne- Romanée	📞 +33 3 80 62 13 70
@ contact@liger-belair.fr	👤 Louis-Michel Liger-Belair

 www.liger-belair.fr	 Vosne Romanée [map]
 11 ha; 30,000 btl	Vosne Romanée, Petits Monts

The domain as such was created in 2000 by Louis-Michel Liger-Belair, but the name goes way back into the history of Vosne Romanée, starting with the purchase of vineyards in 1815, when General Liger-Belair returned from the Napoleonic wars. In the mid nineteenth century, Comte Liger-Belair owned parts of La Tâche and La Romanée, as well as parts of several premier crus in Vosne Romanée and elsewhere.

Most of the holdings were sold when the estate was dispersed in the early 1930s; the grapes from what remained were sold off or the vineyards were rented out. Two branches of the family own vineyards and have recently resurrected domains, Thibault Liger-Belair in Nuits St. Georges (see profile), and Comte Liger-Belair in Vosne Romanée.

Comte Liger-Belair is a general, but his son Louis-Michel wanted to be a winemaker and started his domain with the 1.5 ha of his father's remaining vineyards, which include the monopole of grand cru La Romanée. He added another 1.5 ha in 2002. Other vineyards are rented in Vosne Romanée and Nuits St. Georges. The smallest parcel from which a single cuvée is made is 0.12 ha. There's a focus on old vines, with most plantings varying from 60 to 90 years old; the domain may be young, but attitudes are quite traditional: "We don't make Pinot Noir, we make Burgundy."

The style here tends to elegance, almost delicacy, with concern to avoid over-extraction. Since the domain started, there's been a change to longer cold soak before fermentation starts and less maceration after fermentation; pumping-over is used rather than punch-down. Wine is kept on the lees, without racking, once malolactic fermentation has finished. The strength of the wines (mostly from Vosne Romanée, after all) calls for reliance on largely new barriques for maturation.

Domaine Méo-Camuzet ★★

11, Rue Des Grands Crus, 21700 Vosne Romanée	📞 +33 3 80 61 55 55
@ information@meo-camuzet.com	👤 Jean-Nicolas Méo
🌐 www.meo-camuzet.com	Vosne Romanée [map]
 18 ha; 130,000 btl	Nuits St. Georges, Les Boudots

Every time I visit Méo-Camuzet, there seems to be a new expansion. The latest is to expand the 100-year old cave underneath the courtyard. A previous effort showed a liking for modernization by adding a striking glass front to the old building. From its inception until fairly recently, the domain was rented out, as founder Étienne Camuzet and his successors were not resident in Burgundy. In 1988, Jean-Nicolas Méo took over the estate, reclaimed the vineyards, and started bottling. (He was helped by Henri Jayer, who had been farming many of the vineyards.) Production is divided between the domain (60%) and purchased grapes, which tend to focus on village wines. The label on domain wines says Domaine Méo-Camuzet, while the negociant label says Méo-Camuzet Frères et Soeurs.

The domain has some remarkable holdings: six grand crus and ten premier crus as well as villages and Hautes Côtes de Nuits. The parcel of Clos Vougeot was originally bought by Étienne Camuzet together with the château itself (which he owned until it became the headquarters of the Confrérie). Most of the holdings are in Nuits St. Georges or Vosne Romanée, but individual cuvées don't necessarily show appellation stereotypes. The estate Nuits St. Georges comes from lieu dit Au Bas de Combe, right at the junction with Vosne Romanée. Vosne Romanée is a blend from two plots, three quarters from a cool spot up the slope, one quarter from the center of the village. Typically the harvest is a week later for the Vosne village wine than for Nuits. "Our Vosne is more structured and our Nuits is more feminine, it all depends on the plot," says Jean-Nicolas.

Vinification varies with the cuvée, for example, with varying extents of destemming. Use of new oak has backed off, and now the lesser wines (Bourgogne or Marsannay) have up to 10% new oak, village wines less than 50%, premier crus 50-60%, and grand crus 80%. I find that the estate wines are stronger and more rounded than the negociant wines, but that may be partly because the estate has such splendid vineyards.

The classic cuvées are Vosne Romanée Brulées, planted in the 1930s (in a plot next to Richebourg), Clos Vougeot, and Cros Parantoux (made famous by Henri Jayer). The style is glossy, with the negociant wines showing red cherry fruits, and estate wines moving more towards black fruits. For the top wines, "There's a window after bottling for two years when they are open—although you would miss the soul of the wine—then forget them for another five years."

Jean-Nicolas is a livewire, and since 2014 he's been making Pinot Noir at his Domaine Nicolas-Jay, in Oregon's Willamette Valley. The wine is in the Burgundian tradition, but doesn't have the breed of Méo-Camuzet.

Domaine Georges Mugneret-Gibourg ★★

5 Rue Communes, 21700 Vosne Romanée	☎ +33 3 80 61 01 57
@ dgm@mugneret-gibourg.com	🧍 Marie-Christine & Marie-Andrée Mugneret
🌐 www.mugneret-gibourg.com	📷 Vosne Romanée [map]
📱🖊️📠🍇⚖️ 8 ha; 30,000 btl	⚑ Nuits St. Georges, Les Chaignots

"Mugneret-Gibourg used to be under the radar but now it's been discovered," says one wine merchant ruefully. Originally there were two domains, Mugneret-Gibourg, created in 1933 by the marriage of Jeanne Gibourg and André Mugneret, and Georges Mugneret, created by their son who purchased additional vineyards in his own name. Georges was a practising physician as well as winemaker. His daughters, Marie-Christine and Marie-Andrée, took over the domains in 1998, and were forced to make wine under both labels until in 2009, "after the stupidity of the French administration, we managed to combine the domains" says Marie-Andrée. Now all the wines are under the single label of Domaine Georges Mugneret-Gibourg. Production increased in 2016 when 2 ha came back to the domain after a sharecropping arrangement terminated.

The domain is located in what looks like an ordinary house around a courtyard, but it extends deceptively far back, opening out on to the domain's major vineyard, from which you can see all the way back to the N74. It's presently a matriarchal domain with two sisters and three daughters involved, but after that, in the next generation there is a boy. It's very hands-on: Lucy Teillaud-Mugneret greeted us when we arrived, then went off to help her aunt Marie-Christine run the bottling line.

Vineyards include Bourgogne, Vosne Romanée and Nuits St. Georges villages, premier crus from Nuits St. Georges and Chambolle Musigny, and grand crus Echézeaux, Clos Vougeot, and Ruchottes Chambertin. Marie-Andrée describes vinification as classic, meaning that there is complete destemming and fermentation with indigenous yeast. "We make the wine in the same way for each appellation because terroir is the most important. The way we make Bourgogne is the same as the way we make grand crus. The only difference is the amount of new oak, of course." There's 20% new oak for Bourgogne, 30% for village, 40% for premier cru, and 75-80% for grand cru.

The style epitomizes the Côte des Nuits, with pure, clean, black fruits tending towards freshness and minerality. Always concerned to maintain freshness, "We are one of the first domains to harvest in Vosne Romanée," says Marie-Andrée, "We want to keep freshness and not have too much sugar. The important thing is to have all the flavors we are waiting for. We lose this if we have too much ripeness." The wines are not exactly stern when young—one French critic calls them "introverted," which is a fair description. Certainly these are not wines for instant gratification; they start tight, develop slowly, and need time to come around.

Going from the village wines to premier crus, there is increasing refinement and silkiness. The grand crus mark the full range of the domain: Ruchottes Chambertin is all silky elegance, Clos Vougeot is unusually elegant for the appellation but shows a sense of soft opulence, and Echézeaux has a deep and broader structure. In premier crus, Nuits St. Georges Vignes Rondes, where there is more clay in the soil, is more typical of the appellation than Les Chaignots, which is on mid-slope with thin soil on limestone, and something of the silky refinement of Vosne Romanée just to its north. "Chaignots is always flattering, you can drink it when it's young," ays Marie-Andrée.

Domaine de La Romanée-Conti   ★★★★

1 Place de l'Église, 21700 Vosne Romanée	📞 *+33 3 80 62 48 80*
@ *secretariat@romanee-conti.fr*	👤 *Aubert de Villaine*
🌐 *www.romanee-conti.com*	📷 *Vosne Romanée [map]*
🚫 🔪 🍇 ⬭ *29 ha; 80,000 btl*	🍷 *Richebourg*

"The typicity of Pinot Noir first is to be Burgundian," says Aubert de Villaine, who has been at the domain since 1965, and indeed DRC is generally acknowledged as the epitome of both Pinot Noir and Burgundy. Ever since the vineyards of Romanée Conti were reunited by Aubert's grandfather, Edmond, who created the Domaine de la Romanée Conti in 1912, and then acquired all of La Tâche in 1933, this has been Burgundy's top domain.

With monopoles of Romanée Conti and La Tâche, and major holdings in Romanée St. Vivant, Richebourg, Grands Echézeaux, and Echézeaux, DRC dominates the grand crus of Vosne Romanée. There is also a small holding in Le Montrachet. The focus is not on power, but on subtlety of expression. "Romanée Conti has a character of softness and length in the mouth that makes it special compared to other wines. But it's a question of taste; some people might prefer Chambertin or La Tâche for their greater body," Aubert explains.

Viticulture is organic, the vineyards are perpetuated by selection massale using stock that goes back to Romanée Conti before it was replanted in 1945, and vinification is traditional (with no destemming). A horizontal tasting here is an exploration of nuances in expression at the most refined level, but it is fair to say that Romanée Conti and La Tâche are sui generis.

Lately DRC has been expanding, first in 2008 by leasing vineyards in three *climats* of Corton from Prince de Mérode, and then by leasing 3 ha of Bonneau du Martray's vineyards in Corton Charlemagne in 2017. The wines are of course fabulously expensive, and unfortunately are now bought more for investment than drinking. Aubert de Villaine also owns a domain in his own name in Bouzeron, where the grape is Aligoté.

Profiles of Important Estates

Domaine Sylvain Cathiard

24 Rue de la Goillotte, 21700 Vosne Romanée	
@ sylvain.cathiard@orange.fr	🧍 Sébastien Cathiard
📅 🏭 🍇 🍷 13 ha	🔴 Vosne Romanée [map]

This small domain has a great reputation with something of a cult following. Grapes were sold to negociants from the 1930s until Sylvain Cathiard took over in 1985; his son Sébastien took over in 2011. Vineyards are mostly in Vosne Romanée; there are 11 plots, with the top being a tiny holding in Romanée St. Vivant. Vines are mostly 40-60-years old. Everything is destemmed; new wood used to be high, up to 100%, but Sébastien has been reducing it.

Domaine Bruno Clavelier

6 RN 974, 21700 Vosne Romanée	📞 +33 3 80 61 10 81
@ domaine-clavelier@orange.fr	🧍 Bruno Clavelier
⊕ bruno-clavelier.com	🔴 Vosne Romanée [map]
📅 🏭 🍇 🗒	6 ha; 30,000 btl

This is an old domain, with many vineyards that were replanted in the 1930s-1940s. Estate bottling started only in 1988, when Bruno took over. There are four village wines from lie-dits in Vosne Romanée, and two premier crus. There are also premier crus in Chambolle Musigny and Gevrey Chambertin, and Corton. The flagship wine is Chambolle Musigny premier cru La Combe d'Orveau, from a plot adjacent to Le Musigny. The only whites are a Bourgogne Aligoté and a Vin de France. Vinification is traditional, with about 30% whole clusters, 20% new oak for village wines, and around a third new oak for premier and grand crus. SO2 is minimized by bottling under inert gas.

Domaine J. Confuron-Cotetidot

10 rue de la Fontaine, 21700 Vosne Romanée	📞 +33 3 80 61 03 39
@ domaine-confuron-cotetidot@wanadoo.fr	🧍 Jack Confuron-Cotetidot
📅 🏭 🍇 🍂 13 ha; 37,000 btl	🔴 Vosne Romanée [map]

The domain was founded by Jack Confuron in 1964, and today it is led by his two sons, Jean-Pierre and Yves, who is not only the winemaker here but also at Domaine de Courcel, Château de la Tour (in Vougeot), and Maison Chanson. Holdings are deep all over the Côte de Nuits, with an impressive panoply of premier and grand crus. The Confurons have a long-term interest in culture and selection of Pinot Noir, and the average age of their vines is about 65 years. Harvesting is late, there is no destemming (irrespective of the vintage), cuvaison is very long, and new oak varies from 10-20% for village wines, up to 50% for grand crus, with élevage of 22 months. Wines are bottled unfined and unfiltered.

Domaine Forey Père et Fils

2, Rue Derrière Le Four, 21700 Vosne Romanée	📞 +33 3 80 61 09 68
@ domaineforey@orange.fr	🧍 Regis Forey
📅 🏭 🍇 🖇 10 ha; 35,000 btl	🔴 Vosne Romanée [map]

The domain was founded in 1840. Régis Forey took over from his father Jean in 1989. The domain owns about half its vineyards and leases the other half. Vineyards are mostly in Nuits St. Georges, Vosne Romanée, and Flagey-Echézeaux, but there are some in Clos Vougeot and Morey St. Denis. The domain's top wine came from a lease on La Romanée in Vosne Romanée, but lost this when Liger-Belair took it back in 2001. Régis managed to replace it with

Echézeaux and Vosne Romanée Les Gaudichots. Vinification starts with 3-4 days cold maceration, cuvaison lasts 3-4 weeks with punch-down, and the wine ages in barriques for 16-20 months with up to 80% new oak for grand crus, but some larger barrels used for village-level wines to reduce oak impact.

Domaine Mongeard-Mugneret

16 Rue De La Fontaine, 21700 Vosne Romanée	📞 +33 3 80 61 11 95
@ *info@mongeard.com*	👤 *Vincent Mongeard*
🌐 *www.mongeard.com*	🔘 *Vosne Romanée [map]*
🗓 ⛏ 🍇 ⌚ *30 ha; 170,000 btl*	🍾 *Vosne Romanée*

The domain goes back to the seventeenth century, and has been known as Mongeard-Mugneret since 1945, following the marriage in the 1920s of Eugène Mongeard and Edmée Mugneret. Their son Jean Mongeard started estate bottling after the domain took its new name. A well known figure in Vosne Romanée, he handed over to his son, Vincent, in 1985. There are important holdings in Nuits St. Georges and Vosne Romanée, including top premier crus, and four grand crus: Echézeaux, Grands Echézeaux, Clos Vougeot and Richebourg. The wines were powerful yet beautifully balanced until the late 1980s, but since then seem to have lost some of their luster. The domain has gone into oenotourism indirectly by offering packages in connection with the hotel Le Richebourg (which arranges visits to the domain).

Vignoble Georges Noëllat

1 Rue des Chaumes, 21700 Vosne Romanée	📞 +33 3 80 61 11 03
@ *mc.noellat@free.fr*	👤 *Maxime Cheurlin*
🗓 ⛏ 🍇 ⌚ *18 ha*	🔘 *Vosne Romanée [map]*

Two Noëllat domains, Michel and Georges, are run by grandsons of Ernest Noëllat, the brother of Charles Noëllat, who had a famous domain (incorporated into Domaine Leroy in 1988). Georges Noëllat sold its production after 1990 under a twenty-year contract to Jadot and Drouhin. George's grandson, Maxime Cheurlin, took over in 2010 and resumed estate production from the vineyards in Vosne Romanée and Nuits St. Georges. Maxime is something of a modernist, with destemming, light punch-downs, 30-100% new oak, aging for 14-20 months, and bottling without fining or filtration.

Domaine Michel Noëllat

5 Rue La Fontaine, 21700 Vosne Romanée	📞 +33 3 80 61 36 87
@ *contact@domaine-michel-noellat.com*	👤 *Sophie Noëllat*
🌐 *www.domaine-michel-noellat.com*	🔘 *Vosne Romanée [map]*
🗓 ⛏ 🍇 🚜	*25 ha; 80,000 btl*

Now in its fifth generation, the domain was founded in the nineteenth century. Brothers Alain and Jean-Marc took over in 1989. Jean-Marc's son Sébastien is now involved in winemaking, and Alain's daughter Sophie on the commercial side. Located in a quiet street of Vosne Romanée (actually next to Domain Leroy) the property looks like a private residence. Underneath is a vaulted cellar that Michel Noëllat constructed in 1980, now used as the barrel cellar, and there is a cuverie on the D974, constructed in 2007. Vineyards are divided into 100 plots all along the Côte de Nuits, and some smaller holdings on the Côte de Beaune. Everything is completely destemmed, reds have 3 days cold maceration before fermentation, cuvaison lasts for 14 days, with punch down every couple of days, and aging in barriques lasts for 15-18 months with 30% new oak for village wines and 50% for premier and grand crus.

Domaine Emmanuel Rouget

18 Route Gilly Les Citeaux, 21640 Flagey Échézeaux	📞 +33 3 80 62 86 61
@ domaine.clf@wanadoo.fr	👤 Emmanuel Rouget
🔲 〰 🍇 🚜 7 ha	🔴 Flagey-Echézeaux [map]

Emmanuel Rouget is Henri Jayer's nephew, and started working with his uncle in 1976. Henri handed his domain over to him as he retired gradually between 1996 and 2001. The domain includes the plot of Cros Parantoux in Vosne Romanée that was Henri Jayer's most famous cuvée. Emmanuel started bottling wines under his own name from various family vineyards in 1985, and included some from the Jayer vineyards after 1996 although Henri Jayer continued to bottle some wine until 2001, but since then all production has been labeled as Emmanuel Rouget. Winemaking follows Henri's precepts, with complete destemming, pre-fermentation cold maceration, up to 100% new oak, all aimed at bringing out fruit.

Domaine Vigot Fabrice

20, Rue De La Fontaine, 21700 Vosne Romanée	📞 +33 3 80 61 13 01
@ webmaster@domainevigot.com	👤 Christine Vigot
🌐 www.domainevigot.com	🔴 Vosne Romanée
🏭 🍇 🍂	3 ha; 18,000 btl

Fabrice Vigot created the domain in his own name in 1990 with 4 ha in Vosne Romanée and Nuits St. Georges that came from his mother. When he married Christine in 1996, he reversed the name to become Domaine Vigot Fabrice. Gevrey Chambertin came from Christine's family in 2000. A new winery was built in 2006. Fabrice's father, and then Fabrice, farmed some of the vineyards of Domaine Mugneret-Gibourg (see profile) under a share-cropping arrangement in which they shared the grapes, but this came to an end in 2016 as the result of a series of vintages with very low yields. Until then almost half the vineyards were in Vosne Romanée, with smaller holdings (less than a hectare each) in Gevrey Chambertin, Nuits St. Georges, Echézeaux, and Bourgogne; now the estate produces wine only from its own vineyards in Vosne Romanée, Nuits St. Georges, and Gevrey Chambertin. Winemaking uses about 30% whole clusters, with fermentation in stainless steel, followed by aging for 14-18 months in barriques with 20-30% new oak.

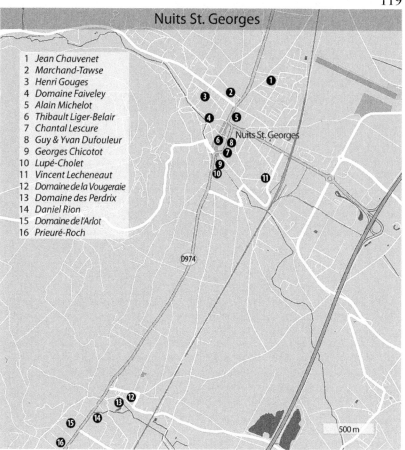

Nuits St. Georges

1 Jean Chauvenet
2 Marchand-Tawse
3 Henri Gouges
4 Domaine Faiveley
5 Alain Michelot
6 Thibault Liger-Belair
7 Chantal Lescure
8 Guy & Yvan Dufouleur
9 Georges Chicotot
10 Lupé-Cholet
11 Vincent Lecheneaut
12 Domaine de la Vougeraie
13 Domaine des Perdrix
14 Daniel Rion
15 Domaine de l'Arlot
16 Prieuré-Roch

Profiles of Leading Estates

Domaine de l'Arlot *

14 RD974, 21700 Premeaux-Prissey	📞 *+33 3 80 61 01 92*
@ *contact@arlot.fr*	👤 *Geraldine Godot*
🌐 *www.arlot.com*	🟢 *Nuits St. Georges [map]*
📅 🏭 🍇 🥄	🍾 *Nuits St. Georges, Clos de l'Arlot*
15 ha; 60,000 btl	*Nuits St. Georges, Clos de l'Arlot*

Clos de l'Arlot was part of negociant Maison Belin until it was bought in 1987 by insurance giant AXA, in collaboration with winemaker Jean-Pierre de Smet. When Jean-Pierre retired in 2006, AXA took complete control. Olivier Leriche became the winemaker, then in 2011 Jacques Devauges arrived, and when he left for Clos de Tart in 2014, Geraldine Godot took over. Buildings are located around a gracious courtyard right on the N74, with old cellars underneath.

Most of the vineyards are in two monopoles: 7 ha Clos des Forêts St. Georges is just up the road; and 4 ha of Clos de l'Arlot surround the winery. Across the N74 is the Clos du Chapeau that produces a Côtes de Nuits Villages. The other holdings are smaller parcels in Vosne Romanée Les Suchots and Romanée St. Vivant. There are no village wines: the line goes straight from the regional Côtes to the premier (and grand) crus.

The domain is unusual in producing white wine on the Côte de Nuits. About half of the Clos de l'Arlot now produces white wine. The wine from the younger vines, and from plots with atypical terroir, is declassified to Nuits St. Georges, La Gerbotte. "La Gerbotte is very fresh, Clos de l'Arlot is more complex," Geraldine says. Vinification is similar, with élevage in 20% new oak, but Clos de l'Arlot shows more finesse.

The reds start with the light, fresh Clos du Chapeau, and then jump to the elegance of Clos de l'Arlot, which often strikes me as stylistically close to the reds of Beaune. There's almost as big a jump going to the next wine of the lineup. "Vosne Romanée Suchots comes after Clos de l'Arlot and before Clos de Forêts because the tannins of Suchots are very fine and Forêts is more muscular," Geraldine explains. Les Suchots has something of the minerality of Clos de l'Arlot, but with greater fruit density. This is where the transition from red to black fruits occurs in the range, and where the identity of the Côte de Nuits becomes clear. Clos des Fôrets is more obviously structured with blackberry fruits, rather firm, but still showing the freshness of house style. "We don't have to extract a lot, the tannins are here already," Geraldine says. Romanée St. Vivant shows grand cru breed, interpreted through the domain's fresh style, finer rather than more powerful. One consequence of the fresh style is that most wines stay around 13% alcohol.

Domaine David Duband *

12 rue du Lavoir, 21220 Chevannes	📞 *+33 3 80 61 41 16*
@ *domaine.duband@wanadoo.fr*	👤 *David Duband*
🌐 *www.domaine-duband.com*	🟢 *Nuits St. Georges*
📅 🏭 🍇 🛢 🥄 *20 ha; 100,000 btl*	🍾 *Chambolle Musigny, Les Sentiers*

Chevannes is in the hills of the Hautes Côtes de Nuits at the end of a narrow twisting road. The domain is on the edge of the little village, in a large modern warehouse-like building built in 2007. It's a practical facility with winemaking on the upper level and a large storage space on the lower level. Wines come from 25 AOPs, varying from 2 to 40 barrels; grapes are purchased for about 25% of production.

David's father created the domain in 1965 when he cut down woods and planted vines on the hillside facing Chevannes. Then he rented vineyards in Nuits St. Georges. David started to make wine in 1991, and took over in 1995. He also makes the wines for Domaine François Feuillet, which has top holdings on the Côte de Nuits, including the old Truchot domain. Wines may be labeled with either name but are the same.

David is frankly unimpressed by very old wines and doesn't see the point of extended aging. "I think that a well made wine with mature tannins can be drunk young. I want the wine to be good when it's bottled, I don't want to make wines that are closed when young." The Hautes Côtes de Nuits has 30% new oak, and the premier and grand crus have 40%. The style is silky with a faint glycerinic sheen, and elegant tannins are usually only just in evidence. Red fruits on the light side favor elegance over power, giving a clean impression. Everything is filtered through the prism of Duband's ultra-modern take on Burgundy.

Domaine Faiveley   ★★

8, Rue De Tribourg, 21700 Nuits St. Georges	📞 +33 3 80 61 04 55
@ contact@domaine-faiveley.com	👤 Erwan Faiveley
🌐 www.domaine-faiveley.com	🗺 Nuits St. Georges [map]
	🍷 Clos des Cortons

Dating from 1825, Faiveley is one of the major domains in Burgundy, with almost half of its vineyards on the Côte d'Or in premier and grand crus, as well as being an important negociant. The source is indicated on the label, as Domaine Faiveley for estate wines, and Joseph Faiveley for wines from purchased grapes. The focus has been on red wines, but the domain has been expanding overt the past decade by purchasing other domains and vineyards, most recently Dupont-Tisserandot in Gevrey Chambertin (see profile) and Chablis producer Billaud-Simon. Faiveley also has significant holdings on the Côte Chalonnaise, especially in Mercurey.

The style of the reds has always been sturdy, but became more extracted and harder in 1993. "For a long time Faiveley was famous for vins de garde for long aging, but we thought it should be possible to produce wines for aging that would be more drinkable young," says Jérôme Flous, explaining that after Erwan Faiveley (then aged 25) took over from his father François in 2004, he started to soften the style. (An abrupt handover seems to be the Faiveley style, as Erwan's father, François, took over from his father in 1976, also at age 25.) A Faiveley vertical shows the old style before 1993, the heavily extracted style until 2006, and since then a more forward fruity style.

Picking today is faster so fruit is fresher, fermentations have been shortened and there is less maceration; pressing is gentler with a new vertical press, and the barriques are higher quality. To compensate for the increased softness, new oak usage has increased: it is up to 15% for village wines, 15-40% for premier crus, and 40-100% for grand crus. The best known wine is perhaps the Clos des Cortons monopole. The strongest suite in reds is a series of premier and grand crus in Gevrey Chambertin, with Les Cazetiers typifying the style. The reds are back on form, and I admit I always found them more interesting than Faiveley's whites before Faiveley started buying significant white grape vineyards.

In 2020, Faiveley made its first major investment in wine outside Burgundy, buying a minority share in famed Pinot Noir producer William-Selyem (see profile in *Guide to Sonoma* of California's Russian River Valley. Faiveley's other interests are quite different: Faiveley Transport is involved in producing the TGV.

Domaine Henri Gouges **

21704 7 rue du Moulin, 21701 Nuits St. Georges	📞 +33 3 80 61 04 40
@ domaine@gouges.com	👤 Gregory & Antoine Gouges
🌐 www.gouges.com	🔴 Nuits St. Georges [map]
📅 🗲 🍇 🍸	🍷 Nuits St. Georges, Les Pruliers
15 ha; 50,000 btl	Nuits St. Georges, Les Perrières

This is one of the most traditional producers in Nuits St. Georges, and the first time I visited, the premises matched my expectations. But a new cuverie was constructed in 2007—in a large courtyard behind the unassuming house—whose existence you would scarcely imagine from the street. Things have not changed with regards to winemaking, however, because "it is the grapes that count." The old cement tanks were moved into the cuverie. The most significant change is that pumping has been eliminated; everything is gravity driven now.

Pierre Gouges says that changes in style are due more to the current age of the vines than anything else; the new cuverie maintains better freshness, so the wine is fruitier, perhaps also due to the lack of pumping. Cousins Pierre and Christian Gouges ran the domain until a recent change to the next generation, Gregory and Antoine, "but we haven't gone very far," Pierre says.

Gouges used to be known for a rather tough style when young, requiring time for the tannins to soften. The changes in the new cuverie have lightened the style, and certainly I notice increased purity of fruit, but although the wines are more accessible, still they are not really intended for early drinking.

Most of the wines come from Nuits St. Georges, including six premier crus as well as the village wine. Les Pruliers is perhaps the most refined, and Les St. Georges the strongest. In addition to the reds, there are also two white wines, from Clos des Porrets St. Georges and Les Perrières, which come from a from a rare albino clone of Pinot Noir observed in the Perrières vineyard. The wines are therefore Pinot Blanc rather than Chardonnay, and the cultivar is now known as the Gouges clone of Pinot Blanc.

Domaine Hoffmann-Jayer *

1 rue du Meix Grenot, 21700 Magny-lès-Villers	📞 +33 3 80 62 91 79
@ domaine@hoffmann-jayer.com	👤 Alexandre Vernet
🌐 www.hoffmann-jayer.com	🔴 Hautes Côtes de Nuits
📅 🏭 🍇 🍸	10 ha; 50,000 btl

Under its original name of Jayer-Gilles, this was considered to be one of the most artisanal domains of the Côte d'Or. A cousin of Henri Jayer, Robert Jayer-Gilles created the domain, and his son Gilles took over when he retired in 1998. Most of the vineyards are on the Hautes Côtes; the village of Magny-lès-Villers is at the junction of the Hautes Côtes de Beaune and Hautes Côtes de Nuits, so there are cuvées from both, although the vineyards are in the same village. Unusually for the area, they are planted at the same 10,000 vines per hectare as the top vineyards of the Côte d'Or. Small holdings in Nuits St. Georges and Echézeaux total 1 ha. Not long before he died, Gilles sold the estate in 2017 to Swiss billionaire André Hoffman of Hoffmann-La-Roche, and the name was changed to Hoffman-Jayer. Winemaker Alexandre Vernet says that, "We don't have any plans to expand the domain except perhaps for another white."

The domain was famous for its stern winemaking policy, with 100% new oak for all cuvées, something that few producers could pull off on the Hautes Côtes. Policy remains generally the same under the new ownership, and Alexandre says that, "I want to maintain the artisanal reputation and even to increase it, from moving viticulture to organic to having very long vinification with lots of extract." The only change is that, "I'm reducing new oak a bit for the lower-level wines to make them more immediately approachable."

There are both whites and reds from both Hautes Côtes. In each case, there is a little more power to the Hautes Côtes de Nuits, but the difference is more marked with the reds. The whites both contain 30% Pinot Blanc with 70% Chardonnay and give a finely textured impression. The red Hautes Côtes de Beaune seems more elegant while the Hautes Côtes de Nuits seems more powerful.

The artisanal style is evident in the Côtes de Nuits Villages, which comes from two parcels in Corgoloin. Perfumed black fruits are elegant, but with a definite tannic edge. Nuits St. Georges shows more aromatics and tannins kick in on the finish. In Echézeaux, the aromatics move more towards tobacco, the palate shows precision of black fruits, but tannins really grip the finish. The domain's reputation is for lots of extraction, but although tannins certainly grip the finish when the wines are young, the style is quite perfumed and elegant.

Maison Dominique Laurent   ★★

2 rue Jacques Duret, 21700 Nuits St. Georges	📞 *+33 3 80 61 31 62*
📠 *+33 3 80 62 32 42*	👤 *Dominique Laurent*
	🔵 *Nuits St. Georges*
🚫🌱🍷🚜 *7 ha; 300,000 btl*	🍷 *Gevrey Chambertin, Cazetiers*

A pastry chef before he went into wine, Dominique Laurent made his name as a negociant. He became famous for the technique of using 200% new oak, meaning that the wine is racked from new oak barrels into a second set of new oak barrels. Attempts to discuss his methods are firmly rebuffed. "Like any artisan, I have no wish or need to discuss; my experiences and research are secret and from a commercial point of view can't be explained, you understand my position? I have even less wish to discuss a subject which has caused me so much criticism from the most stupid people... You'll have to give just another opinion based on tasting." Recently, Dominique appears to have decided that 100% new oak is enough, because he has supplies of higher quality oak; he selects the trees himself in the Tronçais forest.

Insofar as it's possible to form any single opinion, my impression is that sometimes the approach works, and sometimes it overwhelms the wine. An interesting comparison is between the Laurent's Gevrey Chambertin premier cru Clos St. Jacques with the corresponding cuvée from Sylvie Esmonin, from whom he buys the grapes. In 2002, the Laurent wine was richer and rounder, but in 1999 the fruits could not show through Laurent's oak.

Focused on Gevrey Chambertin (although not necessarily making the same cuvées every year), the Laurent wines are always powerful. The style certainly comes over as unusually powerful in, for example, Chambolle Musigny where the usual delicacy of the appellation gives way to overt richness; the richer fruits in, say, Charmes Chambertin, carry the style better, but in Vosne Romanée the combination of Laurent's style with the power of the appellation can be overwhelming.

I think it's fair to say that Dominique's style dominates over appellation, partly because of strong oak, partly because of the use of vendange entière, which together can give an acerbic note and overly structured impression to the finish. When the wines are young, the intensity of the fruits can carry the structure, but as fruits thin out with age, the use of whole bunches can become more obvious. Since 2006, Dominique has also been making wine with his son Jean from vines rented in Vosne Romanée.

Marchand-Tawse   *

9 rue Julie Godemet, Bp 76, 21700 Nuits St. Georges	📞 +33 3 80 20 37 32
@ *contact@marchandtawse.com*	👤 *Pascal Marchand*
🌐 *www.marchand-tawse.com*	🔴 *Nuits St. Georges [map]*
📅 🍷 🚜 🛢 🍇	🍾 *Vosne Romanée*
8 ha; 170,000 btl	*Meursault, Les Charmes*

NUITS-SAINT-GEORGES
AUX BOUDOTS
PREMIER CRU

MARCHAND-TAWSE
PASCAL MARCHAND

"I'm from Montreal, I came to Burgundy thirty years ago, I was a régisseur in Pommard at Comte Armand, then I was with Vougeraie for seven vintages. In 2006 I decided to create my own label," says Pascal Marchand. "I started by renting premises, and making 5 wines and 1,000 cases." Starting as a negociant, Pascal expanded by forming a partnership in 2010 with Canadian banker Moray Tawse, and the firm became Marchand-Tawse. In 2012 they purchased Domaine Maume in Gevrey Chambertin, which brought premier and grand cru vineyards to the portfolio. The negociant wines are labeled as Marchand-Tawse, and the estate wines as Domaine Tawse. Production is about 120,000 bottles of Marchand-Tawse and 50,000 bottles of Domaine Tawse. Pascal bought his own space in the center of Nuits St. Georges in 2011, with buildings surrounding a handsome courtyard, a large warehouse-like facility on the other side of the street, and extensive cellars underground. He also makes wine in Western Australia under the Marchand & Burch label.

The estate vineyards are about half in Bourgogne, with the rest divided between villages and premier or grand crus. Today production is about half from his own vineyards and half from purchased grapes (where half are premier or grand cru, and most of the rest are communal). Altogether there are about 60 wines, many in small quantities, sometimes only 1-3 barrels. 30% is white; about half is Côte de Beaune and half is Côte de Nuits. At the moment, all the wines have the same label but Pascal says that, "In the long run I want to distinguish between the negociant parts and the wines from our own vineyards." There's a family resemblance between the wines going from Nuits St Georges to Vosne

Romanée to Gevrey Chambertin: refinement is the common feature that runs through all.

Domaine Daniel Rion et Fils   **

Route Nationale 74, 21700 Premeaux-Prissey	📞 +33 3 80 62 31 28
@ contact@domaine-daniel-rion.com	👤 Pascale Rion
🌐 www.domaine-daniel-rion.com	🔴 Nuits St. Georges [map]
😊 🏭 🚜 ⛓ 15 ha; 100,000 btl	🍷 Nuits St. Georges, Vieilles Vignes

"The domain started with a few parcels of vines in 1955. Slowly we've added more parcels," says Pascale Rion, who runs the domain together with her two brothers. Driving along the N74, you cannot miss the domain because the adjacent house has "Daniel Rion" in huge letters facing the road. The domain itself is in a large building just off the road. Production is only red wine. One third is regional, a third is in Nuits St. Georges and Vosne Romanée, and a third is in premier or grand crus.

"We try to keep freshness, to have ripe fruits, but not over ripe," is how Pascale describes the style. "We destem 100%. We try to harvest the vineyards so that each is at the same stage of maturity." There is 40% new oak for villages and premier crus. Élevage depends on vintage but is usually 16-18 months.

The style is modern and pure, expressing ripe, round, but fresh, black fruits. Going up the range, the difference is not so much the flavor spectrum as the texture and structure. First the texture becomes finer, then the structure becomes more obvious. There are three different cuvées from Nuits St. Georges: the village wine, a lieu-dit, and the Vieilles Vignes. "We have all the vineyards that my father planted between 1960 and 1967." Moving from the Nuits St. Georges village wine to the lieu-dit, Les Grandes Vignes, the fruits become darker and there is more obvious sense of structure; and with the Vieilles Vignes, the main difference is not in flavor or intensity, but increased refinement of tannins, which are so fine and silky they make the wine more approachable. With the premier crus, Hauts Pruliers is yet more refined, and Aux Rondes Vignes a touch more obviously structured.

Going from Nuits St. Georges to Vosne Romanée, there is an increased sense of reserved power, with more of a glycerinic sheen moving through to the premier crus. Vosne Romanée village wine comes from two plots. "Every year we taste each plot separately, but we always prefer the blend." In premier crus, Beaumonts has increased finesse, Chaumes is more granular, and then coming to the grand crus, Echézeaux has more weight but less refinement, and Clos Vougeot shows its opulence up front. There's a textbook impression of the differences in appellation level all the way from village level to grand cru.

Domaine de La Vougeraie   *

7bis Rue de L'Église, 21700 Premeaux-Prissey	📞 +33 3 80 62 48 25
@ vougeraie@domainedelavougeraie.com	👤 Sylvie Poillot
🌐 www.domainedelavougeraie.com	🔴 Nuits St. Georges [map]
◐ 🍷 🍇 ◯	🍷 Vougeot, Les Cras
44 ha; 130,000 btl	Clos Blanc de Vougeot

One of the newest, and most rapidly growing, domains in Burgundy, Domaine de la Vougeraie brings together several old domains under a new name. The driving force is Jean-Charles Boisset (see profile), who together with his sister Nathalie, has become Burgundy's largest producer by acquiring several houses in Burgundy. These continue to run independently, but Domaine de la Vougeraie amalgamates holdings from four old domains: Claudine Deschamps (the original Boisset family estate in Premeaux, where a new winemaking facility has now been constructed), Pierre Ponnelle, Louis Voilland, and L'Héritier Guyot.

Starting in 1999, winemaker Pascal Marchand went for a powerful style, and then the style is supposed to have lightened after Pierre Vincent took over as winemaker for 2006. He uses 30% new oak for the village wines, 40% for the premier crus, and 50% for grand crus, with an élevage of 18 months. However, I still find the wines to be on the powerful side: the white Clos Blanc de Vougeot, for example, shows a mass of new oak and is all up-front power, compared with the more classic style it used to have when made by L'Héritier Guyot. But you could say the same of many wines in Burgundy, so the fair comment may be that these are definitely wines in the modern style, with something of an influence from the New World.

Profiles of Important Estates

Domaine d'Ardhuy

Clos Des Langres, 21700 Corgoloin	📞 +33 3 80 62 98 73
@ domaine@ardhuy.com	👤 Vincent Bottreau
⊕ www.ardhuy.com	◉ Nuits St. Georges
🗓 🏭 🍇 ◌	40 ha; 200,000 btl

The domain is poised between the Côte de Beaune and the Côte de Nuits. Its nineteenth century house is surrounded by the monopole of the Clos des Langres—the *clos* is in effect the garden of the house—which is in the Côte de Nuits Villages, but the wall of the *clos* is the border with the Côte de Beaune. The domaine dates from 1927. A marriage with the André family in 1947 brought Château Corton André and negociant Reine Pédauque into the family holdings, but these were sold in 2007. The 200 parcels of vineyards extend from Puligny Montrachet to Gevrey Chambertin and make 45 cuvées, 90% red. The domain is strong in Corton, where it has Hautes Mourottes, Clos du Roi, Les Pougets, and Les Renardes, as well as Corton Charlemagne.

Maison Jean-Claude Boisset

5, Quai Dumorey, 21700 Nuits St. Georges	📞 +33 3 80 62 61 00
@ contact@boisset.fr	👤 Jean-Charles Boisset
⊕ www.boisset.com	◉ Nuits St. Georges
🚶 🏭 🍇 🚜	4,500,000 bottles

This was a traditional negociant until Jean-Charles took over in 2002 and transformed it into a mega holding company. Wine is made under the Boisset name at the winery Les Ursulines (a former convent) in Nuits St. Georges, but the most important holdings are under other names. Domaine de la Vougeraie (see profile) amalgamates holdings from four old domains, including l'Héritier Guyot in Premeaux where the wines are now made; other producers functioning under their own names are Bouchard Aîné in Beaune, Ropiteau Frères in Meursault, Maison Jaffelin (in Beaune), Ropiteau Frères (originally in Meursault but now with a broader range),

Antonin Rodet in Mercurey, Château de Pierreux in Beaujolais, J. Moreau in Chablis, Henri Maire (in the Jura), and a series of producers in California grouped under Boisset Wines USA.

Domaine Jérôme Chezeaux

6, Route de Nuits St Georges, 21700 Premeaux-Prissey	📞 +33 3 80 61 29 79
@ jeromechezeaux@wanadoo.fr	👤 Pierrette & Jérôme Chezeaux
🌐 domaine-jerome-chezeaux.jimdosite.com	⬤ Nuits St. Georges
🚜	12 ha

Julien Missery founded the domain in 1930, his son -in-law Bernard Chezeaux took over in 1971, and Bernard's son Jérôme took over in 1993. Jérôme moved into estate bottling and direct sales. Vineyards are in Nuits St. Georges, Vosne Romanée, and Vougeot, and include 6 premier crus and Clos Vougeot. Winemaking starts with 4 days cold maceration, cuvaison lasts 3 weeks, with both pump-over and punch-down, and aging takes place for 18-24 months in barriques with 25-33% new oak.

Domaine Georges Chicotot

15 Rue Général De Gaulle, 21700 Nuits St. Georges	📞 +33 3 80 61 19 33
@ chicotot@aol.com	👤 Pascale & Clément Chicotot
🌐 www.domaine-chicotot.com	⬤ Nuits St. Georges [map]
📅 🏭 🍇	7 ha; 25,000 btl

Georges Chicotet is the seventh generation at this family domain, located on the N74 just south of the town of Nuits St. Georges. The domain had only 5 ha of vineyards in Nuits St. Georges until some additions in Ladoix and Aloxe Corton. Georges, who took over in 1971, was a follower of Guy Accad, a controversial oenologist who believed in extended cold soaks to get more color and tannin in wines. There is no destemming, and cuvaison is long, although new oak is limited to about 10%. Georges's wife Pascale has been the winemaker since 1993; their son Clément is in charge of the vineyards. The top wines are premier crus from Nuits St. Georges, Les Vaucrains and Les Saint Georges. The wines are not filtered or fined at bottling. They are tight when young and need time.

Domaine Jean-Jacques Confuron

D974, 21700 Premeaux-Prissey	📞 +33 3 80 62 31 08
@ jj.confuron@wanadoo.fr	👤 Sophie & Alain Meunier
🌐 domainejeanjacquesconfuron.com	⬤ Nuits St. Georges
📅 🍇 9 ha	🍾 Nuits St. Georges, aux Boudots

The domain was founded as the result of the marriage in 1926 of Jean Confuron of Vosne Romanée with Marie Bouchard of Premeaux, with vines from both sides of the family. Subsequently the estate was split between their sons Christian and Jean-Jacques. After Jean-Jacques fell ill in 1982, his daughter Sophie took over his domain, and after she married Alain Meunier, they started estate bottling in 1988. Their son Louis is now at the domain, and another son, Paul, has a domain in the south of France. There are village and premier cru wines from Vosne Romanée, Chambolle Musigny, and Nuits St. Georges, and grand crus Romanée St. Vivant and Clos Vougeot. Use of whole clusters varies but is usually slight, cold maceration before fermentation is 3-4 days, fermentation lasts about 14 days, and the wine ages in barriques with 50% new oak for village wines, 70% for premier crus, and 80% for the grand crus.

Domaine Guy & Yvan Dufouleur

15, rue Thurot, 21700 Nuits St. Georges	📞 +33 3 80 61 09 35

@ contact@domaineguyetyvandufouleur.fr	👤 Guy & Yvan Dufouleur
🌐 www.domaineguyetyvandufouleur.fr	🔴 Nuits St. Georges [map]
📅 🍷 🍇 🥄	30 ha; 160,000 btl

The Dufouleurs trace their winemaking in Nuits St. George to 1596: Yvan is the fourteenth generation. Guy was his father; now he makes wine with his uncle, Xavier. Until 2006, Dufouleur was both a domain and a negociant, but they sold the negociant, and although it still carries the name of Dufouleur Père et Fils, it's no longer connected with the domain. They produce white wine from the Hautes-Côtes-de-Nuits and Nuits St. Georges premier cru Clos des Perrières, and reds extending from Santenay at the southern end of the Côte de Beaune to Fixin at the northern end of the Côte de Nuits. The largest holding is in the Fixin premier cru, Clos du Châpitre.

Domaine Didier Fornerol

15 Place de la Mairie, 21700 Corgoloin	📞 +33 3 80 62 93 09
@ contact@bourgognefornerol.com	👤 Didier Fornerol
🌐 www.bourgognefornerol.com	🔴 Nuits St. Georges
🧍 🍷 🍇 🌿	7 ha; 25,000 btl

Didier Fornerol started making wine with his father, became the the vineyard manager and cellarmaster with Jean-Pierre de Semt at Domaine de l'Arlot from 1982 until 1998, and then took over his family estate at Corgoloin. Jean-Pierre, although formally retired, leds a hand. Vineyards are in Bourgogne (producing red, white, Aligoté, and Passetoutgrain) and on Côtes de Nuits Villages.

Domaine Jean Chauvenet

6 Rue de Gilly, 21700 Nuits St. Georges	📞 +33 3 80 61 00 72
@ domaine-jean.chauvenet@orange.fr	👤 Christophe Drag
🌐 domainejeanchauvenet.fr	🔴 Nuits St. Georges [map]
📅 🍷 🍇 🌿	9 ha; 35,000 btl

The Chauvenets are an old winemaking family in Nuits St. Georges, and it was Jean Chauvenet who really created the domain after 1966 when he expanded vineyard holdings and estate bottling. There are village wines from Vosne Romanée and Nuits St. Georges, including two lieu-dits, and seven premier crus. The wines were known as typical examples of Nuits St. Georges, rather solid or even rustic in their youth, but the style lightened after Jean's son-in-law, Christophe Drag, took over in 1999, together with Jean's daughter, Christine. The cellar was renovated in 2016. Grapes are destemmed, then there is cold maceration, and aged with 20-33% new oak, depending on the cuvée.

Domaine Philippe et Vincent Lécheneaut

14 rue-des-Seuillets, 21700 Nuits St. Georges	📞 +33 3 80 61 05 96
@ lecheneaut@wanadoo.fr	👤 Vincent Lécheneaut
🌐 www.domaine-lecheneaut.fr	🔴 Nuits St. Georges [map]
🚫 ✂️ 🍇 🚜	10 ha; 55,000 btl

The first vineyards were purchased by Fernand Lécheneaut, while he was working at Maison Morin, and he formed the domain when Morin folded in 1980. It really took its present form under his sons, Philippe and Vincent, who took over in 1985, built up the vineyards, and moved to estate bottling. Vineyards are highly fragmented into 70 different plots, and make 18 cuvées. Destemming is common, but some whole clusters are kept, with the proportion increasing in richer vintages. There is a cold soak, fermentation in cement, and then aging in 33-100% new oak.

Domaine Chantal Lescure

34 A Rue Thurot, 21700 Nuits St. Georges	📞 +33 3 80 61 16 79
@ *contact@domaine-lescure.com*	👤 *François Chavériat*
🌐 *www.domaine-lescure.com*	⬤ *Nuits St. Georges [map]*
🈹 🏭 🍇 🍷	*18 ha; 70,000 btl*

Chantal Lescure was married to Xavier Machard de Gramont, and they founded a 32 ha estate with vineyards all over the Côte d'Or. After Chantal died in 1996, the estate was split into three: Bertrand Machard de Gramont is a 6 ha estate around Nuits St. Georges; Domaine Machard de Gramont in Premeaux has 20 ha with many of the holdings from the Côte de Beaune; and Chantal Lescure now has 18ha, owned by her sons Aymeric and Thibault, and run by winemaker François Chavériat. Vineyards are split between the Côte de Beaune and Côte de Nuits. New oak is 30-50% for most cuvées, but more for Vosne Romanée and Clos Vougeot.

Domaine Thibault Liger-Belair

40 rue du 18 Décembre, 21700 Nuits St. Georges	📞 +33 3 80 61 51 16
@ *contact@thibaultligerbelair.com*	👤 *Thibault Liger-Belair*
🌐 *www.thibaultligerbelair.com*	⬤ *Nuits St. Georges [map]*
🈹 🍷 🍇 🛢 ◖	*8 ha; 40,000 btl*

The Liger-Belair family have been making wine in the Côte de Nuits since the eighteenth century, but sold most of the vineyards in the 1930s, when two branches of the family split. In the twenty-first century, they both resurrected domains from their remaining holdings. Comte Liger-Belair established his domain in 2000 in Vosne Romanée (see profile). Thibault Liger-Belair created his domain in Nuits St. Georges with family vineyards that had been rented to other producers; in 2003 he established a negociant activity under the name of Thibault Liger-Belair Successeurs. He also started Domaine des Pierres Roses in Beaujolais in 2009. The domain in Nuits St. Georges has two cuvées of village wine, a premier cru, Vosne Romanée premier cru, and Richebourg and Clos Vougeot. The negociant adds village wines, premier and grand crus from Aloxe-Corton, Chambolle Musigny, and Gevrey Chambertin. Usually each plot is harvested twice: the first crop is fermented as whole clusters, and the second is destemmed. New oak is usually 20-30%, with a maximum of 50%.

Maison Lupé-Cholet

17 Avenue Du Général De Gaulle, Bp 71, 21700 Nuits St. Georges	📞 +33 3 80 61 25 02
@ *bourgogne@lupe-cholet.com*	👤 *François Denis*
🌐 *www.lupecholet.com*	⬤ *Nuits St. Georges [map]*
◌ 🍷 🍇 🛢 🚜	*25 ha*

Lupé-Cholet is principally a negociant, formed by a partnership between Alexandre de Mayol de Lupé et Félix de Cholet in 1903. It was purchased by negociant Albert Bichot in 1987, becoming part of portfolio that also includes Domaine du Clos Frantin in Vosne Romanée, Clos du Pavillon in Pommard, and Long-Depaquit in Chablis. Lupé-Cholet owns Château Gris in Nuits St. Georges and Château Viviers in Chablis, and is Bichot's vinification center for the Côte de Nuits. Under the Lupé-Cholet label, there are Chablis, Mâcon, Mercurey, Beaujolais, Chablis, as well as a wide range from the Côte de Beaune and Côte de Nuits.

Bertrand & Axelle Machard de Gramont

13, Rue De Vergy, 21700 Nuits St. Georges	📞 *+33 3 80 61 16 96*
@ *bertrandmacharddegramont@aliceadsl.fr*	👤 *Axelle Machard de Gramont*
🌐 *www.bertrand-macharddegramont.com*	🔴 *Nuits St. Georges*
📅 🍇 ⚒	*6 ha; 20,000 btl*

This is the smallest of the three domains resulting from the breakup of the old Chantal Lescure estate, founded by Bertrand Machard de Gramont in 1984 after he left Domaine Comte Georges de Vogüé. His daughter Axelle joined him in 2004, and her name was added to the label in 2015. (Domaine Machard de Gramont in Premeaux is another part of the original estate; see profile). The official address of the domain is in Nuits St. Georges, but actually it's located in the hamlet of Curtil-Vergey, up in the Côtes de Nuits. Most of the vines are in Nuits St. Georges, from which there are four cuvées: Les Haut-Pruliers, Aux Allots, Les Vallerots, and Terrasses des Vallerots, the latter two located above premier cru Les Vaucrains, comprising plots that had been abandoned after phylloxera and which Bernard replanted in 1987 and 2001. A village Vosne Romanée is a blend from four parcels. Axelle has reduced the time spent in oak to 12-14 months to lighten the style.

Domaine Machard de Gramont

105 rue Pique, 21700 Premeaux-Prissey	📞 *+33 3 80 61 15 25*
@ *scemacharddegramont@orange.fr*	👤 *Arnaud Machard de Gramont*
🍇 🚜 *20 ha*	🔴 *Nuits St. Georges*

Chantal Lescure and Xavier Machard de Gramont had a 32 ha domain that was split into three parts in 1983: Domaine Chantal Lescure (18 ha in Nuits St. Georges), Bernard Machard de Gramont (see profile; 6 ha in Côtes de Nuits), and Domaine Machard de Gramont (in Premeaux). Arnaud runs Domaine Machard de Gramont with his sons Alban and Alexis. Vineyards are on both the Côte de Nuits and Côte de Beaune, with an average age of 30 years. Winemaking uses a small amount of whole clusters, and wines age with 20-30% new oak, one unusual feature being the use of some American as well as French oak.

Maison Louis Max

6, Rue De Chaux, 21700 Nuits St. Georges	📞 *+33 3 80 62 43 01*
@ *louismax@louis-max.fr*	👤 *Jean-François Joliette*
🌐 *www.louismax.com*	🔴 *Nuits St. Georges*
🏭 🍇 🛢 🚜	

Louis Max founded the negociant in 1859. A winery built in 1899 in Nuits St. Georges is still used today, although the company has much expanded to include vineyards in the south of France as well as Burgundy, and there is also a modern winery on the outskirts of Nuits St Georges. The 230 ha of vineyards include estates in Rully and Mercurey, and Château Pech-Latt in Corbières and Domaine la Lyre in Côtes-du-Rhône. The family sold the company in 2007 to Stanko Subotic, from Geneva. avid Duband (see profile) from the Côte de Nuits was brought in as technical director in 2014. A very wide range of wines covers all Burgundy, from Chablis, through the Côte d'Or, to Mâcon.

Domaine Alain Michelot

6 Rue Camille Rodier, 21700 Nuits St. Georges	📞 *+33 3 80 61 14 46*
@ *domalainmichelot@orange.fr*	👤 *Élodie Michelot*
📅 🏭 🍇 🍂 *8 ha; 35,000 btl*	🔴 *Nuits St. Georges [map]*

Founded in 1880, the domain is now its fourth generation, although Alain is handing over to his daughter Élodie and her husband Christophe. Vineyards are in Nuits St. Georges, with seven premier crus, and village and premier cru Morey St. Denis. Clos Vougeot was added in 2010. The domain is known for its powerfully structured wines, although grapes are mostly destemmed and new oak is only 25-30%.

Domaine des Perdrix

Rue des Écoles, 21700 Premeaux-Prissey	📞 *+33 3 80 61 26 53*
@ *contact@domainedesperdrix.com*	👤 *Amaury & Aurore Devillard*
🌐 *www.domainedesperdrix.com*	◉ *Nuits St. Georges [map]*
⬤🌢🍇🌣	*15 ha; 70,000 btl*

This domain is less well known than it might be, because since its purchase in 1996 by the Devillard family, it has in effect played second fiddle in their holdings to the Château de Chamirey in Mercurey. While Domaine des Perdrix is not open for visits, the wines can be tasted at Château de Chamirey, together with those from other Devillard properties. Holdings for Domaine des Perdrix are concentrated around Nuits St. Georges, with the flagship being the monopole premier cru of Aux Perdrix. The cuvée Les 8 Ouvrées comes from a plot of the oldest vines, planted at very high density in 1922.

Laurent Ponsot

10 rue des Cerisiers, Za Petite Champagne, 21640 Gilly-lès-Cîteau	📞 *+33 3 80 41 03 27*
@ *contact@laurentponsot.com*	👤 *Anne-Sophie Lhoste*
🌐 *www.laurentponsot.com*	◉ *Nuits St. Georges*
⬤🌢🍇🚜	*7 ha; 80,000 btl*

Laurent Ponsot took over Domain Ponsot (see profile) from his father in 1981 and built the estate into a major domain by the time he left in 2017 (presumably as a result of family disagreements). He started a new domain with his son Clément, setting up at Gilly-lès-Cîteaux a couple of miles to the south, with his own small vineyard holdings (including the Ponsot holding in Clos St. Denis), and most grapes purchased via a negociant activity. Cellarmaster Arnaud Rouellat came with him from Domaine Ponsot. Laurent describes himself as 'an haute couture negociant.' "Many people in Burgundy, with 3,500 growers, can grow outstanding grapes—maybe better than me," he says A modern approach is indicated by the labels, almost the antithesis of the traditional label of Domaine Ponsot, sleek and modern, with the name of the domain in green neon. Laurent is continuing the innovations he made at Domaine Ponsot, using inert gas instead of sulfur, avoiding new oak, using a new synthetic closure instead of cork, thermo-sensors to indicate if a case has been subjected to high temperatures. The domain started with 26 cuvées and still expanding; a new winery will allow for production up to 350,000 bottles annually.

Domaine Prieuré-Roch

6 D974. 21700 Premeaux-Prissey	📞 *+33 3 80 62 00 00*
@ *domaine.prieure.roch@wanadoo.fr*	👤 *Yannick Champ*
🌐 *domaine-prieure-roch.com*	◉ *Nuits St. Georges [map]*
▣🌢🍇🌣	*21 ha; 80,000 btl*

The domain has connections as Henry-Frédéric Roch's family is a part owner of Domaine de la Romanée-Conti. The domain was created in 1988 when Henry-Frédéric bought some parcels from DRC (which was selling them because it was buying the old Marey-Monge estate that it had been leasing until then). Prieuré does not have any particular connection except to lend gravitas to the name. Henry was the son of Lalou Biz-Leroy's older sister and he was a director of DRC until he died in 2018. His longtime second in command, Yannick Champ, took over. The domain has grown to have a series of holdings in top premier and grand crus, the largest being 5 ha in Nuits St. Georges Les Corvées the purchase of the 6 ha monopole of Domaine des Varoilles in Gevrey Chambertin in 2021. Other holdings are 1 ha or less, including Vosne Romanée Les Suchots, Clos Vougeot, and Close de Bèze. The domain started in a converted garage in Nuits St. Georges (the large doors on the left as you go north through the center of town carry the name of the domain), but this was cramped, and the cellar has now moved to larger premises in Premeaux. Henry-Frédéric was a person of strong views, and The approach is really traditional, using 100% whole clusters for fermentation, which you can see in the hardness of the wines when they are young. Fermentation usually lasts ten days, with punch-down twice daily. Most of the wines get 100% new oak. These are not wines for immediate gratification.

Domaine Michèle et Patrice Rion

1, Rue De La Maladière, 21700 Premeaux-Prissey	📞 +33 3 80 62 32 63
@ contact@patricerion.com	👤 Maxime Rion
🌐 www.patricerion.com	🔘 Nuits St. Georges
🏠 🍴 🍇 🛢 🌿	7 ha; 40,000 btl

Patrice Rion began his career making wine at his family estate, Domaine Daniel Rion (see profile). Together with his wife, Michèle, he started his own small domain in 1990, starting with only 1 ha. He left Daniel Rion and built his own winery in 2000, expanded the domain, and his son Maxime joined him in 2005. There is also a negociant activity for expanding the range into Côte de Nuits Villages and Bourgogne. Most of the plots are in Nuits St. Georges, including premier crus Clos des Argillières and Clos Saint Marc (a monopole of less than 1 ha); there's also Chambolle Musigny premier cru Les Cras. The wines are red except for a Nuits St. Georges blend of 90% Chardonnay and 10% Pinot Blanc from 1.3 ha in Les Terres Blanches, at the top of the slope in Premeaux. About 70-80% of the grapes are destemmed, there is a cold maceration for a few days followed by fermentation for 18-21 days, and wines are aged in a reductive environment, with no racking; élevage lasts 15-18 months, with 40% new oak for village and premier crus alike. Patrice describes his winemaking philosophy by saying, "we do not believe that the 'maximum' is the 'optimum."

Domaine Robert Chevillon

68 Rue Félix Tisserand, 21700 Nuits St. Georges	📞 +33 3 80 62 34 88
@ detb@domainerobertchevillon.fr	👤 Denis & Bertrand Chevillon
🌐 www.domainerobertchevillon.fr	🔘 Nuits St. Georges
🚫 🍴 🍇 🌀	13 ha

The domain is one of the old estates in Nuits St. Georges, with an impressive range of premier crus. Founded at the start of the twentieth century by Symphorien Chevillon, the domain was built up by Robert Chevillon in the 1960s, who moved into bottling all production at the estate. His sons Denis and Bertrand joined him in 1990 and took over in 2003. Cuvées include Bourgogne, and both red and white village Nuits St. Georges (the white is Pinot Blanc from the Gouges strain), but the heart of the domain is the 8 premier crus, which account for half the domain: Les Chaignots, Les Bousselots, Les Roncières, Les Perrières, Les Pruliers, Les Cailles, Les Vaucrains, and Les Saint-Georges. Most of the vines are 50-70 years old. Winemaking starts with complete destemming, cold maceration for one week followed by fermentation, and then aging for 20 months in barriques with 20% new oak for village wines and 30% for premier crus. Bertrand describes Les Chaignots as the most aromatic (so it always starts a horizontal tasting) Les Cailles as the most feminine wine, smooth and silky, and Vaucrains as the most muscular and powerful (so it always ends the tasting, even after Les Saint Georges). Few domains can offer such a complete view of Nuits St. Georges.

Côte de Beaune

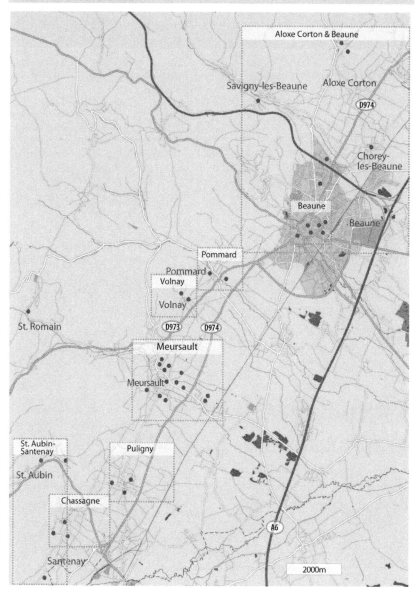

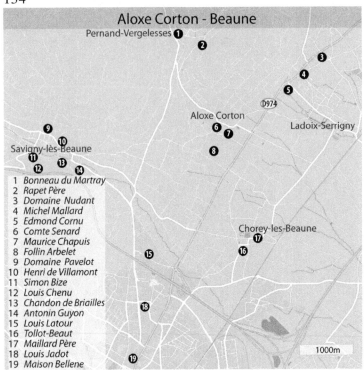

Aloxe Corton - Beaune

Pernand-Vergelesses **1**

2

3

4

5

D974

Aloxe Corton

6
7

Ladoix-Serrigny

9

10

8

Savigny-lès-Beaune

11

13

12

14

1 Bonneau du Martray
2 Rapet Père
3 Domaine Nudant
4 Michel Mallard
5 Edmond Cornu
6 Comte Senard
7 Maurice Chapuis
8 Follin Arbelet
9 Domaine Pavelot
10 Henri de Villamont
11 Simon Bize
12 Louis Chenu
13 Chandon de Briailles
14 Antonin Guyon
15 Louis Latour
16 Tollot-Beaut
17 Maillard Père
18 Louis Jadot
19 Maison Bellene

Chorey-les-Beaune

17

16

15

18

19

1000m

Profiles of Leading Estates

Domaine Comte Senard   *

1 rue des Chaumes, 21420 Aloxe-Corton	📞 *+33 3 80 26 41 65*
@ *office@domainesenard.com*	👤 *Lorraine Senard-Pereira*
🌐 *www.domainesenard.com*	📍 *Aloxe Corton [map]*
🙂 🏭 ❌ 🍇 🚜	*10 ha; 45,000 btl*

The domain was founded in 1857 with a couple of hectares, and is still in the hands of the founding family. Lorraine Senard Pereira, the fifth generation, took over from her father Philippe in 2005. The domain is still headquartered in Aloxe Corton, where it's right in the center of the village, opposite the church. Oriented towards oenotourism, there is a tasting room and shop, and a table d'hôte for lunch). It's a good place to go if you want to understand Corton and Aloxe Corton. The old cellars here date from the 13th or 14th century and are interesting to visit, although they are no longer used; wine has been made in a modern facility in Ladoix since 2012.

The vineyards have remained the same for generations, and are almost all in Aloxe-Corton and Corton (including six climats); most production is red. The domain is in fact in the center of grand cru Corton, and the Clos de Meix monopole, the flagship of the domain, runs right up to the cellars. Walking out to the vineyards, you see the elevation, with a view over the surrounding vineyards and countryside.

There are two interesting white cuvées. The Aloxe-Corton white is not Chardonnay but is Pinot Gris (called Pinot Beurot locally), coming from a plot of very old vines. (It's legal to produce Pinot Gris from existing vines, but not to replant it, so quantity is declining and is now down to 600 bottles per year.) A little spicy, it shows more exotic notes and aromatic lift than Chardonnay, and should be drunk within about six years after release. It's quite a transition to the white Corton, which comes from Chardonnay planted 25 years ago on a strip of limestone running through Clos de Meix, and is close to the mineral style of Corton Charlemagne. The whites have 50% new oak, but it's not obvious.

Reds go from the elegant mineral impression of the village Aloxe-Corton to the richer impression of premier cru Valozières (both have one third new oak), while the grand cru Corton shows more rounded fruits with greater depth and a glossy sheen from Clos du Roi, more sense of richness and completeness from Clos dui Meix, but both maintaining the elegance of the house style. Aged in 50-60% new oak, these are never over-extracted wines. A classic representation of Pinot Noir from the Côte de Beaune, they can be started soon after release, but age quite slowly.

Maison Louis Latour ★

18, Rue des Tonneliers, BP 127, 21204 Beaune	📞 +33 3 80 24 81 00
@ contact@louislatour.com	👤 Anne Charpin
⊕ www.louislatour.com	⊙ Aloxe Corton [map]
🗓 🖌 🍇 🛢 ⌾	⌷ Aloxe-Corton
48 ha; 6,000,000 btl	⌷ Chassagne Montrachet

"I don't want our Pinot Noir or Chardonnay to be too light, we want the power. I think some people are too obsessed about acidity, I think people are missing full, rich wines," says Fabrice Latour. "We've always had a relatively rich style, a bit of richness is good, we try not to harvest too early."

Louis Latour is one of the most important growers and negociants in Burgundy, with estate vineyards all over the area, and a large negociant activity. The house is one of the largest holders of grand crus on the Côte de Nuits. Still family owned, the company is presently run by Fabrice, sometimes known as Louis VII. Offices are in the center of Beaune, wines are produced at the winery built in Aloxe-Corton in 1832 with a rather splendid gravity-feed system using wagons on rails to move grapes to open-topped wood vats, and bottling is done at a modern facility on the outskirts of Beaune.

Unoaked whites from Ardèche IGP or Mâcon or Pouilly Fuissé are fresh, and a jump in style occurs with the Côte d'Or villages, which are given 15% new oak. There's increased sense of depth with the premier crus, with 35-50% new oak. Chassagne Caillerets is broad while Puligny Sous les Puits has more tension. Grand crus have 100% oak. The flagship Corton Charlemagne is full and opulent, in fact the most opulent Corton Charlemagne of all, while Bâtard Montrachet has minerality to cut the opulence.

The Pinot Noir from southern Beaujolais is more exotic than Burgundy, while Mercurey is a pure expression of Pinot Noir in stainless steel, and then the slightly plusher expression of Marsannay, also in stainless steel, brings you to the Côte d'Or. Aloxe-

Corton (with 15% new oak) typifies the AOP with a characteristic glossy sheen, there is more earthiness as you move to Beaune premier crus (35% new oak), and minerality in the Chassagne Montrachet Morgeot red. Volnay En Chevret is very fine with a great sense of purity.

Going up the scale in Aloxe-Corton, you see the glossy sheen of the village wine, restrained by more structure in the premier crus, with more overt structure in Corton itself. Château Corton Grancey, which is not a single plot but a blend from four climats behind the winery, is the most sophisticated of all. In reds, Louis Latour remains controversial for using pasteurization at bottling, which some critics believe impedes aging, but a vertical of Château Corton Grancey identifies it as one of the more ageworthy Cortons.

Instead of competing for land and grapes in the Côte d'Or, Louis Latour has expanded elsewhere, starting in the 1970s with the Ardèche Chardonnay. Recent plantings include Chardonnay in the Auxerrois and Pinot Noir in Beaujolais. Latour has also bought Simonnet-Febvre in Chablis, and Domaine Henry Fessy in Beaujolais.

Profiles of Important Estates

Domaine Chapuis

3, Rue Boulmeau, 21420 Aloxe-Corton	📞 +33 3 80 26 40 99
@ info@domainechapuis.com	👤 Pierre Chapuis
🌐 www.domainechapuis.com	◉ Aloxe Corton [map]
📅 ⛏ 🍇 🚜	12 ha; 25,000 btl

The domain started with less than a hectare in Corton Charlemagne in 1850. It's named for the grandson of the founder, who ran the domain between the first and second world wars. (Originally it was Domaine Louis Chapuis, then Maurice & Anne-Marie Chapuis.) Pierre Chapuis took over from his parents, Maurice and Anne-Marie, in 2018. The domain's largest single holding is in Aloxe-Corton village, comprising several plots totaling almost 4 ha; and there are plots around 1 ha each in Corton Charlemagne, Corton Languettes (within the area of Corton Charlemagne but planted with Pinot Noir), Corton Perrières, Corton Chaumes, and Aloxe-Corton premier cru. Pierre Chapuis says that Corton-Languettes (made by only two domains) is about finesse, whereas traditional Corton is more powerful and structures, and Languettes can be difficult to identify in blind tastings. There are also plots in Savigny-lès-Beaune and Chorey-lès-Beaune (the other white besides Corton Charlemagne). New oak is fairly restrained, about 30% in the Corton Charlemagne.

Edmond Cornu et Fils

6 Rue du Bief, 21550 Ladoix-Serrigny	📞 +33 3 80 26 40 79
@ domaine@cornu-edouard-et-fils.fr	👤 Pierre Cornu
🌐 www.bourgogne-vigne-verre.com/fr/6-domaine-e-cornu-et-fils	◉ Ladoix-Serrigny [map]
📅 ⛏ 🍇 🍷	17 ha; 80,000 btl

This family estate originated some time after 1800 and is located at the north of the Côte de Beaune, close to the border with the Côte de Nuits. Edmond Cornu took over in 1956 and began estate-bottling in 1959. His son Pierre joined in 1985 and has run the estate since 1990 with his cousin Emmanuel Boireau. Plantings are 13.5 ha Pinot Noir, 1.5 ha Chardonnay, and 0.5 ha Aligoté. Vineyards are in Ladoix, Chorey, Aloxe Corton, and Savigny-lès-Beaune on the Côte de Beaune, with a small holding at Corgoloin in Côte de Nuits Villages. Harvesting is by machine: Pierre believes that the reliability outweighs other factors. There are five cuvées from Ladoix, one white and four red, including two red premier crus, La Corvée from the north (more powerful, resembling the Côte de Nuits) and Le Bois Roussot (more elegant from a plot close to Aloxe Corton). For winemaking, all grapes are destemmed. There is a five day cold maceration before fermentation. The reds ferment in stainless steel and then age in barrique for 15-20 months. The Chardonnay whites see only a small amount of new oak.

Domaine Follin-Arbelet

Les Vercots, 21420 Aloxe-Corton	📞 *+33 3 80 26 46 73*
@ *franck.follin-arbelet@wanadoo.fr*	👤 *Franck Follin-Arbelet*
🌐 *www.domaine-follin-arbelet.com*	🔴 *Aloxe Corton [map]*
📋 ⚒ 🐛 ᗧ	*4 ha; 25,000 btl*

Franck Follin-Arbelet founded this small domain in 1992 with his father-in-law's vineyards. He has premier crus in Aloxe-Corton and Pernand-Vergelesses as well as grand cru Corton and Romanée St. Vivant. The domain is located in old family building in the center of Aloxe-Corton. Reds are destemmed and wines aged in new oak varying from 15% for village wine to 75% for grand cru. The only white was the Corton Charlemagne until two new appellations were added in 2018, Pernand-Vergelesses village and the premier cru En Caradeux white.

Domaine Michel Mallard et Fils

43, Route De Dijon, 21550 Ladoix-Serrigny	📞 *+33 3 80 26 40 64*
@ *contact@domaine-mallard.com*	👤 *Patrick Mallard*
🌐 *www.domaine-mallard.com*	🔴 *Ladoix-Serrigny [map]*
📋 ⚒ 🐛 ᗧ	*11 ha; 40,000 btl*

Michel Maillard is the third generation at the domain and took over from his father in 2005. (The domain took its name from Michel's grandfather.) He also worked for Domaine Engel in Vosne Romanée. The largest holding is in Ladoix, with village wines and premier crus in both red and white. There are also Chorey-lès-Beaune, premier cru Serpentières in Savigny-lès-Beaune, a small holding in Aloxe Corton and three climats of Corton (Maréchaudes, Rognet, Renards) as well as Corton Charlemagne. Winemaking is traditional, with some use of whole clusters (up to 50%), and use of new oak ranging from 20% for village wines to 70-90% for the grand crus.

Domaine Nudant

11 Route Nationale 74, 21550 Ladoix-Serrigny	📞 *+33 3 80 26 40 48*
@ *contact@domaine-nudant.fr*	👤 *Guillaume Nudant*
🌐 *www.domaine-nudant.fr*	🔴 *Ladoix-Serrigny [map]*
📋 ⚒ 🐛 🚜	*16 ha; 100,000 btl*

The Nudant family has been making wine in Ladoix since Guillaume Nudant purchased his first vineyard in 1792. Jean-René took over from his father in 1978, and his son Guillaume took over in 2003. Vineyards are in Ladoix, and all around in Pernand-Vergelesses, Aloxe-Corton, Savigny-lès-Beaune, and Chorey-lès-Beaune. Most of the plots are around the hill of Corton, with the top parcels in Corton Charlemagne, Corton Bressandes, and Echézeaux, as well as four premier crus. Winemaking is traditional, with in barriques with one third new oak, for 8-10 months for whites, and 12-18 months for reds.

Pernand Vergelasses

Profiles of Leading Estates

Domaine Bonneau du Martray ***

2 rue de la Frétille, 21420 Pernand Vergelesses	📞 +33 3 80 21 50 64
@ contact@bonneaudumartray.com	👤 Thibault Jacquet
🌐 www.bonneaudumartray.com	🗺 Pernand Vergelesses [map]
🚫 🏭 🍇 📖 11 ha; 25,000 btl	Corton Charlemagne

The most aristocratic domain in Corton, Bonneau du Martray has a single block of 11 ha between Pernand and Aloxe Corton. The domain has no other vineyards, and makes just two wines. The winery is located in the center of Pernand-Vergelesses, where its buildings have been renovated and there is a stylish tasting room underneath. Jean-Charles le Bault de Morinière abandoned his architectural practice in Paris to take over Bonneau du Martray only in 1993, although he was present for all vintages after 1969.

"You can find Corton Charlemagne producers all around the hill and this produces big differences in the wines according to exposition, slope, style of producer," he says, "We have all the variations between Pernand and Aloxe." The single cuvée of Corton Charlemagne is an assemblage from 90% of the estate; the rest is a red Corton coming from four blocks. Jean-Charles is an enthusiast for biodynamics. "The texture is different, it sits on the mid palate, there is a more mineral style, more clarity, purity, volume." The Corton Charlemagne is barrel fermented, spends 12 months in élevage with about a third new oak, and is transferred to stainless steel with all the fine lees for 6 months. "My wines show well in the year after bottling, then they shut down. In the past they used to shut down so much you could not see anything. They still shut down but since 2005 they have been more approachable and understandable, they never become invisible. They open up after 3-4 years," he says.

Given the history of the domain in one family for two hundred years, it created a shockwave when it was announced in 2016 that the domain was being sold to American businessman Stanley Kroenke, owner of Screaming Eagle in Napa Valley; apparently there was no family member interested in continuing the succession. There will be a little less wine in the future, as 3 ha were then leased to DRC, because the domain was felt to be too large to handle in continuing its biodynamic principles.

Domaine Rapet Père et Fils *

2 Pl. de la Mairie, 21420 Pernand Vergelesses	📞 +33 3 80 21 59 94
@ vincent@domaine-rapet.com	👤 Vincent Rapet
🌐 www.domaine-rapet.com	🗺 Pernand Vergelesses [map]
🚫 🖊 🍇 🌿	🍾 Savigny-lès-Beaune, Les Fourneaux
20 ha; 80,000 btl	Pernand Vergelesses, Clos du Village

Located right by the church in the center of the village of Pernand-Vergelesses, this is a very old domain, going back at least to the mid eighteenth century. Originally its vineyards were all around the village; that remains true of the whites, which come from Pernand-Vergelesses, its crus, and Corton Charlemagne, but today the reds are scattered

all over the Côte de Beaune, coming from Pernand-Vergelesses, Aloxe Corton, Savigny-lès-Beaune, and Beaune. Around 1980 when Vincent's grandfather died, the vineyards weren't in great shape, so most of the domain was replanted, using a mixture of clones and selection massale; the domain has increased just a little in size since then.

Vincent takes a thoughtful approach to viticulture and vinification. When asked how things have changed since he took over, he says that working the soil is better, there's better canopy management, and vendange vert is done when necessary. A sorting table was introduced in 2004, there's no pumping in the cuverie, and nitrogen is used when bottling the whites to avoid premox. There's a real focus on improving each stage to get quality in viticulture and vinification. "The style of the grand années remains the same, it's the style of the minor years that has changed," he says. "The wine used to require three years, now it's drinkable straight away." The whites can be quite full; there's always some proportion of whole cluster for the reds, giving a structured background to the generally silky style.

Profiles of Important Estates

Domaine Aurélie Berthod

8 Chemin des Vignes Blanches, 21420 Pernand-Vergelesses	📞 +33 6 36 16 93 13
@ *aurelie.berthod@sfr.fr*	👤 *Aurélie Berthod*
⊕ *www.aurelieberthod.com*	🗺 *Pernand Vergelesses*
🧍🏭🍇☯	*6 ha*

Aurélie Berthod comes from Alsace, married winemaker Vincent Fournier, managed her in-laws estate, the Domaine de la Galopière in Bligny les Beaune, and in 2017 purchased the Roger Jaffelin estate in Pernand Vergelesses, where she established her own domain. The Pernand Vergelesses Blanc village wine and the premier cru Creux de la Net both age in barriques for 9-12 months before release. Reds start with the Haut Côtes de Beaune (aged in vat); Chorey-les-Beaune, Pernand Vergelesses village and premier crus, and Beaune premier cru Belissand, age in barriques for 9-12 months.

Chorey-lès-Beaune

Profiles of Leading Estates

Domaine Tollot-Beaut et Fils   *

Rue Alexandre Tollot, 21200 Chorey-lès-Beaune	📞 *+33 3 80 22 16 54*
@ *domaine@tollot-beaut.com*	👤 *Nathalie, Jean-Paul & Olivier Tollot*
	🔵 *Chorey-lès-Beaune [map]*
🔲🖊🍇🕒 *24 ha; 150,000 btl*	🍾 *Savigny-lès-Beaune, Les Lavières*

The domain was founded in Chorey-lès-Beaune just around the time of phylloxera. Very much a family affair, it's run today by a group of family members headed by Nathalie Tollot. With the sale of the other large individual producer in Chorey (Château de Chorey), Tollot-Beaut is really the only major producer dedicated to Chorey. For many years Tollot-Beaut was synonymous with good value wines from the appellation, but in fact the Chorey and generic Bourgogne account for only about half the vineyards. Other holdings extend into Savigny-lès-Beaune, Beaune (including premier crus Grèves and Clos du Roi), and Aloxe Corton (including small plots of Corton grand cru and Corton Charlemagne).

The Chorey-lès-Beaune red, which is the principal cuvée, is an assemblage from all three areas of Chorey. The best wine from Chorey comes from the lieu-dit of Pièce du Chapitre, a monopole of Tollot-Beaut since 2001. Most of the other holdings outside Chorey are small enough that the wines represent individual plots. All grapes are destemmed, but vinification varies with the year. Prefermentation maceration is used only in good years. Cultivated yeasts are used in difficult years, indigenous in good years. All wines are treated the same, with 16-18 months in barrique; the proportion of new oak depends on the cuvée, extending from around 20% for village wines to 60% for grand crus. I've always found the style to be very reliable, with no disappointments.

Profiles of Important Estates

Maillard Père et Fils

2, rue Joseph Bard, 21200 Chorey-lès-Beaune	📞 *+33 3 80 22 10 67*
@ *contact@domainemaillard.com*	👤 *Pascal Maillard*
🌐 *www.domainemaillard.com*	🔵 *Chorey-lès-Beaune [map]*
🎎🍇🕒	*19 ha; 100,000 btl*

The family has been making wine in Burgundy since 1776, and the domain dates from 1952 when Daniel Maillard purchased the property in Chorey-lès-Beaune. His son Pascal is in charge today. Vineyards extend from Chorey-lès-Beaune (both red and white) to reds from Aloxe-Corton, Corton Rénardes, Savigny-lès-Beaune, Beaune, Ladoix, and Volnay, and whites from Corton and Meursault. The Chorey-lès-Beaune village wines are almost half of production. Winemaking is traditional, with fermentation lasting 12-20 days with punch down once or twice per day, followed by élevage in barriques for 12-18 months with 25-80% new oak going from village to grand cru.

Savigny-lès-Beaune

Profiles of Leading Estates

Domaine Simon Bize   *

12 Rue Chanoine Donin, 21420 Savigny-lès-Beaune	📞 *+33 3 80 21 50 57*
@ *contact@domainebize.fr*	👤 *Chisa Bize*
🌐 *www.domainebize.fr*	🟢 *Savigny-lès-Beaune [map]*
🔲🏭🍇🚜	🍾 *Savigny-lès-Beaune, Les Fourneaux*
22 ha; 100,000 btl	⬜ *Savigny-lès-Beaune, Les Vergelesses*

The Bize family arrived in Savigny in the middle of the nineteenth century. Simon Bize worked at other domains, and little by little built up his own domain. His son took over after the first world war; and his wife (known as Grandma Bize) was a dominant influence. Estate bottling started in 1926, but complete estate bottling only happened a generation later. Patrick Bize started in 1978, and took over in 1988; he expanded the domain with additional vineyards, and built a new cuverie. Under his leadership—sadly he died in 2013—the domain became a reference for Savigny.

You enter in a charming courtyard that appears almost residential, but behind is a huge warehouse facility with an extensive barrel room underneath. Vineyards are mostly in Savigny-lès-Beaune, where there are six premier crus in red and one in white. There's also a little Corton and Corton Charlemagne, and Latricières Chambertin. Overall production is 70% red.

Reds are vinified as whole clusters in large wooden vats (there is some destemming in some years), fermentation is relatively warm, élevage lasts about a year, but there is no new wood. Whites are pressed, go into stainless steel to settle, and then into barriques to ferment. Although vinification is traditional, the style of the reds is modern, almost slick, with a crowd-pleasing suppleness, and never any evident tannins; even lesser vintages leave an opulent impression. I find the reds more successful than the whites.

The most recent development, starting with the 2018 vintage, is the introduction of some 'natural' wines, made with minimal intervention and no added sulfur.

Profiles of Important Estates

Domaine Chandon de Briailles

Rue Soeur Goby, 21420 Savigny-Lès-Beaune	📞 *+33 3 80 21 52 31*
@ *francois.de.nicolay@chandondebriailles.com*	👤 *François de Nicolay*
🌐 *www.chandondebriailles.com*	🟢 *Savigny-lès-Beaune [map]*
🚶🏭🍇⭕	*14 ha; 55,000 btl*

The manor house and gardens where the domain is headquartered were built at the end of the seventeenth century by the same architect who designed Versailles. This has been a family estate since it was purchased in 1834; present owners Claude and François de Nicolay, the seventh generation, took over in 2001. Vineyards are in the vicinity, which is to say Savigny, Pernand and Aloxe. Most production is red: there is little destemming, and aging takes place in old barriques with almost no new oak.

Domaine Clos de la Chapelle

14 Grande Rue, Au Château, 21200 Bligny-lès-Beaune	📞 +33 9 81 83 29 04
@ info@closchapelle.com	👤 Mark O'Connell
🌐 www.closchapelle.com	🔘 Savigny-lès-Beaune
🄳 🏭 🍇 🍷	4 ha; 16,000 btl

Clos de la Chapelle is the new name for an old domain, founded in 1865 when Victor Boillot bought Volnay premier cru Clos de la Chapelle (named for the chapel in the center), which was originally part of what is now the Bousse d'Or premier cru. The domain later added premier crus Volnay en Carelle and Pommard Les Chanlins. It stayed in the Boillot family as Domaine Louis Boillot until it was purchased in 2011 by American Mark O'Connell, who then added 8 further plots, all in premier or grand crus, including Volnay Taillepieds, Pommard Grands Epenots, Beaune Champs Pimont, Teurons, and Reversées, Corton Bressandes, and Corton Charlemagne. Destemming varies with the cuvée. There's one punch-down daily during fermentation. All the plots are small, which limits flexibility in the use of new oak: élevage lasts for 24 months, in barriques where the oldest are 2-year. The cellars moved to Bligny-lès-Beaune, across the D974 from Volnay, in 2017.

Domaine Louis Chenu et Filles

12, Rue Joseph De Pesquidoux, 21420 Savigny-lès-Beaune	📞 +33 3 80 26 13 96
@ juliette@louischenu.com	👤 Caroline Chenu
🌐 www.louischenu.com	🔘 Savigny-lès-Beaune [map]
🄳 🏭 🍇 🍷	10 ha; 45,000 btl

The domain is 90 years old, but started bottling its own wines only when sisters Juliette and Caroline took over from their father Louis in 2007. Located almost entirely in Savigny, the focus is largely on Pinot Noir. The sisters describe their style as "elegant not extracted, refined in that just enough oak is used to provide shoulders for the wine." In whites, the Bourgogne Blanc is close in style to the Savigny-lès-Beaune, both showing a smoky nose with hints of gunflint following on the palate in quite a mineral style. In reds, the style remains elegant, and the Savigny Vieilles Vignes adds a layer of extra richness compared with the Bourgogne. The Aux Clous premier cru shows a more precise edge and greater grip on the palate. But in both reds and whites, the bargain that typifies the elegant house style is the Bourgogne.

Domaine Cruchandeau

4 Rue Robert, 21700 Chaux	📞 +33 6 74 85 79 62
@ domaine.cruchandeau@gmail.com	👤 Julien Cruchandeau
🌐 www.domaine-cruchandeau.com	🔘 Savigny-lès-Beaune
🄳 🍇 ☙	7 ha

Julien Cruchandeau comes from Burgundy, but not from a winemaking family, and worked in restaurants before he returned to Burgundy to focus on wine. He worked at Domaine France Lechenault in Bouzeron on the Côte Chalonnaise from 2001 to 2005, and he founded his own domainin 2003 with a hectare in Bouzeron. In 2007 he moved to a house with a vat room and cellars in Chaux, on the Hautes Côtes de Nuits. Bringing in investors in 2009, he was able to extend his vineyards. Between 2004 and 2010 he was also performing as an electronic music artist; the domain took off when he switched full time to viticulture. Vineyards are scattered in several appellations, with Hautes Côtes de Nuits red and white, Ladoix and Savigny-les-Beaune reed, Nuits St. Georges village, and Puligny Montrachet premier cru Hameau de Blagny. Wines from Hautes Côtes de Nuits to Savigny-les-Beaune age in barriques for 12-15 months with 20% new oak, Nuits St. Georges ages for 14-18 months with a third each of new, 1-year, and older barriques, and Hameau de Blagny ages for 12-15 months with 30% new oak. There are also Crémant and Crémant rosé.

Domaine Antonin Guyon

2 Rue de Chorey, 21420 Savigny-lès-Beaune	📞 +33 3 80 67 13 24
@ domaine@guyon-bourgogne.com	👤 Dominique Guyon
🌐 www.guyon-bourgogne.com	🔵 Savigny-lès-Beaune [map]
📅 🍴 🍇 🥄	48 ha; 200,000 btl

A large estate for Burgundy—in fact one of the largest family-owned wineries in the region—the domain started in the 1960s with parcels extending from Meursault to Gevrey Chambertin. During the 1970s Antonin Guyon's sons Dominique and Michel extended the domain by assembling 350 different parcels representing 25 appellations, including a 22 ha block on the Hautes Côtes de Nuits that was assembled from 80 parcels. Dominique's daughter Hombeline manages the estate today, together with her father. There are 4 white cuvées and 16 reds, with a range from village wines to grand crus. White grapes are pressed as whole bunches, fermented in barrique with weekly battonage, and bottled after 12 months (18 months for the grand crus). Reds are destemmed, held for a week of cold maceration, fermented in open-topped vats, and then given a another week of maceration before aging in barriques. There's been some backing off from new oak, with the current maximum now 50% for grand crus.

Domaine Jean-Marc & Hugues Pavelot

1 Chemin Guetottes, 21420 Savigny-Lès-Beaune	📞 +33 3 80 21 55 21
@ info@domainepavelot.com	👤 Hugues Pavelot
🌐 www.domainepavelot.com	🔵 Savigny-lès-Beaune [map]
📅 🍴 🍇 🌿	17 ha; 60,000 btl

This domain has been passed from father to son for several generations. Hugues has now taken over from his father Jean-Marc. The winery is a large building purchased from negociant La Reine Pedauque in 1989. Vineyards are mostly in Savigny-lès-Beaune, with some plots in neighboring communes. Planting are 90% Pinot Noir and 10% Chardonnay, with a good proportion of old (30-80-year) vines. About half the domain is in village Savigny; the largest premier crus are aux Guettes (1.5 ha) and the flagship La Dominode (2 ha). The oldest vines are the 80-year-old plantings in Les Narbantons. The other premier crus in Savigny are Les Lavières, Les Peuillets and aux Gravains. There are also Les Vergelesses in Pernand-Vergelesses, Bressandes in Beaune, and some white Corton. Destemming varies with the vintage and the cuvée. There is no new oak on village wines, and 20-25% on premier crus.

Maison Henri de Villamont

Rue Du Docteur Guyot, 21420 Savigny-lès-Beaune	📞 +33 3 80 21 50 59
@ contact@hdv.fr	👤 Pierre Jhean
🌐 www.henridevillamont.fr	🔵 Savigny-lès-Beaune [map]
📅 🍴 🍇 🍷 🌿	10 ha; 350,000 btl

This is a large negociant based in Savigny-lès-Beaune. The origins of today's producer actually have nothing to do with Henri de Villamont, who apparently was a Knight who retired from the Crusades to Savigny. The name was adopted by the Swiss group Schenk Holdings to describe their production facility in Savigny, which they bought in 1964. (The château itself was built by Léonce Bocquet, who owned Clos Vougeot, at the end of the nineteenth century.) Schenk supplies supermarkets with a vast amount of wine. By 2004, production in Burgundy was 20 million bottles, but then Henri de Viillamont became the base for Schenk's more up-market operations, although the estate vineyards are only part of production today, which ranges from Chablis to Mâcon. I've always found the wines to be a bit on the light side

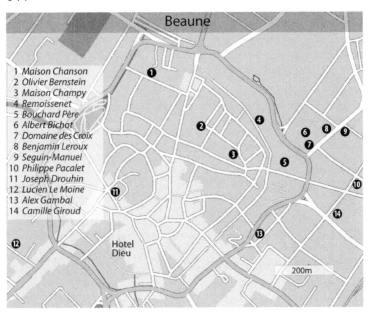

Beaune

1 Maison Chanson
2 Olivier Bernstein
3 Maison Champy
4 Remoissenet
5 Bouchard Père
6 Albert Bichot
7 Domaine des Croix
8 Benjamin Leroux
9 Seguin-Manuel
10 Philippe Pacalet
11 Joseph Drouhin
12 Lucien Le Moine
13 Alex Gambal
14 Camille Giroud

Hotel Dieu

200m

Profiles of Leading Estates

Domaine de Bellene   *

39 Faubourg St Nicolas, 21200 Beaune	📞 +33 3 80 20 67 64
@ contact@domainedebellene.com	👤 Nicolas Potel
🌐 www.domainedebellene.com	🖥 Beaune [map]
📅🏭🍇🥃	🍾 Nuits St. Georges, Les Boudots (Maison Roche de Bellène)
22 ha; 70,000 btl	🍾 Meursault, Les Forges

Nicolas Potel has a chequered history as a both a grower and negociant. His father, Gérard Potel, managed the Domaine de la Pousse d'Or, but after his death in 1997 and the subsequent sale of the estate, Nicolas established his own negociant business. Maison Nicolas Potel became well respected, but was sold to the large negociant Labouré-Roi in 2004.

After leaving in 2007, Nicolas founded a double business, Domaine de Bellène, making wine from its own vineyards, and Maison de la Roche Bellène, a negociant. The domain has its headquarters on the main road going north out of Beaune: behind the double doors it's quite startling to discover vast premises running back from the road. The domain is much smaller than the negociant, which has a separate winery.

Why have both a domain and a negociant? "I come from a domain, it's my background. I was a negociant by force. When I sold the negociant (Maison Potel) I'd started the domain, but my customers wanted me to continue as a negociant." What's the difference between them? "The wines have different goals. You don't have the same control over the vineyard with the Maison. The wines already have an imprint coming from the growers. I'm not going to impose a style on them. The Maison has an easier style, a bit rounder, something that will drink in the next 3-4 years. About 60-70% of the wines are the same every year, but the rest come from sporadic purchases. The domain is biodynamic. Winemaking is minimalist."

The stylistic objective for both domain and maison is "a lean style, not too fat or heavy." Nicolas explains that his focus is switching to the domain. "The domain is still growing but the Maison is contracting, it's a matter of balance, they run separately."

Olivier Bernstein ★★

4 rue Jean Belin, 21200 Beaune	📞 *+33 3 80 22 49 48*
@ *contact@olivierbernstein.com*	👤 *Olivier Bernstein*
🌐 *www.olivierbernstein.com*	⚫ *Beaune [map]*
📓🥒🍇🛢️ 🍷 *7 ha; 25,000 btl*	🍷 *Gevrey Chambertin, Cazetiers*

MAZIS-CHAMBERTIN
GRAND CRU
BY OLIVIER BERNSTEIN

2007

"It's interesting to have someone like me here, in the most conservative region of France, as I'm not from here, I'm not obliged to make wine," says Olivier Bernstein, who comes from a musical background, but became a micro-negociant in 2007. Olivier makes 3 premier crus, 7 grand crus, and village Gevrey Chambertin in a renovated building in a back street of Beaune. Production focuses on reds from the Côte de Nuits. Quantities are small but not miniscule. "There are 4-8 barrels of each wine, I like to have at least four barrels, I don't want to bottle one barrel, that's a nonsense," Olivier says. The boundary between negociant and domain has blurred as Olivier was able to buy 2 ha in 2012, but this doesn't make much difference as he farms all the plots himself anyway. "So I don't really like to be called a negociant," he says.

Winemaking is modern, with maturation entirely in new barriques, although Olivier says, "It's not the new wood that's interesting for me, it's the oxygenation." Except for Chambolle Lavrottes, vines are 40-80 years old. "We only have very old vines because they are much better than recent plantings." The style is finely structured, with Lavrottes the lightest, Gevrey Chambertin remarkably pure, Clos de la Roche and Clos de Bèze very tight when young, and fleshiness only just showing on Clos Vougeot behind that tight, precise house style. These beautifully balanced wines should come into their own about six years after the vintage.

Domaine Bouchard Père et Fils ★

15 Rue du Château, 21200 Beaune	📞 *+33 3 80 24 80 24*
@ *contact@bouchard-pereetfils.com*	👤 *Philippe Prost*
🌐 *www.bouchard-pereetfils.com*	⚫ *Beaune [map]*
📓🏭🍇🛢️🍷	🍷 *Beaune, Grèves Vigne de l'Enfant Jésus*
132 ha; 3,000,000 btl	🍷 *Beaune, Clos St. Landry*

146

"It was magic when Joseph Henriot bought us," says Philippe Prost, winemaker at Bouchard from 1992 to 2012. "The purchase was the first week of July 1995, and one week later Joseph turned up and said, 'Philippe, I've bought you some grand crus, Bonnes Mares, Echézeaux, and Clos Vougeot'." Bouchard has been expanding ever since, starting with the purchase of Ropiteau Mignon in 1998, which brought 32 ha in Meursault, including many premier crus. It is now one of the largest negociant-growers, with vineyards all over the Côte d'Or.

Dating from 1731, this is one of the oldest estates in Burgundy. (Another member of the family founded Bouchard Aîné in 1750; it is a separate producer now owned by Jean-Charles Boisset.) The Bouchard family remained in control for more than two centuries, but at the end of the period, the wines were distinctly under performing. After the sale to Henriot Champagne, it was revived by new investment, including the construction in 2005 of a new gravity flow winery just north of the city.

The domain is housed in the Château de Beaune, a fifteenth century fortress within the walls of the old city of Beaune (with very impressive cellars underneath). Bouchard is the largest owner of premier and grand crus on the Côte d'Or, and these total two thirds of the estate holdings. Estate grapes account for a third of production overall.

Among the best-known wines are some of the premier cru vineyards in Beaune, the Clos St. Landry (a monopole which produces one of the rare whites from Beaune), and Vigne de l'Enfant Jésus (from the center of the Grèves premier cru, a red with more power than usually found in Beaune). Whether due to the new cellar—"with gravity-feed you don't get the bitterness that can come from pumping," says Philippe—or other changes, the reds have become much finer: Beaune Grèves is firm, Volnay Caillerets has the crystalline purity of the appellation, Le Corton is deep and earthy but delicate, and all have a hallmark silkiness on the palate. The whites also show a very fine texture, sometimes inclining to a saline minerality. Meursault Genevrières is the standout among premier crus. There is never more than a subtle touch of oak. "The maximum is 15% new oak for whites because we want to be discrete," Philippe says. Reds are mostly 35%, and up to 45% new oak.

Maison Joseph Drouhin **

7, Rue d'Enfer, 21200 Beaune	+33 3 80 24 68 88
maisondrouhin@drouhin.com	Frédéric Drouhin
www.drouhin.com	Beaune [map]
	Beaune, Clos des Mouches
80 ha; 3,600,000 btl	Chassagne Montrachet, Marquis de Laguiche

Joseph Drouhin started as a negociant in Beaune in 1880. When his son Maurice took over in 1918, he began the move to becoming a negociant-grower by buying vineyards in Beaune's Clos des Mouches and in Clos Vougeot. Today one of the larger negociant-growers, and one of the few still in the old city of Beaune, Drouhin remains located in its old cellars, some dating back to the twelfth or thirteenth centuries. The firm is presently run by four siblings of the fourth generation. Drouhin has also invested in Oregon, where it produces both Pinot Noir and Chardonnay in Willamette Valley. Winemaker Véronique Drouhin oversees the harvest in Beaune and then flies to Oregon to make wine there.

The range in Burgundy extends from the entry-level Laforêt Bourgogne (both red and white) to the top Grand Crus of both Côte de Beaune and Côte de Nuits. Wines come from around 90 appellations, all across the Côte d'Or, and stretching to Chablis and to Beaujolais. Vinification is traditional, with partial destemming (decreased since 2005), fermentation in open-topped containers, and pump-over or punch-down depending on conditions. Oak is handled lightly, almost always using less than 30% new wood. The Drouhin style is elegant, yet clearly devoted to bringing out the fruits. Clos des Mouches is always a textbook example of Beaune, for either red or white. Drouhin started producing Chassagne Montrachet from the core holding of the Marquis de Laguiche, based on a handshake; for years the wine was labeled only as Chassagne, but more recently has been labeled as premier cru Morgeot. Otherwise, the top whites are the Pulignys, and the top reds are the grand crus from Gevrey Chambertin.

Maison Alex Gambal   *

14, Boulevard Jules Ferry, 21200 Beaune	📞 +33 3 80 22 75 81
@ info@alexgambal.com	👤 Alex Gambal
🌐 www.alexgambal.com	⬤ Beaune [map]
📅 🏭 🍇 🛢 🥃	🍷 Beaune, Grèves
4 ha; 60,000 btl	⚱ Saint-Aubin

Chambolle-Musigny
Les Charmes
2007
ALEX GAMBAL

There's an unexpectedly modern warehouse building behind the extended façade on the ring road around Beaune, although the cellars underneath date from 1800. The building was originally part of Bouchard Aîné, and then was sold off and became an art gallery; Alex Gambal bought it in 2003 and renovated the building to become a gravity-feed winery. An American who came to Beaune because of his interest in wine, and leaned the business by working with broker Becky Wassermann, Alex has been slowly making the transition from negociant to grower. "I started in the business in 1997 as a classic negociant buying semi finished wine, then the next year I started buying grapes. Then I started buying vineyards. We now have 4 ha which are just about a third of our production. I'm planning to add 8 ha which would triple the domain," Alex says.

There's a wide range of wines from Bourgogne to premier and grand crus from all over the Côte d'Or, with a little more white than red. Everything is destemmed, then fermentation with indigenous yeast is followed by élevage of up to 16 months. New oak is 10-15% for Bourgogne, 20-25% for village wines, a third for premier crus, and 50-100% for grand crus. "But the percentage of new oak is not so important as the barrels you are using, it's a matter of how the oak and toast interact with the juice," Alex says. Style tends to a light elegance rather than power, but always with a sense of underlying structure.

Alex sold the domain in 2019 to Jean-Claude Boisset (owner of Domaine de la Vougeraie and other estates), but it continues to run independently.

Maison Louis Jadot   **

21, Rue Eugène Spuller, 21200 Beaune	📞 +33 3 80 22 10 57
@ visit@louisjadot.com	👤 Pierre Henry Gagey
🌐 www.louisjadot.com	⬤ Beaune [map]
📅 🏭 🍇 🛢 👓	🍷 Chambolle Musigny, Les Baudes
140 ha; 10,000,000 btl	⚱ Puligny Montrachet, Clos de la Garenne

Maison Louis Jadot is one of the most important negociant-growers in Burgundy, with more than half of their holdings on the Côte d'Or consisting of premier or grand crus. They produce more than a hundred different wines. They have also expanded significantly to the south, buying some top producers in the Beaujolais (Château des Jacques) and Pouilly-Fuissé (Feret). The latest acquisition, on the Côte de Beaune, was Domaine Prieur-Brunet, with 18 ha in several villages.

The firm originated as a negociant in 1859, and was run by the Jadot family until it was purchased by their American importer, Kobrand, in 1985. The old cuverie in the center of Beaune was replaced in 1995 by a modern building on the outskirts, which was expanded further in 2010.

Most (60%) of Jadot's production in the Côte d'Or is from estate vineyards; the rest is purchased as grapes from more than 200 growers (on rare occasions they buy finished wine; sometimes they will exchange wine with a grower in order to get a barrel of a specific appellation.) Jacques Lardière was in charge of Jadot's winemaking since 1970 and believes in minimal intervention. "The impression that you can determine quality by controlling winemaking is crazy, you need to have the confidence to work with Nature and allow the terroir to express itself. It is man who makes the mistakes," he says. One of Burgundy's major figures, Jacques retired in 2012, and is now making the wines at Jadot's latest venture, the Resonance Vineyard in Oregon.

Lucien Le Moine ***

1 ruelle Morlot, 21200 Beaune	📞 +33 3 80 24 99 98
@ llm@lucienlemoine.com	👤 Mounir Saouma
🌐 www.lucienlemoine.com	🗺 Beaune [map]
🚫 🍷 🛢 🚜	🍷 Gevrey Chambertin, Cazetiers
0 ha; 30,000 btl	🥂 Chassagne Montrachet, Morgeots

Located just outside the town center, from outside the property looks a little run down, but the interior has been handsomely renovated, practical rather than flashy, but with a certain contemporary flair. Lucien Lemoine is the creation of Mounir and Rotem Saouma, who have been making wine here since 1999. This may be Burgundy's top micro-negociant. The name reflects Mounir's past experience (Lucien, meaning light, is a translation of Mounir, and Le Moine, the monk, refers to when Mounir learned winemaking in a monastery).

There are typically about 80 different wines each year, extending from a basic Bourgogne to the premier and grand crus that form the main focus. Production scale is tiny: just one to three barrels (less than 1,000 bottles) from each cru. The approach to winemaking is direct: let the wine have a slow and very long fermentation, and keep it on full lees for élevage. "We have very cold cellars so we never complete fermentation before ten months after harvest," Mounir explains. There's minimal manipulation at bottling, and the wines often have a little residual carbon dioxide, and so need decanting.

For me, these wines are completely natural, with a wonderful purity of fruit allowing terroir to show itself at every level of the range. The reds are exceptionally refined; even the Bourgogone really highlights the style, deep, black, and pure, it could easily be a village wine from the Côte de Nuits. The whites are mineral and smoky when young; they sometimes show the results of low sulfur in aging more rapidly than you might expect. The wines are expensive and hard to find, but an eye opener as to the potential for minimal manipulation. Since 2009 there has also been a winery in the Rhône called Clos Saouma.

Maison Benjamin Leroux   *

5 rue Colbert, 21200 Beaune	📞 *+33 3 80 22 71 06*
@ *contact@benjamin-leroux.com*	👤 *Benjamin Leroux*
🌐 *www.benjamin-leroux.com*	🖼 *Beaune [map]*
🕮 ⚗ 🍇 🛢 🍂	📍 *Savigny-lès-Beaune*
8 ha; 180,000 btl	*Chassagne Montrachet, Morgeots*

Benjamin Leroux started his negociant company in 2007, but continued to be the winemaker at Comte Armand in Pommard until 2014, when he became a full time negociant. "After fifteen years in Pommard, I have a true idea of what is a domain, I want to do the same thing, but as a negociant," he says. He rents a cavernous space in a large old winery just off the ring road around Beaune, and has now managed to purchase his first vineyards. "Seven years ago, everything came from grape purchases, today it is the strong majority, and ideally in the future it would be half," he says. "Everything is under the same name, I don't distinguish between domain and negociant."

Production is equal white and red, with grand cru about 10%, and premier cru and village about 30% each. "I started with lots of regional villages and where I grew the most was premier and grand cru." There are 30 different wines altogether; the largest cuvées are Bourgogne and Auxey-Duresses, a few thousand bottles each, but others may be as small as only a single barrel. Vinification depends on vintage. "We are wrong if we destem every year and wrong if we always do vendange entière; you have to adjust to the vintage," Benjamin says. The house style for whites shows citrus fruits with faintly piquant lime on the finish and a suspicion of herbal savory notes that will add complexity as the wine ages. The reds are always ripe with good supporting structure, with an approachable, firm style.

Remoissenet Père et Fils   *

20, rue Eugène Spuller, 21200 Beaune	📞 *+33 3 80 26 26 66*
@ *brepolt@remoissenet.com*	
🚶 🏭 🛢 🚜 *14 ha; 200,000 btl*	🖼 *Beaune [map]*

Remoissenet is a classic Burgundian negociant, with minimal vineyard holdings, but a very large range of cuvées from all over the Côte de Beaune and Côte de Nuits. Founded in 1877, it was run for the last thirty years under family ownership by Roland Remoissenet from an old building in Beaune, with a cuverie outside the city. Remoissenet was known for its extensive holdings of old vintages, slowly released on the market at quite reasonable prices. When Roland retired in 2005, the company was sold to New York financiers. Supposedly over a million bottles of old vintages were included in the sale.

The last years of the family regime were marked by a noticeable decline in quality, and the wines gave an impression that they were going through the motions, but under the new ownership the firm has begun to revive and also to purchase some vineyards on its own account. As a negociant, everything depends on the quality of purchases and vinification; a major asset is Remoissenet's longstanding relationship with Baron Thénard, the largest holder of Le Montrachet, which has been their top wine for many years. In fact, the whites have always been regarded as better than the reds.

Profiles of Important Estates

Maison Albert Bichot

6bis Boulevard Jacques Copeau, 21200 Beaune	📞 +33 3 80 24 37 37
@ *bourgogne@albertbichot.com*	👤 *Albéric Bichot*
🌐 *www.albertbichot.com*	📍 *Beaune [map]*
🗓️🍷🍇🛢️🚜	*103 ha; 650,000 btl*

The company was founded as a negociant in 1831, and took its name from the third generation, Albert Bichot, who established it in Beaune. It was generally an underperformer until Albéric Bichot took over in 1996. It owns several individual estates (collectively described as Domaines Albert Bichot): Long Depaquit in Chablis, Clos Frantin and Château-Gris in Nuits St. Georges, Domaine du Pavillon south of Pommard, Domaine Adélie in Mercurey, and Domaine de Rochegrès in Moulin-à-Vent. Each has its own winery, but the general mandate is that wines should be approachable when young. Wines under the Albert Bichot label come from the negociant and are aged in the large underground cellars in Beaune. Only Domaine Long Depaquit is open for visits and tastings (and for purchasing the wines of all the estates).

Maison Bouchard Aîné et Fils

4, Boulevard Maréchal Foch, Hôtel Du Conseiller Du Roy, 21200 Beaune	📞 +33 3 80 24 06 66
@ *magasin@bouchard-aine.fr*	👤 *Vincent Bottreau*
🌐 *www.bouchard-aine.fr*	📍 *Beaune*
🚶🏭🍇🛢️🚜	*25 ha; 350,000 btl*

Bouchard Aîné was founded in 1828 when the eldest son in the family of Bouchard Père et fils (see profile) started a negociant business. A new era started in 1993 when it was bought by Jean-Claude Boisset (see profile). Headquarters are in a gracious old building on the ring road around Beaune, where there is now an extensive program in oenotourism. Wines are made in a new cuverie, constructed in 2000, just north of Beaune. Production comes mostly from grapes purchased on long-term contracts and covers most of the communes on the Côte d'Or, mostly at village level, but with some premier crus. It extends northwest to Chablis and south to the Côte Chalonnaise and Mâcon and Beaujolais.

Maison Camille Giroud

3 Rue Pierre Joigneaux, 21200 Beaune	📞 +33 3 80 22 12 65
@ *contact@camillegiroud.com*	👤 *Carel Voorhuis*
🌐 *www.camillegiroud.com*	📍 *Beaune [map]*
🗓️🏭🍇🛢️🚜	*1 ha; 100,000 btl*

The house started as a small negociant in 1865. In the first half of the twentieth century, it was known for its policy of purchasing wine rather than grapes, relying on the palate of owner Lucien Giroud. After Lucien died in 1989, the policy changed and the house followed a more traditional policy, buying grapes and even some plots of vines. In 2001 the house was sold to the Colgins of Napa Valley. David Croix came as winemaker, and was succeeded in 2016 by Carel Voorhuis. The house has become somewhat of a micro-negociant, with its production coming from 30 different appellations.

Maison Champy

12 place de la Halle, 21200 Beaune	📞 +33 3 80 23 75 21
@ visites@maisonchampy.com	👤 Dimitri Bazas
🌐 www.champy.com	🔵 Beaune [map]
📅 🏭 🍇 🛢 🥂	22 ha; 500,000 btl

Founded in 1720, this is one of the oldest negociants in Beaune. Ownership has changed in rapid succession. Financial difficulties caused Champy to be sold to Jadot in 1990, then Pierre Meurgey bought it back without its vineyards. More recently it was bought by Pierre Beuchet in 2012, and then sold in 2016 to Advini, a holding company with several wineries in France and South Africa. Champy owns Domaine Laleure-Piot, which is run independently, and also bought the Louis Boillot domain in Volnay, which it renamed as Domaine Clos de la Chapelle. Dimitri Bazas has been the winemaker since 1999, and Champy is still located in its historic cellars in Beaune. I have never found the wines to have much character.

Chanson Père Et Fils

10 Rue Paul Chanson, 21200 Beaune	📞 +33 3 80 25 97 97
@ caveau@domaine-chanson.com	👤 Maxime Montaldi
🌐 www.domaine-chanson.com	🔵 Beaune [map]
📅 🏭 🍇 🛢 🥂	45 ha; 1,000,000 btl

This is an old negociant, established in 1750, and sold to its manager, Alexis Chanson, in 1847. A decline in quality led to its purchase by Bollinger in 1999. Jean-Pierre Confuron was brought in to help with production and Gilles de Courcel to help with commercialization. Wines are still aged in the old cellars in a bastion in Beaune, but there's a modern production facility outside the town. Vineyards include 25 ha in Beaune premier crus, and provide about a quarter of the grapes. Whites are vinified as whole clusters and there is no destemming of reds. Wines age for 12-20 months in barriques with 20% new oak.

Domaine des Croix

2 Rue Colbert, 21200 Beaune	📞 +33 3 80 22 41 81
@ contact@domainedescroix.com	👤 David Croix
📅 🏭 🍇 🍷 8 ha; 30,000 btl	🔵 Beaune [map]

David Croix worked with Benjamin Leroux at Comte Armand in Pommard, and then became the winemaker at negociant Camille Giroud from 2002 to 2016, when he left to become the winemaker at Domaine Guy Roulot. In 2005, together with a group of investors, he bought the 5 ha of Domaine Duchet, which became the basis for Domaine des Croix, with vineyards in Beaune and Corton. Further vineyards were added later. David makes ten cuvées at Domaine des Croix (which is located next door to Benjamin Leroux), including four premier crus and village wine from Beaune, and Corton. One objective is to show what the terroirs of Beaune can do. Production is mostly red, but there is also Corton Charlemagne. Use of new oak is moderate. There's a sense of experimentation and change at the domain; the conventional use of SO2 solutions has been replaced by using sulfur mined in Poland, which because it's more active, allows lower amounts to be used. The one thing that seems to be sure is that things will continue to be questioned.

Domaine Newman

29, Boulevard Clémenceau, 21200 Beaune	📞 *+33 3 80 22 80 96*
@ *info@domainenewman.com*	👤 *Christopher Newman*
🌐 *www.domainenewman.com*	🏠 *Beaune*
🚜	*6 ha*

Robert Newman was part of an American syndicate led by Alexis Lichine that bought Château Lascombes in Bordeaux in 1951. A year later he bought some plots in Mazis and Latricières Chambertin and Bonnes-Mares and arranged for Alexis Lichine to manage the vineyards and make the wine. This was probably the first time a foreigner acquired vineyards in Burgundy. By 1974 the vineyards needed replanting, but Robert did not want to take that on. His son Christopher, who grew up in New Orleans, bought Alexis Lichine's share, and took over the vineyards. There are now holdings in Pommard and Beaune, including two premier crus, and the Côte de Beaune. Chris sold the Latricières Chambertin, and lost control of the Mazis Chambertin and Bonnes Mares until they reverted to him in 2008, so there was a period when the domain did not produce grand crus. Grapes are mostly destemmed (some years there is some use of whole clusters), there is punch-down or pump-over depending on conditions, new oak is 50-60% for the grand crus. Australian Jane Eyre has been making the wines since 2004, and also makes wines under own label in Australia.

Philippe Pacalet

12 Rue de Chaumergy, 21200 Beaune	📞 *+33 3 80 25 91 00*
@ *contact@vins-philippe-pacalet.fr*	👤 *Philippe Pacalet*
🌐 *www.philippe-pacalet.com*	🏠 *Beaune [map]*
🗓🏭🍇🛢🚜	*16 ha; 70,000 btl*

Philippe Pacalet started making wine with his uncle, Marcel Lapierre, in Beaujolais. After six years, in 1991 he became winemaker at Prieuré-Roche in Nuits St. Georges. In 2001, he set up on his own as a negociant, and in 2007 he acquired spacious premises in an old warehouse near the railway station. Today he makes wine from several appellations on the Côte de Nuits and Côte de Beaune, as well as having projects in Moulin-à-Vent in Beaujolais and Cornas in the Northern Rhône. Grapes for the cuvées in Burgundy are purchased; the Moulin-à-Vent comes from an estate vineyard. His specialty is finding plots of old Pinot Noir. Reds are made by whole cluster fermentation without any addition of sulfur. Philippe considers himself a minimalist—he's often described as a 'natural wine' maker—as there is little temperature control (doing gradual punch-downs is used to keep temperature down), and there is no racking or fining. Wines age in barriques for a year with little new oak, and then spend 6 months in cuve. With 25 different cuvées, it is not surprising Philippe calls himself a "revealer of terroirs."

Domaine Seguin-Manuel

2 Rue de l'Arquebuse, 21200 Beaune	📞 *+33 3 80 21 50 42*
@ *contact@seguin-manuel.com*	👤 *Thibaut Marion*
🌐 *www.seguin-manuel.com*	🏠 *Beaune [map]*
🗓🏭🍇🛢🚜	*9 ha; 100,000 btl*

Seguin-Manuel was founded in 1824 by the Manuel family, changed its name when Marguerite Manuel married Félix Seguin, and under their son Félix in 1934 acquired the fourteenth century buildings in Savigny-lès-Beaune that originated as part of the monastery of Cîteaux. Everything changed completely when Thibaut Marion left his family winery, Chanson Père et Fils (see profile), and bought Seguin-Manuel in 2004. The original vineyards were in Savigny-lès-Beaune, and Thibaut has added plots in Beaune, Pommard, Puligny Montrachet, Meursault, and Vosne Romanée, as well as expanding the range further on the Côte d'Or, and to the Côte Chalonnaise, Mâcon, and Chablis, by adding a negociant activity. There are more than 50 cuvées. Wines from estate vineyards are labeled as Domaine Seguin-Manuel, while negociant wines are labeled only as Seguin-Manuel, with otherwise identical labels that are reproductions of the label from the early twentieth century. The winery moved to Beaune in 2005. Production has doubled since Thibaut took over. New oak varies from about 20% for village wines to up to 50% for premier or grand crus.

154

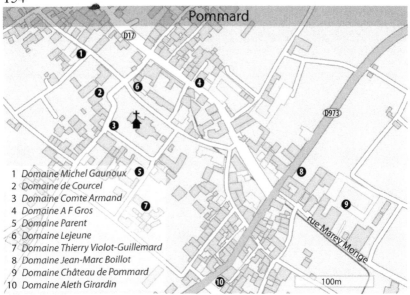

1 Domaine Michel Gaunoux ❺
2 Domaine de Courcel
3 Domaine Comte Armand
4 Domaine A F Gros
5 Domaine Parent
6 Domaine Lejeune
7 Domaine Thierry Violot-Guillemard
8 Domaine Jean-Marc Boillot
9 Domaine Château de Pommard
10 Domaine Aleth Girardin

Profiles of Leading Estates

Domaine Jean-Marc Boillot ★★

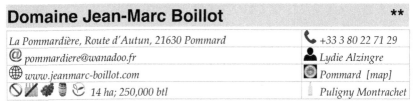

La Pommardière, Route d'Autun, 21630 Pommard	📞 +33 3 80 22 71 29
@ pommardiere@wanadoo.fr	👤 Lydie Alzingre
🌐 www.jeanmarc-boillot.com	Pommard [map]
🚫 🔪 🍇 🛢 ❄ 14 ha; 250,000 btl	Puligny Montrachet

This domain started with a family division. Jean-Marc Boillot had made 13 vintages at the family domain, when he left in 1984 after a disagreement with his father, Jean Boillot, because he was unable to make the sort of wines he wanted. After four years as winemaker at Olivier Leflaive, while also making his own wine from a couple of rented hectares, he became independent.

He now has half the vineyards from his paternal grandfather, Henri Boillot, plus some vineyards from his maternal grandfather, who was Etienne Sauzet. The domain is run from his grandfather's house in Pommard. Holdings are split more or less equally between Puligny Montrachet (including four premier crus and some Bâtard Montrachet) and reds from Pommard, Beaune, and Volnay. The style is undeniably rich and powerful (and interestingly has been so successful that the family domain, now called Henri Boillot after Jean-Marc's brother, subsequently moved in the same direction). Whites see 25-30% new oak, reds get 50% new oak.

For me, the style comes off better in whites than reds, where sheer power can overwhelm the delicacy of an appellation such as Volnay. The Pulignys tend to be powerful rather than mineral. Whether red or white, this is very much a domain in the modern idiom. In 1998 Jean-Marc extended his activities into the Languedoc, where he produces IGP d'Oc wines under the labels of Domaine de la Truffière and Les Roques.

Domaine Comte Armand ***

Place De L'Église, 21630 Pommard	📞 +33 3 80 24 70 50
@ epeneaux@domaine-comte-armand.com	🧑 Paul Zinetti
🌐 www.domaine-comte-armand.com	🔘 Pommard [map]
🛢🗑🍇⭕ 10 ha; 40,000 btl	🍷 Pommard, Clos des Epeneaux

One of the key domains in Pommard, Comte Armand carries as a subtitle, Le Domaine des Epeneaux, reflecting its holding of the monopole of Clos des Epeneaux, one of the best premier crus in Pommard. The same family has owned the domain since before the Revolution; the present Comte Armand is a lawyer in Paris.

The domain was devoted exclusively to Pommard until it expanded in 1994 by purchasing vineyards in Volnay and Auxey-Duresses. The wines increased in elegance under winemaker Benjamin Leroux, who took over winemaking in 1999 (when he was 23), and stayed until 2014, when he left to make his own wine as a micro-negociant. Paul Zinetti took over, but says, "The only thing that changed is me, we want continuity."

The top wine here is always the Clos des Epeneaux, which expresses the generosity of Pommard. In fact, the wine is a blend: "The magic of the clos is that you can do an assemblage from four different areas," Paul says. The quarters are divided by location (upper versus lower) and age of vines (35- to 90-years). Each part is vinified separately, and assemblage occurs at the end of élevage. Typically all the lots go into the final blend, but occasionally one is declassified. Tasting barrel samples shows that each brings its own character: the youngest vines give wine that is tight and fresh, the plot of 55-year old vines in the lower part gives more aromatics, turning from red to black fruits, 65-70-year old vines on the calcareous terroir at the top give more aromatic lift with an impression of elegance as well as power, and this sample is perhaps the most complete in itself, while the oldest vines, from the lowest part, give less aromatics but more structure. Tasting the blend, assembled from samples half way through élevage in a beaker, shows that greater complexity, with black fruit aromatics balancing chocolaty tannins.

When lots are declassified, there may be a Pommard Premier Cru tout court, which shows a flatter profile than the Clos des Epeneaux. Outside Pommard, the Volnay is fine, and Volnay Fremiets is more elegant compared to the village wine. The red Auxey-Duresses is an unusual example of a wine from that appellation with real character along the lines of Pommard, but less elegant, with its concentration partly explained by the old age (35-60-years) of the vines. The Auxey-Duresses premier cru (a blend of two premier crus) is powerful and ripe. New oak varies from 10% for Auxey-Duresses to 25% for the Volnay and Pommard premier crus. The domain is at the top of its game.

Domaine de Courcel ***

29 place de l'Eglise 21630 Pommard	📞 +33 3 80 22 10 64
@ courcel@domaine-de-courcel.com	🧑 Yves Confuron
🌐 www.domainedecourcel-pommard.fr	🔘 Pommard [map]
🛢🗑🍇🍾 11 ha; 30,000 btl	🍷 Pommard, Epenots

"The wines are the equivalent on the Côte de Beaune of Domaine de la Romanée Conti on the Côte de Nuits," according to eminent French wine critics Bettane and Desseauve. The distinctive approach to winemaking was introduced by Yves Confuron, who has been the winemaker since 1996. "Yves developed a method—well his father was involved at the domain in Vosne Romanée—for carbonic maceration à la froide. We believe it is a wonderful method to extract everything from the grapes," explains Alain Bommelaer, whose wife Anne is one of four siblings who are the present owners of the estate. It has been in the hands of the Courcel family for 400 years. The domain has a splendid residence in the main square in Pommard, just across from the church; next to it is the winery, with old caves underground.

"The other thing Yves insisted on was to have extremely ripe grapes. People don't do this in general because we are always afraid here of the weather, and we need to harvest before it turns bad. We want to have extremely ripe grapes because is no destemming—well, just a little to get some juice to start with—and you can't do this unless the stems are ripe." Winemaking starts with cold maceration under carbon dioxide for a few days before fermentation is allowed to begin. After fermentation, maceration continues for three weeks under a blanket of carbon dioxide. The wine goes into casks after 4-5 weeks. The main difference between cuvées is the duration of maceration.

"Only old oak is used. We keep the stems, so we don't want any more tannins from the wood," Alain adds. "Most wine is drunk too young, we all know this, this is why we make a point of keeping back some bottles. One of the major mistakes in Burgundy in the late 1980s was to make wines immediately drinkable, supposedly good after three years. This is why we like our method of winemaking, we think it brings out the specificity of terroir."

The domain focuses on Pommard premier crus (although there is also a Bourgogne), and there is a view that some of them justify grand cru status in Courcel's hands. The same powerful style resonates from the Bourgogne, through the Pommard premier crus, to the Grand Clos des Epenots. Even the Bourgogne has a sense of tannic grip to the palate. Pommard Epeneaux, which comes from the oldest vines, planted in 1936, is aromatically complex, with an impression of rich black cherry fruits. Rugiens is a real vin de garde with less immediate fruits and greater sense of structure. Grand Clos des Epenots is not a wine for the fainthearted, with a powerful structure that takes time to resolve to allow flavor variety to show. These are wines for the ages.

Profiles of Important Estates

Domaine Michel Gaunoux

Rue Notre Dame, 21630 Pommard	📞 +33 3 80 22 18 52
📠 +33 3 80 22 74 30	👤 Alexandre Gaunoux
📅 🍇 🚜 7 ha; 40,000 btl	🌐 Pommard [map]

The estate was founded by Alexandre Gaunoux in 1885, Michel Gaunoux joined in 1957, the domain took his name after it was split following Henri's death in 1972, and Madame Gaunoux ran it after he died young in 1984, until his children Alexandre and Anne were able to take over in 1990. Pommard is the heart of the domain, with premier crus Rugiens-bas and Grand Epenots, and a premier cru cuvée blended from Les Arvelets, Combes, and Charmots. Various plots in Beaune, including some premier cru, go into the single red cuvée from Beaune. The domain is often described as traditional, but this is misleading because grapes are destemmed and new oak is only 15-20%. The domain is known for holding back some production so as to be able to offer old vintages. Tastings are unusual here, because the domain does not believe in tasting from barrique, and allows only bottled wines to be sampled.

Domaine Aleth Girardin

21 Route d'Autun, 21630 Pommard	📞 *+33 3 80 22 59 69*
@ *alethgirardin@orange.fr*	👤 *Aleth Le Royer*
🌐 *www.alethgirardin-pommard.com*	🗺 *Pommard [map]*
🗓 🐝 🚜	*7 ha; 30,000 btl*

The domain was called Armand Girardin until his daughter Aleth Le Royer took over in 1995. She had planned to be a lawyer, but did not like it, and returned to the family domain in 1978. The only change in style is that Armand did not destem, but Aleth destems completely. She also uses cold maceration before fermentation. Most of the vineyards are in Pommard: there are five premier crus, with Rugiens-bas, where the vines date from 1906, the flagship of the domain. The average age of other parcels is 65 years. Vinification and aging are identical for all cuvées, in order to showcase terroir; new oak is usually one third.

Domaine A. F Gros

1 place de l'Europe, 21630 Pommard	📞 *+33 3 80 22 61 85*
@ *contact@af-gros.com*	👤 *Caroline Parent-Gros*
🌐 *www.af-gros.com*	🗺 *Pommard [map]*
🗓 🏭 🐝 🛢 🚜	*14 ha; 80,000 btl*

This is one of the many Gros estates, although located in Pommard, whereas the others are in Vosne Romanée. Anne-Françoise is one of three siblings who inherited the Jean Gros estate. She married winemaker François Parent, whose sisters run Domaine Parent (see profile) in Pommard; Anne-Françoise and François combined their vineyards to form Domaine A. F. Gros (not to be confused with domaine Anne Gros in Vosne Romanée). Now their son Mathias Parent has taken over, together with his sister Caroline. Coming from both sides of the family, there are plots in Pommard, Savigny-lès-Beaune, Chambolle Musigny, and Flagey-Echézeaux. Winemaking starts with destemming, there is cold maceration for 4-5 days, followed by cuvaison in stainless steel for 2-3 weeks, with both punch-down and pump-over. The wine ages for 12 months, with 40% new oak for village wines, 66% for premier cru, and 100% for grand cru. There is also a negociant activity, with wines labeled as Maison Parent-Gros.

Domaine Lejeune

1 Place De L'Église, La Confrèrie, 21630 Pommard	📞 *+33 3 80 22 90 88*
@ *commercial@domaine-lejeune.fr*	👤 *Aubert Lefas*
🌐 *www.domaine-lejeune.fr*	🗺 *Pommard [map]*
🧍 🏭 🐝 🛢	*10 ha; 50,000 btl*

The domain is located in the village square in Pommard. François Jullien de Pommerol, Professor of Oenology in Beaune, introduced estate bottling in 1977 after he inherited this family estate, which had been passed from aunts to nieces for several generations. His son-in-law, Aubert Lefas, has been in charge since 2005. Aside from some Bourgogne, the wines are all red and come from Pommard, with three premier crus. There is no destemming, and there is a small amount of carbonic maceration to start off fermentation. New oak is 25-35%, except for Rugiens and Grands Epenots at 50%.

Domaine Parent

3, rue de la Métairie, 21630 Pommard	📞 *+33 3 80 22 15 08*
@ *contact@domaine-parent.com*	👤 *Anne Parent*

158

🌐 www.domaine-parent.com	🅞 Pommard [map]
🗄 ⛏ 🍇 🍂	10 ha; 78,000 btl

Located right in the center of Pommard, opposite the church, the domain was founded in 1803, although the family had already been making wine for a couple of centuries. Jacques Parent handed over to his daughters Anne (winemaker) and Catherine (sales) in 1998; their brother François married Anne-Françoise Gros and went to make wine at A. F. Gros (see profile). All plantings are Pinot Noir. Plots are mostly in Pommard, with some also in Beaune and Corton. Bourgogne is produced under a negociant license as well as from their own plots. Winemaking starts with 3-5 days cold maceration, cuvaison lasts 16-18 days, and then Bourgogne ages with no new oak, village wines age in 30% new oak, premier crus in 40% new oak, and Corton grand cru in 50% new oak.

Château de Pommard

15, Rue Marey Monge, 21630 Pommard	📞 +33 3 80 22 07 99
@ concierge@chateaudepommard.com	👤 Concierges du Château de Pommard
🌐 www.chateaudepommard.com	🅞 Pommard [map]
🚶 ⛏ 🍇 🛢 🗒	20 ha; 80,000 btl

This large estate—the largest monopole in Burgundy—had somewhat lost its luster by the time it was sold to Silicon Valley entrepreneur Michael Baum in 2014. The monopole is Clos Marey-Mange, a 20 ha plot surrounded by a 2km wall. This produced only a single cuvée, labeled Clos Marey-Mange, until the Cuvée Simone, from an 0.5 ha plot of very dense clay, was bottled separately in 2010. It represents one of seven distinct terroirs within the clos. The château is into oenotourism, with a wine school, tours and tastings, and a gift shop. It's a serious endeavor: "One of the biggest mistakes we made was making the experiences too short and inexpensive, which attracted people who weren't serious about wine," Michael says. Now it's the base of a wine-education enterprise that includes events elsewhere. Under the name of Famille Carabello-Baum there is also a range of negociant wines from both the Côte de Beaune and Côte de Nuits.

Domaine Thierry Violot-Guillemard

7-9 rue Sainte Marguerite, 21630 Pommard	📞 +33 3 80 22 49 98
@ contact@violot-guillemard.fr	👤 Thierry, Estelle & Joannès Violot-Guillemard
🌐 www.violot-guillemard.fr	🅞 Pommard [map]
🗄 ⛏ 🗒 🍇 🍂	8 ha; 36,000 btl

There are two Violot-Guillemard domains in Pommard: Thierry and Christophe. Thierry, who is the fifth generation here, has been in charge of his domain with his wife Estelle since 1980. His son Johannès is now taking over. Plots are predominantly in Pommard, with some small holdings in Beaune, Volnay, and Meursault. Most of the vines are quite old, around 60 years. The top holdings are in premier crus Pommard Epenots, Rugiens, Platière, and Derrière Saint-Jean, and Beaune Clos des Mouches. In recent vintages, when yields have been reduced by frost, some grapes have been bought from neighbors to make Pommard Arvelets and Volnay Santenots. Starting with Bourgogne, one unusual cuvée is the Pinot Beurrot (an old name for Pinot Gris). The reds typically have a short pre-fermentation cold maceration, followed by cuvaison lasting 10 days, and then age in barriques with 50% new oak for 14-18 months. Whites usually age for 11 months before release.

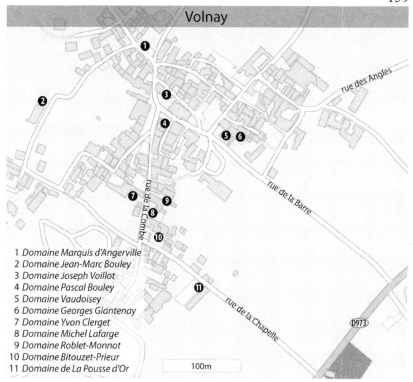

1 Domaine Marquis d'Angerville
2 Domaine Jean-Marc Bouley
3 Domaine Joseph Voillot
4 Domaine Pascal Bouley
5 Domaine Vaudoisey
6 Domaine Georges Glantenay
7 Domaine Yvon Clerget
8 Domaine Michel Lafarge
9 Domaine Roblet-Monnot
10 Domaine Bitouzet-Prieur
11 Domaine de La Pousse d'Or

100m

Profiles of Leading Estates

Domaine Marquis d'Angerville ★★

Rue De Mont, 21190 Volnay	📞 *+33 3 80 21 61 75*
@ *info@domainedangerville.fr*	👤 *Mathilde Reboux*
🌐 *www.domainedangerville.fr*	🔲 *Volnay [map]*
🗑🎋🍇⬭ *15 ha; 55,000 btl*	🍴 *Volnay, Les Caillerets*

The domain takes its name from the Marquis d'Angerville, who inherited the estate in 1906, but its origins go back at least a century earlier. The Marquis was involved in re-establishing the estate as a leading producer of Pinot Noir after the ravages of phylloxera, and during the 1930s became one of the leaders of the grower movement against the large negociants who dominated Burgundy at the time, initiating the move to estate bottling.

After 1952, his son Jacques d'Angerville built up the estate's reputation for the sheer precision and elegance of its wines. It's a measure of the commitment to Pinot Noir that a low-yielding, small-berried clone developed from their vineyards is now known as the d'Angerville clone. Jacques was succeeded in 2003 by Guillaume d'Angerville, who had been working at Chase Manhattan Bank.

160

Most of the holdings are in Volnay, with a roll call of premier crus, headed by the monopole Clos des Ducs, adjacent to the domain, which occupies a splendid nineteenth century maison, just behind the church in Volnay. Other top holdings include Caillerets and Taillepieds. The wines always had a wonderful taut precision under Jacques d'Angerville, but seem since then to have become broader and less focused. One change in winemaking has been the introduction of a small proportion (up to 20%) of new oak. Guillaume has expanded his operations by purchasing two estates in the Jura in 2012, followed by another in 2014: wines are labeled as the Domaine du Pélican.

Domaine Michel Lafarge ✱

Rue de La Combe, 21190 Volnay	📞 +33 3 80 21 61 61
@ contact@domainelafarge.com	👤 Frédéric Lafarge
🌐 www.domainelafarge.fr	📍 Volnay [map]
📅 🔪 🍇 🛢 🍷	🍾 Volnay, Vendanges Sélectionnées
12 ha; 55,000 btl	Beaune, Les Aigrots

This is one of the most distinctive domains in Volnay. The Lafarge's have been making wine since the nineteenth century, and started estate bottling in the 1930s. The winery is at an unassuming address in a back street of town, and the rambling cellars underneath are ancient. Vineyards are in 38 separate parcels, divided roughly into a third each of Bourgogne, village wines, and premier crus. In addition to Volnay and its premier crus, which are the heart of the domain, there are holdings in Beaune (white as well as red), Meursault, and Pommard. More recently, the Lafarge's have expanded into Beaujolais with the creation of Domaine Lafarge-Vial.

The style here is traditional in making no concessions to the current trend for immediate gratification: vertical tasting shows that these wines need time, as you dig back far enough for the sheer purity of the fruits to be able to shine though. The wines are taut, precise, and elegant when they come around. Although keeping up with the latest thinking in converting to biodynamics, Frédéric Lafarge points out that this is in line with their care for the soil and the vines. "We did not fall for the fad of clonal fashions or the heavy fertilization in the 1960s," he says, "and part of the reason for our quality is that the plants are obtained by selection massale in which each generation has continued the match of terroir and cépage."

All the reds age for 12 months in barriques; new oak reaches 20% for the premier crus. Even the Bourgogne Passetoutgrains, a 50:50 blend of Pinot Noir and Gamay coplanted in a 90-year old vineyard, shows the tight house style, with red fruits behind acerbic tannins. Volnay village wine shows tight cherry fruits with hints of tobacco-like tannins on the finish when young, Beaune Les Aigrots is softer and rounder, but you have to go to the monopole Clos du Château des Ducs from Volnay to get a silky sheen in a young wine. The Lafarge Volnays can typify the crystalline purity of the appellation, but I would not try to drink any except the very lightest vintages within the first decade. The style of the whites is as lean as the reds.

Domaine Hubert de Montille ✱✱

Rue Pied de la Vallée, 21190 Volnay	📞 +33 3 80 21 39 14
@ contact@demontille.com	👤 Etienne de Montille

⊕ *www.demontille.com*	🌑 *Volnay [map]*
📅 🏭 🍇 🛢 🗍 *37 ha; 200,000 btl*	⚑ *Volnay, Taillepieds*

The great reputation of this old domain started after Hubert de Montille took over in 1947, when it had been reduced to 3 ha in Volnay. A lawyer by profession, he continued to practice law as well as to run the domain. His son Etienne joined in 1983, took over the cellars in 1990, and has been in charge since 1995. The domain has expanded all over the Côte d'Or, and has three quarters of its holdings in premier and grand crus, mostly red. De Montille took over the Château de Puligny Montrachet, which had been languishing, and since 2017 its wines have been labeled as Domaine de Montille.

There's been a softening of style with the change of generations. "Hubert's winemaking style was highly extracted and more austere," says winemaker Brian Sieve, who makes the wines for the domain and also for its negociant activity. Initially called Deux Montille, the negociant was created to complement the domain by producing white wines, extending from the Côte de Beaune into extended into Côte Chalonnaise and Chablis. It was run by Etienne's sister, Alix (who is married to Jean-Marc Roulot, another famous white winemaker). Alix stopped making wine in 2014, and the name of the negociant changed to Maison de Montille.

Wines for both domain and negociant have been made in a single spacious facility in Meursault since 2005 (previously the domain was vinified in Volnay and the negociant in Beaune). "There are no style differences between the negociant and the domain: everything is handled in exactly the same way," Brian explains. There's extensive use of whole clusters for reds; new oak varies from 20-50%, and is usually higher for the Côte de Nuits. The domain is known for the purity of its wines, and the style is precise and elegant, showing textbook illustrations of differences due to terroir.

Domaine de La Pousse d'Or   *

Rue De La Chapelle, 21190 Volnay	📞 *+33 3 80 21 61 33*
@ *marleen@lapoussedor.fr*	👤 *Benoît Landanger or Marleen Nicot*
⊕ *lapoussedor.fr*	🌑 *Volnay [map]*
🚫 ✏ 🍇 🗍 *18 ha; 90,000 btl*	⚑ *Volnay, Clos de la Bousse d'Or*

I remember the wines of Pousse d'Or from the early nineties as among the most elegant in Volnay, with an indefinably delicate expression of Pinot Noir. Then with Gérard Potel's death in 1997 the domain somewhat fell out of view. Patrick Landanger, who had been an engineer and inventor, bought the domain. He started by employing a general manager, but "he was told that if he wanted to regain confidence he would need to make the wine himself. So he went to oenology school... The first vintage he made was 1999, which was well received," explains commercial manager Marleen Nicot.

There's been major investment in a new building that houses a gravity-feed winery, with three levels built into the side of the hill. Patrick is still inventing, as seen in a new glass device that has replaced bungs in barrels (so topping up is required less often).

Production is focused on red wine. The heart of the domain remains the premier crus from Volnay, but Patrick has expanded, first by purchasing two vineyards in Corton, and then by adding a village wine and four premier crus in Chambolle Musigny. The only white comes from Puligny Caillerets; it is less interesting than the reds. For all the premier crus there is one third new oak, one third one-year, and one third two-year; grand Crus have 40-45% new oak. Larger barrels (350 liter) are used for the white wine. The wines from Volnay give a precise yet intense expression; the Chambolles seem a little rounder and more feminine.

Profiles of Important Estates

Domaine Bitouzet-Prieur

19, Rue De La Combe, 21190 Volnay	📞 *+33 3 80 21 62 13*
@ *francois@bitouzet-prieur.com*	👤 *Vincent & François Bitouzet*
🌐 *www.bitouzet-prieur.com*	🛢 *Volnay [map]*
🗓 📊 🍇 🔥	*13 ha; 55,000 btl*

The hyphenated name reflects the union of the Prieurs of Meursault and the Bitouzets of Volnay. Vincent Bitouzet can trace his family in Volnay back to 1804—the domain was founded in 1860—and his wife, Annie Prieur comes from a long established family of growers in Meursault. The domain is accordingly split between its major holdings in Volnay and Meursault (which accounts for about a third of the total). Their son François joined the domain in 2005. Reds are produced in the rue de la Combe in Volnay, a couple of doors along the street from Michel Lafarge; whites are produced in Meursault. Holdings in Volnay include 2 ha of village plots, and premier crus Les Aussy, Taillepieds, Clos des Chênes, Pitures, Caillerets, and Mitans. In Meursault there are plots in two well-known lieu-dits, Les Corbins and Clos du Cromin, and the three premier crus Charmes, Perrières, and Santenots. Whites age for 15-18 months. Reds are completely destemmed, and then ferment at relatively high temperature, with cuvaison lasting 2 weeks, and punch-down twice a day. Use of new oak is moderate, usually up to 20%. There are also cuvées of Beaune premier Cru and Puligny Montrachet, as well as Bourgogne.

Domaine Jean-Marc Bouley

Chemin De La Cave, 21190 Volnay	📞 *+33 3 80 21 62 33*
@ *domaine@jean-marc-bouley.com*	👤 *Thomas Bouley*
🌐 *www.jean-marc-bouley.com*	🛢 *Volnay [map]*
🗓 📊 🍇 🍂	*9 ha; 35,000 btl*

The name of the domain has officially been changed to Jean-Marc & Thomas Bouley to reflect the fact that Thomas joined the domain in 2002 and has been in charge since 2012. There has been a Bouley family estate in Volnay for several generations; this domain was created when Jean-Marc founded his own domain in 1974 with 2.5 ha of rented vineyards; ten years later he inherited the family vineyards. Wines are red, from Volnay, Pommard, and Beaune, except for a Bourgogne Aligoté. There is usually no destemming. Bourgogne sees only old barriques, village wines get 30% new oak, and premier crus 30-50%, with 18-20 months aging.

Domaine Pascal Bouley

Place De L'Église, 21190 Volnay	📞 *+33 3 80 21 61 69*
@ *bouleypascal@wanadoo.fr*	👤 *Pierrick Bouley*
🌐 *www.pascalbouley.com*	🛢 *Volnay [map]*
🚶 📊 🍇 🚜	*10 ha; 30,000 btl*

Pierrick Bouley is the sixth generation at this family estate; he joined the domain in 2005, and took over from his parents, Pascal and Réyanne, in 2016. The cellars are in the center of the village of Volnay. The wines may be labeled either as Réyanne & Pascal Bouley (in France) or

163

as Pierrick Bouley (exports). The focus is on Volnay, with some plots also in Pommard, Monthélie, and Saint Romain; there's also an Aloxe-Corton. The only white is Morgeot from Chassagne Montrachet. There are 3.5 ha in village Volnay and five premier crus (all the premier crus are from plots less than a third of a hectare). All grapes are destemmed. The village Monthélie has now new oak, other village wines have around 10%, and premier crus have up to 25%. Use of SO2 is light. Pierrick is regarded as a rising star, and the style tends to elegance, even a touch of austerity, rather than power.

Domaine Yvon Clerget

12 Rue de La Combe, 21190 Volnay	📞 +33 3 80 21 61 56
@ thibaud@domaine-clerget.com	👤 Thibaud Clerget
🌐 www.domaine-clerget.com	🔘 Volnay [map]
📆 🏭 🍇 🥄	6 ha; 22,000 btl

This is effectively a new domain, although the Clergets have been making wine here since the thirteenth century. Under Yvon Clerget the wines were workmanlike but not very interesting. There was an inter-regnum after Yvon retired in 2009, and grapes were sold off until his son Thibaud was ready to take over the domain in 2015. Vineyards include four premier crus in Volnay, Rugiens in Pommard, one of Beaune, and Clos Vougeot. The only white comes from a small plot in Meursault. Fort reds, grapes are destemmed and wine ages for 18 months. There are high expectations for success.

Domaine Georges Glantenay et fils

3 rue de la Barre, 21190 Volnay	📞 +33 3 80 21 61 82
@ contact@domaineglantenay.com	👤 Sarah Glantenay
🌐 www.domaineglantenay.com	🔘 Volnay [map]
🏃 🏭 🍇 ☕	8 ha; 36,000 btl

There are two Glantenay domains in Volnay: Georges Glantenay and Bernard & Thierry Glantenay. Domaine Georges Glantenay was founded in 1893, and brother Guillaume (winemaker) and sister Sarah (sales) are the fourth generation. The cellars were completely renovated in 2014. Vineyards are in the immediate area in Volnay, Pommard, Monthélie, and Meursault and there is also a holding in Chambolle Musigny. The range starts with Bourgogne (Aligoté, Chardonnay, and Pinot Noir) and Crémant de Bourgogne. The village wines from Volnay, Pommard, and Chambolle Musigny have 7 days cold maceration before fermentation, with cuvaison then lasting 21 days, followed by aging in barriques with 20% new oak. The wines are racked from barrel to barrel to allow some oxygen exposure. The only village white is a Meursault, which ages in 40% new barriques. There are three premier crus in Volnay, which have similar vinification to the village reds, except that cuvaison lasts for 30 days, and new oak is 35-40%. Village wines are just over a third of production; Bourgogne and premier crus are each a little less.

Domaine Roblet-Monnot

11 Rue La Combe, 21190 Volnay (tastings)	📞 +33 3 80 21 22 47
52 Grande Rue de Curtil, 21200 Bligny-lès-Beaune (cellars)	
@ robletmonnot@yahoo.fr	👤 Pascal Roblet
📆 🏭 🍇 🔘 9 ha	🔘 Volnay [map]

The domain was created in 1865 by Pascal Roblet's maternal great grandfather. He can trace the family in Volnay back to the seventeenth century on his mother's side, and four generations on his father's side. This was Domaine Monnot until Pascal took over in 1990 and renamed it as Roblet-Monnot. The major part of the domain is 6 ha in Volnay; the rest is in Pommard, Meursault, and Hautes Côtes. Pascal has been replanting the domain gradually at the very high density of 12,000 vines/ha. All grapes (except for Volnay Pitures) are destemmed, and there is cold soak for 2-3 days before fermentation, which takes place in open-topped tanks (mostly stainless steel). The Bourgogne Rouge ages for 18 months in 2-4-year barriques and 300-liter barrels, and there is also a Vieilles Vignes cuvée, vinified the same way. Volnay St. François is not just a village wine as it includes lots from premier crus Robardelle and Mitans (and sometimes Pitures). The premier cru cuvées are Santenots (actually the vineyard is across the border in Meursault), Volnay Brouillards, Volnay Taillepieds, and Pommard Arvelets. They age for 18-24 months in barriques with up to 30% new oak. The winery has moved across the N74 but the wines can be tasted in the village.

Nicolas Rossignol

22, rue Jean François Champollion, 21200 Beaune	📞 *+33 3 80 24 35 62*
@ *contact@nicolas-rossignol.com*	👤 *Nicolas Rossignol*
🌐 *nicolas-rossignol.com*	◉ *Volnay*
📅 ⚒ 🍇 ℮	*20 ha; 110,000 btl*

The fifth generation in his family to make wine, Nicolas Rossignol started by making wine at the family estate, Rossignol-Jeannie, in Volnay. He created his own estate, starting with 3 ha in Volnay, and has been expanding it ever since; there are presently more than 30 cuvées. In 2011 he moved from Volnay to a new winery just south of Beaune, and combined the family domain with his own venture, making all the wines under his own name. The wines have become finer, and Nicolas describes the change made possibly by the new winery as "moving from extraction to infusion." The wines are almost all red, including seven Volnay premier crus and eight Pommard premier crus. He usually sells the small amount of white he produces to a negociant. "Bourgogne or Aligoté is not so interesting and I don't have that much of a feeling for white wine." The Bourgogne Rouge is a bit of a throwback as it comes from vines planted in 1922 by his grandfather; he treats it in the same way as the premier crus. Winemaking varies quite a bit with the vintage, using punch-down or pump-over, new oak varying up to 50%, and aging from 10-20 months.

Domaine Christophe & Pierre Vaudoisey

Place de l' Église, 21190 Volnay	📞 *+33 3 80 21 20 14*
@ *christophe.vaudoisey@wanadoo.fr*	👤 *Laurence Vaudoisey*
🌐 *www.domainechristophevaudoisey.com*	◉ *Volnay [map]*
📅 ⚒ 🍇 ℮	*10 ha; 30,000 btl*

The domain dates from 1804, and Christophe Vaudoisey and his wife Laurence took over in 1985. They restored the family house in the center of the village, constructed a new cuverie, and created a tasting room. Their son Pierre's name was added to the domain when he joined. Black grapes are destemmed and go into stainless steel for 10 days of fermentation, followed by élevage of 16-18 months with up to 30% new barriques. Reds include Monthélie, Volnay, with four premier crus (Clos des Chênes, Caillerets, Mitans, and Ronceret), and Pommard with two premier crus (Chanlins and Clos Micault). The white is a Meursault from lieu-dit Vireuls, and ages for 12 months. There are also Bourgogne (Aligoté, Chardonnay, and Pinot Noir).

Domaine Joseph Voillot

Place de l'Église, 21190 Volnay	📞 *+33 3 80 21 62 27*
@ *joseph.voillot@wanadoo.fr*	👤 *Etienne Chaix*
🌐 *www.joseph-voillot.com*	◉ *Volnay [map]*
📅 ⚒ 🍇 ℮	*8 ha; 35,000 btl*

Split between Volnay and Pommard, the domain was run from 1995 by Jean-Pierre Charlot, formerly a professor in Beaune, and son-in-law of Joseph Voillot. When he retired, his nephew Etienne Chaix (Joseph's grandson) took over. Production is almost entirely red, much of it from premier crus (four in Volnay and four in Pommard). Holdings are divided into 35 plots, with the largest being 1 ha of Volnay Champans. Most of the vines are old, ranging from 30- to 60-years old. "We work very traditionally, all our vineyards are worked the same way, vinification is the same for all cuvées, we want to show the differences in the vineyards," says cellarmaster Etienne Chaix. "We are interested in freshness and fruit, we don't want to mask them with oak, so we use only 10-15% new oak for the premier crus." The style is traditional in the sense that the wines can be tight and linear when young. Bourgogne Pinot Noir is the lightest, Volnay is a little earthier, and Pommard has more weight and structure. In premier crus, Beaune Aux Coucherais has classic tightness, Volnay Fremiets has more sense of fruits, with some elegance, Champans has more presence with a light sheen on the palate, Pommard Clos Micault actually displays an elegance more resembling Volnay, and Pommard Pèzerolles and Rugiens show more the classic firmness of Pommard and mature in an earthy direction. Two whites from Meursault, lieu-dit Chevalières, and premier cru Les Cras, are upright with increasing sense of salinity.

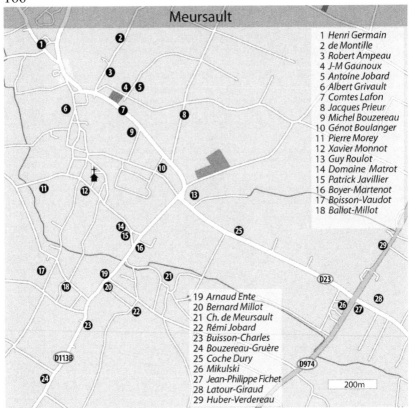

Meursault

1 Henri Germain
2 de Montille
3 Robert Ampeau
4 J-M Gaunoux
5 Antoine Jobard
6 Albert Grivault
7 Comtes Lafon
8 Jacques Prieur
9 Michel Bouzereau
10 Génot Boulanger
11 Pierre Morey
12 Xavier Monnot
13 Guy Roulot
14 Domaine Matrot
15 Patrick Javillier
16 Boyer-Martenot
17 Boisson-Vaudot
18 Ballot-Millot

19 Arnaud Ente
20 Bernard Millot
21 Ch. de Meursault
22 Rémi Jobard
23 Buisson-Charles
24 Bouzereau-Gruère
25 Coche Dury
26 Mikulski
27 Jean-Philippe Fichet
28 Latour-Giraud
29 Huber-Verdereau

200m

Profiles of Leading Estates

Domaine Robert Ampeau et Fils ★★

6, Rue Du Cromin, 21190 Meursault	📞 +33 3 80 21 20 35
@ michel.ampeau@wanadoo.fr	👤 Michel Ampeau
	🗺 Meursault [map]
🏭🍾🚜🚜	🍷 Blagny, La Pièce Sous le Bois
10 ha; 50,000 btl	🍾 Meursault, Les Charmes

Robert Ampeau marches to the beat of a different drum: the concept of the current release has no meaning here. The imperatives of winemaking, or to be more precise, of commercializing the wines, are, to say the least, unusual. Wines are released when they are ready, or perhaps more to the point, when the domain feels like selling them. Both reds and whites from the mid 1990s are on sale now, giving consumers the opportunity to start with mature wines. Tastings start where others leave off: on my most recent visit, we tasted wines from 2002 to 1976. Production is 60% red and 40% white. Since Robert's death in 2004, Michel Ampeau has been making the wines.

There are holdings in ten premier crus, including four in Meursault. The wines are meant to age, and have reached an interesting stage of maturity when released. Since current releases haven't really reached the era of premox, it's impossible to say if that will be a problem for the whites, but typically they peak around fifteen years of age and hold until twenty. I suspect that the traditional style of winemaking in an oxidative manner will avert any problem.

The style of the whites is rich and full, although Michel says he is an early picker. Meursault shows a classically nutty flavor spectrum, Meursault La Pièce Sous le Bois adds hints of honey and spices, and the Charmes premier cru adds a subtle hint of minerality. The complexity of Meursault Perrières shows why it is a candidate for promotion to grand cru, with seamless layers of flavor. This is the epitome of the classic style of Meursault. Puligny Combettes is a textbook example of purity and precision. The general style of the whites shows an intriguing combination of minerality and development.

The reds combine a sheen to the palate that masks the fruit density, with the structure of supple tannins in the background. A sense of liveliness gives an impression of being a decade younger than the real age. Savigny-lès-Beaune and La Pièce Sous le Bois from Blagny age much longer than you might expect for those appellations, in the general soft, earthy style of the house. Auxey-les-Duresses Les Ecussaux adds faintly herbal notes. Beaune Clos du Roi shows a smooth opulence, Pommard is broader but still sophisticated, while the Volnay Les Santenots premier cru tends to earthiness. Reds age easily for 30 years.

Wines from the great appellations show great typicity and ageability, but the surprise and the bargain are the wines from lesser appellations: and the domain is also remarkable for its ability to produce high quality in lesser years; vintages such as 1994 or 1997 show well more than 20 years later.

Domaine Michel Bouzereau et Fils   ★★

5 Rue Robert Thénard, 21190 Meursault	📞 +33 3 80 21 20 74
@ *michel-bouzereau-et-fils@wanadoo.fr*	👤 *Jean-Baptiste Bouzereau*
🌐 *www.michelbouzereauetfils.com*	📷 *Meursault [map]*
📅 🏭 🍇 🍷 12 ha; 65,000 btl	*Meursault, Les Tessons*

French inheritance laws explain why there are so many Bouzereau domains in Meursault. "Bouzereau has been important in Meursault for seven generations, although it's only four generations we've been concerned exclusively with viticulture. In my grandfather's time we had four domains, now we have five domains with the name Bouzereau. I have my grandfather's domain, but the vines have been shared at each generation, of course, so we have all the appellations," says Jean-Baptiste Bouzereau.

Domaine Michel Bouzereau has 14 appellations, 11 in white and 4 in red. A splendid modern underground cave was constructed in 2008. Jean-Baptiste says, "I look for elegance and finesse, and to harvest mature but not too mature to keep freshness." There is 15-30% new wood, with higher levels used for premier crus. The whites are Meursault and Puligny, the reds are Volnay, Pommard, and Bourgogne. The three lieu-dits from Meursault show a range from the breadth of Tessons to the tension of Limousin (which is just next to Puligny). The three Meursault premier crus show greater breadth, with complexity increasing from Charmes and Genevrières to Perrières, the last two along the lines of what a Meursault grand cru might offer if one existed. The Puligny premier crus, Champs Gain and Caillerets, are more tightly wound. What you see here across the whole range is how purity of the fruits highlights the characters of the individual terroirs.

Domaine Jean-François Coche Dury   ★★★★

9 rue de Charles Giraud, 21190 Meursault	📞 *+33 3 80 21 24 12*
📠 *+33 3 80 21 67 65*	🧑 *Rafaël Coche*
	🔘 *Meursault [map]*
◎ 🗡 🍃 ☙	🍾 *Auxey Duresses*
10 ha; 45,000 btl	*Meursault*

One of the great names of white Burgundy, Coche Dury is difficult to taste in depth, partly because quantities are so small, partly because Jean-François Coche verged on reclusive. Jean-François retired officially in 2010, with his son Raphaël taking over. This remains a hands-on operation; Raphaël turned up for our tasting on his tractor direct from the vineyards. The house on the road through Meursault is surrounded by vines; you can see the church a couple of hundred yards away. Round the back is a second building that has just been extended.

Raphaël is the fourth generation. "My great grandfather worked at a domain in Meursault and started to make his own wines after returning from the 1914 war. He continued to have a day job and accumulated vineyards. When my father (Jean-François) started in the 1970s, there were many good opportunities to buy vineyards and he expanded the domain—today this would not be possible because vineyards are so expensive. Jean-François started by setting up his own domain, but when my grandfather retired in 1985, his vineyards came to Jean-François." This was when the domain was named Coche-Dury. Vineyards come from the old Coche family holdings plus those brought by Jean-François's marriage to Odile Dury in 1975. About half are in Meursault, with the rest spread around Puligny Montrachet, Auxey-Duresses, Monthelie, and Volnay. Appellation Meursault is the largest holding at just over 4 ha.

The style has not changed since Raphaël took over. "Élevage is always for 18 months; we are not going to change it. After the first winter, the wine is soft, then it takes on the permanent character. The whites are structured, with tannins if you like." 25% new oak is more or less the same for all the village wines, premier cru, and grand cru. There is very little battonage. The style here is steely and intensely mineral, right through the range. Going past the smoke and gunflint, the layered palate offers the richness of the Côte d'Or, with precisely delineated fruits, and evident but beautifully integrated oak. The modest alcohol level contributes to elegance.

The village Meursault shows the style to powerful effect, and it intensifies in the Meursault lieu-dit Chevalier (if you can find it). (Chevalier and Rougeots are the only two lieu-dits identified as such on the label: other lieu-dits within Meursault may be bottled separately, but just labeled as Meursault.) The difference between Meursault and Puligny is clear from the Enseignères lieu-dit from Puligny, which is more linear and precise. By contrast, the Caillerets premier cru from Meursault has more breadth but less precision. Genevrières is more backward and structured. "It always has that tannic impression," Raphaël says. The most powerful of the premier crus, always needing more time, Perrières shows the most penetrating minerality. Corton Charlemagne has the greatest concentration and roundness; "it's the softness of Charlemagne," Raphaël says.

As good as it gets for white Burgundy, Coche Dury whites are always expensive. Under the negociant label of Domaine & Selection, there is a Meursault from the Vireuls lieu-dit produced by Coche Dury, at slightly more reasonable prices. When is the right time to drink the whites? "The minimum is after five years but they are formidable after ten years. For Corton Charlemagne they will be even better at fifteen years," Raphaël says. For the reds everything is destemmed. Bourgogne Rouge comes from two parcels close to the house, Auxey Duresses is charming, and Meursault is more reserved.

Domaine Arnaud Ente   ★★★

12, Rue De Mazeray, 21190 Meursault	📞 +33 3 80 21 66 12
📠 +33 3 80 21 66 12	👤 Arnaud Ente
	🖥 Meursault [map]
📅 🍷 🌿 ☕ 4 ha; 20,000 btl	Meursault

Arnaud Ente is sometimes described as a rising star in Meursault, but as evidenced from the price of his wines, he is now solidly established with something of a cult following. Although there are vineyards in the family, they have been run by other members. Arnaud started working at Coche Dury, then in 1991 began producing wine from vineyards rented from his father in law. Individual vineyard holdings are tiny, with nothing as much as a hectare, and most well under half a hectare. This tiny domain is run by Arnaud, his wife Marie-Odile, and two workers.

Initially the wines were made in an opulent style from grapes picked quite late, but since 2000 a policy of earlier picking has focused more on bringing out minerality (and also results in moderate alcohol). Impressions of gunflint and salinity are reminiscent of Coche Dury, but the palate still has a more opulent sheen.

The affordable wines are Aligoté, Bourgogne Blanc, and Meursault, mostly vinified in demi-muids. The village Meursault comes mostly from the clos of En l'Ormeau, where production is divided into three cuvées: Meursault AOP, Clos des Ambres (old vines), and La Sève du Clos, from very old (around 100 year) vines. There is also some Meursault premier cru Goutte d'Or and a Puligny Les Referts, as well as a little Volnay premier cru. Oak is fairly restrained these days, down to 20% new barriques for the top cuvées compared with 35% in the early years, reflecting the change of focus.

Domaine Henri Germain et fils   ★

2 Bis Rue Du Moulin Judas, 21190 Meursault	📞 +33 3 80 21 22 04
@ domaine.h.germain-et-fils@orange.fr	👤 Jean-François Germain
📅 🍷 🌿 ☕ 8 ha; 30,000 btl	🖥 Meursault [map]
🍷 Meursault, Limozin	🍾 Chassagne Montrachet

"The domain is very recent, started by my parents in 1973 with only 1.5 hectares," says Jean-François Germain. The official address takes you to a courtyard with the bureau on one side, and his parents' house on the other. The winery is 100 yards away, around a corner in the next street. Behind the ordinary looking garage doors is a long courtyard with some old buildings lining one side, and a vineyard at the end. There are very old caves underneath.

Production is three quarters white, with 13 separate cuvées, focusing on Meursault village, lieu-dits, and premier crus. "All whites get the same 20% new oak whether it's Bourgogne or premier cru, and there's no battonage," says Jean-François. The lack of battonage contributes to the impression of elegance in the house style. The Bourgogne comes from vineyards around Meursault and has an unusually fine impression for the level of appellation. The village wine moves in a more citrus direction with some hints of minerality. Coming from mid slope, the lieu-dit Chevalier is more inclined to minerality, and from the bottom of the slope, lieu-dit Limozin is fatter. The premier crus are more complex, moving from the silky elegance of Poruzot, to the more mineral character of Charmes, and the more powerful impression of Perrières. Moving to Chassagne, the Morgeot comes from a single parcel and is quite fat by comparison with Meursault.

The same policy of equal treatment applies to the reds, which get 18 months élevage. Usually everything is destemmed—only an unusually rich vintage will see some stems included. The style is relatively soft, increasing in intensity and roundness from the Bourgogne to the Chassagne to the Meursault lieu-dit Clos des Mouches. Beaune Bressandes is the finest of the reds.

Domaine Albert Grivault ***

7, Place Du Murger, 21190 Meursault	📞 +33 3 80 21 23 12
@ *albert.grivault@wanadoo.fr*	👤 *Claire Bardet*
	🌐 *Meursault [map]*
📅 🥃 🍇 🍷 6 ha; 35,000 btl	*Meursault, Clos du Murger*

The domain occupies a lovely maison, graciously set back from the main street of Meursault. It feels like a residence in the town, but walking out of the back of the house into the courtyard behind, winery buildings are on either side, and the Clos du Murger is immediately behind. The caves date from 1865.

"The domain has the name of my grandfather," explains Michel Bardet. "He bought the Clos des Perrières, which was the most famous vineyard in Meursault at the time, just after phylloxera, and established a domain of 12 ha. Because of difficulties with estate taxes, my mother sold some of the estate to Alexis Lichine and to Bize-Leroy's father. Before I became involved, I was an engineer (at Honeywell Bull). Slowly I phased out as an engineer and came to run the domain together with my sister." Today the domain has the monopole of Clos des Perrières, part of Les Perrières ("we are the largest proprietor"), and a vineyard in the village. There is also a hectare of Clos Blanc in Pommard.

The white wines are Bourgogne, Meursault Clos du Murger, Perrières, and Clos des Perrières). "Clos du Murger is a marque. Because my mother left one part of the Clos du Murger unplanted for thirty years, it lost the right to the Meursault appellation." So today the village Meursault comes from the old vines planted in two thirds of the Clos du Murger, and the other third (planted in 2001) is used for the Bourgogne Blanc (but an application has been made to restore it to Meursault AOP). The two top wines of the domain are Perrières, which comes from the major part of the 1.7 ha holding—"We sell some Perrières to Leroy, and we had to use biodynamics for the parcel, it was very complicated"—and Clos des Perrières (just 1 ha). Clos des Perrières was replanted between 1986 and 1989. The only red is the Clos Blanc of Pommard.

The style is restrained, even austere at premier cru level in cool vintages. The Bourgogne has no new wood, there is a little for the Meursault, the premier crus have 20%. The Bourgogne has unusual elegance for the appellation level, the Meursault Clos du

Murger is more stony, Perrières is fine and silky, and Clos des Perrières is more tightly coiled. "Meursault does not have a grand cru, but if it did it would be Perrières or certainly Clos des Perrières," Michel says. "Les Perrières has 50-year-old vines, but you see more intensity in Clos des Perrières. Someone who wants to drink the wine immediately will miss the point, Clos des Perrières doesn't reach its peak until 15 years." Indeed, Clos des Perrières may be one of the most ageworthy whites in Burgundy; the 1985 was still vibrant and lively in 2017.

Domaine Antoine Jobard ★★

2, Rue De Leignon, 21190 Meursault	📞 *+33 3 80 21 21 26*
@ *antoine.jobard@orange.fr*	👤 *Antoine Jobard*
	◉ *Meursault [map]*
◌◪❧🍂 *7 ha; 40,000 btl*	🍾 *Meursault, en la Barre*

The Jobards go back five generations in Meursault, but the two Jobard domains of today date from the division of the Pierre Jobard domain in 1971 between two brothers. One half was first known as Domaine François Jobard. When François's son Antoine joined in 2002, the name was changed to François and Antoine Jobard, and then in 2007 it was changed to Antoine Jobard when François nominally retired. François was famous for his reserve; Antoine is more forthcoming.

The domain is adjacent to the lieu-dit En La Barre (which can be relied upon to outperform the village level). The domain is exclusively white and all Meursault except for one very small parcel in Puligny Montrachet. The cuvées in Meursault include two lieu-dits, and four premier crus. (There was some red in Blagny, but it's been replaced with Chardonnay.) Under François, the reputation of the domain was for bucking the trend to big, buttery Meursaults and producing a taut, mineral style. Fashion has now caught up, so the Jobard Meursaults are more in the mainstream.

Élevage is long (18-24 months), but uses little new oak, "maximum 20%," says Antoine. There is little battonage. "We make wines that are more reserved," is Antoine's description. The minerality of the style gives an impression moving in the direction of Puligny, yet there is a glossy sheen to the palate, with a sense of richness at the end. I especially like en la Barre for its balance of minerality and opulence; the premier crus are more opulent.

Domaine Rémi Jobard ★★

12, Rue Sudot, 21190 Meursault	📞 *+33 3 80 21 20 23*
@ *contact@domaineremijobard.fr*	👤 *Rémi Jobard*
	◉ *Meursault [map]*
🗓 ⛿ ❧🍂 *9 ha; 40,000 btl*	🍾 *Meursault, Les Narvaux*

The domain started with Charles, when he inherited half of the Pierre Jobard domain in 1971, and has been less well known than the domain of his brother François. The domain became Charles & Rémi Jobard when Charles's son Rémi joined in 1991, and has now become simply Rémi Jobard. Rémi has been making the wine since 1993, although Charles still drops in, and the wines have become increasingly elegant.

The main focus of the domain (and its reputation) rests with the estate vineyards in Meursault, where nine separate parcels include three premier crus, but production has been expanded by a small negociant business, and there is also red wine from Monthélie and Volnay. New presses have been installed to allow slower and gentler pressing. Fermentation is unusually slow: "We have a special system in which it's done outside, so the cold weather blocks its progress in October-November," Rémi explains.

The style minimizes oak influence by using barrels made by Stockinger in Austria with oak from Austria, Germany, and France. All wines age in a mix of large or small foudres and barriques. Élevage lasts a year in oak, followed by six months in cuve. New oak is 15% for Bourgogne Blanc, 20% for premier cru whites, and 25% for the two reds. "I like wine with lots of purity and energy," Rémi says. "Everything ages in wood, but I look for oak that does not give classic aromas like toast, I want the oak to bring out the natural aromas of the wine."

The Bourgogne Côte d'Or Blanc is something of a baby Meursault, showing purity of lines with fruits veering towards citrus. There are four cuvées from different lieu-dits in Meursault. "They are bottled individually because I've tried assemblage but I prefer the separate cuvées." The style is modern, meaning clean and pure. Sous La Velle is less overt than the Bourgogne, but has more of a sheen to the palate, Luraule (a little-known lieu-dit next to premier cru Gouttes d'Or) is rounder and more powerful, Les Narvaux is smoother and more upright, and Chevalières is the best of the lieu-dits, with more sense of restraint and minerality. In premier crus, Poruzot Dessous makes a broader impression, Charmes moves more towards minerality, and 60-year old vines make Genevrières more structured and reserved. The style is modern, in the direction of an opulent glycerinic sheen rather than the old butter and nuts, and the mineral edge of the New Meursault shows increasingly underneath going up the hierarchy.

Domaine Comtes Lafon   ***

5, Rue Pierre Joigneaux, 21190 Meursault	📞 *+33 3 80 21 22 17*
@ *domaine@comteslafon.fr*	👤 *Dominique Lafon*
🌐 *www.comtes-lafon.fr*	📍 *Meursault [map]*
🚫🔪🍇⚪ *16 ha; 80,000 btl*	*Meursault, Clos de la Barre*

Dominique Lafon's great-great grandfather started the domain. "The big step was when my father took over in 1956, but he was also an engineer, it was not his main job. The vineyards were under a sharecropping agreement, so my father was not managing them himself. I took over in 1984 and stopped the sharecropping. The contracts are for 9 years, so it was 1993 until I took all of them over." The domain has been expanded by splitting the purchase of the Labouré-Roi vineyards with Dominique's friend Jean-Marc Roulot, and Dominique has put his stamp firmly on the domain. "All the work we've done has been focused on a move towards elegance. We use just enough new oak for each vineyard, but I don't want to taste it in the wine. The objective was to get the wines to my taste."

The domain has become one of the reference points for Meursault with a splendid array of lieu-dits and premier crus, but the reds from Volnay show the same hallmark elegance and precision. The village Meursault is a blend of various plots, sometimes including declassified lots from premier crus. Clos de la Barre comes from the vineyard next to the winery and captures the house style. "There's always more tension here," says Dominique. Another lieu-dit, Desirée, is always fatter. Terroir shows itself in the approachability of Bouchères, the roundness of Poruzots, power of Genevrières, steely backwardness of Charmes, and smoky, stony, depth of Perrières.

Lafon also created a domain in Mâcon in 1999. And in addition to the domain in Meursault, Dominique started his own label in 2008, making wine from 4.5 ha of vineyards in Meursault, Puligny-Montrachet, Volnay, and Beaune. This allows him to experiment beyond the confines of the domain. The wines are in a similar style to the domain, but to my palate do not seem to reach the same heights of refinement.

Domaine Matrot   ★★

12, Rue De Martray, Bp 12, 21190 Meursault	📞 *+33 3 80 21 20 13*
@ *info@domaine-matrot.fr*	👤 *Adèle & Elsa Matrot*
🌐 *www.domaine-matrot.fr*	🗺 *Meursault [map]*
🎁 🏭 🍇 🛢 🍷 ♺	🍾 *Meursault*
24 ha; 160,000 btl	*Meursault*

The estate is now in its sixth generation. It owes its present form to Joseph Matrot, who took over in 1914 and started estate bottling. His son Pierre took over in 1937 and expanded the estate, and Pierre's son Thierry took over in 1976. Today the estate is run by Thierry's daughters, Elsa (winemaking) and Adèle (marketing). "Father has officially retired but continues to take care of the vineyards," Elsa says. The estate has had some changes of name as generations have succeeded one another, to Pierre Matrot, and then since 2009 to Thierry and Pascale Matrot, but policies have stayed the same.

Half the vineyards are red and half are white, but the white includes the Bourgogne Chardonnay, which accounts for about half of all production. (It comes mostly from around Meursault but includes about 20% sourced from elsewhere.) The Matrots have their own view of winemaking, partly reflecting their own traditions, but also modernizing when they feel it to be appropriate. The Bourgogne Chardonnay and the half bottles are all under screwcap. "Screwcaps are more reliable and uniform. A case of bottles under screwcap are all the same, but under cork they are all different. Screwcaps are very good for half bottles because they age more slowly," Elsa explains.

The use of new oak is unusual. "We do the opposite of other winemakers, we use the new oak for the Bourgogne, and then we use the one-year-old barrels for the Meursault and premier crus, which have only barrels of 1-5 years. We don't want the taste of new oak in the premier crus. There is no battonage unless there is a problem with reduction. Too much battonage tires the wine, we prefer minerality and freshness."

Asked to define house style, Elsa says that the terroirs determine character. The premier crus all come from different terroirs but winemaking is the same. "Puligny, Meursault, and Blagny premier crus are in a small triangle, but are completely different." In whites, Meursault tends to minerality; usually this intensifies in Meursault-Blagny which may even acquire a hint of salinity; and Puligny has a fine quality with great purity. Reds are well structured, building from Maranges to Auxey Duresses to Meursault, all a little tight at first and needing time after release to soften, with Blagny Pièce sous le Bois the most generous and rounded—"this is the signature of the domain."

Domaine Pierre Morey   ★★

13 rue Pierre Mouchoux, 21190 Meursault	📞 *+33 3 80 21 21 03*
@ *contact@morey-meursault.fr*	👤 *Anne Morey*
🌐 *www.morey-meursault.fr*	🗺 *Meursault [map]*
🌥 🏭 🍇 🍷 *10 ha; 50,000 btl*	🍾 *Meursault, Les Tessons*

174

"The domain is very old," says Anne Morey, who has been making the wine since 1998. "The Morey family arrived in France in the fifteenth century, and started in Chassagne. They moved to Meursault just after the Revolution." Production is two thirds white and a third red. "We work four villages, Puligny, Meursault, Pommard and Monthelie, and make 7 white and 5 red wines." The cuverie was extended in 2010 to allow gravity-feed winemaking. "We want to produce vins de garde, with long élevage sur lies, we keep lots of lees. Malo occurs late because we have very cold cellars."

Whites are fermented in barrique, with 40-50% new wood as the maximum for grand crus. Battonage is done only up to malolactic fermentation. For the reds everything is destemmed. "But I have the impression that you deprive the grapes of something by destemming, I dream of being able to adjust destemming to the vintage and to use a proportion of vendange entière."

The reds are precise and the whites tend to a tight, steely character, not surprising as Anne's father Pierre was winemaker at Domaine Leflaive as well as running his own domain. In addition, there is a negociant activity, Morey-Blanc, which is almost entirely white, and was started in 1992, to replace vineyards when the contracts expired on plots rented from Lafon. Today this is being cut back a bit. "It can be frustrating not to work the vines," Anne says, but the style is similar to Pierre Morey itself.

Domaine Jacques Prieur   *

6, Rue Des Santenots, 21190 Meursault	📞 +33 3 80 21 23 85
@ domaine-jprieur@prieur.com	👤 Edouard Labruyère
🌐 www.prieur.com	Meursault [map]
🗓🍷🍇	Clos Vougeot
21 ha; 100,000 btl	Meursault, Clos de Mazeray

The domain was founded by a couple in the silk business in Lyon; they gave it to their nephew, Jacques Prieur, who became a significant figure in Meursault. In 1988, most of his children decided to sell their share to the Labruyère family. "We come from Moulin-à-Vent where we have owned 14 ha for 7 generations," Edouard Labruyère explains. "I was a courtier in Bordeaux until I came here to run the domain in 2008. My goal was clear. Jacques Prieur is fantastic in terms of terroir—we own 9 grand crus and 14 premier crus. I asked the team to make wines that represent the terroir. The signature of Prieur was too evident in the bottle, we were more known by the label than the terroir. I wanted to change that." Behind the stone façade is a modern cuverie, with separate facilities for red and white. "We modernized everything in 2009, no renovation had been made since 1958."

Production is half red and half white. Meursault Clos de Mazeray is the only village wine in the portfolio. Vinification is traditional, with limited destemming and fermentation in open wood vats. Ageing is 18-24 months with no racking. "I stopped battonage for whites in 2008. I believe we have enough natural richness, I didn't want to add more fat." The reds of the Côte de Beaune have an unusual elegance, while those from the Côte de Nuits tend to be sterner. The whites are relatively sturdy, but good representations of their appellations. Labruyère also owns Château Rouget in Pomerol, and have started a new Champagne house, Champagne JM Labruyère.

Domaine Guy Roulot ★★★

1 Rue Charles Giraud, 21190 Meursault	📞 *+33 3 80 21 21 65*
@ *roulot@domaineroulot.fr*	👤 *Jean-Marc Roulot*
	🔵 *Meursault [map]*
🚫🍂🍇🛢 *15 ha; 85,000 btl*	*Meursault, Les Tessons*

The domain was established by Jean-Marc Roulot's parents in the fifties, but, "I wanted to be an actor—I went to Paris—it wasn't entirely successful but it didn't work so badly, I was a professional actor for ten years. When my father died we employed a régisseur, then my cousin Grux managed the vintages until 1988, and then I came back to run the estate," Jean-Marc explains. "I still spend 20% of my time acting, but it's no different from having another estate; it takes less time than making Beaujolais."

The domain is famous for its focus on the lieu-dits of Meursault. "My father had no premier crus, but he wanted to distinguish the different lots—he was one of the first to do this—and the style was defined by the decision to separate the cuvées." Jean-Marc has lengthened élevage to 18 months, with 12 months in barrique followed by 6 months in cuve, all on the lees. "The wine needs something to eat." There's no new oak for Bourgogne Blanc or Aligoté, village is 15-18%, and premier crus are 25-33%. The domain increased by 3 ha when Jean-Marc got half the vineyards of the old Labouré-Roi domain.

The focus is on Meursault, with 6 lieu-dits and 4 premier crus, but there are also Bourgogne, Auxey-Duresses, and Monthelie (in red as well as white). Aided by an emphasis on early picking, the style is crisp and elegant, with moderate alcohol. "In 2009 we were among the first in the vineyard. I don't like high alcohol, I'm very comfortable with 12.5-12.8%."

Profiles of Important Estates

Domaine D'Auvenay

Village Bas, 21190 Meursault	📞 *+33 3 80 21 23 27*
@ *domaine.leroy@wanadoo.fr*	👤 *Lalou Bize-Leroy*
🚫🍂🍇🛢 *4 ha; 11,000 btl*	🔵 *Meursault*

This is Lalou Bize-Leroy's family estate, which she and her sister inherited in 1980. When she established Domaine Leroy (see profile) in 1990, she bought out her sister's share. She expanded the holdings and keeps them separate from Domaine Leroy. The wines are made in the original cellar near Saint Romain. The original parcels in Meursault and Auxey-Duresses are the heart of the estate, but there are now also tiny plots in several premier and grand crus. The domain is mostly white, with 2.6 ha Chardonnay, 0.8 ha Aligoté, and 0.5 ha Pinot Noir (but the reds are Bonnes Mares and Mazis Chambertin). The domain is run in the same way as Domaine Leroy, with a strong commitment to biodynamics in the vineyards, no destemming in the cellar, and winemaking by the lunar calendar.

Domaine Ballot-Millot & Fils

9 rue de La Goutte d'Or, 21190 Meursault	📞 *+33 3 80 21 21 39*
@ *charles.ballot@ballotmillot.com*	👤 *Charles Ballot*
⊕ *www.ballotmillot.com*	🔵 *Meursault [map]*
🔲🏔🍇🌿	*10 ha; 55,000 btl*

The roots of this family domain go back to the seventeenth century. Charles Ballot, the fifteenth generation, took over in 2000. Whites are 60% of production, with the heart in Meursault, where there are three top premier crus including Les Perrières, and some lieu-dits. For whites, there is no battonage during aging for a year in barriques with no more than 25% new oak. In reds there are three premier crus from Pommard and also Volnay and Beaune. Reds are destemmed and spend 18 months in barriques, with 15-20% new oak depending on the cuvée.

Domaine Bernard Boisson-Vadot

1 Rue Moulin Landin, 21190 Meursault	📞 +33 3 80 21 21 66
@ boisson-vadot@orange.fr	👤 Pierre Boisson
🏃 🏭 🍇 🚜 10 ha; 55,000 btl	🏵 Meursault [map]

The Boissons have been making wine in Meursault for two centuries, and from their cellars in the heart of the village, Bernard Boisson and his son Pierre produced wine under four labels: Boisson-Vadot, Bernard Boisson, Pierre Boisson, and Anne Boisson. The labels reflect the pattern of family ownership of the vineyards; Bernard and his wife own about half, Pierre and his sister Anne own the rest. Bernard retired in 2020, and after this only the Anne Boisson and Pierre Boisson labels are being used. Most of the wine is white, from Meursault, including three lieu-dits, Sous la Velle, Grands Charrons, and Chevalière, and the Genevrières premier cru. Élevage is relatively long at 19-22 months, but new oak is moderate, with no more than 25-35%, depending on the cuvée. There is a little red from Hautes Côtes de Beaune. Monthélie, Auxey-Duresses and Pommard. The wine is mostly sold to private customers in France.

Domaine Bouzereau-Gruère et Filles

22a Rue De La Velle, 21190 Meursault	📞 +33 3 80 21 20 05
@ contact@bouzereaugruere.com	👤 Marie Laure & Marie Anne Bouzereau-Gruère
🌐 www.bouzereaugruere.com	🏵 Meursault [map]
🏃 🏭 🍇 🚜	10 ha; 36,000 btl

Hubert Bouzereau came from a winemaking family in Meursault and Marie-France Gruère from Chassagne Montrachet. They established their estate in 1970, and in 2001 the domain took the name of Bouzereau-Gruère et Filles when their daughters joined; Marie-Anne is the winemaker, while Marie-Laure manages the domain. Most of the cuvées come from the villages or premier crus of Meursault or Chassagne Montrachet, but there are also Puligny Montrachet and Saint Aubin. Production is three quarters white, but there's also a little Chassagne red and two tiny red plots in Corton Bressandes and Santenay. None of the plots are as large as a hectare. The flagship wine comes from 40-45-year-old vines in Blanchots Desssous in Chassagne Montrachet.

Domaine Yves Boyer-Martenot

17 rue de Mazeray, 21190 Meursault	📞 +33 6 91 95 99 38
@ contact@boyer-martenot.com	👤 Hélène Brissard or Vincent Boyer
🌐 www.boyer-martenot.com	🏵 Meursault [map]
🏃 🏭 🍇 🛢 🚜	11 ha; 45,000 btl

The domain goes back four generations, and after a brief period working with his father, Vincent Boyer took over in 2002 and renovated the winery in 2003. His sister Sylvie was involved in marketing at first, and then ran a negociant business before moving on. The domain has plots in some top premier crus, Perrières, Charmes, and Genevrières in Meursault, and Caillerets in Puligny, and has a focus on single-vineyard wines including four lieu-dits in Meursault. All production is white, and the wines are aged in one third new oak. All the village wines come from estate grapes, and grapes are purchased for the Aligoté and Bourgogne Blanc.

Domaine Buisson-Charles

3 Rue De La Velle, 21190 Meursault	📞 +33 3 80 21 22 32
@ dombuissoncharles@wanadoo.fr	👤 Patrick Essa
🌐 www.buisson-charles.com	🔘 Meursault [map]
🚶🏭🍇🍷🥃	7 ha; 45,000 btl

Michel Buisson was the third generation of winemakers and established the domain in the 1960s; he officially handed over to his daughter Catherine and son-in-law Patrick Essa in 2001. Based in Meursault, the domain has 4 ha of Meursault and its premier crus, but added more vineyards including a hectare in Puligny Montrachet in 2016. All this is white, but there is a little red from premier crus in Volnay and Pommard. In 2001 a negociant activity was added to widen the range, and this is the source of the Corton Charlemagne and Chablis. New oak is from 20-40% depending on the cuvée.

Domaine Jean-Philippe Fichet

2, Rue De La Gare, 21190 Meursault	📞 +33 3 80 21 69 34
@ contact@domaine-fichet-meursault.com	👤 Jean-Philippe Fichet
🌐 www.domaine-fichet-meursault.com	🔘 Meursault [map]
📅✏️🍇🍷🌿	7 ha; 70,000 btl

The focus at this domain is on exquisite definition of terroirs. Jean-Philippe started as a grower in 1981, but had to restart in the early 1990s when he lost his sources. In 2000, he moved production to space that he renovated in an old building near the Hôpital de Meursault, and in 2001 he created the domain. The heart of production is in Meursault, where there are 4 lieu-dits (around 0.5-1.0 ha each) and a village wine (coming from five lieu-dits but with a total area under a hectare). There are tiny amounts of Puligny Montrachet premier cru Les Referts, Auxey-Duresses, Monthélie, and Bourgogne Blanc. The domain is basically white wine except for two small holdings of Bourgogne Rouge and Auxey-Duresses premier cru. Wines age for 12 months, using a mixture of barriques and 500-liter barrels with less than 30% new oak, followed by six months in cuve. There is very little battonage, to avoid excessive extraction. Jean-Philippe's attitude is summarized when he says, "Tiny crops are never the best: without enough juice in the grapes, the wines can be too powerful, or even heavy."

Domaine Jean-Michel Gaunoux

1 Rue De Leignon, 21190 Meursault	📞 +33 3 80 21 22 02
@ jean-michel.gaunoux@wanadoo.fr	👤 Jean-Michel Gaunoux
🌐 www.jean-michel-gaunoux.com	🔘 Meursault [map]
📅🏭🍇🌿	6 ha; 40,000 btl

Henri Gaunoux was a well known vigneron before and after the second world war. When he died in 1972 the estate was divided between his sons. François established a domain based on the vineyards in Meursault, and Michel founded one with the vineyards from Pommard (see profile). François's son, Jean-Michel, started with his father, but left to form his own domain in 1990, with three premier crus in Meursault as well as the village wine, and reds from premier crus in Pommard and Volnay. New oak is moderate, with 15-30% depending on the cuvée, and aging lasts 15-16 months.

Domaine Génot Boulanger

21190 25 rue de Cîteaux, Meursault	📞 +33 3 80 21 49 20
@ contact@genot-boulanger.com	👤 Guillaume Lavollée
🌐 www.genot-boulanger.com	🔘 Meursault [map]
📅🏭🍇🥃	22 ha; 80,000 btl

The domain was founded in 1974 when Charles-Henri Génot and his wife, Marie Boulager bought vineyards and a nineteenth century château (at first the domain was known as Château Génot-BouLager). In 1995 they expanded from the Côte de Beaune into the Côte de Nuits; subsequently they also started to produce Crémant. In 1998, their grandson François Delaby took over, and he was succeeded in 2008 by his daughter Aude and son-in-law Guillaume Lavollée. There is an unusually wide range of wines, including more than 30 cuvées. Reds are partly destemmed. All wines see 25-35% new oak. The domain now also has a modern production facility in an industrial park near Meursault.

Maison Vincent Girardin

5 Impasse des Lamponnes, 21190 Meursault	📞 +33 3 80 20 81 00
@ vincent.girardin@vincentgirardin.com	👤 Marco Caschera
🌐 www.vincentgirardin.com	📍 Meursault [map]
🚫🍷🍇🛢 🕒 14 ha; 500,000 btl	Puligny Montrachet, Les Folatières

The domain was sold in 2012 to La Compagnie des Vins d'Autrefois, a negociant in Beaune. Winemaker Eric Germain has stayed on. Vincent Girardin started with an initial 2 ha that he obtained from his parents in 1982. The family had been making wine in Santenay since the seventeenth century. Expansion focused mostly on the white wines of the Côte de Beaune, which are 80% of estate production, but the negociant activity of Maison Girardin extended the range significantly (and is known for its affordable Bourgogne, Emotion), as also did a large purchase of vineyards in Chénas from La Tour du Bief (which added another 200,000 bottles per year). Production moved in 2002 from the old cuverie in Santenay to a purpose-built facility in the industrial estate east of Meursault. Half of the 42 individual parcels are in Puligny and Chassagne Montrachet. The domain was converting to biodynamics, but backed off, although it still follows many biodynamic practices. There is extensive sorting here—Girardin is one of the few in Burgundy to run to an optical sorting machine—and fermentation is allowed to occur naturally. Use of new oak is claimed to be moderate—10 to 35% depending on appellation—but I find oak to be quite evident in the young wines, which tend to power, sometimes at the expense of finesse: these are strong wines.

Domaine Huber-Verdereau

23 RD 974, 21190 Meursault	📞 +33 6 80 01 90 77
@ contact@huber-verdereau.com	👤 Thiébault Huber
🌐 www.huber-verdereau.com	📍 Meursault [map]
📅🏭🍇🍷	9 ha; 45,000 btl

Thiébault Huber founded the domain in 1994. His grandfather, Raoul Verdereau, owned vines, and Thibault's parents, who lives in Alsace, rented out the 3 ha they inherited until Thiébault changed from being a sommelier in Strasbourg to qualify in viticulture and oenology and decided to make wine. Expanding his estate, Thiébault now owns half his vineyards and leases the other half. The range is expanded by a negociant activity to produce 16 whites, 12 reds, and Crémant. Vineyards are in 32 parcels, the largest cuvées being red, from Bourgogne (just across the D974 from Volnay) and almost 2 ha in Bourgogne Hautes-Côtes de Beaune (which includes a good percentage of Pinot Gris). From Volnay there is a village wine, a lieu-dit (Robardelles), and Les Frémiets premier cru. From Pommard there is the Clos du Colombier, next to Thiébault's house, which he bought in 2010. It's partly classified as premier cru and partly at village level; Thiébault makes a single cuvée with Pommard AOP but premier cru pricing. He also makes premier cru Les Bertins from vines planted in 1959. Winemaking follows the principle of avoiding too much extraction, and Volnay ages in 20% new oak, with Pommard getting 25%; the village wines and premier crus age for 12-14 months. There are also white cuvées at regional level and one cuvée each from Meursault and Puligny Montrachet.

Domaine Patrick Javillier

19, place de l'Europe (shop)	☎ +33 3 80 21 27 87
9 rue des Forges, 21190 Meursault	
@ contact@patrickjavillier.com	👤 Marion Javillier
🌐 www.patrickjavillier.com	◉ Meursault [map]
🧍🏭🍇🍷	10 ha; 70,000 btl

Raymond Javillier built up the domain after the second world war. Patrick took over in 1974 and expanded further, partly by acquisition, partly from his wife's vineyards (the source of the red wines in Santenay). His daughter Marion took over making the red wines in 2008. The domain is best known for its whites, which are sometimes felt to be on the austere side when young, but a change to shorter aging in barriques and more time spent in cuve has made them more approachable. New oak policy is hard to pin down because it varies with conditions. Reds are completely destemmed, there is cold maceration before fermentation, and aging lasts for 18 months.

Domaine Latour-Giraud

6 RD 974, 21190 Meursault	☎ +33 3 80 21 21 43
@ domaine-latour-giraud@wanadoo.fr	👤 Jean-Pierre Latour
🌐 www.domaine-latour-giraud.com	◉ Meursault [map]
📅🏭🍇🍷	11 ha; 55,000 btl

Latour-Giraud takes its name from the marriage in 1958 between a Latour, whose history in Meursault dates from the seventeenth century, and a Giraud, from a family who had owned a distillery in Meursault since 1845. The domain has been run since the 1990s by Jean-Pierre Latour and his sister Florence. The domain is known for its extensive holdings in the top premier crus of Meursault, including Charmes, Perrières, and Genevrières (the flagship wine, where Latour-Giraud's 2.5 ha make it the largest owner). Full of flavor, with a mineral tang, the Genevrières can really be enjoyed in the first years after release. White wine is 85% of production. Reflecting the focus on premier crus, the wines tend to be powerful; village wines see 25-33% new oak, and premier crus 40-70%.

Domaine du Château de Meursault

Rue Du Moulin Foulot, 21190 Meursault	☎ +33 3 80 26 22 75
@ tourisme@chateau-meursault.com	👤 Stéphane Follin-Arbelet
🌐 www.meursault.com	◉ Meursault [map]
🧍🏭🍇🚜	60 ha; 300,000 btl

The château stands in a 2 ha park with buildings dating from the seventeenth century. The ancient cellars underneath are the largest in the region. It stayed in the hands of one family from the nineteenth century through 1973; since then it has belonged to two moguls. André Boisseaux, whose family founded the Patriarche negociant and Kriter sparkling wine, purchased and restored it in 1973. His son, Jacques Boisseaux, was in charge until 2012, when it was sold to Olivier Halley, an owner of Carrefour supermarkets and head of H partners, which owns several wine brands, and also purchased the Château de Marsannay. There has been significant investment, including an optical sorter, which is rare in Burgundy. Stéphane Follin-Arbelet came from Bouchard to be the winemaker. The extensive land holdings are all over the Côte de Beaune, with 110 separate parcels in 35 appellations, and are split equally between red and white. Whites age for 12 months in 20-25% new oak; reds are destemmed and age for 12-15 months in 25-40% new oak.

Domaine François Mikulski

7 Rd 974, 21190 Meursault	📞 +33 3 80 21 25 11
@ contact@domainemikulski.fr	👤 François Mikulski or Thomas Boccon
🌐 www.domainemikulski.fr	⊙ Meursault [map]
🗓 🔪 🍇 🥃	10 ha; 50,000 btl

François Mikulski is a first generation winemaker: his mother was Burgundian and his father escaped from occupied Poland in 1939. After spending time at wineries in California, François worked with his uncle, Pierre Boillot, from 1984 to 1991, and then rented the family vineyards to create his own domain. Most of the vineyards today are rented. The original intention was to sell the wine to negociants, but prices were so low at the time that the Mikulskis decided to bottle it themselves. Production is three quarters white. François's aim is to bring out minerality, and new oak is moderate at 20-30%.

Domaine Bernard Millot

27, Rue De Mazeray, 21190 Meursault	📞 +33 3 80 21 20 91
@ contact.millotb@domaine-millot.com	👤 Émilien Millot
🌐 www.domaine-millot.com	⊙ Meursault [map]
🗓 🍺 🍇 🚜	8 ha; 30,000 btl

The Millot family is now in its fourth generation at the domain, with Émilien working with his parents Bernard and Sylvie. Vines are relative old, with an average age around 20 years in Meursault and 35-40 years in Puligny. There is a village Puligny Montrachet (Les Corvées), while from Meursault there are three lieu-dits and premier crus Goutte d'Or and Perrières, as well as a red. There is also a red Beaune Les Sizies. Both reds and whites age in barriques for 12 months, and the whites then spend an extra 6 months in stainless steel before release. The proportion of new oak is quite low, around 10%.

Domaine Xavier Monnot

Domaine René Monnier, 6 Rue du Dr Rolland, 21190 Meursault	📞 +33 3 80 21 29 32
@ xavier-monnot@orange.fr	👤 Xavier Monnot
🏃 🍺 🍇 ⏱ 18 ha; 120,000 btl	⊙ Meursault [map]

This was Domaine René Monnier until 2005, when René's grandson, Xavier Monnot, renamed it. Previously it was run by René's daughter and her husband, together with Xavier, who took over in 1994, replanted parcels, and renovated the cellar. Vineyards are quite dispersed all over the Côte de Beaune, extending to the Côte Chalonnaise, split equally between red and white. One of the best cuvées is the Beaune premier cru Toussaints.

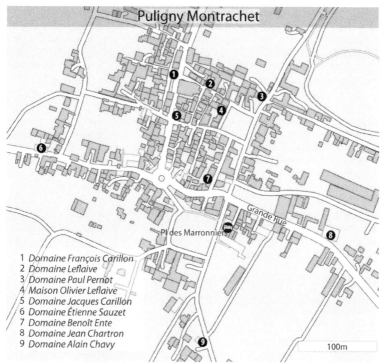

Puligny Montrachet

1 Domaine François Carillon
2 Domaine Leflaive
3 Domaine Paul Pernot
4 Maison Olivier Leflaive
5 Domaine Jacques Carillon
6 Domaine Étienne Sauzet
7 Domaine Benoît Ente
8 Domaine Jean Chartron
9 Domaine Alain Chavy

Profiles of Leading Estates

Domaine François Carillon   *

2-4 Place de l'Église, 21190 Puligny Montrachet	📞 +33 3 80 21 00 80
@ contact@francoiscarillon.com	👤 François Carillon
🌐 www.francoiscarillon.com	🗺 Puligny Montrachet [map]
🚫 📏 🍇 🛢 🍂	16 ha; 200,000 btl

When the Louis Carillon domain was split between brothers François and Jacques in 2010 after 24 years of partnership, Jacques stayed in the old cellars but changed the domain name to Jacques Carillon (see profile), while François set up his own domain just across the street. He created his own marque but the barriques are stamped with Carillon 1611 to show his pride in the family history of winemaking. The Louis Carillon domain became famous for its white wine, but actually started growing Chardonnay only in 1960.

Vineyards are mostly in Puligny Montrachet (some coming from Louis Carillon but augmented by purchases to increase the size of the domain from its initial 5 ha), with some small plots in Chassagne and Saint Aubin, but the only holding larger than a hectare is the village Puligny. There are 19 white cuvées from estate vineyards, and some grapes are purchased for the three red cuvées.

"We look for purity of style and elegance, we want wines that go with food," says Maître de Chai, Thomas Pascal. "We respect each vintage, there is no chemical transformation. We use five different tonneliers to get a light touch in the wood, we don't want the signal of the oak in the wine."

The style is relatively understated, starting with the Bourgogne, which comes from vines just outside the Puligny appellation; with 12% new oak it makes a fresh citric impression. St. Aubin, even at premier cru level, seems a bit angular by comparison. The Puligny village wine has more sense of minerality, but still staying in a fresh mineral direction. Premier cru Champs Gains makes a more subtle, elegant impression, with some stone fruits showing on the palate. Folatières makes a richer impression and becomes more savory. Combettes is the first in the line really to show any direct impression of new oak, with greater breadth on the palate. "Combettes gives us all by itself what we search for, elegance and power," Thomas says. Perrières, which has the maximum new oak of the house at 25%, is the only cuvée that really seems to need much time to be ready after release.

All the wines spend 11 months in barriques, followed by a few months in cuve to maintain freshness, before they are bottled. There is some experimentation with oak here, including smaller and larger barrels, and a vertical cask resembling an egg with the top cut off. The objective is to mature the wines without undue external influence.

Domaine Jacques Carillon   *

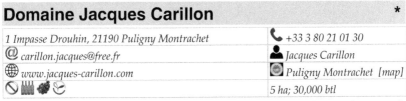

1 Impasse Drouhin, 21190 Puligny Montrachet	📞 +33 3 80 21 01 30
@ carillon.jacques@free.fr	👤 Jacques Carillon
🌐 www.jacques-carillon.com	🍷 Puligny Montrachet [map]
🚫 🏭 🍇 🌱	5 ha; 30,000 btl

"I worked with my father and brother until 2010 when we split the domain. We haven't changed anything in the style because I made the wines at Louis Carillon and I haven't changed," says Jacques Carillon. I remember the old Louis Carillon domain as a reliable source of white Burgundy, perhaps rarely scaling the heights but always offering well-made reflections of the vintage. The domain took its modern form with Louis's father, then his sons came into the domain in the eighties, Jacques to make the wine and François to manage the vineyards. After 24 years, the domain was split between Jacques and François, each of whom now has their own domain. Continuing the tradition of the Louis Carillon domain, Jacques remains in the old cellars, although the name on the label has changed to Jacques Carillon.

Jacques has stayed with the vineyards inherited from Louis Carillon, mostly in Puligny, plus some Chassagne Village. All are white, except for the St. Aubin Pitangerets, presently red, but likely to be replaced with Chardonnay when the vineyard comes up for replanting. "My grandfather and father planted red in St. Aubin when it was impossible to sell the whites," Jacques says.

Grapes are pressed pneumatically, the juice is transferred into barriques, goes through alcoholic and malolactic fermentation, and ages on the lees for a year with minimal battonage and racking, before aging in a further six months in vats before bottling. "We use little new oak, 15% for village wines and 20% for premier crus. We don't want the aromas of oak in the wine," Jacques says. Bienvenues Bâtard Montrachet is an exception that comes from such a small plot (0.12 ha) that there are usually only a couple of barriques (one is new).

The Puligny village wine is attractive and fruity; "it's an assemblage of 7 lieu-dits from all around, so it's really representative of the appellation," Jacques says. The Chassagne is softer and broader. In Puligny premier crus, Champs Canet moves in a slightly nuttier direction, perhaps reflecting its location on the border with Meursault. Perrières sees the first signs of minerality, flavorful and moving in a more savory direction. "It's always rich and broad, and it could end short, but the acidity gives it length," Jacques says. Les Referts shows more sense of tension, not as rich as Perrières, but more mineral, and perhaps the most typical of Puligny. Bienvenues Bâtard shows that unique Grand Cru combination of power and tension. The style is understated, but relatively broad.

Domaine Leflaive ★★★★

Place du Pasquier de la Fontaine, 21190 Puligny Montrachet	📞 +33 3 80 21 30 13
@ *domaine@leflaive.fr*	👤 *Brice de la Morandière*
🌐 *www.leflaive.fr*	◉ *Puligny Montrachet [map]*
🖉 🍇 ◯ 48 ha; 250,000 btl	*Puligny Montrachet, Clavoillon*

The atmosphere has certainly changed since I first visited Domaine Leflaive. Twenty-five years ago, I called one morning for an appointment. Anne-Claude answered the phone herself and said, come along this afternoon for a tasting. Today, emails to the domain get an automated response saying that visits can be arranged only through your local distributor.

One of the leading producers in Puligny Montrachet since the 1920s under Vincent Leflaive, the domain rose to the summit under his daughter Anne-Claude, who took over in 1990. Anne-Claude was one of the first in Burgundy to convert to biodynamic viticulture, and the wines have gone from strength to strength. Sadly Anne-Claude died in 2014, and her nephew, Brice de la Morandière, returned from a career running international companies to take over in 2015. Pierre Vincent came from Domaine de la Vougeraie as winemaker in June 2017. The domain's headquarters are an imposing set of buildings round a courtyard occupying one side of the Place des Marronniers, but Brice has expanded the original cellars, close by in Rue l'Église, which are now used for fermentation and first-year aging as well as for tastings.

The domain's style is the quintessence of Puligny: ripe stone fruits, tempered by a steely, mineral structure. New oak is moderate. "At Domaine Leflaive, there is only one method," Brice says. "We haven't changed anything. "One year in barriques is followed by one year in steel. First the wine likes to have the oxygen from the barriques, then it likes to have the mass from the stainless steel." The only difference is the proportion of new oak, rising from 10% for Bourgogne to 15% for village wines, 20% for premier crus, and 25% for grand crus."

The same style runs with increasing intensity from the village wine through the premier crus. Clavoillon shows the smoke and gunflint that is classic for Leflaive's Pulignys. Some people consider it a little obvious compared to Les Folatières and Les Combettes, but it can be the most consistent of the premier crus. Les Pucelles is certainly the top premier cru, and can come close to grand cru standard, moving towards smoothness and roundness, but always retaining that sense of minerality. Moving out of Puligny, Sous le Dos d'Âne from Meursault is sweeter and broader, less austere, with less obvious minerality. There are four of the five grand crus: Chevalier Montrachet, Bâtard-Montrachet, Bienvenues-Bâtard-Montrachet, and a tiny holding in Le Montrachet itself. Going up the hierarchy, there is greater refinement rather than greater power. At the other end of the

184

range, Leflaive has been expanding its offerings in Mâcon (see *Guide to Southern Burgundy*). There are also negociant wines, labeled as Leflaive & Associés, and Anne Claude bought the Clau de Nell in the Loire.

Maison Olivier Leflaive Frères   *

10, Place Du Monument, 21190 Puligny Montrachet	📞 +33 3 80 21 37 65
@ contact@olivier-leflaive.com	👤 Olivier Leflaive
🌐 www.olivier-leflaive.com	Puligny Montrachet [map]
😊 👥 ✖ 🍇 🍶 🌱 19 ha; 650,000 btl	Puligny Montrachet

Officially retired, but in practice evident everywhere, Olivier Leflaive is a force of nature. He was involved in managing Domaine Leflaive from 1982 to 1994, started as a negociant in 1984, and this became his full time activity from 1994. More recently he has acquired vineyards (including an inheritance of some that had been part of Domaine Leflaive). (The domain wines are indicated as Récolte du Domaine on the label).

Given the family history, the focus is on white wine. His first winemaker was Jean-Marc Boillot, who now runs his own domain, and since 1988 Frank Grux has been the winemaker. "In terms of philosophy and character of wine, I was born in Leflaive style which is finesse and elegance," Olivier says. The house style shows good extraction and the wines are flavorful, first showing fruit, but then with a savory edge behind. They are reliable and consistent. In addition to the main focus on Chassagne and Puligny Montrachet, there are also wines from Chablis and some reds from the Côte de Beaune.

Olivier is known as a small, quality negociant, but in fact, including the estate and negociant activity, wine is made overall from around a hundred hectares, so this has grown into a sizeable operation. But Olivier has extensive control of the vineyards, and says firmly, "I am a winemaker, not a negociant." The entrepreneurial spirit has shown itself also in the establishment first of a restaurant in the village square in Puligny Montrachet, and most recently in a hotel.

Domaine Paul Pernot   **

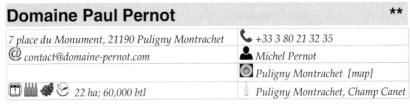

7 place du Monument, 21190 Puligny Montrachet	📞 +33 3 80 21 32 35
@ contact@domaine-pernot.com	👤 Michel Pernot
	Puligny Montrachet [map]
📋 👥 🍇 🌱 22 ha; 60,000 btl	Puligny Montrachet, Champ Canet

Paul Pernot is still running the domain that he founded in 1959. The Pernot's have been in Puligny for a long time. "My great grandfather was already here even before we were involved with wine. Wine comes from both my mother's and father's sides," Paul says. "I have two sons who work with me. Michel does marketing, Jean-Marc does winemaking and viticulture. My third son thinks the métier is too difficult." Paul is still closely involved: the day after our visit, we encountered him driving out in his Mercedes convertible to check on the work in the vineyards. First impressions at the domain are somewhat traditional: it occupies a series of old warehouse-like buildings along a vast courtyard just off the main square of Puligny. Paul Pernot comes across from the family house for the tasting, which is held in a cavernous space used for stockage.

Vineyards are mostly in Puligny, with some in Meursault-Blagny and in Chassagne, and some premier crus in Beaune. There are splendid holdings in Puligny, where cuvées include one village wine, and several premier and grand crus. "We have many parcels but we don't make lieu-dits, just one cuvée," Paul explains. "Usage of new oak is very light, but we have lots of barriques of 2-3 years age." The village Puligny is a marker for the village, with a characteristic linear purity, and a touch of steel. Champs Canet is broader, showing a more evident touch of oak, while Chalumeaux is fuller, with the fruits more in evidence. Clos de la Garenne (the cru is shared between Pernot and Duc de Magenta), is waiting to uncoil with time. More restrained, Folatières is holding back, and needs longer. There are a lot of old vines here: Garenne (60 years), Chalumeaux (70 years), and Folatières (55 years).

Les Pucelles is the most complex premier cru aromatically. The two grand crus typify the difference between Puligny and Chassagne Montrachet, as Bienvenues Bâtard Montrachet (all within Puligny) is precise, while having the depth of the grand cru without being at all heavy, while Bâtard Montrachet (coming from a plot on the Chassagne side) is broader. This is often felt to be one of the keynote domains of the village.

Domaine Étienne Sauzet ★★

11 rue de Poiseul, 21190 Puligny Montrachet	☎ +33 3 80 21 32 10
@ etienne.sauzet@wanadoo.fr	👤 Benoit Riffault & Emilie Boudot
⊕ www.etiennesauzet.com	📍 Puligny Montrachet [map]
◐ ▨ ❀ ▤ ▢ 10 ha; 100,000 btl	Puligny Montrachet, Les Champs Canet

When Etienne Sauzet founded the domain in the 1930s he was a negociant in gateaux as well as a vigneron. "It's bizarre but his deuxième métier allowed him to buy vines. It was common in that period when things weren't too good to use the second job to buy vines," explains Benoît Riffaut, who married Etienne's granddaughter; management of the domain jumped a generation when he took over in 1974. Now his daughter and son-in-law are involved. He's supposed to retire next year but plans to carry on unofficially. "It's impossible to stop when you are used to this métier. I won't be in charge but I'll be here," he says. The domain has a complicated organization because it was divided among three siblings in 1991, and formally functions as a negociant buying grapes from the various parts, but little by little the original vineyards are being reincorporated into the domain.

All cuvées come from Puligny, except for the Bourgogne, which comes from vines just outside the appellation. The village wine comes from 7 plots spread around the village, and there are 9 premier crus—"that's our specialty," says Benoît. Backing off from new oak has changed the style a bit: today it is often 20-25%, and the maximum is 30% for the grand crus. "Vanilla and aromatics of oak are artificial for us," says Benoît. I remember vanillin in the wines from two decades ago, but today the style shows a steely minerality, with emphasis on richer stone fruits as opposed to citrus increasing up the hierarchy.

Profiles of Important Estates

Domaine Henri Boillot

Les Champs Lins, 21190 Puligny Montrachet	📞 *+33 3 80 21 68 01*
@ *henri@boillotvins.fr*	👤 *Guillaume Boillot*
🌐 *www.henri-boillot.com*	🏠 *Puligny Montrachet [map]*
🔷🗡🍇🍶	*15 ha; 70,000 btl*

The domain started as Jean Boillot, but there was a family split when his son, Jean-Marc, who had made the wine for several years, left in 1984 after a disagreement because he wanted to make wines in a more forceful, modern style (see profile). Jean's other son, Henri took over the domain, and in 2005 renamed it as Henri Boillot. Previously (in 1996) he had created a negociant business, which he still runs. At the domain, Henri now makes the white wines, and his son Guillaume has made the red wines since 2006. Production is divided more or less equally between red and white. Wines for both domain and negociant are made in a modern facility in Meursault. The same label is used for both, but estate wines are labeled Domaine Henri Boillot, while negociant wines are labeled just Henri Boillot. The style is not as powerful as Jean-Marc Boillot. Oak exposure is about 10% for Bourgogne, 25% for village wines, 60% for premier crus, and 100% for grand crus.

Domaine Jean Chartron

8 Grande Rue, 21190 Puligny Montrachet	📞 *+33 3 80 21 99 19*
@ *info@jeanchartron.com*	👤 *Anne-Laure or Jean-Michel Chartron*
🌐 *www.jeanchartron.com*	🏠 *Puligny Montrachet [map]*
🚶🏭🍇🍶	*15 ha; 80,000 btl*

This old domain in Puligny Montrachet, founded in 1959, has been led by Jean-Michel Chartron since 2004. Vineyards are mostly in Puligny Montrachet, with a majority in premier and grand crus. There are five premier crus in Puligny, one in Chassagne, and two in St. Aubin. Grand Crus include Le Montrachet. Vineyards are almost all white, with small plots of red in Bourgogne and (unusually) in Puligny Caillerets. In the past, I have generally found the wines to be unexciting, but a heavier style of the early years has been lightened by reducing the reliance on new oak since 2009, which is now 10-40% depending on the cuvée.

Maison Chartron et Trébuchet

RN 74, 21190 Puligny Montrachet	📞 *+33 3 80 21 32 85*
@ *contact.france@bejot.com*	👤 *Vincent Sauvestre*
🌐 *www.groupegcf.fr*	🏠 *Puligny Montrachet*
🚶🏭🛢🚜	*16 ha; 600,000 btl*

The large negociant of Chartron et Trébuchet was founded in 1984 by Jean-René Chartron (of Domaine Jean Chartron: see profile) and Louis Trébuchet (who managed the negociant Jaffelin in Beaune). In addition to producing wines under its own name, it distributed the wines of Jean Chartron. The negociant got into financial difficulties and was sold in 2004 to Bejot Vins, a large negociant with interests in Burgundy, including Moillard and Corton-André (Reine Pedauque) and 260 ha of vineyards, as well as 270 ha in Southern France. Bejot Vins was sold in 2015 to the conglomerate Les Grands Chais de France, and all the holdings in Burgundy, amounting 300 ha of vineyards and the negociant interests, are now collected under the rubric of La Maison François Martenot. Moillard is now effectively the flagship of François Martenot. Moillard and Corton-André are workmanlike if somewhat four-square. I have never found the wines of Chartron and Trébuchet to be very interesting.

Domaine Alain Chavy

5 Rue du Creux de Chagny, 21190 Puligny Montrachet	📞 *+33 3 80 21 39 27*
@ *chavya@wanadoo.fr*	👤 *Alain Chavy*
📅 ⚒ 🍇 🍷 *10 ha; 80,000 btl*	🍂 *Puligny Montrachet [map]*

The Chavy's have been in Puligny for two hundred years. Alain Chavy and his brother Jean-Luis worked with their father at Domaine Gérard Chavy until he retired in 1997. Then in 2003 they decided to divide the domain. Alain moved to an old house in the Puligny Montrachet and constructed a new underground cellar (unusual in Puligny). His son Corentin has now joined him. Alain's plots are mostly in Puligny, including Pucelles, and old vines in Clavoillons (the Chavy's are the only owners aside from Domaine Leflaive), Folatières, and Champs Gains. Alain started with 6.5 ha but has now expanded to 10 ha, adding Les Charmes. Chevalier Montrachet is the only grand cru, but makes only 2 barrels. Alain is one of the first to pick in the village, aiming for a crisp style with minerality. Wines are barrel-fermented and then age for 12 months in barriques with about 20% of larger (400-liter) barrels, followed by 6 months in stainless steel. Wines are also bottled under the label of Chavy-Martin.

Domaine Comtesse de Chérisey

4 bis Hameau de Blagny, 21190 Puligny-Montrachet	📞 *+33 9 66 89 59 40*
@ *contact@domainecomtessedecherisey.com*	👤 *Laurette Martelet*
🌐 *www.domainecomtessedecherisey.com*	🍂 *Puligny Montrachet [map]*
📅 ⚒ 🍇 🍂	*9 ha; 45,000 btl*

The domain is actually in the hamlet of Blagny, a mile or so to the north of the village of Puligny Montrachet, and its vines, all around Blagny, are more or less divided between the AOPs of Puligny Montrachet and Meursault. There is a high concentration of old vines, the Blagny premier cru rouge coming from the oldest (1934), followed by the white (1946-1955). The Blagny premier cru Genelotte is a monopole of the domain. Aside from the plot of old Pinot Noir, plantings are all white. The vines for the Puligny premier cru Hameau de Blagny were planted in 1950. The vineyards come from the family of Hélène, winemaker Laurent Martelet's wife. The domain is named for her mother. White grapes are pressed, the juice settles for 12 hours, and then is racked into barriques, except for Meursault cuvée Léo, which ferments and ages in stainless steel.

Domaine Benoît Ente

4 Rue Mairie, 21190 Puligny Montrachet	📞 *+33 3 80 21 93 73*
@ *domainebenoit-ente@orange.fr*	👤 *Benoît Ente*
🌐 *www.benoit-ente.fr*	🍂 *Puligny Montrachet [map]*
📅 ⚒ 🍇 🍷	*5 ha; 35,000 btl*

Benoît is the younger brother of Arnaud Ente in Meursault (see profile), making wine from a tiny domain based on old vineyards (planted in the 1950s) he inherited in 1997. His style has evolved from gaining richness through battonage with reliance on new oak to a more minimalist approach; new oak is now less than 30%. He's considered to be a rising star in the village, and only the small size of the domain prevents greater acclaim.

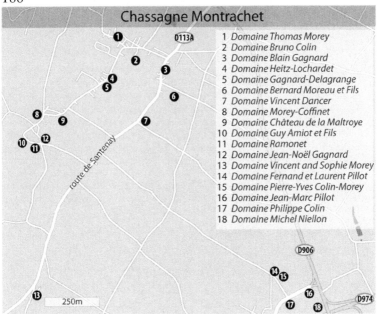

Chassagne Montrachet

1 Domaine Thomas Morey
2 Domaine Bruno Colin
3 Domaine Blain Gagnard
4 Domaine Heitz-Lochardet
5 Domaine Gagnard-Delagrange
6 Domaine Bernard Moreau et Fils
7 Domaine Vincent Dancer
8 Domaine Morey-Coffinet
9 Domaine Château de la Maltroye
10 Domaine Guy Amiot et Fils
11 Domaine Ramonet
12 Domaine Jean-Noël Gagnard
13 Domaine Vincent and Sophie Morey
14 Domaine Fernand et Laurent Pillot
15 Domaine Pierre-Yves Colin-Morey
16 Domaine Jean-Marc Pillot
17 Domaine Philippe Colin
18 Domaine Michel Niellon

Profiles of Leading Estates

Domaine Guy Amiot et Fils   **

13, Rue Du Grand Puits, 21190 Chassagne Montrachet	📞 +33 3 80 21 38 62
@ domaine.amiotguyetfils@wanadoo.fr	👤 Fabrice Amiot
🌐 www.domaine-amiotguyetfils.com	◉ Chassagne Montrachet [map]
🚫 🌿 🍇 🥄	🍷 Chassagne Montrachet, Vieilles Vignes
10 ha; 60,000 btl	🥂 Puligny Montrachet, Les Champs Gains

"I would describe our philosophy for winemaking as traditional not modern, in the sense that we favor long aging, at least two years," says Fabrice Amiot, who works with his brother Thierry, the winemaker, at this family domain. The family originally had a laundry business in Paris, but bought the house and surrounding vineyard (Cailleret) in the 1920s. By the 1930s they owned more vineyards, and Pierre Amiot became one of the first growers in the town to bottle his own wines. Domain Guy Amiot was created in 1985 as part of a move to expand to markets beyond France. The tasting room is in the original house, on one side of a covered courtyard surrounded by winery buildings.

"The domain has a lot of old vines because it was grandfather who really developed the vineyards," Fabrice says. "All our holdings are in Chassagne, we have all the aspects of Chassagne, and there is a plot in Puligny." The domain's reputation rests on its whites, which include eight premier crus in Chassagne, Les Demoiselles in Puligny, and Saint

Aubin, not to mention 0.1 ha in Le Montrachet. Many of the vineyards were leased out until they reverted to the domain in the late 1990s. The domain has expanded beyond the Côte d'Or by buying a vineyard of old vines Aligoté in Bouzeron in 2015. "We could afford to buy it, because it's not expensive and it's very close," Fabrice explains. The wine is very good, with the old vines really showing.

Elegant is the word most often used to describe the style. "Oak is much less than ten years ago, Thierry has reduced new oak to less than 35-30%, and there is a better expression of terroir," Fabrice says. The Vieilles Vignes Chassagne comes from a dozen plots in the village, with an average age of 50 years; it's attractive with a fine granular texture. Les Vergers, from 70-year old vines at the top of the slope, has a little more weight. Les Macherelles is spicier, and Les Champs Gains in smooth, silky, and more complex with faint herbal undertones. Cailleret makes the finest impression of all the Chassagne premier crus. Les Demoiselles from Puligny Montrachet is more linear, with great fruit purity. The comparison defines the difference between Puligny and Chassagne Montrachet. Reds from Santenay and Chassagne Montrachet account for about half of production; the style is precise and linear.

Domaine Jean-Marc Blain Gagnard   *

15 Route de Santenay, 21190 Chassagne Montrachet	📞 +33 3 80 21 34 07
@ domaine-blain-gagnard@wanadoo.fr	👤 Jean-Marc Blain
	⊚ Chassagne Montrachet [map]
🗓📗🍇🥂	▮ Chassagne Montrachet, Morgeot
8 ha; 72,000 btl	Chassagne Montrachet

Jean-Marc Blain is proud of the genealogy of his family, with several domains that have descended from the old domain of Delagrange-Bachelet. Jean-Marc married Claudine Gagnard, youngest daughter of the Gagnards of Domaine Gagnard Delagrange (see profile), and they created their domain in 1980 with vineyards from Claudine's family. Their son Marc-Antonin is now involved, makes the wine at Gagnard Delagrange, makes wine under his own name from some small family plots, and also founded a domain in 2014 in Beaujolais together with his sister, Blain Soeur et Frère.

Blain-Gagnard is located in the old cellars of Delagrange-Bachelet. "We are a typical family domain with holdings broken up into about 40 plots, in 15 different appellations," Jean-Marc says. Production is 60% white (9 cuvées) and 40% red (6 cuvées). "Our style is traditional, producing vins de garde. Our wines need 5-6 years, they have purity and good tension, although they are getting richer because of global warming." Actually, I think Jean-Marc underrates the appeal of his wines when they are young.

White Chassagne Montrachet is just over half of production. Coming from 6 plots all around the village, it includes 30% of grapes from premier crus. "It's a representation of all Chassagne," Jean-Marc says. It's fresh and fruity, with a textured palate showing stone fruits with a touch of citrus that characterizes the house style. Puligny comes from a single plot (in lieu-dit Rue aux Vaches) and shows greater tension and purity. In Chassagne premier crus, Clos St. Jean from calcareous terroir is deeper but more delicate, Boudriotte (within Morgeot) is more upright but covered by a smooth sheen, and Morgeot itself shows more powerful stone fruits with a phenolic texture. Caillerets is more subtle and complete, with a mix of tension and granularity. The tiny production of Criots Bâtard Montrachet is finer and tighter yet, while Bâtard Montrachet is broader and richer, but more restrained at first. All whites spend 11 months in barriques, with the same 15% new oak for village wine and premier crus, but 30% for grand crus. Reds age for 15-18 months in oak.

In reds, the village Chassagne shows typical lightness. Clos St. Jean—"always the lightest and most delicate, this is the Volnay of Chassagne"—has a sense of precision. Morgeots is deeper—"this is a vin de garde par excellence"—and has a sense of power. Volnay Pitures is tighter and purer, Volnay Champans has more lifted aromatics approaches a crystalline purity.

Domaine Bruno Colin   *

3 Impasse des Crets, 21190 Chassagne Montrachet	📞 +33 3 80 24 75 61
@ contact@domainebrunocolin.com	👤 Bruno Colin
🌐 www.domaine-bruno-colin.com	📍 Chassagne Montrachet [map]
🗄 🏭 🚐 🍇 🛢 🚜 9 ha; 70,000 btl	🍷 Chassagne Montrachet

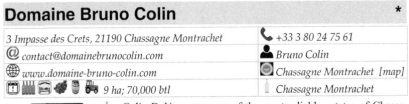

Colin-Deléger was one of the most reliable estates of Chassagne Montrachet, where Bruno worked with his father Michel from 1993 until the domain was divided between Bruno and his brother Philippe when Michel Colin retired in 2003. (Michel held on to three parcels, and continued to make Chassagne en Remilly, Puligny Les Demoiselles, and Chevalier Montrachet under the Colin-Deléger label (see profile) for a while. Philippe's wines are well thought of, but haven't achieved as high a reputation as Bruno's: see profile.)

Located in the old buildings of the original premises in the heart of the village, Bruno focuses on Chassagne Montrachet, including 8 premier crus, plus 2 Puligny premier crus and some St. Aubin. Sources are supplemented by purchasing some grapes. The 15 white cuvées make up 60% of production. There are 6 red cuvées, including the only one of the 30 estate parcels to be larger than a hectare (in Chassagne). Premier crus account for 14 of the 21 cuvées.

When Bruno was involved in making the wines at Colin-Deléger, the style was never to excess; the wines were never flamboyant, always solid representations of their appellations, but Bruno's style seems to have become more elegant now. Bourgogne Chardonnay, which comes from around Chassagne, predicts the house style, inclines to soft citrus fruits. Chassagne village is a little more textured, broader on the palate, and a fraction nutty. In premier crus, Chaumées jumps in style to show a strong minerality. "It always makes a more woody impression," says Antoine Laisney at the domain. Morgeots has a more understated style, with a more subtle impression of minerality. Its sense of finesse extends to Maltroye, which is less mineral, and softer and delicate.

Moving away towards the grand crus, en Remilly is more linear, setting a saline minerality against a citrus palate. The sense of linearity intensifies with Puligny Truffières, which is fin tight with gunflint minerality in the background. The peak is reached with Les Demoiselles (suspended until 2018 vintage because of replanting all 7 rows), and Chevalier Montrachet, which leans more towards Chassagne than Puligny, setting white flowers against a subtle, nutty, textured background.

Élevage for whites is 12 months in 350 liter barrels with 10-15% new oak. "We switched to larger barrels in 2015 because they are better for everything, we use barriques only when there isn't enough wine to fill a 350 liter barrel," Antoine says. Reds include Bourgogne Pinot Noir, the deeper Santenay Vieilles Vignes, fruiter Chassagne Vieilles Vignes, Maranges Fussières with more lifted aromatics, the earthy Santenay Gravières, and Chassagne Maltroye, which has the most grip and structure of all.

Domaine Pierre-Yves Colin-Morey ★★

4, rue de la Murée, 21190 Chassagne Montrachet	📞 +33 3 80 21 90 10
@ *contact@pierreyvescolinmorey.fr*	👤 *Pierre-Yves Colin-Morey*
	🔘 *Chassagne Montrachet [map]*
🚫🏷️🍇🛢️ 🍂 *7 ha; 85,000 btl*	*Saint Aubin, Le Chatenière*

While he was making wine with his father at the family domain of Marc Colin, Pierre-Yves started the Colin-Morey negociant in 2001 with his wife Caroline (formerly Morey). Then in 2005 the family domain was divided and he started to make wine from his 6 ha share. All the wines go under the label of Colin-Morey. The domain vineyards are mostly in St. Aubin, with some in Chassagne Montrachet, but the negociant wines (which amount to about a third of all production) extend over all the white wine appellations of the Côte du Beaune. In 2014, Caroline inherited 7 ha in Chassagne Montrachet and Santenay, and makes wine from them under the separate label of Caroline Morey.

Pierre-Yves is simply fascinated by white wine. The St. Aubins are fine examples of the appellation as his vineyards are all on the slopes; there's a gradation in interest going from the lieu-dits Pucelle to the Perrières or en Remilly premier crus, which are very good value. The lieu-dit Les Ancegnières from domain vineyards in Chassagne Montrachet performs above appellation level. The Champs Gains premier cru in Chassagne is always excellent.

Grapes are pressed as whole bunches, wines are matured mostly in 350 liter barrels rather than the usual 228 Burgundy barriques, and the wines stay on their lees without battonage for a year. There's about 30% new oak on average, but it can be evident when the wines are young, and it's best to give it time to resolve. The style has become increasingly mineral in recent years, with an increase in minerality going from St. Aubin (where the top premier crus are close in style to Chassagne), to Chassagne Montrachet (a touch softer and more textured than Puligny) to Puligny Montrachet (the most intense). Pierre-Yves is generally considered to be one of today's rising stars.

Domaine Vincent Dancer ★★

23 Route de Santenay,21190 Chassagne Montrachet	📞 +33 3 80 21 94 48
@ *vincentdancer@free.fr*	👤 *Vincent Dancer*
🌐 *www.vincentdancer.com*	🔘 *Chassagne Montrachet [map]*
📅🏭🍇🍂 *6 ha; 15,000 btl*	*Chassagne Montrachet, La Romanée*

Since the domain was founded in 1996 with vineyards inherited from Vincent's mother in Chassagne and his father in Puligny Montrachet, Vincent has built a reputation as a rising star; indeed, the wines are on their way to achieving cult status. Vincent grew up in Alsace, but after studying engineering went to Burgundy, where his family owned plots that were being rented out. He took them over and founded the domain, which continues with just the original parcels.

All holdings are very small, including lieu-dits and premier cru Les Perrières in Meursault, two parcels in Chassagne's top premier cru, Morgeots (La Romanée and Tête du

Clos), and a plot in Chevalier Montrachet so small as to make only one barrel. Vincent is reserved to the point at which detailed information is hard to come by, but he's proud of being the first producer in Chassagne to become organic, and he practices a minimalist approach with no battonage, fining, or filtration. New oak is about 25% for the village wines, 50% for the premier crus, and is 100% for the single barrique of Chevalier Montrachet.

The great reputation here is for the whites, where the new wave style is poised between minerality and opulence; going from the lieu-dits in Meursault to the premier cru in Chassagne, the balance shifts towards greater texture and more intensity. There are also reds from Chassagne (from Morgeots, no less), and from Pommard and Bourgogne. The domain is difficult to visit.

Domaine Jean-Noël Gagnard   *

9, Place Des Noyers, 21190 Chassagne Montrachet	📞 +33 3 80 21 31 68
@ contact@domaine-jean-noel-gagnard.com	👤 Caroline Lestime
🌐 domaine-gagnard.com	Chassagne Montrachet [map]
🚫 🍷 🍇 🍷	Chassagne Montrachet, l'Estimée
11 ha; 50,000 btl	Chassagne Montrachet, Les Masures

Right in the center of Chassagne Montrachet, the family residence is on one side of the courtyard, and you go down to the old cellars underneath for the tasting. Jean-Noël had an accident in 2015 and hurt his leg, so he had to retire. His daughter, Caroline, is the winemaker, and her husband Hubert came to join her at the domain in 2016. Hubert also runs a shop (called Vignes et Verges) in the village where people can taste the Noël-Gagnard wines and other organic wines. "The shop is focused on everything organic," he says.

"The domain goes back several generations, before the Revolution. We are focused on Chassagne with three communal wines and six premier crus." Red wine is about 20% of production. "We don't want to do everything in white, it's more famous, but we want to keep the character of Burgundy." In addition to Chassagne, there are wines from Santenay and the Hautes Côtes de Beaune. The domain mostly rests on long-term holdings, with many of the vineyards acquired by Jean-Noël in the 1960s. Many of the plots are very small. The latest acquisition was in premier cru Les Chaumées: "it's only five rows but they are pretty long rows."

The style is light and elegant in the modern idiom, with a focus on freshness. "We use oak for sure, but not in excess, we should not even taste the oak, it is for the oxygenation, we use only 30% new oak on average, a little bit more for the grand cru, less for the Hautes Côtes or village wine. Battonage is quite limited, the more battonage the more richness there is, and that is not what we are looking for, we are looking for tension and elegance." The style of the whites is restrained, with a slight citrus or mineral edge to offset against the light impression of oak; the reds follow the house style of elegance.

There's increasing emphasis on expressing individual terroirs. Two Chassagne village wines come from different plots. "Les Masures is not very far from Les Chaumes but we find it much more complex." In premier crus, there are multiple cuvées from within Morgeot. "Jean-Noël mixed Boudriotte and Petit Clos to make a Morgeot, but Caroline decided to separate them to bring out the terroir. The idea is to go even farther in the process of separating the vineyards," Hubert explains.

Domaine Fernand et Laurent Pillot   **

2, place des Noyers, 21190 Chassagne Montrachet	📞 +33 3 80 21 99 83
@ contact@vinpillot.com	👤 Laurent Pillot
🌐 www.vinpillot.com	🗺 Chassagne Montrachet [map]
😊 🏭 🍇 🍷	🍾 Beaune, Boucherottes
15 ha; 70,000 btl	Chassagne Montrachet, Les Chênes

This dynamic domain makes wine from 64 different plots. There's a tasting room in the family house in Chassagne, but the winery is just outside the village in a practical building near the N74. A new extension has a stylish tasting room overlooking the vineyards. Laurent Pillot has been making the wines since 1994. He turned up for our tasting on his tractor, from the vineyards, which are quite spread out. The original Pillot vineyards are mostly in Chassagne, with some in Meursault and St. Aubin, but Laurent's wife, Marie-Ann, inherited half of the Pothier-Rieusset domain in Pommard, and later they bought the other half. This is very much a family business; Laurent's son Adrian took over winemaking in 2017.

Chassagne Montrachet is the focus for whites, with the village wine coming from several plots in the center ("we sell off grapes from some of the plots at the edge"), lieu-dits, and five premier crus. The house style shows that sense of purity of fruits more commonly associated with Puligny. Palates show complex stone fruits with a subtle touch of oak. "My father likes to have just a slight taste of the barrel," Adrian says. "This is typical of our style. Usually we buy one third new oak and we sell the 3-year barrels." New oak runs from 25% for village wines to 40-60% for premier crus, depending on the cru.

The Les Chênes lieu-dit in Chassagne is close to premier cru quality, Les Vergers premier cru shows a touch more concentration and greater purity, Champs Gains is a little broader, Morgeot is the fattest, Vide Bourse is distinctive as the most delicate and elegant, and Grandes Ruchottes brings out that soft Chassagne style with more depth and power. Laurent looks for elegance. "We work with coopers to extract tannins during barrel production, so that we get elegance in the wine," he says.

The reds are precise. "Normally I destem most of the grapes," Laurent says, "although in 2015 more whole clusters were used because the grapes were so ripe." The Volnay is a blend from all the plots in Volnay, "about a quarter come from premier cru, but the plots are too small to separate." Beaune Boucherottes has a sense of purity and precision that recalls Volnay; with greater fruit concentration pushing the tannins back, Pommard Charmots adds weight to the precision of the red cherry fruits.

Domaine Jean-Marc Pillot   *

Le Haut des Champs, 21190 Chassagne Montrachet	📞 +33 3 80 21 92 96
@ jeanmarc.pillot@wanadoo.fr	👤 Jean-Marc Pillot
📅 🏭 🍇 🍷 13 ha; 70,000 btl	🗺 Chassagne Montrachet [map]
Chassagne Montrachet, Les Vergers	🍾 Chassagne Montrachet, Macherelles

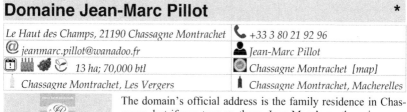

The domain's official address is the family residence in Chassagne, but if you turn up there, Jean-Marc's mother gives you directions to the winery, which has been located since 1988 in a modern building in Le Haut Champ, just down the road off the RN6. Originally there was one Pillot domain, but in 1988 Jean Pillot split it with his brother Fernand. Jean worked with his son, Jean-Marc, who took over in 1991, and now Jean-Marc's son, also named Jean-Marc, has been working with his father for seven years. The domain has equal plantings of black and white grapes. "The unusual proportion of reds goes back to my grandfather who had more red; and my father believed the history showed well for reds, and there are some terroirs, such as St. Jean, better suited to reds," explains Jean-Marc.

The whites have an approachable style. The village wine has 25% new oak, but 2-year oak is the oldest. Premier crus have up to 30% new oak. Élevage is 12 months in wood and 6 months in cuve, with battonage. The fruits on the village Chassagne are somewhat obvious, then become less overt on the premier crus, with Champs Gains, Maltroye, Les Vergers, and Macherelles showing stone fruits. The two classiest premier crus are Morgeot, which is more restrained, but shows greater sense of depth and texture, and Les Caillerets, which shows the greatest purity. Even barrel samples, a few months before bottling, seem more or less ready to drink.

Reds have 20% new oak for village wines and 25% for premier crus. Reds are typical for Chassagne, quite approachable, and making a light impression, from the direct fruits of the Santenay Champs Claude or Chassagne Vieilles Vignes, to the lightly structured impression of Macherelles, and the fine sense of purity and precision in Morgeot. The top red is Clos St. Jean, rounder and more structured, supporting Jean Marc Senior's point.

Domaine Ramonet ★★

4, Place-des-Noyers, 21190 Chassagne Montra-chet	☎ +33 3 80 21 30 88
@ ramonet.domaine@wanadoo.fr	👤 Jean-Claude Ramonet
	🌐 Chassagne Montrachet [map]
🚫 🍷 🍇 🚜 17 ha; 100,000 btl	Chassagne Montrachet, Les Boudriottes

This old-line domain has long been considered by many to be the best in Chassagne Montrachet. Pierre Ramonet purchased his first vineyards in the 1920s and 1930s, and then built up the domain after the second world war; it passed to his grandsons, Noël the winemaker, and Jean-Claude vineyard manager, in the 1980s. Since Noël retired in 2013, the labels have said Jean-Claude Romanet. His two daughter are now also in the domain. Conscious of its fame, the domain goes its own way and does not take criticism kindly: requests to visit can be rebuffed.

Ramonet has an important diversity of holdings, with six premier crus in Chassagne Montrachet, and four grand crus. There is also village wine from Puligny as well as Chassagne, and small amounts of premier cru from Puligny and St. Aubin. Vinification is traditional, but there is unusually extended lees contact and no battonage. New oak is stated to be around a third for the premier crus, but tastes stronger in the wines. Through the nineties these wines had a powerful yet balanced expression of Chassagne in a relatively creamy style, showing a characteristic sweetness of oak and fruits on a rich and viscous palate.

While I did not have problems with premox in the 2000s, the wines seemed to become heavier, with more phenolic overtones, giving the impression of a heavier-handed use of oak. Now they seem to have lightened up, with more mineral impressions to Boudriottes and Morgeots, which for me are the two most typical premier crus (and the largest holdings). Although there are some reds from Chassagne and from three of the premier crus, they have never been as interesting as the whites.

Profiles of Important Estates

Domaine Vincent Bachelet

27 Route de Santenay, 21190 Chassagne-Montrachet	📞 *+33 3 80 21 37 27*
@ *contact@vincent-bachelet.com*	👤 *Vincent Bachelet*
🌐 *www.vincent-bachelet.com*	🅖 *Chassagne Montrachet*
🕴🏭🐜🚜	*17 ha*

This is a typical family estate with many small plots distributed around the Côte de Beaune. Vincent is the third generation of winegrowers in the family: he started working with his father Bernard before setting up his own estate in Chassagne Montrachet. Now he works with his daughter Aurore and son Etienne. Production is 70% red. The range starts with regional wines, Bourgogne, Hautes Côtes de Beaune, and Côtes de Beaune Villages for red, and Bourgogne for white, all aged for 11 months in new and 1-year oak. A red from 50-year-old vines in the Chassagne lieu-dit Les Benoites ages for 15 months, and one from 60-year-old vines in Maranges premier cru La Fussière ages for 18 months. In whites, the village Puligny, Chassagne, Meursault Clos du Cromin, and St. Aubin premier cru En Remilly, age for 12 months in new and 1-year barriques.

Domaine Colin-Deléger

3 impasse-des-Crêts, 21190 Chassagne Montrachet	📞 *+33 3 80 24 75 61*
@ *domainebrunocolin@wanadoo.fr*	👤 *Michel Colin-Deléger*
🚫🍷🚜 *1 ha; 5,000 btl*	🅖 *Chassagne Montrachet*

Michel Colin-Deléger created this domain in Chassagne Montrachet in 1987. The style was always mainstream, never falling into excess of either of the extremes of buttery notes or minerality. When Michel retired in 2003, the vineyards were divided between his sons Philippe and Bruno, who now have their own domains (see profiles), but Michel kept back three small parcels (totaling less than a hectare) from which he made wine until 2015: En Remilly premier cru in Chassagne, Les Demoiselles premier cru in Puligny, and Chevalier Montrachet grand cru.

Domaine Philippe Colin

ZA du Haut-des-Champs, 21190 Chassagne Montrachet	📞 *+33 3 80 21 90 49*
@ *domainephilippecolin@orange.fr*	👤 *Philippe Colin*
🚫🍷🐜🕯 *13 ha*	🅖 *Chassagne Montrachet [map]*

When Michel Colin retired in 2003, the Colin-Deléger domain was divided between his son Bruno (see profile) and Philippe. Each got 9 ha, and Philippe has since acquired another 4 ha. Bruno kept the original premises, and Philippe built a new winery on the edge of the village. For a small domain there are a lot of different cuvées, partly representing Philippe's interest in terroir and his wish to represent each plot individually. Most production is white, and there are 7 white crus in Chassagne Montrachet alone. The oldest vines, about 80 years of age, are in Chenevottes. Village wines age in 20-25% new oak, and premier crus get 35%.

Domaine Fontaine-Gagnard

19 Route de Santenay, 21190 Chassagne Montrachet	📞 *+33 3 80 21 35 50*
@ *domainefontainegagnard@wanadoo.fr*	👤 *Céline Fontaine*
🌐 *www.domaine-fontaine-gagnard.com*	🅖 *Chassagne Montrachet*
🚫🍷🐜🚜	*12 ha*

The domain originated in the holdings of Gagnard-Delagrange (see profile) as Richard Fontaine married Jacques Gagnard's eldest daughter Laurence in 1982. Their daughter Céline is in charge today. Holdings are almost all in Chassagne Montrachet, including premier crus Boudriotte, Caillerets, Clos St. Jean, Maltroie, Morgeot, La Romanée, and Vergers, and grand crus Criots-Bâtard-Montrachet (where they own the largest part of this tiny cru), Bâtard-Montrachet and Montrachet. The focus is on whites, but there are also Bourgogne and Chassagne Montrachet red, and Volnay premier cru Clos des Chênes. Premier crus generally age for 11 months in barriques with a third each of new, 1-year, and 2-year oak.

Domaine Gagnard-Delagrange

26 Rue Charles Paquelin, 21190 Chassagne Montrachet	📞 +33 3 80 21 31 40
@ mariejosephegagnard@gmail.com	👤 Marie-Josèphe Delagrange
🚫 🗡 🍇 ℃ 2 ha; 10,000 btl	◉ Chassagne Montrachet [map]

Domaine Gagnard-Delagrange was created in 1959 when Jacques Gagnard married Marie-Josèphe Delagrange. The domain included several premier crus in Chassagne Montrachet and grand crus. Jacques Gagnard had a restrained style, which he passed on to his grandson, Marc-Antonin Blain-Gagnard, who has been making the domain wines since Jacques died in 2009 (and is now also involved at Domaine Blain-Gagnard: see profile). Many of the vineyards were distributed in the family when Jacques died, but the domain retained 7 ha.

Domaine Heitz-Lochardet

24 Rue Charles Paquelin, 21190 Chassagne-Montrachet	📞 +33 6 50 72 87 10
@ moderation@armandheitz.com	👤 Armand Heitz
⊕ armandheitz.com	◉ Chassagne Montrachet [map]
🗓 🏭 🍇 ℃	8 ha; 80,000 btl

Dating from 1857, the domain belonged to the Lochardet family during the twentieth century. Originally 20 ha, it was divided by inheritance, and Heitz-Lochardet acquired its name for Brigitte Lochardet's share of the estate when she married Christian. From 1988 to 2013, the grapes were sold to Joseph Drouhin. Then Armand Heitz qualified in oenology, took over the vineyards, and started to produce wine from Chassagne Montrachet, Meursault, Pommard, Volnay, and a little Bourgogne. As more vineyards have returned to family control, doubling from its original size, the range has widened, and now includes premier crus Maltroye, Chenevottes, and Morgeot divided into three cuvées) in Chassagne, Clos des Poutures, Pezerolles, and Rugiens in Pommard, and Volnay Taillepieds. Production is 60% white. Pinot Noir fermented as 50-100% whole clusters for village wines, and 100% whole clusters for premier crus, there is cold maceration for 3-7 days before fermentation, which lasts 10-15 days, and only pump-over. Whites are pressed as whole clusters. Aging lasts 10-15 months with 15% new oak for Bourgogne, and 25-30% for village wines and premier crus. In addition to wines from the domain, a negociant line started in 2017, extending the range of village wines, labeled simply Armand Heitz. This is used also for the Connivence cuvée, made as a collaboration with a different friend each year. Crémant comes from purchased grapes. Armand also makes wine with his brother-in-law at the 6 ha Domaine la Combe-Vineuse in Juliénas (Beaujolais).

Domaine Château de la Maltroye

16, Rue de la Murée, 21190 Chassagne Montrachet	📞 +33 3 80 21 32 45
@ chateau.maltroye@wanadoo.fr	👤 Jean-Pierre Cournut
🚫 🗡 🍇 ℃ 15 ha; 60,000 btl	◉ Chassagne Montrachet [map]

The Château de Maltroye occupies an eighteenth century house set back from the road though the village. Its caves date from the fifteenth century. The Picard family purchased the house and the vineyards that came with it in 1940. André Cornut purchased the property in 1993 after a dispute about inheritance, and his son Jean-Pierre took over in 1995. Immediately behind the house are the vineyards of the Maltroie premier cru. Vineyards are in Chassagne except for 2 ha in Santenay, and just over half are white grapes. There's village wine from Chassagne, several premier crus, and Bâtard Montrachet. The whites tend to be rich, too rich and powerful for my palate, which may be due to the use of high proportions of new oak.

Domaine Bernard Moreau et Fils

3 Route Chagny, 21190 Chassagne Montrachet	📞 *+33 3 80 21 33 70*
@ *domaine.moreau-bernard@wanadoo.fr*	👤 *Benoit Moreau*
📅 🏭 🍇 🍂 *14 ha; 75,000 btl*	🔴 *Chassagne Montrachet [map]*

Auguste Moreau built a cellar at the Champs Gain vineyard in 1809, but the current domain basically dates from its expansion under Marcel Moreau in the 1930s. Bernard Moreau took over in the early 1960s, when he was very young, and gave his name to the domain in 1977. After working in the New World, his sons took over in 1999, with Benoît looking after the vineyards and Alexandre in charge of the cellar. Vineyards are all in Chassagne except for a tiny plot in St. Aubin. The approach to winemaking is traditional, with village wines seeing 25% new oak, premier crus 30-50%, and grand crus (Bâtard and Chevalier Montrachet) receiving 100%. Élevage was lengthened to 18 months in 2004. There's a large plot of red Chassagne Montrachet and a little red premier cru; otherwise plantings are white.

Domaine Morey-Coffinet

6 Place Du Grand Four, 21190 Chassagne Montrachet	📞 *+33 3 80 21 31 71*
@ *morey.coffinet@orange.fr*	👤 *Thibault Morey*
🌐 *www.domainemoreycoffinet.com*	🔴 *Chassagne Montrachet [map]*
🚫 🍷 🍇 🍶 🎱	*9 ha; 45,000 btl*

The domain was established in the 1970s by Michel Morey and his wife Fabienne with vineyards that came from both sides of the family. Their son, Thibaut, joined the domain in 2000 and is now taking over. (Michel's father's domain, Marc Morey, was run by his sister.) The domain is located in an eighteenth century house with sixteenth century cellars that Michel Morey bought when the domain was created. The estate vineyards are almost all in Chassagne Montrachet, but the range is extended by a negociant activity under the name of Maison Morey-Coffinet. Whites are three quarters of production and include Bourgogne, village Chassagne, six premier crus, and Bâtard Montrachet, and there are also cuvées from Puligny, Meursault, and Corton Charlemagne. Wine age for only 11 months in barriques in order to retain freshness and be approachable when young.

Domaine Thomas Morey

9 rue Nord, 21190 Chassagne Montrachet	📞 *+33 3 80 21 97 47*
@ *domainethomasmorey@orange.fr*	👤 *Thomas Morey*
🌐 *www.thomasmorey-vins.com*	🔴 *Chassagne Montrachet [map]*
🚫 🍷 🍇 🍶	*13 ha; 60,000 btl*

After Bernard Morey retired in 2005, his sons Thomas and Vincent formed their own domains by dividing the vineyards in 2007. Thomas purchased some additional plots, and in 2011 was offered a rental of 3 ha from his neighbor in Chassagne. Altogether he owns 8 ha and rents 5 ha. Alcoholic and malolactic fermentation are rapid, and the wines are aged for only 11 months. Thomas has an unusual policy with regards to sulfur: in order to keep a low dose at bottling, he adds very small doses regularly over the year. White wines are in the majority and include a wide range: Bourgogne, Saint Aubin, Chassagne Montrachet (including several premier crus), Puligny Montrachet, and Bâtard Montrachet.

Domaine Vincent and Sophie Morey

3 hameau de Morgeot, 21190 Chassagne Montrachet	📞 *+33 6 76 25 58 35*
📠 *+33 3 80 20 62 37*	👤 *Vincent Morey*
🌐 *www.morey-vs-vins.com*	🔘 *Chassagne Montrachet [map]*
📅 🏭 🍇 🕭	*20 ha; 60,000 btl*

Vincent Morey and brother Thomas (see profile) each formed their own domains in 2007 after their father Bernard Morey retired in 2005. Vincent took over Bernard's old premises in the heart of Morgeot and formed a domain with his wife Sophie, who comes from Santenay. Vineyards come from both sides of the family. Vincent and Sophie both had plots in premier cru Les Embrazées, so the combination became their largest holding. There are vineyards also in other premier crus of Chassagne, and in Puligny and Bâtard Montrachet, and of course Santenay. Unusually for a domain in Chassagne, a majority of the vineyards (11 ha) are red, mostly in Santenay. Aging is similar for all cuvées, with www.lapaulee.com 40% new oak for the whites and 50% for the reds.

Domaine Michel Niellon

Le haut des champs, 21190 Chassagne Montrachet	📞 *+33 3 80 24 70 17*
@ *domainemichelniellon@orange.fr*	👤 *Michel Coutoux*
🚫 🔪 🍇 🕭 *8 ha; 45,000 btl*	🔘 *Chassagne Montrachet [map]*

Three generations are involved at this tiny domain. Michel Niellon began estate-bottling with his father Marcel in the 1960s (when the estate was only 4 ha), since 1991 has been working with his son-in-law, Michel Coutoux, and more recently also with his grandson, Mathieu Bresson. Two thirds of production is white, with a full range from Bourgogne, through Chassagne village and several premier crus, to Chevalier Montrachet. New oak is moderate, varying from 20-30%, but the style is relatively rich.

Domaine Paul Pillot

3 Clos Saint Jean, 21190 Chassagne Montrachet	📞 *+33 3 80 21 31 91*
@ *info@pressoir.wine*	👤 *Thierry Pillot*
🍇 🕭 *13 ha*	🔘 *Chassagne Montrachet*

The domain was founded in 1900 and is now in the hands of the fourth generation under Thierry, who joined in 1999 and took over in 2004 from his father, Paul, who had expanded the domain to its present size. He works with his sister, Crystelle, who is married to Arnaud Mortet of Domaine Denis Mortet in Gevrey Chambertin. The range starts with Bourgogne (red, white, and Aligoté), with white village wines from Saint Aubin and Chassagne Montrachet, and reds from Santenay and Chassagne Montrachet (both Vieilles Vignes cuvées from vines over 50 years old). The heart of the domain is in the 6 premier crus from Chassagne Montrachet, and Bâtard Montrachet and Corton Charlemagne. Thierry has reduced use of new oak, and introduced 350-liter barrels as well as barriques. Most wines age in the larger barrels with 10% new oak.

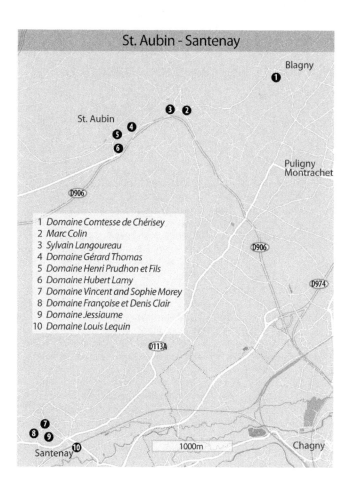

St. Aubin - Santenay

Blagny

St. Aubin

Puligny
Montrachet

D906

1 Domaine Comtesse de Chérisey
2 Marc Colin
3 Sylvain Langoureau
4 Domaine Gérard Thomas
5 Domaine Henri Prudhon et Fils
6 Domaine Hubert Lamy
7 Domaine Vincent and Sophie Morey
8 Domaine Françoise et Denis Clair
9 Domaine Jessiaume
10 Domaine Louis Lequin

D906

D974

D113A

1000m

Chagny

Santenay

Profiles of Leading Estates

Domaine Anne-Marie et Jean-Marc Vincent   *

3 rue Sainte-Agathe, 21590 Santenay	📞 *+33 3 80 20 67 37*
@ *vincent.j-m@wanadoo.fr*	👤 *Jean-Marc Vincent*
	◉ *Santenay [map]*
🗓 🏭 🍇 🛢 ⚲	🍷 *Santenay, Passetemps*
7 ha; 35,000 btl	*Santenay, Beaurepaire*

The cellars date from the fourteenth century, but this is a new domain. The vineyards belonged to the family, but they were not vignerons. "Jean-Marc's father was an engineer in Colmar. Jean-Marc didn't want to follow that and went to oenology school at Dijon in 1993. We were in Nuits St Georges before we came here, we didn't know what we were getting into," says Anne-Marie, a fraction ruefully. Established eighteen years ago, this remains a very hands-on operation: Anne-Marie had a second job until 2000, and the first real employee was hired only in 2009. "When we started all the equipment was old and we had to replace everything, but we did it slowly," Anne-Marie recollects. For the first two years, grapes were sold to negociants, but since then all production has been estate-bottled.

There are separate cellars for whites and reds in the heart of the village (the old cellars were purchased by Ann-Marie's grandfather in 1950). Viticulture has moved progressively in a more organic direction. New plantings use selection massale rather than clones, planting density is being increased, with a quarter of the vineyards now at more than 14,000 vines/ha, and a technique of braiding, when shoots are knotted together, is being used instead of trimming. There's the same élevage for all cuvées, with about 25% new oak. Since 2018, aging has been moved to 18 months in barriques, rather than 12 months in barriques followed by 6 months in cuve. No sulfur is used during vinification and only minimal amounts at bottling.

The whites have an intriguing blend of fruits and herbs when young, which strengthens to a delicious savory quality as they age. The reds are round, with a touch of tannin showing for the first couple of years, and the premier crus are quite Beaune-like. You might think that given their delicious quality when young, these wines don't need to age, but they do benefit from time in the bottle, becoming deeper with time, and peaking a few years after the vintage. All the wines come from estate grapes, except for the Montagny white, from purchased grapes.

Profiles of Important Estates

Domaine Bachelet Monnot

15 Grande Rue, 71150 Dezize-lès-Maranges	📞 *+33 3 85 91 16 82*
@ *bachelet-monnot@wanadoo.fr*	👤 *Marc & Alexandre Bachelet*
🗓 🍇 🛢 *22 ha; 100,000 btl*	◉ *Maranges*

Brothers Marc and Alex Bachelet formed their own domain in 2005, with vineyards from their father, Jean-François Bachelet, who made the wine at Domaine Bernard Bachelet, and their uncle Monnot. The winery is in Maranges, at the southern end of the Côte de Beaune. Production is more or less half red and half white, but the whites have the better pedigree. Reds come mostly from Maranges or Santenay, while most of the whites come from Puligny or Chassagne

Montrachet, including some premier and grand crus, with other plots in Saint Aubin or Maranges. Their largest holding is the Maranges premier cru Clos de la Boutière (adjacent to Santenay), of which they own half. Wines mostly age for 12 month in barriques with 25% new oak followed by another 6 months on the lees in stainless steel for whites or concrete for reds. The style shows tension, and the wines can sometimes start out a little austere.

Domaine Chevrot et Fils

19, Route De Couches, 71150 Cheilly-lès-Maranges	📞 +33 3 85 91 10 55
@ contact@chevrot.fr	👤 Pablo & Vincent Chevrot
🌐 www.chevrot.fr	⚫ Maranges
📅🏭🍇🍷	20 ha; 80,000 btl

At the far south of the Côte d'Or, beyond Santenay, the domain produces both Maranges and Santenay, including village wines and premier crus from both appellations, Bourgogne, and Hautes Côtes de Beaune. The vineyards were mostly purchased two generations ago, then Fernand Chevrot took over, before handing over to his sons Pablo and Vincent. A start-of-the-art winery was completed in 2020, and the brothers say this has improved vinification. Some of the vineyards are worked by horse. Grapes go directly into fermentation, usually with 10-15% stems for red, with punch-down daily, and then aging for 12 months with 5-10% new oak for village wines and 20-30% for premier crus. The domain also has some Aligoté including both the Vert subcultivar and the higher quality Doré. "Lots of old vines are disappearing because the image of Aligoté wasn't good," Pablo Chevrot says, "but we really trust in it, and believe it is good." He makes two cuvées: Cuvée des Quatre Terroirs from a sandstone slope, and Tilleul, from 60-year-old vines, aged in barrique.

Domaine Françoise et Denis Clair

14 Rue de la Chapelle, 21590 Santenay	📞 +33 3 80 20 61 96
@ fdclair@orange.fr	👤 Jean-Baptiste Clair
📅🏭🍇⛄ 14 ha; 75,000 btl	⚫ Santenay [map]

Denis Clair founded the domain in 1986 with vineyards that the family had long owned, but from which production had been sold to negociants. His wife Françoise comes from St. Aubin. Their son Jean-Baptiste joined in 2000, and makes the white wines. The domain has 9 ha in Santenay (mostly black plantings) and 5 ha in St. Aubin (all white plantings). The whites ferment in barrique, with 15% new oak for the village Santenay, and 15-25% new oak for the Santenay and St. Aubin premier crus; aging lasts 10 months. Reds are entirely or almost entirely destemmed; Santenay Clos Genet and premier crus Clos des Mouches and Clos de la Comme, age in barriques for 12 months with 20-25% new oak, whereas St. Aubin premier cru Sur le Sentier du Clou ages in a mix of vat and barriques.

Domaine Jessiaume

10 Rue de La Gare, 21590 Santenay	📞 +33 3 80 20 60 03
@ info@jessiaume.com	👤 Stéphanie Chagnard
🌐 www.jessiaume.com	⚫ Santenay [map]
📅🏭🍇🍷	14 ha; 75,000 btl

The domaine was founded in 1850 by the Jessiaume family, and they ran it until 2006, when they sold to Sir David Murray, the fifth richest man in Scotland, who made his fortune in minerals. The Jessiaumes stayed at the domain for a transition until 2013 (when they went to make the wine at Maison Chanzy on the Côte Chalonnaise). A new team took over in 2014, and the winery was renovated. Sir David then sold Jessiaume to Jean-François Le Bigot, of the pharmacological company Oncovita, in 2020. Located at the southern end of the Côte d'Or, the domain has strong holdings in Santenay—almost half the vineyards are in premier cru Les

Gravières, and there are also premier cru La Combe and lieu-dit Clos du Genet—and Auxey-Duresses (village and premier cru), and also in Volnay (village and Les Brouillards premier cru), Pommard (lieu-dit La Combotte), and Beaune (premier cru Cent Vignes). The range was extended by adding a negociant activity in 2008, and now extends all the way up the Côte de Beaune and into the Côte de Nuits.

Domaine Louis Lequin

2, Rue Du Pasquier De Pont, 21590 Santenay	📞 *+33 3 80 20 63 82*
@ *info@louis-lequin.com*	👤 *Antoine Lequin*
⊕ *www.louis-lequin.com*	⬤ *Santenay [map]*
📅 🏭 🍇 🗤	*7 ha; 40,000 btl*

The Lequin family bought their first plot in Santenay in Le Clos Genet in 1669 on a 120-year mortgage. The first Louis Lequin founded the domain in 1852. It expanded, acquiring plots in both the Côte de Beaune and Côte de Nuits. The present Louis Lequin took over in 1993. There are plots in Santenay (premier cru La Comme), Chassagne Montrachet (premier cru Morgeot, both red and white), Bâtard Montrachet, Pommard, Corton, Corton Charlemagne, and Nuits Saint Georges. The whites age in a third each of new, 1-year, and 2-year barriques, with battonage every day. Black grapes are destemmed. spend 6 days in cold maceration, ferment for 12-15 days with pump-over, and age in 25% new barriques for 16-18 months.

Domaine Lucien Muzard et Fils

11 Bis, Rue De La Cour Verreuil, 21590 Santenay	📞 *+33 3 80 20 61 85*
@ *lucienmuzard71@gmail.com*	👤 *Claude & Hervé Muzard*
⊕ *www.facebook.com/domainemuzard*	⬤ *Santenay [map]*
📅 🏭 🍇 🛢 🗤	*19 ha; 100,000 btl*

The Muzard family has been in Santenay since the seventeenth century. Brothers Claude and Hervé Muzard, who are the ninth generation, took over domain from their father Lucien in 1995 and started estate-bottling. The majority of vineyards are in Santenay, including five premier crus; other plots are in Maranges and Chassagne Montrachet. Their largest holding is in Santenay premier Cru Maladière. A small negociant activity (about 10% of production) extends the range into some extra appellations. Red is 80% of production. Until recently reds were all destemmed, but now a small amount of whole clusters is used. Wines are aged in barriques of up to four years age, but there are now also some experiments with larger barrels.

Monthélie

Profiles of Leading Estates

Domaine Henri et Gilles Buisson   *

Impasse Du Clou, 21190 Saint-Romain	📞 *+33 3 80 21 22 22*
@ *contact@domaine-buisson.com*	👤 *Franck Buisson*
🌐 *www.domaine-buisson.com*	🔘 *Saint-Romain*
📋🏭🍇🛢 *20 ha; 85,000 btl*	*St. Romain, Le Jarron*

The Buissons have been making wine in Saint Romain for eight generations, but the domain was established when Henri Buisson decided to start bottling his own wines in 1947 instead of selling them to the negociants. The domain continued under his son Gilles, and now is run by two grandsons, winemaker Frédéric and marketing manager Franck. The winery is in the heart of the village, nestled under the rocky hills that surround Saint-Romain. "We've been here for generations, and we've expanded by buying the neighbors," explains Franck as he points to several surrounding buildings that are now part of the domain. This is the most important, and one of the best, domains in the appellation, with its 11 ha in Saint-Romain making up over 10% of the small AOP.

The first estate vineyards were in Saint Romain, where there are cuvées from separate lieu-dits. "We thought of doing an assemblage for a village Saint-Romain," says Franck, "but we prefer to use some grapes in the blend to make a good Bourgogne rather than to make a weak Saint-Romain." Saint Romain is a little over half of production overall, and each of the three cuvées in Saint Romain (one red and two white) carries the name of a lieu-dit. Vineyards elsewhere in the Côte de Beaune include Meursault and Corton, and some Bourgogne near Saint-Romain.

Production is two thirds red to one third white. All wines spend about a year in barrique, depending on vintage. New oak ranges from 20% for Saint Romain to 60% for Corton. The style is clean and pure, and tends to elegance, sleek for the reds, linear and precise for the whites. The Saint-Romain red Sous Roche shows a light, nutty character, a little reminiscent of Chassagne Montrachet. Corton-Renardes is sleek and elegant. In whites, Saint-Romain Perrières comes from a partly north-facing plot with thin soils, and shows a linear style of yellow fruits, more saline than mineral. Sous Château comes from the other side of the hill, on soils with more clay facing full south, and is more textured with a broader palate, but still reflecting the purity of house style.

The focus has been on organic viticulture since the 1970s; the extreme manifestation is the production of the Absolu cuvées, one red and one white, from Saint Romain, which have no added sulfur. The crisp, sleek style is accentuated in the Absolu cuvées.

Domaine Marc Colin et Fils   **

Gamay, 21190 Saint-Aubin	📞 *+33 3 80 21 30 43*
@ *contact@marc-colin.com*	👤 *Caroline & Damien Colin*
🌐 *www.marc-colin.com*	🔘 *Saint-Aubin [map]*
🌙🏭🍇🕒 *12 ha; 80,000 btl*	*Saint-Aubin, en Remilly*

Starting with 7-8 ha, Marc Colin began to make wine with his brother Jacques around 1970, and created the domain in 1979. Marc retired in 2008, and the domain is now run

by his sons Damien and Joseph, and their sister Caroline. (The domain was larger until brother Pierre-Yves, who had been the winemaker together with his father, took out his 6 ha share to run separately as Domaine Pierre-Yves Colin-Morey.)

Winemaking is centered in some old buildings in the main street of St. Aubin, and a bit farther along is a modern tasting room. The Colins own about half the vineyards, and the other half is rented. About 80% is Chardonnay, with the rest split between Aligoté and Pinot Noir. There are 12 different cuvées from St. Aubin, and also Chassagne and Puligny Montrachet. "As we look more and more for finesse, freshness, and minerality, we have reduced new oak and battonage," Damien says. "St. Aubin has 15% new oak, whereas eight years ago it was 30%. St Aubin is cooler so we always have freshness and minerality. Puligny is sometimes like St. Aubin but can be more floral. Chassagne is usually a bit fatter."

The house style is elegant and precise. The St. Aubins are unusually fine for the appellation, but the Puligny shows a touch more tension, and the Chassagne is indeed fatter. It would be good policy to drink St. Aubin and the Chassagne lieu-dit first, while waiting for the Puligny and Chassagne premier crus to come around.

Domaine Hubert Lamy   *

20 Rue Des Lavières, 21190 Saint-Aubin	📞 *+33 3 80 21 32 55*
@ *hubertlamydomaine@gmail.com*	👤 *Olivier Lamy*
🌐 *www.domainehubertlamy.com*	📷 *Saint-Aubin [map]*
🚫🌿🍇🍷 *19 ha; 110,000 btl*	*Saint-Aubin, en Remilly*

The Lamy's have been making wine in St. Aubin since the seventeenth century. The domain is located just off the main street in a workmanlike building, somewhat like an oversize converted garage. Hubert Lamy started bottling his own wine in 1973, when the domain was created with 8 ha; it increased significantly during the 1990s. All wine has been estate bottled since Olivier took over in 1996. Now there are 47 parcels altogether, two thirds in St, Aubin, but there are small holdings also in Puligny Montrachet, Chassagne Montrachet, and Santenay. More than three quarters are Chardonnay. Some parcels of Pinot Noir have been replanted with Chardonnay. "My father started the switch to white wine in 1970," says Olivier, "It's not the terroir, it's not the typicité, it's commercial. But this is a return to the situation of many years ago, when production was white." There are 5 red cuvées and 16 white, including 7 premier cru St. Aubin.

The style has lightened since Olivier started. "When I was younger I worked at Coche Dury and with Henri Jayer, and wanted to make wines like they do, but if I use the same techniques in St. Aubin, I won't make the same wines." He describes his target now as wines that are "ripe, fresh, and round, which can be a difficult combination. When I was young, I tried to copy Puligny, but my tastes have changed in twenty years and I try to make wine that expresses the terroir of St. Aubin."

Winemaking uses 2-3 days' cold maceration, followed by a two-week fermentation, and then a year or longer in barriques followed by a year in stainless steel on the lees. New oak has backed off from 30% ten years ago. "Now we are using less and less." The most interesting wines here are white (it was a good decision to focus on Chardonnay). St. Aubin premier cru Clos de Meix has more stone fruits than citrus but plays to freshness, Derrière Chez Edouard is fuller and more structured, Frionnes is tighter with more sense of purity, en Remilly is fine and textured and resembles the Puligny, and Clos de Chatenière comes even closer to Puligny with a steely sense of minerality. The best from St. Aubin is usually the premier cru Les Murgers des Dents de Chiens. The Puligny village wine itself is tight and pure, and Chassagne is broader. Making some of the best wine in the appellation, the domain is one of the benchmarks of St. Aubin, and actually I prefer the St. Aubins to the Chassagnes. The house style shows stone fruits with a characteristic catch of lime at the end, and has focused more on minerality in the past ten years. The tipping point for developing away from primary character is 5-6 years, and most people will want to drink them in that span.

Profiles of Important Estates

Domaine Christophe Buisson

21190 Saint-Romain	📞 *+33 3 80 21 63 92*
@ *domainechristophebuisson@wanadoo.fr*	👤 *Christophe Buisson*
🌐 *www.christophe-buisson.com*	◉ *Saint-Romain*
🗓️ 🏭 🍇 🚜	🍾 *Saint Romain, Absolu*
43 ha; 220,000 btl	🍶 *Meursault, Marguerite*

Located in Saint Romain, this family-run domain also has vineyards elsewhere on the Côte de Beaune (Meursault, Auxey Duresses, Volnay, and Pommard) and in Corton. The focus is on natural wine. Chemical products are limited in viticulture (herbicides and pesticides are not used). Vinification uses indigenous yeast and tends to be protracted. Elevage on the lees lasts a year in barriques (with 10% new oak). Sulfur usage is minimal, and the two Absolu cuvées (one St. Romain white and one red) have zero sulfur added during vinification. Production of Absolu is small: a thousand or so bottles of each color. When asked if the wines are stable with no protection against oxidation, third generation winemaker Frédérick Buisson shrugs and says, "try them." At least when young there certainly seems to be no problem. The style of the whites tends toward minerality; the reds are elegant and can be a little spicy.

Domaine de Chassorney

Rue Chevrotin, 21190 Saint Romain	📞 *+33 3 80 21 65 55*
@ *chassorney@orange.fr*	👤 *Frédéric Cossard*
🌐 *www.chassorney.com*	◉ *Saint-Romain*
🗓️ 🍇 🚜	*10 ha*

Frédéric Cossard started in the milk trade, became a wine merchant, and then created his domain from scratch in 1996 by renting vineyards. He also makes wine as a negociant, simply using the label Frédéric Cossard (grapes come from growers who follow his rule book for viticulture). The wine was made at first in rented space in the village of Saint Romain, then in 1998 Frédéric bought a house and made the wine in the cellars underneath, and then as he expanded, he purchased an old pig farm a mile outside the village and built a new winery there. He makes natural wines, avoiding sulfur dioxide to the extent of cleaning his barrels with ozone. White grapes are pressed directly to barrique in oxidative conditions, the idea being that this protects against future oxidation; there is no battonage because fermentation lasts long enough to keep the wine turbid. The wine is usually bottled the following September, still with some carbon dioxide, which takes another year to assimilate. Reds ferment as whole bunches in open vats. Because there s no sulfur, the wines go straight on to malolactic fermentation. Barriques are a mix of new and 1-3-year. Red wines include Saint Romain, Auxey-Duresses, Savigny-lès-Beaune, Volnay and three Volnay premier crus, and Pommard Les Pezerolles. Whites are Saint Romain and Auxey Duresses. Frédéric also makes wine under his own name from grapes purchased from other place, including Beaujolais, Jura, and Languedoc.

Domaine Darviot Perrin

22 Grande Rue, 21190 Monthélie	📞 *+33 3 80 21 27 45*
@ *domaine.darviot-perrin@wanadoo.fr*	👤 *Didier Darviot*
🌐📄 *11 ha*	📍 *Monthélie*

Didier Darviot created the domain in 1989 with his wife Geneviève, whose family provided the Perrin half of the vineyards. Their daughter Alix now makes the wine with her father. The domain is based in Monthelie, but most of its holdings are in Meursault, Chassagne Montrachet, and Volnay. The holdings in Meursault include the three top premier crus, Charmes, Genevrières, and Perrières, offering an unusual opportunity for direct comparison. Chassagne Montrachet includes premier cru Blanchots-Dessus, just under Le Montrachet; and there is also premier cru Volnay. Average vine age is 60 years, with the oldest around 90 years. Reds are destemmed and whites are pressed as whole bunches. The cellars are very cool, and malolactic fermentation has been known to take up to a year. The wines age in 25% new barriques, and often are released a year after other growers. The domain is really best known for its whites. The Meursault lieu-dit, Sous la Velle, seems a little obvious, with impressions of sweet new oak actually more evident in young wines than in the premier crus, where the style tends perhaps more to salinity than minerality but is complex and long.

Domaine Dujardin

1 Grande Rue, 21190 Monthélie	📞 *+33 3 80 21 20 08*
@ *domaine.dujardin@orange.fr*	👤 *Ulrich Dujardin*
🌐 *www.domaine-dujardin.com*	📍 *Monthélie*
📅🏭🍇🌿	*9 ha; 40,000 btl*

Based in Monthélie, just north of Meursault, this small family domain produces wines from the surrounding appellations. Ulrich Dujardin, who had been at the domain since 1990, took over in 2007 when the owners, the Bouzerands, retired. Ulrich added a negociant activity in 2014. The cellars date from the twelfth and fifteenth century, excavated by Cistercian monks. Production is split between red and white. The reds comprise Monthélie and two premier crus, Les Vignes Rondes and Les Champs Fulliot, and a village Beaune. Whites comprise village wines from Monthélie, Auxey-Duresses, and Meursault. Reds age in barrique for 18-24 months, whites for 12-18 months. The domain also cultivates escargots.

Domaine Alain Gras

Rue Sous-la-Velle, Village Haut, 21190 Saint Romain	📞 *+33 3 80 21 27 83*
@ *contact@domaine-alain-gras.com*	👤 *Alain Gras*
🌐 *www.domaine-alain-gras.com*	📍 *Saint-Romain*
📅🏭🍇🌿	*14 ha; 80,000 btl*

Alain took over his family vineyards in 1979. Located on top of a hill, the winery has panoramic views over Saint Romain. Vineyards are mostly in Saint Romain (including the recent acquisition of a couple more hectares), but extend to Meursault and Auxey Duresses. Reds are destemmed and get about 15% new oak; whites are fermented as partial whole clusters and get about 20% new oak. This is generally regarded as the top producer in Saint Romain, and the wines are well represented in restaurants in France.

Sylvain Langoureau

20 Rue de la Fontenotte, 21190 Saint-Aubin	📞 *+33 3 80 21 39 99*
@ *domainesylvainlangoureau@orange.fr*	👤 *Sylvain & Nathalie Langoureau*
📅🏭🍇🌿 *10 ha; 65,000 btl*	📍 *Saint-Aubin [map]*

Sylvain Langoureau and his wife Nathalie founded this small domain in 1988. Sylvain is the fifth generation of growers in his family, but the first to bottle wine instead of selling to negociants. Based in the hamlet of Gamay between St. Aubin and Puligny Montrachet., the domain has plots mostly in St. Aubin but also in Meursault, Puligny, and Chassagne Montrachet. Plantings are three quarters Chardonnay, with 15% Pinot Noir and 10% Aligoté. There are 6 premier crus in St. Aubin: Sur Gamay, Les Frionnes, Le Champlot, Bas de Vermarain, Derrière chez Edouard, and (especially) en Remilly. There are also premier crus Les Chalumeaux and La Garenne from Puligny, Meursault premier cru Blagny, and Chassagne lieu-dit Les Pierres. Chassagne Les Voillenots Dessous is red. The Bourgogne is Aligoté. Wines age in 20-30% new barriques without any battonage.

Château de Monthelie

21190 Monthélie	☏ *+33 3 80 21 23 32*
@ *desuremain@wanadoo.fr*	👤 *Dominique de Suremain*
⊕ *www.domaine-eric-de-suremain.com*	🖼 *Monthélie*
🎛 🏭 🍇 🍶	*11 ha; 45,000 btl*

The Château de Monthélie, which dates from the sixteenth century, has been in the de Suremain family since 1903. Eric de Suremain took over in 1978 and made the domain into a leader in biodynamic viticulture. Vineyards are split almost equally between Monthélie, just to the west of Volnay, and Rully, on the Côte Chalonnaise. Cuvées from Monthélie are labeled as Château de Monthélie, while those from Rully are labeled as Eric de Suremain. Four plots make up almost a hectare of village Monthélie, and there are five premier crus, all rather small except for the 3 ha of Sur La Velle.

Domaine Henri Prudhon et Fils

32, Rue Des Perrières, 21190 Saint-Aubin	☏ *+33 3 80 21 36 70*
@ *contact@henri-prudhon.fr*	👤 *Vincent & Philippe Prudhon*
⊕ *www.henri-prudhon.fr*	🖼 *Saint-Aubin [map]*
🎛 🏭 🍇 🌿	*15 ha; 90,000 btl*

Henri Prudhon and his wife Marguerite established this domain in 1945 with vineyards from both sides of the family. Their son Gérard expanded into Chassagne and Puligny Montrachet, and started estate-bottling in 1983. His sons Vincent and Philippe have now taken over. There are about 2 ha in Bourgogne (Aligoté, Chardonnay, and Pinot Noir). In St Aubin, there are 5 ha of Chardonnay (including village wine and 7 premier crus: Les Castets, Sur le Sentier du Clou, Les Perrières, Sur Gamay, La Chantenière, en Remilly, and Murgers Dents de Chien) and 6 ha of Pinot Noir (including village wine and 3 premier crus: Les Frionnes, Sur le Sentier du Clou, and Les Rouges Gorges). There's also one lieu-dit and one premier cru in each of Chassagne and Puligny Montrachet. The whites age with no new oak for village wine, 20-35% depending on the site for the St. Aubin premier crus, 30% or 50% in Chassagne and Puligny premier crus. Very little new oak is used for the reds. Aging lasts 9-12 months.

Domaine Gérard Thomas et Filles

6, Rue Des Perrières, 21190 Saint-Aubin	☏ *+33 3 80 21 32 57*
@ *domaine.gerard.thomas@orange.fr*	👤 *Isabelle et Anne-Sophie s*
🎛 🏭 🍇 🚜 *12 ha; 30,000 btl*	🖼 *Saint-Aubin [map]*

Gérard has run this estate since 1982, with his daughters Isabelle and Anne now taking over. Vineyards are focused on St. Aubin, but Gérard has expanded into Puligny and Chassagne Montrachet. The largest holdings are almost 2 ha in premier cru Les Murgers de Dents de Chien and more than 1.5 ha in lieu-Dit Champ Trant in St. Aubin. Most production is white, and other cuvées include premier crus La Chatenière, Frionnes, and Combes from St. Aubin, lieu-dit Le Trezin and premier cru La Garenne from Puligny, and Meursault Blagny premier cru. Red comes from Chassagne premier cru Les Chenevottes. The whites receive 25% new oak and age in barrique for 10 months.

Côte Chalonnaise

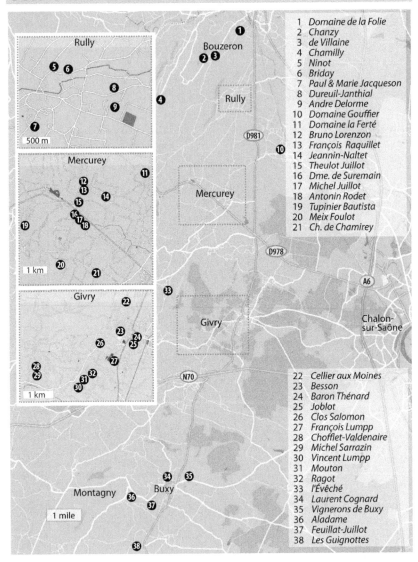

1	Domaine de la Folie
2	Chanzy
3	de Villaine
4	Chamilly
5	Ninot
6	Briday
7	Paul & Marie Jacqueson
8	Dureuil-Janthial
9	Andre Delorme
10	Domaine Gouffier
11	Domaine la Ferté
12	Bruno Lorenzon
13	François Raquillet
14	Jeannin-Naltet
15	Theulot Juillot
16	Dme. de Suremain
17	Michel Juillot
18	Antonin Rodet
19	Tupinier Bautista
20	Meix Foulot
21	Ch. de Chamirey

22	Cellier aux Moines
23	Besson
24	Baron Thénard
25	Joblot
26	Clos Salomon
27	François Lumpp
28	Chofflet-Valdenaire
29	Michel Sarrazin
30	Vincent Lumpp
31	Mouton
32	Ragot
33	l'Évêché
34	Laurent Cognard
35	Vignerons de Buxy
36	Aladame
37	Feuillat-Juillot
38	Les Guignottes

Bouzeron

Profiles of Leading Estates

Domaine Aubert et Pamela De Villaine *

2, Rue De La Fontaine, 71150 Bouzeron	📞 +33 3 85 91 20 50
@ contact@de-villaine.com	🧑 *Pierre De Benoist*
⊕ *www.de-villaine.com*	⬤ *Bouzeron* [map]
🏠🏭🌿🍷	🍷 *Mercurey, Les Montots*
303 ha; 140,000 btl	*Bourgogne, Les Clous*

DOMAINE A. ET P. DE VILLAINE
Propriétaire à Bouzeron

Bouzeron

Appellation Bouzeron Contrôlée

Mis en Bouteille au Domaine

In addition to running Domaine de la Romanée Conti, Aubert Villaine, together with his wife Pamela, makes wine at this domain in the Côte Chalonnaise. The Villaines purchased and revived the domain in the seventies, expanding it from its original 8 ha. The domain has been managed since 2000 by Aubert's nephew, Pierre de Benoist. Almost half of the domain's vineyards are in Bouzeron, planted with Aligoté Doré on the tops of the slopes; Chardonnay and Pinot Noir are planted lower. The Aligoté makes the Bouzeron appellation wine.

Aubert became one of the spokesmen for Aligoté when he was involved in obtaining appellation status for Bouzeron, and the domain wine is one of the flagships for the appellation, showing citrus fruits, sometimes a touch spicy, in a light and attractive style. The Chardonnay and Pinot Noir are the basis for the various Bourgogne Côte Chalonnaise cuvées: Les Clous and Les Clous Aimé in whites; Les Clous, La Fortune, and La Digoine in reds. The domain expanded into Rully with a purchase of 10 ha, for both red and white, in 2015 and 2016, followed by the purchase of the 12 ha of Domaine de Rully Saint Michel (where the last vintage under this name was 2017). The cuverie needed to be expanded to handle the new vineyards.

For the Bourgogne and Rully, the house style for Chardonnay shows as a delicious acidity balancing between citrus and stone fruits with a nicely textured finish: both the Les Clous and Les Clous Aimé are a cut above the usual generic Bourgogne Blanc. Among the reds, I prefer the Mercurey to the Bourgogne cuvées. The domain produced wine exclusively from the Côte Chalonnaise until it expanded by purchasing a small parcel of Pinot Noir in Santenay in 2011 followed in 2014 by a parcel of white in St. Aubin premier cru les Perrières.

Profiles of Important Estates

Maison Chanzy

1, Rue De La Fontaine, 71150 Bouzeron	📞 +33 3 85 87 23 69
@ domaine@chanzy.com	🧑 *Karine Moréteaux*
⊕ *www.domaine-chanzy.com*	⬤ *Bouzeron* [map]
🚶🏭🌿🍷🍷	*80 ha; 500,000 btl*

Bought out of bankruptcy in 2012 by a private equity fund based in Paris, Bouzeron-based Chanzy is now the center of Groupe Chanzy, which also owns Domaine Pagnota, based in

Chagny just to the north of Bouzeron. Together the two houses are the largest landowner on Côte Chalonnaise, and also produce wines from the Côte d'Or. The group also owns Château Signac in the southern Rhône. Chanzy's estate wines are labeled as Domaine Chanzy, and negociant wines as Maison Chanzy. Winemaking was entrusted to the Jessiaume family, after they sold their own domain in Santenay, with Jean-Baptiste making the reds, his father Marc making the whites, and uncle Pascal in charge of the vineyards. Max Blondelle came as winemaker in 2019. A brand called "B" is targeted at the luxury market, in an overtly commercial approach.

Rully

Profiles of Leading Estates

Domaine Vincent Dureuil-Janthial ***

Rue De La Buisserolle, 71150 Rully	📞 *+33 3 85 87 26 32*
@ *vincent.dureuil@wanadoo.fr*	🧑 *Vincent Dureuil*
🌐 *dureuiljanthial-vins.com*	📀 *Rully [map]*
📅 🏭 🍇 🍂	🍾 *Rully, Maizières*
20 ha; 100,000 btl	*Rully, Margotés*

The range and quality of wines justify this estate's reputation as the most important domain in Rully. At the back of the town, a tasting room in a charming house on one side of the street is run by Vincent's father, and a practical winery, more or less a warehouse, extends along the opposite side of the street. The domain was started by Vincent's grandfather; Vincent took over twenty years ago when he was 24. There is also a small negociant activity under the name of Céline et Vincent Dureuil.

The domain's holdings are a bit complicated: Vincent has 3 ha in his own name, his father has some, his father-in-law has 1 ha (premier cru in Nuits St. Georges), and 6 ha are rented on long term contracts. "There's no land for sale in Rully, so it's impossible to buy more vineyards," Vincent explains. Vineyards are organic, because "biodynamic is just too expensive for the Côte Chalonnaise."

The 16 cuvées come mostly from Rully, with many premier crus, which we tasted not according to terroirs, but in order of vine age, which Vincent evidently views as a more important determinant of quality. The oldest vineyard is in Meix Cadots (the Vieilles Vignes cuvée, planted in 1920, now giving yields of 30 hl/ha.) "For the money it would be better to plant new vines and get 55 hl/ha, but it's four generations of work," Vincent says ruefully. The style shows minerality and precision. The whites are the glory of the domain, at their best a lesser man's Puligny. Reds show the limitations of the Chalonnaise, but with characteristic precision for Rully and earthy breadth for Mercurey.

Maison P. et M. Jacqueson *

12 Rue Saint Laurent, 71150 Rully	📞 *+33 3 85 43 26 05*
@ *marie@jacqueson-vins.fr*	🧑 *Pierre& Marie Jacqueson*
🌐 *www.jacqueson-vins.fr*	📀 *Rully [map]*
📅 🏭 🍇 🛢 🍃	🍾 *Rully, Cloux*
18 ha; 130,000 btl	*Rully, Margotés*

The long building that dominates the street was built in 2013; previously the domain was in much smaller space across the road. Marie Jacqueson's grandfather started the domain in 1946 with some vines from his parents. He had another job, working for a domain in Mercurey, but slowly he bought vines. Her father took over in 1972, and Marie took over in 2006. Vineyards continue to be added, and the domain has now almost doubled in size from when Marie's father started.

The domain is principally in Rully but also has some Bouzeron and Mercurey. Overall it is 60% white. There are 18 different cuvées from Bourgogne Aligoté through Rully premier cru in whites and reds, and a Passetoutgrains—"We have everything," Marie says. "Our specialty with the Bouzeron is the élevage of Aligoté entirely in fûts (but no new wood, of course)."

The heart of the domain lies in the Rully premier crus, Grésigny (with the oldest vines of the domain, planted by Marie's grandfather 60 years ago), La Pucelle, Raclot, and Les Cordères in white, and Les Naugues and Les Cloux in red. "All the white Rully premier crus are treated the same way and have 20% new oak. Any differences are due to terroir," Marie says. For reds there is complete destemming and 25% new oak. The house style with whites is quite fat, more stone fruits than citrus, with a texture on the palate approaching the style of the Côte d'Or. Reds can be tight at first, then broaden and become earthy after a year or so.

Profiles of Important Estates

Domaine Michel Briday

31, Grande Rue, 71150 Rully	📞 *+33 3 85 87 07 90*
@ *domainemichelbriday@orange.fr*	👤 *Sandrine Briday*
🌐 *www.domaine-briday.com*	🗺 *Rully [map]*
☺ 🏭 🍇 ❧	*15 ha; 55,000 btl*

Michel Briday founded the domain in 1976 by renting 6 ha of vineyards. The first estate vineyards were purchased in 1996. Michel's son, Stéphane started working with his father in 1988, and took over the domain in 2000. The estate expanded beyond Rully into Bouzeron and Mercurey. Most (60%) of production is white. The focus is on Rully, where there are cuvées of village wine, a single-vineyard wine from a lieu-dit, and 5 white and 2 red premier crus. There are also a Bouzeron, two Mercureys, a Bourgogne Rouge, and a Crémant. The village Rully white ages mostly or entirely in vat, and the lieu-dit, Clos des Remenots, and the premier crus age in barriques with up to 10% new oak. Clos de Remenots lies between two premier crus and can be more powerful. The red Rully premier crus age in barriques with 25% new oak. Stéphane does not like obviously oaky aromas, and has been moving from 225-liter barriques to larger barrels of 300- or 400-liters that reduce oak contact and increase freshness.

Domaine de la Folie

71150 Chagny	📞 *+33 3 85 87 18 59*
@ *contact@domainedelafolie.fr*	👤 *Clémence & Baptiste Dubrulle*
🌐 *www.domainedelafolie.fr*	🗺 *Rully [map]*
📅 🏭 🍇 🚜	*12 ha; 50,000 btl*

Located in Chagny on the northern border of the Côte Chalonnaise, the domain has been in the family for five generations, but Clémence and her husband Baptiste Dubrulle are the first actually to live and make wine there. When they took over in 2010, the domain was quite run down, and they spent the first two years bringing it back up to speed. All the vineyards are in Rully. The communal plots are in the Clos la Folie. There are two premier crus for white wines, both monopoles: Clos de Chaigne is more powerful, and Clos St Jacques is more elegant. The two reds come from the premier cru Clos de Bellecroix: the Croix de Bellecroix cuvée comes from north-northeast-facing vineyards, while the richer Cuvée Marée comes from east-facing vineyards. The Clos la Folie white and the Clos de Bellecroix red age in cuve; the other cuvées age in barriques with 20% new oak.

Maison André Delorme

11 Rue Des Bordes, 71150 Rully	📞 *+33 3 85 87 10 12*
@ *caveau@andre-delorme.com*	👤 *Rose Leguissimo*
🌐 *www.andre-delorme.com*	🔘 *Rully [map]*
🚶🏭🍇🛢🚜	*70 ha; 800,000 btl*

There really was an André Delorme, who founded a negociant in Rully when he returned from the war in 1942. The Maison grew to become a producer of Bourgogne Crémant and a major producer on the Côte Chalonnaise. It owns two domains, Domaine de la Vigne au Roy and Domaine Les Vignes de l'Ange, but wines come mostly from purchased grapes. In 2005, it was sold to Veuve Ambal, the largest producer of Crémant in Burgundy, formerly also located in Rully, now located in new cellars just south of Beaune. There has been some investment, and a new winemaking team took over. Veuve Ambal also owns the negociant Prosper Maufoux (Maison des Grands Crus) in Santenay.

Domaine Ninot

Le Meix Guillaume, 2 Rue De Chagny, 71150 Rully	📞 *+33 3 85 87 07 79*
@ *ninot.domaine@wanadoo.fr*	👤 *Erell & Flavien Ninot*
🌐 *www.domaineninot.com*	🔘 *Rully [map]*
📅🏭🍇🍂	*14 ha; 50,000 btl*

"We've been barrel makers and winemakers since the fourteenth century," says Erell Ninot, who has runs the domain since 2003 with her brother Flavien. The domain had a difficult patch when her grandfather died when Erell's father was only 14, and the estate was divided, but her father rebuilt the domain from his share of 5 ha. Cuvées are divided between Rully and Mercurey, half red and half white. Wine making uses a mixture of vats (to keep freshness) and barriques (with little new oak), and both reds and whites age for 12-18 months before release. Rully Chaponnière is the flagship red; top whites are La Barre and Gresigny.

Domaine Jean Baptiste Ponsot

26, Grande Rue, 71150 Rully	📞 *+33 3 85 87 17 90*
@ *domaine.ponsot@orange.fr*	👤 *Jean-Baptiste Ponsot*
🌐 *domaine-jean-baptiste-ponsot.fr*	🔘 *Rully*
📅🏭🍇🌿	*9 ha*

The domain was established by Lucien Ponsot in 1954. His son, Bernard, expanded the vineyards and sold the fruit to negociant Olivier Leflaive. Bernard's son, Jean-Baptiste, took over in 2000 (he was only 20 at the time), planted new vineyards on land that had not previously been cultivated, and moved into estate-bottling. He built a new cellar in 2005. All the vineyards are in Rully, with one third in the village AOP (include the lieu-dit En Bas de Vauvry, which is a monopole) and two thirds in premier crus (Molesme, Montpalais, and La Fosse); production is two thirds white and a third red. Wines move into barriques for malolactic fermentation and then age for 12 months.

Domaine Rois Mages

21 Rue des Buis, 71150 Rully	📞 *+33 6 80 38 66 16*
@ *debavelaere_f@hotmail.com*	👤 *Félix Debavelaere*
🌐 *rois-mages.com*	🔘 *Rully*
🚶🏭🍇🚜	*11 ha*

Burgundian Anne-Sophie Debavelaere founded this domain with the purchase of vineyards in Rully in 1954, later expanding into Bouzeron and into Beaune. Her son Félix joined her and took over in 2009. Vineyards are in several of the *climats* of Rully village plus premier cru Les Pierres. Each lieu-dit is vinified as a separate cuvée. There are whites from all the plots, and reds from the Chaponières lieu-dit and the premier cru. The other cuvées are the Aligoté from Bouzeron and a red from Beaune premier cru Les Sceaux. All the wines age in barriques for 12 months followed by a further 6 months on the lees in stainless steel.

Montagny

Profiles of Leading Estates

Domaine Stéphane Aladame ✳

Rue Du Lavoir, 71390 Montagny-lès-Buxy	☎ +33 3 85 92 06 01
@ aladame@wanadoo.fr	👤 Stéphane Aladame
🌐 www.aladame.fr	Montagny [map]
🍷 🏭 🍇 🛢 🛢 8 ha; 40,000 btl	Montagny, Les Maroques

The domain is located in a group of old buildings around a courtyard, just above the town of Montagny. "I created the domain in 1992 when I bought 2.5 ha from a vigneron who was retiring. I was eighteen at the time," recollects Stéphane Aladame. Since then, it's been built up slowly to its present size, and now there are six cuvées of Montagny premier cru plus a Crémant. There are no vines in Montagny village, but Stéphane has a negociant activity to produce Montagny AOP.

Cuvée Decouverte is an assemblage of premier crus from young vines (less than 20 years old), vinified in cuve for 10 months, with some lees. Cuvée Selection Vieilles Vignes comes from four different premier cru parcels (older than 40 years), and is matured 60% in oak with 10% new. Most of the premier crus are matured in proportions of old barriques and cuve, but the premier crus with the oldest vines (Les Coères at 45 years and Les Burnins at 90 years) are matured exclusively in old barriques.

The style tends to elegance, with smooth fruits, and a characteristic catch of lime at the end, reflecting the emphasis on maintaining freshness and precision. "I don't look for wines with too much maturity, too heavy. I harvest relatively early and want to keep acidity. I may have a degree less of alcohol, usually it's 12.5-13%. I look for minerality rather than richness," Stéphane says. Fruit concentration and the sense of texture resulting from oak exposure intensify going up the hierarchy.

Château de Chamirey ✳

Rue du Château, 71640 Mercurey	☎ +33 3 85 45 21 61
@ contact@domaines-devillard.com	👤 Amaury Devillard
🌐 www.chamirey.com	Mercurey [map]
😊 🏭 🍇 🏭	Mercurey, Clos du Roi
37 ha; 200,000 btl	Mercurey, en Pierrelet

The vineyards of this estate are exclusively in Mercurey, concentrated around the rather splendid château, which was added to the estate two generations ago in 1931. The modern winery has a spacious tasting room. The fifth generation of the Devillard family run the estate today. Across from the château is a modern winery, with a spacious tasting room and restaurant. Vineyards are two thirds black to one third white, with 15 ha in premier crus. The whites are fruit-driven and nicely rounded, very attractive for short or mid-term drinking, but not likely to be especially long-lived.

The village wine is matured in 400 liter casks to preserve its minerality, with no new oak; the top white is a premier cru, the monopole La Mission, which is aged for 15 months in barriques with one third new oak. The red Mercurey comes from several plots, six from the village AOP, and includes two from premier crus, to increase quality, which has an influence especially in cooler years. Premier cru Ruelles is a monopole, but the top red is Les Cinq, a blend of the best lots from each of the five premier crus (production is small, only 1,900 bottles in 2010).

All wines, especially the reds, have evident notes of ripeness approaching over-ripeness, so it was not a surprise to hear that, "We are always the last in Mercurey to harvest, we pick very late" (for both reds and whites). In addition to Château de Chamirey, the Devillards own Domaine de Perdrix in Nuits St. Georges, Domaine de la Ferté just to the south in Givry, and in 2018 purchased Domaine Rolet in the Jura.

Domaine Joblot   *

4, Rue Pasteur, 71640 Givry	📞 +33 3 85 44 30 77
@ domaine.joblot@wanadoo.fr	👤 Juliettte Joblot
🌐 www.domainejoblot.com	◉ Givry [map]
🚫 🏭 🍇 🍂 14 ha; 65,000 btl	⚑ Givry, Cellier aux Moines

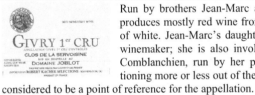

Run by brothers Jean-Marc and Vincent Joblot, this domain produces mostly red wine from Givry, with a small proportion of white. Jean-Marc's daughter Juliette is now taking over as winemaker; she is also involved with Domaine Lienhardt in Comblanchien, run by her partner Antoine Lienhardt. Functioning more or less out of the family property, Joblot is widely considered to be a point of reference for the appellation.

Vineyards in the northern part of Givry are three quarters in premier crus, the best of which are Clos du Cellier aux Moines (the oldest known vineyard in Givry) and Clos de la Servoisine. There are 8 cuvées altogether, 3 white and 5 red (including one red and one white Givry AOP; the rest are premier cru). One unusual feature here is that date of harvest is determined by acidity levels, so the wines have not succumbed to the fashion for increasing ripeness or over-ripeness. With painstaking viticulture, yields are kept low and there is intense selection of grapes at harvest. Grapes are destemmed, and there is long cool maceration before fermentation.

There's extensive use of new oak, but the brothers are very fussy about the extent of toast (it should not be too much); barrels come from a long-standing relationship with François Frères. Vinification is the same for all wines, with the stated aim of minimal intervention to ensure that differences between the cuvées are due solely to terroir. Oak can be evident in young wines, so do not try to drink before, say, three years.

Domaine Michel Juillot   *

59, Grande Rue, 71640 Mercurey	📞 +33 3 85 98 99 89
@ infos@domaine-michel-juillot.fr	👤 Laurent Juillot
🌐 www.domaine-michel-juillot.fr	◉ Mercurey [map]
☺ 🏭 🍇 ✿	⚑ Mercurey, Clos Tonnerre
33 ha; 180,000 btl	Mercurey, Vignes de Maillonge

Located on the main road through Mercurey, the tasting room of this domain seems continually thronged with visitors. The domain is now in its fourth generation, under Laurent

2006

Domaine Michel Juillot

Mercurey

Juillot since 1988 (although his father, Michel, a well known character in the town, remains in evidence). It's expanded greatly under the last two generations, from 6 ha when Michel took it over in 1963.

Two thirds of the vineyards are in Mercurey, mostly red, with a significant proportion in premier crus; in addition there are holdings in Rully and Bourgogne, and also some in Aloxe-Corton and Corton. The range is wide, but the real interest here is to compare the premier crus, vinified in the same way for either whites or reds, to demonstrate terroir. Vinification is traditional, with élevage in barriques for 12 months for whites and 16-18 months for reds. For whites, new oak (25%) is used only for the three premier crus; for reds, new oak varies from 15% for the Mercurey to 35% for the five premier crus. The barriques come mostly from the Vosges. There's an unusual policy of holding stocks from older vintages.

The reds tend to start out a little hard, which is typical of Mercurey, but soften in an earthy direction after a couple of years; they tend to peak around five or six years after the vintage. The whites in my view tend to be more successful; the Mercurey AOP is a bit straightforward in its flavor spectrum, but the premier crus show a nice sense of reserve to the stone and citrus fruits.

Domaine Bruno Lorenzon   *

Rue du Reu, 71640 Mercurey	📞 +33 3 85 45 13 51
@ contact@domainelorenzon.com	👤 Bruno Lorenzon
🌐 www.domainelorenzon.com	Mercurey [map]
📅 🏭 🍇 🍂 8 ha; 35,000 btl	Mercurey, Les Champs Martin

Carline

par

l●renzon
Mercurey.France

2010

In a back street of Mercurey, the domain itself has a somewhat dilapidated appearance; at the main entrance there's a notice directing you to the office around the back, which as likely as not will be closed also. Don't expect to be able to visit, with or without an appointment. Perhaps that is because Bruno Lorenzon is in the vineyards, following up on his favorite saying, "Great berries are 90% of the work."

This small domain is now in its third generation under Bruno, who took over in 1997, after prior experience in foreign countries (he has made wine in South Africa and New Zealand as a consultant), and a stint with the tonnellerie in Mercurey (with whom he remains associated). Bruno runs the domain together with his sister Carline. Barriques come from the tonnellerie (there is 20-40% new wood for whites and 15-40% for reds). Élevage lasts from 9 to 18 months.

Vineyards are almost exclusively in Mercurey, almost all in premier crus, with 4 ha of red and 1 ha of white (including 6 red and 5 white premier crus); there are also Montagny and Corton Charlemagne. The main holding is a large block (3.7 ha) in the center of the steep limestone slope of the Champs Martin premier cru. This is planted with both Pinot Noir and Chardonnay. The style is modern, tending to good color and extraction. It reaches its peak in the vieilles vignes cuvée Carline from Champs Martin (aged for 19 months in 40% new oak), which tends to have more power rather than greater typicity compared with the regular cuvée.

The domain is nominally available for visits on appointment, but don't count on there being anyone there when you turn up.

Domaine François Lumpp ✱

36, Avenue De Mortières, Le Pied Du Clou, 71640 Givry	📞 +33 3 85 44 45 57
@ domaine@francoislumpp.com	👤 Isabelle & François Lumpp
🌐 www.francoislumpp.com	⬤ Givry [map]
🗓️ 🏭 🍇 🚜	10 ha; 55,000 btl

Created when François, who had been making wine in Givry since 1977, split from his brother at the family domain in 1991 to create his own domain, this is considered to be one of the most reliable domains in Givry. (His brother's domain is Vincent Lumpp: see profile.) It is headquartered in a workmanlike building on the main road through town. Starting with 3.5 ha, the domain has slowly expanded. Today there are 7.5 ha of red and 2 ha of white.

The vineyards are exclusively in Givry; there's a village white cuvée and premier cru, and six red premier crus. In fact, the majority of production is in premier crus. François and Isabelle Lumpp have replanted most of their vineyards with closer spacing to reduce yields (using a really dense 11,000 vines per hectare, with vines coming by selection massale from the Côte d'Or). The stated aim is to harvest at "just ripe," rather than over-ripe. The various premier crus are distinguished by position on the slope, with Pied de Clou at the bottom, next to the winery, Crausot at the top, and the best, La Vigne Rouge and Clos du Cras Long, coming from mid-slope. The 2 ha of Vigne Rouge are the most recent acquisition of the estate (in 2007).

New oak barriques can be found in the cellar, up to about 30%, but the aim is that the taste of oak should not be evident in the wine. Following plantings in Givry, the focus is on reds, but the domain has an equally high reputation for its whites. Reception can be on the chilly side for visitors.

Domaine François Raquillet ✱

19, Rue De Jamproyes, 71640 Mercurey	📞 +33 3 85 45 14 61
@ francoisraquillet@club-internet.fr	👤 François Raquillet
🌐 www.domaine-raquillet.com	⬤ Mercurey [map]
🚶 🌾 🍇 🛢 🥂	📍 Mercurey, Les Velley
10 ha; 50,000 btl	📍 Mercurey, Les Veleys

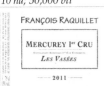

François Raquillet is proud of being the eleventh generation in a line of vignerons passing from father to son since the seventeenth century. The domain was formally established in 1963, and François joined his father in 1984; he took over together with his wife Emmanuelle in 1990. By reducing yields (by removing buds at bud break) and modernizing vinification, in particular increasing the emphasis on the quality of oak barrels (using barriques for reds, and 500 liter barrels for whites, with new oak now up to 30%), François revitalized the domain, which is now considered a reference point for Mercurey.

Holdings are closely focused on the appellation, with vieilles vignes village level white and red, and then a lieu-dit and premier cru white, and four premier cru reds. The estate vineyards in Mercurey have 8 ha of Pinot Noir and 2 ha of Chardonnay, with an average vine age of 35 years. They are supplemented with purchases of grapes from vineyards that François harvests himself, extending the range to a Bourgogne red, and white Rully premier cru and Meursault. After sorting, reds are fermented in concrete, whites in the

500 liter barrels, with little battonage. Elevage lasts a year, longer for the top premier crus. The red premier crus can show unusual minerality and precision for Mercurey. Although the domaine nominally welcomes visits, in practice visitors are likely to find a notice redirecting them to the communal tasting room in the town if they want to try the wines.

Profiles of Important Estates

Domaine Berthenet

Rue du Lavoir, 71390 Montagny-lès-Buxy	📞 *+33 9 65 38 99 03*
@ *contact@vinsberthenet.com*	👤 *Jean Pierre Berthenet*
⊕ *www.vinsberthenet.com*	◉ *Montagny [map]*
🧍🏭🍇🚜	*20 ha; 100,000 btl*

The domain formally dates from 1974, when Jean Berthenet purchased his first small plot of vines, but the Berthenets have been involved with wine in Montagny for four hundred years. Jean-Pierre took over from his parents in 1991, and the modern era started when he left the co-operative in 2001, built a new cellar the following year, and started to produce his own wine. Jean-Pierre was the first to introduce sustainable viticulture in the village. He now works with his son François. Production is focused on the 15 ha of Montagny, with a village wine and 6 premier crus; other cuvées include a Givry, Bourgogne (red, rosé, and Aligoté from a 2 ha plot, divided into the regular and Vieilles Vignes cuvée from vines planted in 1950), and a Crémant. A new machine has been purchased for gentler harvesting. Montagny AOP and premier cru Saint-Morille age in stainless steel, Platières and Montcuchots age in a mix of stainless steel and barriques, Vieilles Vignes and Coères age in barriques, and Symphonie ages in new oak.

Domaine Besson

9 Rue des Bois Chevaux, 71640 Givry	📞 *+33 3 85 44 42 44*
@ *xavierbesson3@wanadoo.fr*	👤 *Xavier & Guillemette Besson*
⊕ *www.domaine-besson-givry.com*	◉ *Givry [map]*
📅🍇♻	*8 ha*

This family domain started in 1938 with a few parcels in the lieu-dit Le Petit-Prétan around the château. Guillemette and Xavier Besson took over in 1989, and their son Henri-Vital joined in 2017. The winery is located in a fortified building dating from the Middle Ages, with a large vaulted cellar. Vineyards have clay soils on a limestone base. There are four white Givry village cuvées, two red village wines, and three red premier crus from Givry, and also a red premier cru from Beaune Les Champs-Pimont. Production is three quarters red. Whites are pressed as whole bunches, reds are destemmed and then have three days cold maceration before fermentation starts. The village wines see 30% new oak, which increases to 50% for the premier crus, using a mix of barriques and 500-liter barrels.

Cave des Vignerons de Buxy

Caveau De Buxy-Maison Millebuis, 4-6 Route De Chalon, 71390 Buxy *& Caveau de Saint Gengoux le National, 1 route de Curtil, 71460 Saint Gengoux le National*	📞 *+33 3 85 92 04 30*
@ *accueil@vigneronsdebuxy.fr*	👤 *Caroline Torland*
⊕ *www.vigneronsdebuxy.fr*	◉ *Montagny [map]*
🧍🏭🍇🚜	*1130 ha; 8,500,000 btl*

Created in 1931, today with 120 members, this cooperative is responsible for the major part of production in Montagny, and also produces wine from Givry, Rully, and Mercurey. It's a dynamic operation that has absorbed some smaller cooperatives, and constructed a new cave in 2004 to cope with expansion. In 2014 Mason Millebuis was introduced for an upper-level line, including single vineyard selections, and 2018 a new tasting room and boutique was opened under the Millebuis name. The cave is into oenotourism and offers a variety of activities.

Domaine du Cellier aux Moines

Clos du Cellier Aux Moines, 71640 Givry	📞 +33 3 85 44 53 75
@ contact@cellierauxmoines.fr	👤 Philippe & Catherine Pascal
🌐 www.cellierauxmoines.fr	🔘 Givry [map]
📅 🏭 🍇 🛢	8 ha; 20,000 btl

As the name indicates, this is an old ecclesiastical property, in fact founded by Cistercian monks from the Abbey de la Ferté around 1130. Located in the hills just west of Givry, in Givry's top premier cru, it was acquired and resurrected in 2004 by Catherine and Philippe Pascal, who came from a background in wine and luxury goods. The winemaker is Guillaume Marko from the Côte de Nuits. A new gravity-feed cellar has been constructed next to the old cellars. Winemaking is traditional: manual harvest, only partial destemming, aging in barriques with a third new oak. Vineyards are around the property, and more plots have since been purchased in Mercurey and Beaune. Local wines include Givry, Givry premier cru, Mercurey, and then from the Côte de Beaune, Santenay, Chassagne Montrachet, and Puligny Montrachet premier crus.

Château de Chamilly

7 allée du Château, 71510 Chamilly	📞 +33 3 85 87 22 24
@ contact@chateaudechamilly.com	👤 Véronique Desfontaine
🌐 www.chateaudechamilly.com	🔘 Mercurey [map]
🚶 🏭 🍇 🥂 🛢	32 ha; 180,000 btl

The château was built in the seventeenth century on the site of a fortified farm from the fourteenth century, located between Bouzeron and Mercurey to the west of the main route through the region. The Desfontaine family bought it at the start of the nineteenth century, and it is run today by Véronique together with her sons Xavier and Arnaud. The main production is split between Mercurey (mostly red) and Montagny, but there are also wines from grapes purchased from Santenay, St. Aubin, Puligny Montrachet, and Corton. The Bourgogne Rouge is a blend from vineyards all over the Côte Chalonnaise. There are three Mercurey reds from specific lieu-dits and premier cru Les Puillets. All age for 12 months in barriques and 6 months in cuve. From Montagny there are two village wines and two premier crus. The tasting room is in the old kitchens of the château and offers a range of tours and tastings.

Domaine Chofflet-Valdenaire

9, rue du Lavoir Russilly, 71640 Givry	📞 +33 3 85 44 34 78
@ chofflet.valdenaire@orange.fr	👤 Denis Valdenaire
🚶 🏭 🍇 🥂 🌀 15 ha; 50,000 btl	🔘 Givry [map]

The domain has been in the family since the early twentieth century. Denis Valdenaire joined his father-in-law, Jean Chofflet, in 1987, and took over in 2000. Located a couple of miles to the west of Givry, all the vineyards are in AOP Givry. There is village Givry in both white (La Pièce) and red (Héritage), and two premier crus: Clos de Choue is in a 6 ha amphitheater facing south, half with very old vines, half planted recently; Clos Jus was an acclaimed site before phylloxera, then abandoned and planted again only relatively recently. It's known for the black-fruit character of the wine, unlike the more common red fruit profile usually associated with Givry. Winemaking starts with complete destemming, followed by several days cold maceration. After fermentation, the village red ages partly in wood and partly in cuve; Clos de Choue ages in 40% in vat and 60% in barriques with 20% new oak; and Clos Jus ages entirely in 20% new barriques. The village white, and the white premier cru Les Galaffres, are vinified in vat with a small percentage in new barriques (5% for village, 10% for premier cru).

Domaine Laurent Cognard

4 Ruelle de la Pompe, 71390 Buxy	📞 +33 6 85 13 91 35
@ laurent@domainecognard.fr	👤 Laurent Cognard
📋 🏭 🍇 🕰 11 ha; 35,000 btl	◉ Montagny [map]

After working in the commercial side of the wine industry, Laurent Cognard returned home to take over his family estate and start estate-bottling. The domain moved to vaulted cellars in the village of Buxy that were used as a prison in the Middle Ages. Most of the vineyards are in Montagny, but there are small holdings in Mercurey that produce red wine. Production has expanded as some vineyards that were leased out have returned to the domain. In addition to the 7 ha on the Côte Chalonnaise, Laurent also more recently took over 4 ha in Pouilly-Loché that came from his grandparents. The Montagny premier crus age mostly in a mix of barriques and 500-liter barrels, with one third new oak, and a small proportion (20%) aged in stainless steel. The Montagny premier cru Les Bassets is a monopole that faces east on a limestone base and is the flagship of the domain.

Domaine de l'Évêché

6 Rue de l'Évêché, 71640 Saint-Denis-de-Vaux	📞 +33 3 85 44 30 43
@ contact@joussier.com	👤 Quentin & Vincent Joussier
🌐 www.domainedeleveche.com	◉ Mercurey [map]
🚶 🏭 🍇 🚲	14 ha; 45,000 btl

The family have been involved with wine for four generations, but the domain is not that old. Vincent Joussier's father bought a 5 ha parcel that was planted with fruit trees, and Vincent took over the domain in 1985. The cuverie was completely renovated in 2018. The majority of production is Bourgogne Côte Chalonnaise, with a regular cuvée and a special cuvée in both red and white The white ages in stainless steel, and the Reviller cuvée ages in 500-liter barrels with 30% new oak. The red ages in 14 hl foudres, and the Edition Limitée ages in100% new barriques. The 4 ha in Mercurey are in two *climats*, Les Murgers and Les Ormeaux, both planted mostly with Pinot Noir, but each making a small amount of white. They age in barriques with a small proportion of new oak. Over half of production is bottled by the estate, with the rest going to negociants. The domain is into oenotourism, offering a variety of tours and tastings.

Domaine la Ferté

13 rue du Closeau, 71640 Mercurey	📞 +33 3 85 45 21 61
@ contact@domaine-de-la-ferte.com	👤 Famille Devillard
🌐 www.domaine-de-la-ferte.com	◉ Mercurey [map]
◖ 🔪 🍇 🕰	3 ha; 15,000 btl

This tiny property, with vineyards in Givry, was purchased from Baron Thénard (see profile) by the Devillard family of Château de Chamirey (see profile) in 2010. (The name comes from a Cistercian abbey; the church and cloister were destroyed, and the remaining building is now the Château de Ferté.) Each of the three parcels of vineyards makes a separate cuvée: village Givry comes from a 1.7 ha plot immediately south of premier cru Servoisine, Clos de Mortières is under 1 ha, and Servoisine is an 0.67 ha plot in the premier cru. The wines can be tasted at Château de Chamirey.

Domaine Feuillat-Juillot

11 route de Montorge, 71390 Montagny-lès-Buxy	📞 *+33 3 85 92 03 71*
@ *domaine@feuillat-juillot.com*	👤 *Françoise Feuillat-Juillot*
🌐 *www.feuillat-juillot.com*	🔴 *Montagny [map]*
🚶 🏭 🍇 🍷	*14 ha; 70,000 btl*

This started out as Domaine Maurice Bertrand in 1989, and then became Domaine Bertrand-Juillot when Françoise Feuillat-Juillot (daughter of Michel Juillot: see profile) joined. After Maurice Bertrand died in 2002, Françoise bought the domain, and renamed it as Feuillat-Juillot. Vineyards are in 13 Montagny premier crus, with a high proportion of old vines. Harvest is manual; vinification is in vat except for Les Bordes and Les Coères, which age in barrique with a little new oak. Les Coères is the top wine.

Domaine Gouffier

11 Grande Rue, 71150 Fontaines	📞 *+33 3 85 91 49 66*
@ *contact@gouffier.fr*	👤 *Fréderic Gueugneau*
🌐 *www.gouffier.fr*	🔴 *Mercurey [map]*
📅 🏭 🍇 🛢 🍇	*6 ha; 40,000 btl*

The domain was in the hands of the Gouffier family for several generations. Frédéric Gueugneau grew up in the neighborhood and used to work at the estate under Jérôme Gouffier; he was working at La Chablisienne when Jérôme died and the family invited him to take over the estate. Frédéric makes the wines, and his partner Benoît Pagot manages the estate and is building a negociant business. The commitment to quality showed in the decision not to release any reds from the 2013 vintage. Vineyards are dispersed (although there are none in the village of Fontaines where the domain is located). At the region level, there are Bourgogne Aligoté and red and white Bourgogne Côte Chalonnaise. There are three red cuvées from Mercurey: Les Murgers comes from calcareous terroir, Clos de la Charmée from iron-rich soil, and Clos l'Évêque is the premier cru. Premier cru Champs Martin was red until it was replanted to white in 2013. From Rully, there are both red and white communal cuvées, including Meix de Pellerey, from east-facing vineyards based on limestone, and several premier crus.

Domaine Jeannin-Naltet

4, Rue de Jamproyes, 71640 Mercurey	📞 *+33 3 85 45 13 83*
@ *domaine@jeannin-naltet.fr*	👤 *Benoît Eschard*
🌐 *jeannin-naltet.fr*	🔴 *Mercurey [map]*
📅 🏭 🍇 🚜	*9 ha; 45,000 btl*

The domain was founded in 1858. Benoît Eschard, who started out as an engineer and constitutes the sixth generation, took over from his uncle, Thierry Jeannin-Naltet, in 2013. Vineyards are in a single block, falling into three climats, including 7 ha in three Mercurey premier crus, Clos de l'Evêque, Clos des Grands Voyens, and Les Naugues. Cuvée Jeanne comes from the best part of Clos des Grands Voyens. They age in barriques for 12 months with 30% new oak (35% for Cuvée Jeanne). A Vieilles Vignes Mercurey comes from 40-year-old vines in a plot below Grands Voyens, and ages with 20% new oak. White Mercurey has 25% new oak.

Domaine Vincent Lumpp

45 rue De Jambles, Hameau de Poncey, 71640 Givry	📞 *+33 3 85 44 52 00*
@ *info@domaine-lumpp.fr*	👤 *Baptiste Lumpp*
🌐 *domaine-lumpp.com*	🔴 *Givry [map]*
📅 🏭 🍇 🍷	*8 ha; 25,000 btl*

Brothers Vincent and François Lumpp inherited the family domain in the late 1970s, and then split in 1991 when François founded Domaine François Lumpp (see profile). Vincent has been working with his son Baptiste since 2001. All Vincent's vineyards are in Givry, divided into 1 ha of Chardonnay and 7 ha of Pinot Noir. The Chardonnay is planted at the bottom of the slope, and the Pinot Noir higher up. The reds include eight premier crus. The top wines are Clos du Cras Long and Clos St. Paul, a 2 ha monopole.

Domaine Masse Père et Fils

Theurey, 71640 Barizey	📞 *+33 3 85 44 36 73*
@ *info@domainemasse.fr*	👤 *Fabrice Masse*
🌐 *www.domainemasse.fr*	🔴 *Montagny*
🚶 👒 🍇 🛢 🍷	*13 ha; 90,000 btl*

Fabrice Masse took over this family domain from his father in 2000. Together with his uncle Roland (formerly the Régisseur at the Hospices de Beaune), he added a negociant activity, buying enough grapes and must to double production. He rebuilt the winery. The estate vineyards are in Givry, from which there are red village cuvées (Vieilles Vignes and Le Creuzot Monopole) and premier crus (Vieilles Vignes, Servoisine, Champ Lalot, and Quintessence), and whites from both village and premier crus (En Choué and En Veau). There are cuvées from all the villages of the Côte Chalonnaise as well as Bourgogne, Mâcon, and St. Véran. Wines age for 10-12 months in barriques with upto 30% new oak.

Domaine du Meix Foulot

Le Meix Foulot, 71640 Mercurey	📞 *+33 3 85 45 13 92*
@ *meixfoulo@club.fr*	👤 *Agnès Dewe De Launay*
🗓 👒 🍇 🍷 *20 ha; 80,000 btl*	🔴 *Mercurey [map]*

Located on a high point overlooking the appellation, this is a family estate with two centuries of history. Paul de Launey took over in 1956, moved to estate-bottling, and established the domain's reputation in the following decade. His daughter Agnès de Launey returned from the United States to take over in 1996. Vineyards are mostly in Mercurey, and typically for the appellation, are 90% red. The top wines are premier cru Veleys, from four plots totaling 1.5 ha, including some very old vines, and the 1.9 ha Clos du Château de Montaigu (at the foot of the ruins of the castle, close to the winery). The wines age in barriques with 20% new oak.

Domaine Laurent Mouton

6, rue de l'Orcène - Poncey 71640 Givry	📞 *+33 3 85 44 37 99*
@ *contact@domainelaurentmouton.com*	👤 *Laurent Mouton*
🌐 *www.domainelaurentmouton.com*	🔴 *Givry [map]*
🗓 👒 🍇 🍷	*12 ha; 60,000 btl*

Faced with a lawsuit from Château Mouton Rothschild in 2014 to change the name of the domain, Laurent Mouton said, "They say that I am a usurper. I wish to preserve the name Domaine Mouton. I do not see why I should justify myself or my name. Their family name is Rothschild, not Mouton." Eugène Mouton created the domain with 1 ha of vines in 1870. His son grew the domain to 3 ha, and then a generation later, Laurent's father expanded and started estate bottling in 1976. All grapes are destemmed, and there is punch-down for reds twice daily during fermentation. There is one red village Givry (aged 75% in barrique) and four premier crus: Clos Charlé (the lightest), La Grande Berge (with some 50-year old vines, getting some new oak) Les Grands Prétans (the most powerful), and Clos Jus (the slowest to develop), all aged in barrique. In whites, the village Givry ages 75% in barriques, and Cuvée Excellence, from two small plots, ages in 400-liter barrels. There is no malolactic fermentation for the whites.

Domaine Ragot

4, Rue de L'Ecole, Poncey, 71640 Givry	📞 +33 3 85 44 35 67
@ givry@domaine-ragot.com	👤 Nicolas Ragot
🌐 www.domaine-ragot.com	🔘 Givry [map]
🏃 🏭 🍇 🍷	9 ha; 45,000 btl

The Ragot family have had vines in Givry since the eighteenth century, originally as part of polyculture; by the 1970s the domain was devoted exclusively to viticulture, with the wines being estate-bottled. It was run by cousins Jean-Paul and Jean-Pierre Ragot, and Jean-Paul's son Nicolas took over in 2008 (although his father stayed involved). Vineyards have 6.5 ha of Pinot Noir, 2 ha of Chardonnay, and a tiny amount of Aligoté. Plantings include a majority of vines over 40-years old. Aside from Crémant and Aligoté, all the cuvées are from Givry, with white village wine and premier cru, and red village wine, vieilles vignes cuvée, and three premier crus. They age mostly in barriques, with up to 20% new oak, but some foudres are also used. "I don't want marked wood taste to my wines," Nicolas says.

Maison Antonin Rodet

55 Grande Rue, 71640 Mercurey	📞 +33 3 85 98 12 12
@ rodet@rodet.com	👤 Josette Thomas
🌐 www.rodet.com	🔘 Mercurey [map]
🏃 🏭 🍇 🚜	124 ha; 100,000 btl

Antonin Rodet founded the Maison and purchased vineyards at the end of the nineteenth century, and the family expanded the business into a major negociant until they sold out in the early 1990s. It ended up with Sequana Capital (a paper manufacturing company), who held it until they sold to Jean-Claude Boisset of the Côte de Nuits in 2009. The purchase brought with it Dufouleur Père et Fils in Nuits St. Georges, which Rodet purchased in 2006, as well as the Château de Mercey and Château de Rully, the two major properties on Côte Chalonnaise. Production is about two thirds red wine. Wines come from a wide range of sources, including the southern part of the Côte de Beaune as well as Chalonnaise. The wines are workmanlike representations of their appellations. Moving into oenotourism, the Maison is receptive to visits, which can be held in English, French, or German.

Domaine du Clos Salomon

16, Rue Du Clos Salomon, 71640 Givry	📞 +33 3 85 44 32 24
@ clos.salomon@orange.fr	👤 Ludovic du Gardin
🌐 www.du-gardin.com	🔘 Givry [map]
📳 🏭 🍇 ✋	10 ha; 50,000 btl

Clos Salomon became a top site in Givry when Hugues Salomon supposedly made it the favorite wine of the Pope of Avignon and Henry IV in the fourteenth century. Its 7 ha is a monopole that comprises most of the estate of the Domaine du Clos Salomon. It has been owned by the present family since 1558 (with some changes of their name due to marriage). They have not always been winemakers, but Ludovic du Gardin's father made the wine in the 1960s. After he died in an accident in 1977, there were various winemakers until Fabrice Perotta came in 1990, and in 1997 he became a partner in the domaine with Ludovic. Clos Salomon makes a single red cuvée, aged for one year in barriques with a third new oak. In 2003, a Givry Blanc from a small (0.4 ha) plot in premier cru La Grande Berge was added, and in 2004 another white from 2 ha in Le Clou in Montagny that were in the family Only a little new oak(10-20%) is used in the Montagny.

Château de Santenay

1, Rue Du Château, 21590 Santenay	📞 *+33 3 80 20 61 87*
@ *contact@chateau-de-santenay.com*	👤 *Gérard Fagnoni*
⊕ *www.chateau-de-santenay.com*	◉ *Mercurey*
🚶🏭🍇🚜	*98 ha; 600,000 btl*

Although this very grand estate, with a medieval castle that belonged to Philip the Bold in the fourteenth century, is located in Santenay, most (72 ha) of its vineyards are in Mercurey, located all over the appellation. It is one of the largest domains in Burgundy. After a difficult period, it was bought by the bank Crédit Agricole in 1997. From Mercurey it produces both white and red village wine, and a series of red premier crus. Délestage (rack and return during fermentation) is used to give the reds a soft structure. Wines age in barrique, including about 20% of new oak. Crédit Agricole extended the holdings into Côte d'Or by purchasing another 7.5 ha in 2019, including a plot in Clos Vougeot.

Domaine Michel Sarrazin et Fils

Charnailles, 71640 Jambles	📞 *+33 3 85 44 30 57*
@ *sarrazin2@wanadoo.fr*	👤 *Jean-Yves & Guy Sarrazin*
⊕ *www.sarrazin-michel-et-fils.fr*	◉ *Givry [map]*
🚶🏭🍇🚜	*35 ha; 200,000 btl*

This family domaine dates from the seventeenth century, and took its modern form when Michel Sarrazin took over in 1964 and started estate bottling. His sons Guy and Jean-Yves took over in the mid 1990s, and now run the estate together. A new cuverie was constructed in 2011. The modern approach is indicated by the use of optical sorting. Located in the hills of the hamlet of Jambles just west of Givry, the domain has 20 h in Givry, including one white premier cru and three red premier crus; there are also Bourgogne and Crémant. Red is two thirds of production. The Sarrazin brothers are known for judging their own wines against the Côte d'Or, as opposed to local competition.

Domaine de Suremain

71 Grande Rue, 71640 Mercurey	📞 *+33 3 85 98 04 92*
@ *contact@domaine-de-suremain.com*	👤 *Loïc de Suremain*
⊕ *www.domaine-de-suremain.com*	◉ *Mercurey [map]*
📅🔪🍇🌿	*19 ha; 60,000 btl*

Located in the Château Bourgneuf in the center of the village of Mercurey, this family domain is now in its seventh generation under Loïc de Suremain and his father Yves, who took over in 1987. Vineyards are in Mercurey, mostly red, and mostly premier cru, including five different premier crus; there is just 1 ha of premier cru in white. The focus is on showing the specificity of each plot—"our young vines and old vines are harvested together to keep the specificity of each terroir and the characteristics of the vintage." Harvest is only manual (not necessarily the case on the Côte Chalonnaise).

Domaine Baron Thénard

7 Rue de L'Hôtel de Ville, 71640 Givry	📞 *+33 3 85 44 31 36*
@ *domainethenard@wanadoo.fr*	👤 *Jean-Baptiste Bordeaux-Montrieux*
🍇🚜 *23 ha*	◉ *Givry [map]*

The Thénard family has owned land in Givry since 1760, and the estate was founded in 1842. In 1872 Baron Paul Thénard bought two parcels of Le Montrachet, becoming the second larg-

226

est landholder in the grand cru (behind Marquis Laguiche). They later bought plots in Corton's Clos du Roi and Grands Echézeaux, and now have 5 ha on the Côte d'Or. The domaine is best known for its Montrachet, which for many years was bottled by Remoissenet. The wines are made at the estate in Givry, where Jean-Baptiste Bordeaux-Montrieux (his branch of the family comes from the Loire, and he is descended on the maternal side from Thénards) has been in charge since the since the early 1980s. There are 2 ha of white Givry and 16 ha of red. The largest holding is 7.5 ha in premier cru Les Bois Cheveaux; the top wine is premier cru Cellier aux Moines. The approach is very traditional; wines are fermented in large wood casks, then aged in a mixture of barriques and foudres.

Domaine Theulot-Juillot

4 rue de Mercurey, 71640 Mercurey	📞 +33 3 85 45 13 87
@ contact@theulotjuillot.eu	👤 Nathalie & Jean-Claud Theulot
🌐 www.theulotjuillot.eu	🟢 Mercurey [map]
🧍🍇🍇🍂	12 ha; 65,000 btl

Since Emile Juillot established the domain, it has been handed down through the women of the family. Emile's granddaughter, Nathalie Theulot, together with her husband Jean-Claude, took over in 1987. (The name changed from Emile Juillot to Theulot-Juillot in 2007.) Half of the vineyards are in village Mercurey, the other half in six premier crus, including the flagship La Caïlloutte. There's also some Bourgogne, making 15 cuvées in total. Winemaking is traditional.

Domaine Tupinier-Bautista

30 ter rue du Liard , 71640 Mercurey	📞 +33 3 85 45 26 38
@ tupinier.bautista@wanadoo.fr	👤 Manu Bautista
🌐 www.domaine-tupinier-bautista.com	🟢 Mercurey [map]
📋🍇🍇🍂🍂	11 ha; 50,000 btl

The family has been growing grapes in Mercurey since 1770. Manu Bautista took over from his stepfather, Jacques Tupinier, in 1997, and increased the estate from its then 8 ha. There are two cuvées of Mercurey red from 50-year-old vines, the Vieilles Vignes from a 1 ha plot (aged in half new and half 1-2-year barriques), and Victoria, from a third of a hectare (aged in half new and half 1-year barriques). Red premier crus are En Sazenay, and Les Vellées (aged like the Vieilles Vignes) and Clos du Roy (25% new and 75% 1-2-year barriques). The whites are the village Mercurey, Cuvée Marie Christine (20% new oak) and premier crus En Sazenay and Les Vellées (40% new oak).

Mâcon

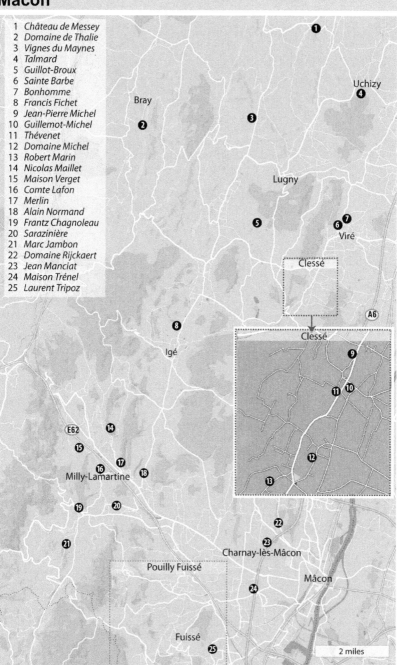

1 Château de Messey
2 Domaine de Thalie
3 Vignes du Maynes
4 Talmard
5 Guillot-Broux
6 Sainte Barbe
7 Bonhomme
8 Francis Fichet
9 Jean-Pierre Michel
10 Guillemot-Michel
11 Thévenet
12 Domaine Michel
13 Robert Marin
14 Nicolas Maillet
15 Maison Verget
16 Comte Lafon
17 Merlin
18 Alain Normand
19 Frantz Chagnoleau
20 Sarazinière
21 Marc Jambon
22 Domaine Rijckaert
23 Jean Manciat
24 Maison Trénel
25 Laurent Tripoz

Uchizy

Bray

Lugny

Viré

Clessé

A6

Clessé

Igé

E62

Milly-Lamartine

Pouilly Fuissé

Charnay-lès-Mâcon

Mâcon

Fuissé

2 miles

Profiles of Leading Estates

Domaine Héritiers du Comte Lafon   *

Les Cartelees, 71960 Milly-Lamartine	📞 *+33 3 85 37 78 09*
@ *comtes.lafon@gmail.com*	🧑 *Caroline Gon*
⊕ *www.comtes-lafon.fr*	🔴 *Mâcon [map]*
◗ 🌡 🍇 ⦿ *21 ha; 140,000 btl*	*Mâcon-Milly-Lamartine*

This is not, as its name might suggest, an old domain inherited in the Comte Lafon family, which for several generations has run a top domain in Meursault. In fact, it was an existing domain in Milly Lamartine that Dominique Lafon purchased and renamed in 1999, when he was the first producer from the Côte d'Or to expand into Mâcon. Further vineyards in Uchizy were added in 2003. The latest addition to the range in 2009 was Viré-Clessé, coming from the vineyards of Château de Viré.

Today the vineyard holdings are divided into three roughly equal parts in Milly-Lamartine, Chardonnay-Uchizy, and Viré-Clessé, so that now the domain produces Mâcon, Mâcon-Villages, Mâcon-Milly-Lamartine, and Viré Clessé, together with five single-vineyard wines. Production is typically Mâconnais, with the basic wines aged in stainless steel, and some large wood containers used at the upper end.

Dominique describes his objectives as, "I'm not going down to Mâcon to make little Meursault. I'm going to make great Mâcon." The wines are perhaps a little richer than typical for the region, but retain subregional character with the Viré-Clessé, for example, more powerful than the Mâcons. The top wine is the Clos de la Crochette in Mâcon-Chardonnay, a 2.6 ha vineyard originally planted by monks at the Abbey of Cluny. Prices are around a tenth of Lafon's more famous wines from Meursault, but comparisons would be foolish.

Domaine Leflaive   *

Place du Pasquier de la Fontaine, 21190 Puligny Montrachet	📞 *+33 3 80 21 30 13*
@ *domaine@leflaive.fr*	🧑 *Brice de la Morandière*
⊕ *www.leflaive.fr*	🔴 *Mâcon Verzé*
◗ 🌡 🍇 ⦿	*24 ha; 130,000 btl*

Famous for its range of steely, mineral wines from Puligny Montrachet, Domaine Leflaive (see profile in *Guide to Burgundy*) moved into Mâcon in 2004. After Anne-Claude Leflaive died in 2014, her nephew, Brice de la Morandière, took over, and expanded the Mâcon holdings from 17 to 24 ha. "Mâcon is treated differently from Puligny," Brice says, "we play more with the contents, using some eggs, some foudres, some vats." The original wine from the area was Mâcon-Verzé, which spends its first year in a mix of stainless steel and concrete, followed by six months in stainless steel. "With the 2017 vintage we decided to start with some single vineyards in Macon, we decided there were differences. We've picked two single vineyards we think are interesting, one west-facing, one north-facing." West-facing Les Chênes has same élevage as Mâcon-Verzé, except that 10% old oak is used. It is deeper and more textured than Mâcon-Verzé. En Vigneraie is a southeast-facing vineyard in Pouilly-Fuissé. It ages the "Leflaive Way," like the Puligny Montrachets, in barriques for the first year (but with only 15% new oak), then spends a year in stainless steel. It comes closer in style to the wines of Puligny, with stone and citrus fruits texturing the palate.

Maison Verget ***

Le Bourg, 71960 Sologny	☎ +33 3 85 51 66 00
@ contact@verget-sa.com	👤 Julien Desplans
🌐 www.verget-sa.fr	⚫ Mâcon [map]
🗓️ 🏭 🛢️ 🚜	▫️ Pouilly-Fuissé, La Roche
0 ha; 200,000 btl	▫️ Chablis, Montée de Tonnerre

"In a good year we make about 55 different wines at Verget. Most of the wines are based on grapes from several growers although for Côte d'Or it may be from a single grower because quantities are small," explains Jean-Marie Guffens. "The philosophy is to make wine that is as good as possible within very complicated rules of the region. Taking in mind that we always prefer precision—we try to make the wines as pure as possible." Verget buys only grapes or must, with the range of cuvées changing from year to year. All wines stay in wood for 8 months and in concrete for 8 months. "You see terroir more clearly if you treat all wines the same," Jean-Marie says.

Created in 1990, Verget is now part of a trilogy of holdings, also including the Guffens-Heynen domain in Mâcon (established in 1979), and Château des Tourettes (purchased in 1997 in the Lubéron). Verget's range includes southern Burgundy (Mâcon, St. Véran, and many cuvées from Pouilly-Fuissé), Chablis (from village wines to Grand Cru), and the Côte d'Or. Verget demonstrates Jean-Marie's view of the potential of an appellation rather than others' historic view of it, with flavorful Pouilly-Fuissé and ripe, intense, Chablis.

The wines from the Guffens-Heynen domain really show what can be done in the region. They have a flavor interest and complexity and texture that in a blind tasting might well be taken for a higher level appellation; in fact it is that deep texture, reminiscent of the Côte d'Or, that for me is Verget's trademark.

Domaine des Vignes du Maynes *

Rue des Moines, Sagy-le-Haut, 71260 Cruzille	☎ +33 3 85 33 20 15
@ info@vignes-du-maynes.com	👤 Julien Guillot
🌐 www.vignes-du-maynes.com	⚫ Mâcon [map]
🗓️ 🏭 🍇 ⚪	▮ Beaujolais-Leynes
8 ha; 85,000 btl	▮ Bourgogne Rouge, Auguste

Located North of Mâcon, but producing wine from both Mâcon and Beaujolais, the domain produces reds from both Gamay and Pinot Noir as well as its white Mâcon. They are proud of the history: vines were first planted here by the monks of Cluny in 910, and pressing takes place on wooden wine presses dating from 1895. (The Maynes in the name is the result of an old mistake, a substitution for Moynes, meaning monks.) The

Guillots have owned the estate since 1954, and it is now in the hands of the third generation, Julien, who took over in 2001.

The estate consists of a single contiguous holding, built up by Julien's grandfather, who started with 4 ha in 1954, and then slowly acquired other plots to reconstitute the original *clos*. A negociant activity started in 2000 to handle grapes from 4 ha of other growers nearby, but has now expanded to amount to almost half of production. The negociant wines are labeled as Alain et Julien Guillot and are organic.

All red wines are made in the same way; the Guillots are followers of Jules Chauvet, and use semi-carbonic maceration; intact berries have ten days of carbonic maceration, and then fermentation is completed conventionally. All wines (red and white) rest on the lees in barriques for eleven months. Cuvée 910 is an unusual Mâcon-Cruzille, made from cofermentation of Pinot Noir, Gamay, and Chardonnay in the ancestral manner.

The Bourgogne Rouge comes from Pinot Noir, but the red wines from Mâcon, like the Beaujolais, come from Gamay. In spite of the difference in grape variety, the same style runs through all red cuvées, with fruits showing purity and precision. You might say that the Guillots are making Burgundian wines in Beaujolais.

Profiles of Important Estates

Domaine David Bienfait

67 Rue de l'Etang, 71960 Bussieres	📞 +33 6 86 72 53 93
@ *davidbienfait@hotmail.fr*	
🌐 *davidbienfait.com*	🍷 *Mâcon Villages*
📅 🏛️ 🍇 🔩	*2 ha*

David Bienfait grew up in Vergisson, but not in a wine estate. After qualifying in oenology and viticulture, he spent time in New Zealand before returning to Mâcon to start his own domain in 2009 with 1.8 ha. He has plots in Charnay, Davaye, and Vergisson, from which he produces Macon Villages, St. Véran, and Pouilly Fuissé. The Mâcon Villages comes from 1.1 ha of young vines and is vinified in vat, St. Véran comes from a tiny parcel of 0.2 ha of young vines facing south, called Clos des Poncetys, and ages 60% in barriques, 40% in vat for 7 months, and Pouilly Fuissé comes from 0.7 ha on a steep, stony, south-facing slope in Les Crays in Vergisson, aged in barriques for 12 months.

Domaine Frantz Chagnoleau

Le Carruge, 18 Chemin Des Prés, 71960 Pierreclos	📞 +33 6 80 65 13 19
@ *domaine.chagnoleau@orange.fr*	👤 *Frantz Chagnoleau & Caroline Gon*
🌐 *www.domainefrantzchagnoleau.fr*	🍷 *Mâcon Pierreclos [map]*
📅 🏛️ 🍇 🔩	*9 ha; 45,000 btl*

Frantz Chagnoleau started making wine with Olivier Merlin (see profile) in La Roche Vineuse. He is married to Caroline Gon, who is the winemaker at Héritiers du Comte Lafon (see profile). To complete the triangle of connections, Olivier Merlin and Comte Lafon collaborate on the Château des Quarts (see profile) in Pouilly-Fuissé. Frantz and Caroline assembled their domain from plots of old vines (average age 50 years), principally in Saint-Albain (in Mâcon Villages), Chasselas (In St. Véran and Mâcon Rouge), Prissé and Vergisson (in Pouilly-Fuissé). The range includes cuvées from Mâcon, Viré-Clessé, St. Véran, and Pouilly-Fuissé, and single parcel wines from St. Véran and Pouilly-Fuissé. Frantz and Caroline describe themselves as minimalists. Most of the wines are bottled shortly after fermentation and malolactic have finished; Pouilly-Fuissé Madrigal, and the St. Vérans La Roche and A la Côte, age for another six months in stainless steel.

Domaine Fichet

651 route Aze, 71960 Igé	📞 +33 3 85 33 30 46
@ contact@domainefichet.fr	👤 Pierre-Yves & Olivier Fichet
🌐 www.domainefichet.fr	Mâcon Igé [map]
🧍🏭🍇🍷	36 ha; 200,000 btl

The Fichet family has been growing grapes for several generations in Igé, and the domain was created when Francis Fichet withdrew from the cooperative in 1976. His sons Pierre-Yves and Olivier joined in 1988 and 1990 to take over vineyard management and winemaking, respectively. When the domain was founded it had 11 ha, mostly of Gamay and Pinot Noir; today the focus is more on Chardonnay (16 ha), with 7 ha of Pinot Noir and smaller holdings of Gamay and Aligoté. A new winery was built in 2006. The brothers focus on individual vineyards, and there are several cuvées from lieu-dits in Mâcon Villages, but the wine for which the domain is best known is Château London from a lieu-dit in Mâcon-Igé, which includes a plot of very old vines and ages 10% in barriques. Wines come from estate grapes, except for 10% from purchased grapes for regional appellations.

Domaine Guillot-Broux

42 Route de Martailly, Lieu-Dit Le Pâquier, 71260 Cruzille	📞 +33 3 85 33 29 74
@ domaine.guillotbroux@wanadoo.fr	👤 Emmanuel & Patrice Guillot
🌐 www.guillot-broux.com	Mâcon [map]
📅🏭🍇🛢🍃	17 ha; 90,000 btl

"The appellation means nothing to us. That's why we don't focus on it. We focus on the individual vineyards," says Emmanuel Guillot. After working in Beaujolais and then in Meursault, Jean-Gérard Guillot returned to Cruzille where he created the domain with only a hectare of vineyards. His parents were pioneers in organic viticulture, starting as early as 1954. His sons Emmanuel and Patrice have been running the domain since he died in 2008. They have restored old vineyards that were abandoned after phylloxera, and they added a negociant activity, Maison Guillot-Broux, in 2014, with grapes sourced only from organic growers. Estate vineyards are in the villages of Cruzille, Grévilly, and Chardonnay, planted at unusually high density, mostly on east-facing slopes. Single-vineyard wines are 70% of production. There are five whites under Mâcon-Cruzille, representing different plots. Les Perrières is the top wine. Les Molières is a little unusual, as the vineyard has the Chardonnay muscaté clone, which is somewhat exotic. Unusually for Mâcon, almost half the vineyards are red, so there is a red Mâcon-Cruzille (Gamay) and two cuvées of Bourgogne (Pinot Noir), with La Myotte coming from the oldest vines, planted in 1956. All the wines are aged in barriques, with 10-15% new oak.

Domaine Marc Jambon et Fils

38 impasse de la Roche, 71960 Pierreclos	📞 +33 6 25 68 80 61
@ contact@domainemarcjambon.fr	👤 Pierre-Antoine Jambon & Michel Prudhon
🌐 domainemarcjambon.fr	Mâcon Pierreclos [map]
📅🏭🍇🍷	12 ha; 30,000 btl

The Jambons have been growing grapes since 1752, but started making wine only after Pierre-Antoine joined his father Marc in 1996. Until then grapes were sent to the coop. Pierre-Antoine took over in 2017 when his father retired, and was joined by partner Michel Prudhon. Vineyards are mostly in Mâcon-Pierreclos, with smaller holdings in Pouilly-Vinzelles. Plantings are 75% Chardonnay; the rest is either Aligoté or Gamay, but planting Pinot Noir started in 2005. The focus here is on producing cuvées from single parcels. The start of the range from Mâcon is the Mâcon-Pierreclos Cuvée Classique, aged in vat. Les Fossils comes from the most calcareous parcels, Terroir de la Roche comes from the oldest vines at La Roche, and Carroge and Cadole come from single parcels. They age in barriques, with a very small amount (5%) of new oak for La Roche. There are also some sweet wines: Caresses de la Saint Martin (previously called Vendanges de la Saint Martin) is harvested the 11th November and has botrytized grapes wit ha sugar level of 50-100g/l; Noblesse du Chardonnay is harvested by successive passes through the vineyard, with higher levels of botrytis, and a sugar level of 180 g/l. There's also an unusual botrytized red from Gamay (with 50 g/l sugar), L'Insolite. In more conventional reds, there are Mâcon-Pierreclos Cuvée Classique (aged in stainless steel) and also the single parcel La Vernillère (aged in barrique), both from Gamay, and the cuvée Parcelle B1106 from Pinot Noir (labeled as Mâcon Rouge) aged in barriques.

Domaine Jean Manciat

557, Chemin Des Gérards, 71850 Charnay-lès-Mâcon	📞 +33 3 85 34 35 50
@ dom.jeanmanciat@orange.fr	👤 Jean Manciat
🗓 🏭 🍇 ☘ 9 ha; 45,000 btl	⊙ Mâcon Charnay les Mâcon [map]

The domain started in 1985 with 3 ha of vines inherited from the family. Jean's father had made wine as a hobby, while raising cattle. Jean has slowly built the domain up to its present size, mostly white with vineyards in Mâcon, some small plots in Pouilly-Fuissé, and some parcels rented in St. Véran. He practices an extreme form of sustainable viticulture: "this is a 'hyper lutte raisonnée,' which I call 'risky' because we intervene only if there is a real danger of compromising the harvest." Production is all white, except for one small plot of Gamay. A mark of the focus on quality is that, unusually for Mâcon, grapes are harvested manually. Wines age in stainless steel.

Domaine Merlin

106 chemin du Lavoir, 71960 La Roche Vineuse	📞 +33 3 85 36 62 09
@ contact@merlin-vins.com	👤 Olivier & Corinne Merlin
🌐 www.merlin-vins.com	⊙ Mâcon La Roche Vineuse [map]
🗓 🏭 🍇 🛢 ☘	15 ha; 150,000 btl

Olivier Merlin started making wine at a cooperative in the Jura, where he met Corinne, and then spent two years making wine in California. In 1987 they rented the Vieux Saint-Sorlin domaine, consisting of a somewhat dilapidated 4.5 ha. Slowly they purchased more vineyards, and in 1997 purchased a winery in La Roche Vineuse, which was renovated further in 2009. Olivier added a negociant activity in 1997, and today makes wine from 15 ha of estate vineyards, supplemented by purchases from 8 ha. Most of the estate vineyards are in La Roche Vineuse, the majority for making white Mâcon, but there is also some Pinot Noir, which makes a Bourgogne Rouge. The top white wines are the cuvées of Pouilly-Fuissé, which come from plots in Fuissé and Vergisson. These wines, together with Les Cras (Mâcon La Roche Vineuse) and Le Grand Bussière (St. Véran), age in barrique with a third to a half new oak. There is also some Beaujolais, where the top wine comes from a 1.5 ha parcel purchased in Moulin à Vent in 2006. Olivier also partners with Dominique Lafon to make the wines from Château des Quarts (see profile).

Château de Messey

71700 Ozenay	📞 +33 6 70 66 32 51
@ chateau@demessey.com	👤 Frédéric Servais
🌐 www.chateaudemessey.com	⊙ Mâcon [map]
🗓 🏭 🛏 🍇 🛠	10 ha; 35,000 btl

Château de Messey was probably making wine when the monks of Cluny owned the land in the twelfth century. The château stands in 100 ha of farmland; 75 ha are used for Charolaise cattle. Wine production stopped there in 1958. It resumed after Marc Dumont, who owns the major negociant Manoir Murisaltien in Meursault and the Château de Belleville in Rully, bought an 8 ha plot of forest at 400m altitude nearby at Cruzille. He planted 5 ha to make the Clos des Avoueries, from which there are five cuvées coming from different parts of the vineyard. In addition, there is a Mâcon-Cruzille from vines planted below the *clos* blended with some lots from within it. A second vineyard, Les Crêts, was planted in 1993 as a single 5 ha block around the Château de Messey, and is a Mâcon-Chardonnay (Chardonnay here referring to the village at the center of the AOP, not to the variety, although of course the grapes are indeed all Chardonnay). Harvest is manual. Vinification is a mix, with free-run juice handled in stainless steel, but barrels or larger wood casks used after pressing. Fermentation is at very low temperature to slow the process.

Domaine Nicolas Maillet

La Cure, 71960 Verzé	📞 *+33 3 85 33 46 76*
@ *nicolas@vins-nicolas-maillet.com*	👤 *Nicolas Maillet*
🌐 *www.vins-nicolas-maillet.com*	⬤ *Mâcon Verzé [map]*
🧍🏭🍂🍷	*8 ha; 50,000 btl*

Now in its fourth generation, this family domain sent grapes to the local cooperative until Nicolas started estate bottling in 1999. Vineyards are mostly around Verzé, planted with all four grape varieties, Chardonnay for the Mâcon white (80% of plantings), with small amounts of Aligoté for the Bourgogne white, Gamay for the Mâcon red, and Pinot Noir for the Bourgogne red. In addition to four cuvées from Mâcon, there is a Pouilly-Fuissé from a plot at Vergisson. All wines are vinified in cuve.

Domaine Sylvaine & Alain Normand

10 Allée en Darèze, La Roche-Vineuse 71960	📞 *+33 3 85 36 61 69*
@ *vins@domaine-normand.com*	👤 *Sylvaine Normand*
🌐 *domaine-normand.com*	⬤ *Mâcon La Roche Vineuse [map]*
🧍🏭🍂🍷	*35 ha; 150,000 btl*

Alain Normand came from the Loire in 1993 to lease an abandoned vineyard of 11 ha in La Roche Vineuse. Alain makes wine from, the best lots, and sells off the remaining grapes to pay the lease. In 2010 his wife Sylvaine inherited vineyards in Chaintré and Solutré, some in Pouilly-Fuissé, some on the lower slopes of the villages and therefore classified as Mâcon. For both Mâcon and Pouilly-Fuissé, the basic cuvée ages in vat, while single-vineyard or vieilles vignes cuvées see some wood. The Pouilly-Fuissé cuvées come from Solutré; the grapes from Chaintré have been sold to negociants. There is now a range of reds as well as whites from Mâcon (including Roche Vineuse and Igé), and St. Véran and Pouilly Fuissé, where the top two cuvées are from *climats* Les Crays and Au Vignerais. The domain has moved into a new cuverie, built in contemporary style with a spacious tasting room. just outside the village.

Domaine de la Sarazinière

1081 Route Alphonse de Lamartine, 71960 Bussières	📞 *+33 6 11 96 85 27*
@ *philippe.trebignaud@saraziniere.com*	👤 *Philippe & Guillaume Trébignaud*
🌐 *www.saraziniere.com*	⬤ *Mâcon Villages [map]*
🗓🏭🍂🍷	*10 ha; 40,000 btl*

Sarazinière is the name of the small river and lieu-dit where Philippe Trébignaud's uncle, Claude Seigneuret, planted Chardonnay and Gamay in 1926. Philippe took over the estate in 1990, and his son Guillaume joined him in 2017. The range includes several single-parcel wines. The Bourgogne Aligoté comes from a parcel planted 20 years ago and ferments and then ages for 18 months in stainless steel. Mâcon Bussières Le Pavillon comes from a rocky lieu-dit and ages for 10 months in vat. The Claude Seigneuret cuvée comes from the original Chardonnay vines, now almost a hundred years old, planted on calcareous soils; it ages for 10 months in barriques that are 1-10 years old. In reds, Mâcon Bussières Coline comes from clay-limestone soils; grapes are destemmed and the wine ages in cuve for 6-10 months. In 2015, Philippe bought a parcel in Serrières, and the Mâcon Serrières rouge comes from granite terroir; it's mostly destemmed, and ages for 10 months in cuve. Mâcon Bussières Les Devants comes from selections made by Claude Seigneuret and planted from the 1930s-1950s on clay-limestone soils; grapes are completely destemmed, and then age in neutral barriques for 10 months.

Domaine Gérald Talmard

685 Route de Chardonnay, 71700 Uchizy	📞 +33 6 03 85 40 59
@ *gerald.talmard@wanadoo.fr*	👤 *Gérald Talmard*
🌐 *www.domainetalmard-gerald.fr*	🔵 *Mâcon Uchizy* [map]
🚶🏭🍇👓	*30 ha; 230,000 btl*

The Talmard family has been growing grapes in Mâcon since 1645. Joseph Talmard sold grapes to the cooperatives, and then in 1975 his sons Philibert and Paul started estate-bottling. The brothers divided the estate into two equal parts of 17 ha each in 1997. Philibert's son, Gérald, now has vineyards mostly in the village of Chardonnay but also in Uchizy. His policy is to pick early to maintain freshness. Wines are aged in stainless steel. Mâcon-Uchizy comes from soil with more clay and less lime than Mâcon-Chardonnay, and is the slightly fuller of the two cuvées. The latest cuvée is Champ Saint-Pierre, which comes from a plot of 75-85-year-old vines, and is harvested later than the other plots.

Domaine de Thalie

La Moutonnerie, 71250 Bray	📞 +33 6 15 07 65 65
@ *domainedethalie@gmail.com*	👤 *Peter Gierszewski*
🌐 *www.domainedethalie.fr*	🔵 *Mâcon* [map]
📅🍇🍶	*5 ha*

After working in viticulture in the arena of garage wines, Peter Gierszewski established this small estate in 2009, at around 300m elevation in the hills above Cluny, with vineyards facing west, planted with Gamay, Pinot Noir, and Chardonnay. In spite of its small size, there is variation in terroir, with clay-limestone soils, marne, and granite. The focus is on artisanal winemaking. "A lot of our work is pure instinct," Peter says. In reds, Balancin is Bourgogne Pinot Noir, from clay-limestone terroir, made by fermenting whole bunches followed by aging in barriques for 10 months. Pierres Levées Mâcon-Bray, from Gamay grown on marne, fermented as whole bunches, and aged in 500-liter barrels for 10 months. Plutonic is an equal blend of Gamay and Syrah, with carbonic maceration for the Gamay and conventional fermentation for destemmed grapes for the Syrah, aged for 8 months in vat. The grape mix makes it IGP Saône et Loire. The whites are all Mâcon-Bray. Atout Vent comes from clay-limestone and ages in vat, Cosmic, from the highest vineyard, facing east, comes from clay-limestone and ages in vat, and Pierres Levées is grown on marne and ages in oak.

Maison Trénel et Fils

33 Chemin du Buéry, 71850 Charnay-lès-Mâcon	📞 +33 3 85 34 48 20
@ *contact@trenel.com*	👤 *Nicolas Dietrich*
🌐 *www.trenel.com*	🔵 *Mâcon Charnay les Mâcon* [map]
🚶🏭🍇🛢🚜	*4 ha; 400,000 btl*

Located in a functional building more or less between Beaujolais and the Mâconnais, this old negociant makes a wide range of wines from both regions. Founded in 1928, Trénel specializes in fruit liqueurs and brandies as well as wines, describing itself as an "artisan liquoriste." It was purchased in 2015 by Michel Chapoutier of Maison Chapoutier in the northern Rhône. Management and winemaker have changed. As a negociant without any vineyards, Trénel sources grapes from a complete range of the Beaujolais Crus and a Mâcon Villages. The wines are workmanlike representations of their appellations, without becoming really exciting.

Maison Céline et Laurent Tripoz

Place De La Mairie, 1073 Chemin Des Boutats, 71000 Loché	📞 *+33 3 85 35 66 09*
@ *cltripoz@free.fr*	👤 *Céline & Laurent Tripoz*
🌐 *www.tripoz.fr*	🗺 *Mâcon Loché [map]*
🔲 🏭 🐌 🍷	*14 ha; 70,000 btl*

Céline and Laurent Tripoz come from Loché, but not from a wine domain, so they started from scratch when they planted vineyards in 1987, with their first vintage in 1990. They aim to get the maximum diversity from their holdings, and have Chardonnay (75% of plantings), Aligoté (10%), Pinot Noir (10%), and Gamay (5%), for producing 11 cuvées under Bourgogne, Mâcon, Mâcon-Loché, Mâcon-Vinzelles, and Pouilly-Loché, as well as Crémant de Bourgogne and an unusual sparkling wine from Aligoté. The conventional still Aligoté, Limoné, ages in stainless steel; the Bourgogne Blanc, Les Chênes, ferments and ages in barriques. Mâcon-Loché and Mâcon-Vinzelles age in stainless steel, while the flagship Pouilly-Loché ages in barriques with 20% new oak. In reds, the Bourgogne is Pinot Noir, while Mâcon and Mâcon-Serrières are Gamay, with the Mâcon fermenting by semi-carbonic maceration; all age in oak.

Profiles of Leading Estates

Domaine André Bonhomme *

Rue Jean Large, 71260 Viré	*+33 3 85 33 11 86*
earl.bonhomme.andre@terre-net.fr	*Aurelia Bonhomme*
www.vireclessebonhomme.fr	*Viré-Clessé [map]*
10 ha; 80,000 btl	*Viré-Clessé, Vieilles Vignes*

Aurélien Bonhomme's great grandfather planted 4 ha, and his grandfather was the first to bottle his own wine locally. Since 2001, Aurélian and his parents have run the domain, which presently consists of 35 different parcels in Clessé and Viré. Chickens run around the elegant courtyard. The house is at one side, with a rather striking aviary outside the winery, which is partly under reconstruction; at the other side is a workmanlike warehouse, built three years ago, small but with everything packed in. There's a couple of hectares behind the house, with the remaining vineyards scattered around the hills of Viré and Clessé.

Estate production is expanded by purchases of grapes harvested with their own pickers; "80,000 bottles would be a large number for 10 ha!", Aurélian says. All the wines are Viré-Clessé except for a little Mâcon Villages (sold in the U.S.) and some Crémant de Bourgogne. The classic part of production is about five wines. Style varies across the range. Les Pierres Blanches (vinified in stainless steel) and Les Brenillons (vinified in foudres) are intended for relatively early consumption, within five to seven years. Cuvée Spéciale (the major part of production) is a blend using both stainless steel and (old) oak; and Vieilles Vignes increases oak usage to 70%, with less than 20% new oak. These are intended to age for fifteen years or so. Where oak is used, "We are moving from barriques to 400 liter casks to get more harmony," Aurélian explains.

Domaine de la Bongran-Gillet *

199 Rue des Gillets, 71260 Clessé	*+33 3 85 36 94 03*
contact@bongran.com	*Gautier Thévenet*
www.bongran.com	*Viré-Clessé [map]*
22 ha; 60,000 btl	*Mâcon, Cuvée Tradition*

Headquarters for the three domains under Jean Thévenet (not to be confused with Jean-Paul Thévenet in Beaujolais or Jean-Claude Thévenet at Pierreclos) is a modern utilitarian warehouse in Clessé. There is the unusual policy here of dividing the vineyards according to terroirs into domains, so each domain represents one terroir (defined by the proportion of clay to calcareous soil). All are in Viré-Clessé.

Domaine de la Bongran, the largest and best known, was the first of the domains, started two generations back, and then expanded by Jean Thévenet, who was one of the first to introduce organic methods in the region. Domaine Emilian Gillet (the original family name) was founded in 1988 with vines that had been rented. And the smallest,

Domaine de Roally, was purchased when its owner retired in 2000 by Gauthier Thévenet, Jean's son.

All three domains are worked in similar ways, but with differences resulting from their characters: fermentation is slower, and élevage is longer for Domaine de la Bongran, so its wines are released later than the others. The wine from Domaine de la Bongran has an exotic quality, the fruits are pushed to the limits of ripeness, and there's a distinct impression of sweetness (the 2006 had 5.5 g/l residual sugar). Perhaps this is the terroir of ripeness. "Wines from this terroir always have residual sugar. But if it's balanced, you don't feel it," says Jean Thévenet. Sometimes there's even a late harvest, botrytized wine.

Profiles of Important Estates

Domaine Guillemot-Michel

664 Route de Quintaine, 71260 Clessé	📞 *+33 3 85 36 95 88*
@ *sceadequintaine@wanadoo.fr*	👤 *Sophie & Gautier Roussille*
⊕ *www.domaineguillemotmichel.net*	◉ *Viré-Clessé [map]*
🗓 ⛏ 🍇 🌀	*7 ha; 40,000 btl*

When Pierrette and Marc Guillemot took over Pierrette's family domain in 1985, the grapes were going to the coop, but they started estate bottling. Marc managed the vineyards and Pierrette made the wine. Since 2013 their daughter Sophie and her husband Gautier have been taking over. Vineyards are on clay and limestone slopes in the hamlet of Quintaine, just north of Mâcon, and the single cuvée is Viré-Clessé. The wine ages on its lees in cement tanks until it is bottled in the Spring following the harvest. The style is to harvest the grapes at high ripeness. Sophie has started to produce a sparkling wine, a mousseux made by the ancestral method from Chardonnay, under her own name.

Domaine Robert et Marielle Marin

256 Route De La Vigne Blanche, 71260 Clessé	📞 *+33 3 85 36 95 92*
@ *marin.robert71@orange.fr*	👤 *Marielle & Robert Marin*
⊕ *www.domaine-marin.com*	◉ *Viré-Clessé [map]*
🗓 ⛏ 🍇 🚜	*22 ha; 50,000 btl*

Robert and Marielle took over the family domain in 1976. They started bottling their own wines when the Viré-Clessé appellation was created in 1998. In 2014, they expanded by taking over some of the vineyards of Gilbert Mornand (a well known grower who was the mayor of Clessé). There is a cuvée of Mâcon-Villages and several cuvées in Viré-Clessé: Cuvée du Clos, Clos du Château, and Breillonde ferment and age in concrete vats, while Cuvée Chartine ferments and ages in used barriques.

Domaine Michel

372 Route de Cray, 71260 Clessé	📞 *+33 3 85 36 94 27*
@ *domainemichelclesse@orange.fr*	👤 *Denis, Franck & Vincent Michel*
⊕ *www.domainemichelclesse.fr*	◉ *Viré-Clessé [map]*
🧍 ⛏ 🍇 🌱	*22 ha; 160,000 btl*

The family has been making wine for six generations, since 1840. The domain was originally called René Michel et ses Fils, but changed to a simpler label when Franck Michel took over from his father, René, in 1996; he works together with his nephew Vincent (whose father looks after the Michael family cattle). (Jean Pierre Michel was at the domain from 1981 to 2004, when he left to form his own domain: see profile.) The Mâcon Villages ages on the lees in stainless steel for 6 months; Viré-Clessé Tradition and Quintaine (the name of the village) also age in stainless steel, but for 12 or 18 months. The Viré-Clessé Vieilles Vignes, Sur le Chêne (this is the name of lieu-dit, where there is more chalk and less clay), ages in 1-5-year barriques with battonage for 12 months, followed by another 12 months in stainless steel. There are also two sweet wines. Levrouté is a late-harvest with some residual sugar. (Franck Michel was Vice-President of the growers' association, and instrumental in getting a change in the rules allowing terms for sweet wines to be used on labels of Viré-Clessé). There is also botrytized dessert wine, Heritage (sugar levels around 50 g/l) from botrytized grapes. Both come from lieu-dit La Barre in vintages when conditions allow.

Domaine Jean-Pierre Michel

955 route de Quintaine, lieu-dit Quintaine, 71260 Clessé	📞 +33 3 85 23 04 82
@ *vinsjpmichel@orange.fr*	👤 Jean-Pierre Michel
🌐 *www.vinsmichel-jeanpierre-clesse71.fr*	🔴 Viré-Clessé [map]
🧍 🏭 🍇 🚜	9 ha

Jean-Pierre was making wine at the family domain (Domaine Michel: see profile) until he set up his own domain in 2004 at Quintaine, halfway between Viré and Clessé. He has 1.5 ha In Mâcon-Villages at the bottom of the slope in Quintaine, and 5 ha at the top of the slope in Viré-Clessé as well as another 1.5 ha in the lieu-dit Sur la Chêne where there is more chalk and less clay. The top cuvée is Sur le Calcaire, which comes from Sur la Chêne, and ages in barriques. There are two cuvées each from Viré-Clessé : Terroirs de Quintaine describes the cuvée blended from several *climats* in Quintaine and ages in stainless steel, while M de Quintaine is a small production aged in barrique. There's also a Terroirs de Quintaine in Mâcon-Villages. Finally there is a sweet wine called Vendange d'Exception du Terroir, made in occasional years when conditions are suitable.

Domaine Sainte Barbe

Rue De La Grappe D'or, Cidex 2109, 71260 Viré	📞 +33 9 64 48 09 44
@ *jean-marie.chaland@orange.fr*	👤 Jean-Marie Chaland
🌐 *www.jeanmariechaland.com*	🔴 Viré-Clessé [map]
🧍 🏭 🍇 🍂	9 ha; 45,000 btl

The Chaland family own two domains in Viré: Sainte Barbe and Des Chazelles. The estate was created in 1967 by Jean-Marie Chaland's parents. Vineyards are divided into 23 plots, with about two thirds in Viré-Clessé, and the rest in Macon Villages and Mâcon, all Chardonnay except for less than a hectare of old Gamay vines acquired in Mâcon-Burgy in 2012. Three quarters of plantings are old vines, ranging from 50- to 100-years. There are five cuvées of Viré-Clessé from Sainte Barbe and two from Des Chazelles (with one Vieilles Vignes cuvée from each, and cuvées from specific locations). La Perrière is a typical example of the Viré-Clessé single parcels: harvest is manual, and after fermentation the wine ages half in stainless steel and half in barrique.

Pouilly-Fuissé

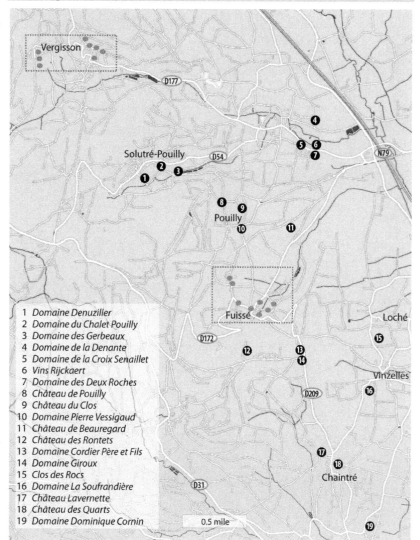

Vergisson

D177

Solutré-Pouilly

D54

N79

Pouilly

Fuissé

Loché

D172

Vinzelles

D209

Chaintré

D31

0.5 mile

1 Domaine Denuziller
2 Domaine du Chalet Pouilly
3 Domaine des Gerbeaux
4 Domaine de la Denante
5 Domaine de la Croix Senaillet
6 Vins Rijckaert
7 Domaine des Deux Roches
8 Château de Pouilly
9 Château du Clos
10 Domaine Pierre Vessigaud
11 Château de Beauregard
12 Château des Rontets
13 Domaine Cordier Père et Fils
14 Domaine Giroux
15 Clos des Rocs
16 Domaine La Soufrandière
17 Château Lavernette
18 Château des Quarts
19 Domaine Dominique Cornin

240

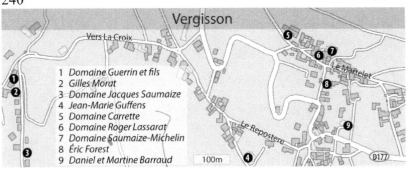

Vergisson

1 Domaine Guerrin et fils
2 Gilles Morat
3 Domaine Jacques Saumaize
4 Jean-Marie Guffens
5 Domaine Carrette
6 Domaine Roger Lassarat
7 Domaine Saumaize-Michelin
8 Éric Forest
9 Daniel et Martine Barraud

100m

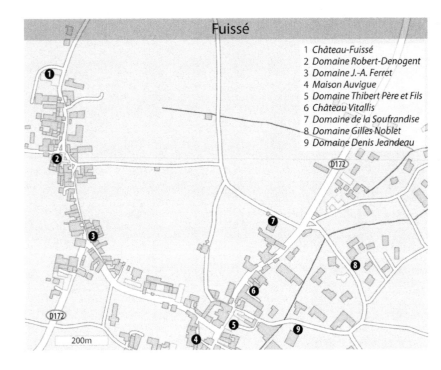

Fuissé

1 Château-Fuissé
2 Domaine Robert-Denogent
3 Domaine J.-A. Ferret
4 Maison Auvigue
5 Domaine Thibert Père et Fils
6 Château Vitallis
7 Domaine de la Soufrandise
8 Domaine Gilles Noblet
9 Domaine Denis Jeandeau

200m

Profiles of Leading Estates

Domaine Daniel et Martine Barraud   *

3 place de la Mairie, 71960 Vergisson	📞 +33 3 85 35 84 25
@ contact@domainebarraud.com	👤 Julien Barraud
⊕ www.domainebarraud.com	⬤ Pouilly-Fuissé [map]
📅 🏭 🍇 🍂 11 ha; 70,000 btl	Pouilly-Fuissé, en France

Although the Barrauds have had vineyards around Vergisson since 1890, the domain was effectively founded by Daniel and Martine Barraud. "We created all the buildings, our parents did not have any buildings, they were small growers" explains Martine. "My husband comes from a family of vignerons in Vergisson and he is the fourth generation. Today our son Julien and his sister are taking over. My husband has reached retirement age, but is still working."

The domain has grown gradually over the years and has now officially become Daniel & Julien Barraud. It's located on the slope of the Roche de Vergisson, and is surrounded by vineyards. Daniel was just visible on his tractor in the vineyards when we arrived at the domain. Although the domain is small, the focus is on single-vineyard wines, with no less than six cuvées from Pouilly-Fuissé, where vineyards are concentrated in Vergisson, but there are also three cuvées each from St. Véran and Mâcon.

The caves are quite modern, and Martine says, "here at this domain we have tradition and modernity. We hold to a very simple, traditional, method of working. My husband always says we are *agriculture des vignes*. Vinification is in barriques and demi-muids, with just a little new oak, 15-30% maximum (for the Vieilles Vignes cuvée)." Elevage lasts 10-15 months, and wines are bottled without fining or filtration.

Mâcon Chaintré is light and attractive. In St. Véran, en Creches is fruity from a southeast-facing vineyard, whereas Les Pommards comes from older vines (planted in 1963) on a northeast-facing slope, giving long hang time, and more presence on the palate. Alliance is the only blended cuvée in Pouilly-Fuissé; the others all represent lieu-dits. "We've always treated the parcels individually, *nous sommes presque toute parcellaire*, we like the principle of showing terroir in each wine."

In Pouilly-Fuissé, en France comes from a lieu-dit with thin soil on bedrock, and is a little rounder than the St. Vérans. La Verchère is the parcel of 60-year-old vines around the house, and is silkier. Les Crays comes from under the Roche de Vergisson; "this gives very small berries and concentrated wine with lots of finesse," says Martine. With a very fine texture, it has a greater sense of minerality, even salinity. La Roche is always the most mineral, coming from 35-year old vines growing at the highest altitudes; en Bulands comes from 80-year-old vines, and is always the last to be harvested, and the richest. Coming from four parcels of 35-60-year-old vines that are too small to vinify separately, Alliance has the same assemblage each year. It's more forceful than the individual cuvées but maintains the same light, airy style. The Pouilly-Fuissés are a classic representation of the appellation.

Château de Beauregard ***

Beauregard, 71960 Fuissé (cellars)	📞 *+33 3 85 35 60 76*
l'Oenothèque Georges Burrier, Rouette du Clos, 71960 Fuissé	
(wine shop)	
@ *joseph.burrier@wanadoo.fr*	👤 *Fréderic Marc Burrier*
🌐 *www.joseph-burrier.com*	🔵 *Pouilly-Fuissé [map]*
📅 🍷 🍇 🛢 🌿 *46 ha; 380,000 btl*	*Pouilly-Fuissé, Vers Cras*

One of the top domains—perhaps the top domain—in Pouilly-Fuissé, Château Beauregard occupies a cluster of old buildings a mile or so out of the town of Fuissé. Beauregard is the largest producer in Pouilly-Fuissé, and also has holdings in Beaujolais. "I feel like a true producer of South Burgundy, I do not see any difference between Beaujolais and here," says Frédéric-Marc Burrier, who is president of the growers association. In that capacity, he is deeply committed to the development of premier crus for the appellation, and his own wines certainly reflect nuances of terroir. There are two communal wines coming from younger and older vines, and then a series of eight single-vineyard wines representing different *climats*.

These are probably the most ageworthy wines in Pouilly-Fuissé, with the top cuvées maturing for thirty years or so. Winemaking is traditional. "There has been no change here, I am making wines just like my father and grandfather," says Frédéric-Marc. "I am the last to use a mechanical press," he adds, explaining that in his opinion the excessive clarity achieved by pneumatic presses can cause early aging. Wines are fermented in barrique, stay in cask for a year, and are racked only at the end. The same 10-15% new oak is used for all cuvées. Beauregard is known as a white wine producer, but the reds from the top crus of Beaujolais have an unusual refinement and elegance that lifts them well above the usual impression of Gamay.

Frédéric-Marc has now taken over—on a 20 year lease—the monopole of Château du Clos (see profile) in Solutré-Pouilly.

There is now a tasting room and shop in the village of Fuissé

Domaine J.-A. Ferret **

61 rue du Plan, 71960 Fuissé	📞 *+33 3 85 35 61 56*
@ *ferretlorton@orange.fr*	👤 *Audrey Braccini*
🌐 *www.domaine-ferret.com*	🔵 *Pouilly-Fuissé [map]*
📅 🍷 🍇 🌿 *18 ha; 100,000 btl*	*Pouilly-Fuissé, Le Clos*

Now part of Jadot's expansion into southern Burgundy, Domaine Ferret started as a family business in 1840. In the present era, Mme. Jeanne Ferret, who took over after 1974 when her husband died, was one of the first to focus on single vineyards. There was some modernization when her daughter, Colette, took over in 1993. In 2006, when Colette died, there was no family to inherit; Jadot had been buying must from Ferret for fifty years, and bought the estate in 2008.

There is a lovely courtyard with the old winery just close to the church, and the vineyards of Le Clos and Les Perrières are on the slope right behind, but wine is now made in a new gravity-feed cellar built a few hundred meters away. The old cellar had the capacity only to vinify 10 ha worth of grapes, because Mme. Ferret sold the rest, but now all the grapes are vinified in the new cellar.

Mme. Ferret divided the wines into three groups: communal, Tête de Cru, and Hors Classe. In the communal wines, Autour de Fuissé comes from around Fuissé, and Sous Vergisson comes from Vergisson. As Tête de Crus there are Le Clos, Clos de Prouges, and Les Perrières; and as Hors Classe there are Les Ménétrières and Tournant de Pouilly. Mme. Ferret used to prefer the fuller weight of wines from Fuissé rather than the more delicate wines of Vergisson, and usually harvested late to increase power. Since Audrey Braccini took over as winemaker for Jadot, harvesting has moved earlier, and the style has lightened.

Château-Fuissé ★★

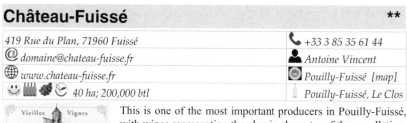

419 Rue du Plan, 71960 Fuissé	📞 *+33 3 85 35 61 44*
@ *domaine@chateau-fuisse.fr*	👤 *Antoine Vincent*
🌐 *www.chateau-fuisse.fr*	🗺 *Pouilly-Fuissé [map]*
☺ 🏭 🍇 ⌚ *40 ha; 200,000 btl*	*Pouilly-Fuissé, Le Clos*

This is one of the most important producers in Pouilly-Fuissé, with wines representing the classic character of the appellation. The Vincent family have been making wine here since 1862: Antoine Vincent, who took over from his father in 2003, is the fifth generation. There are more than a hundred vineyard plots, mostly in Fuissé with some in Pouilly. Holdings have changed little since the addition of Les Combettes twenty years ago. Soils are heterogeneous. "Even in Les Clos, which is 2.5 ha based on limestone soil just behind the winery, there are differences from top to bottom, so the top is vinified in 1- or 2-year-old barriques to respect the minerality, but at the bottom we can use more new oak," Antoine says. Vinification varies with the vintage: malolactic fermentation depends on the acid balance, and some vintages have extensive battonage while others have little.

About 20 lots are vinified individually; the single vineyards remain separate, but others are blended. There are two cuvées at Pouilly-Fuissé village level, Tête de Cuvée and Vieilles Vignes (from 50- to 80-year-old vines in nine plots planted by Antoine's grandfather). There are three single vineyard bottlings, Les Brûlées (relatively powerful), Les Combettes (relatively delicate), and Le Clos (one of the top cuvées of the appellation). The overall style is firm and full-flavored.

In addition to Pouilly-Fuissé, there's some St. Véran and Mâcon, and most recently some Juliénas from Beaujolais (Domaine De La Conseillère). There's also a negociant business under the Vincent label that gives an aperçu into the house style at a lower price level, including Mâcon Villages and St. Véran as well as the Marie Antoinette Pouilly-Fuissé.

Domaine Saumaize-Michelin ★★

51 Impasse du Puits, Le Martelet, 71960 Vergisson	📞 *+33 3 85 35 84 05*
@ *saumaize-michelin@wanadoo.fr*	👤 *Roger & Christine Saumaize*
🌐 *saumaize-michelin.com*	🗺 *Pouilly-Fuissé [map]*
☺ 🏭 🍇 ⌂	*Pouilly-Fuissé, Vignes Blanches*
11 ha; 80,000 btl	*St. Véran, Les Creches*

The Saumaizes have been making wines for generations in Vergisson, but the domain was formally created when Roger Saumaize married Christine Michelin in 1981. Roger received 4 ha of the family vineyards from his father. (His brother also has a domain under the name of Jacques and Nathalie Saumaize.) "We started mostly with renting vineyards," Christine explains, "slowly the domain grew and we bought vineyards." Their son Vivien, now in the domain, expanded it by buying another hectare in Pouilly-Fuissé and a tiny plot in St. Véran in 2020.

A track on the north edge of the village leads up to the domain. Opposite the family house, an old grange was converted into a winery in 1991 and renovated in 2016. "This is Roger's kingdom," Christine says, as we make our way into a vast underground area. "Vergisson is one of the sites of France, so you can only build down, not up," she explains. The cave is stuffed with barriques: all the cuvées are aged in wood, with up to 15% new oak. We tasted at a table outside, under an old vine—"it's 14° in the cave." Walk out into the vineyard behind the house, and you are right under the great rock of Vergisson.

"The vineyards are all around the rock of Vergisson. This gives our wine a strong minerality," Christine says. The vineyards extend into three appellations, with 15 cuvées coming from Mâcon, St. Véran, and Pouilly-Fuissé (all white except for a Mâcon Rouge). The wines are very fine for their appellations. Mâcon Villages opens with obvious fruits, the impression becomes more elegant and precise moving to St. Véran, and then more concentrated for Les Creches, a single-vineyard wine from a very calcareous location just southwest of the rock of Vergisson. There's an increasing sense of minerality with some herbal impressions moving towards Pouilly-Fuissé.

The domain made its first cuvée from an individual parcel in 1985, but now there are many cuvées from different lieu-dits in Pouilly-Fuissé, the distinction being exposure and how calcareous the soil is. Tasting here is an exercise in terroir. Pentacrine comes from the south side of Vergisson, and is named after a fossil that is common in Vergisson; it's aged in 500 liter barrels "to maintain minerality." Coming from north of the rock, Les Courtelongs is fuller-bodied and tends more towards stone fruits. Vignes Blanches is precise, Les Ronchevats is rounder, La Maréchaude comes from a really steep parcel with ferrous rocks—"so steep no machine can go up, you have to use walking sticks"—and is the most saline. "Clos Sous La Roche is a only a few meters away, but there is a complete change of terroir," with white rocks, making the wine very tense and mineral; this is the most subtle of the cuvées. Most cuvées have 10 months élevage, but Ampelopsis has 20 months, and combines the fullness of Courtelongs with the minerality of the Vergisson cuvées. "It's a selection of fûts that particularly please us from all the *climats*," Christine says.

The wines make an airy impression with increasing complexity going up the range, as direct fruits become less obvious, while herbal and mineral impressions increase, with a sense of tension and salinity showing in Pouilly-Fuissé.

Domaine La Soufrandière   *

125 rue aux Bourgeois, 71680 Vinzelles	📞 *+33 3 85 35 67 72*
@ *contact@bretbrothers.com*	👤 *Jean-Philippe & Jean-Guillaume Bret*
🌐 *www.bretbrothers.com*	🔴 *Pouilly-Vinzelles [map]*
📅 🌿 🛢 ⭕ *19 ha; 95,000 btl*	*Pouilly-Vinzelles, Les Quarts*

245

Only a single hectare at the time, the estate was purchased by the Bret family in 1947, but until the late 1990s, grapes were sold to the cooperative. Today the domain is run by three brothers, who produced their first vintage from La Soufrandière in 2000; they created the negociant business of Bret Brothers in 2001. The domain produces about 55,000 bottles from 11 ha, and the negociant buys grapes from another 8 ha to produce 40,000 bottles. A modern cave was built in 2000, and doubled in size in 2011.

Each wine for Bret Brothers comes from a single grower (harvested by Soufrandière's pickers); specializing in micro-cuvées (from 900 to 4,000 bottles), they make about 18 bottlings. Estate vineyards are around the property, which looks out over the Saône Valley from just behind the Vinzelles village at 225 m elevation. The 4 ha of Pouilly-Vinzelles (Les Quartz) are just behind the house, immediately to the west is the small plot of Les Longeays, and there's a hectare of Mâcon Vinzelles coming from the bottom of the slope, below Pouilly-Vinzelles.

Wines are aged for a year in barriques: "All barrels are old, 5-15 years, we don't want any new oak," says Jean-Philippe Bret. The estate wines become increasingly subtle going up the hierarchy. Mâcon-Vinzelles is overtly fruity, Pouilly-Vinzelles shows more restraint and adds some citrus, Les Longeays shows more variety and restraint, and Les Quarts becomes hard to place between stone and citrus fruits. The Bret Brothers wines, which cover a wider range, are a little less intense.

Domaine Thibert Père et Fils   *

20 rue Adrien Arcelin, 71960 Fuissé	+33 3 85 27 02 66
info@domaine-thibert.com	Sandrine Thibert-Needham
www.domaine-thibert.com	Pouilly-Fuissé [map]
30 ha; 160,000 btl	Pouilly-Fuissé

"We are a family domain, my parents come from seven generations of vignerons in Fuissé," says Christophe Thibert. "My parents didn't bottle, everything was sold in barrels, today we bottle everything. My grandfather had 12 children, and each constructed his own domain. We set up here in 1967." The domain lies behind an unassuming entrance in the main street next to the village square. Behind is a vast courtyard with winery buildings all around, constructed successively, most recently in 2005 and 2014. There's a spacious tasting room at the front. It has increased several times in size since 1967.

Aside from the communal Bourgogne, the rosé, and the Crémant, there are 13 cuvées from Mâcon Villages, St. Véran, Pouilly-Loché, Pouilly-Vinzelles, and Pouilly-Fuissé. Vinification follows traditional lines, with Mâcon Verzé aged in 20% old barriques and 80% stainless steel, St. Véran aged in barriques with a maximum of 10% new oak, and a little more new oak used for the cuvées from the Pouillys. "I want to produce wines where I can smell the fruit, the terroir and the minerality, so I am careful with new oak."

Fruits increase in citric intensity going up the range, Mâcon Verzé is faintly herbal, the St. Véran cuvées have a little more bite, and Pouilly-Loché has more forceful fruits in the same citrus spectrum. Pouilly-Fuissé is smoother, starting with the Cuvée Traditionelle. The Vieilles Vignes, from vines that are almost 80 years old, has a stony impression with more weight. Moving in the direction of minerality, the single parcel wines Vignes Blanches and Menétrières are the top of the line, and are worth looking out for.

Profiles of Important Estates

Maison Auvigue

100 Place Saint Germain, 71960 Fuissé	📞 *+33 3 85 34 17 36*
@ *contact@auvigue.fr*	👤 *Sylvain Brenas*
🌐 *www.auvigue.fr*	🔘 *Pouilly-Fuissé [map]*
🚶🏭🍇🍶🚜	*6 ha; 160,000 btl*

The family say they have been making wine since 1929, first in Beaujolais, then around Fuissé, and finally in the village of Solutré Pouilly. In 1946 they converted an old windmill to a winery, and in 1982 they extended production by starting a negociant. A new headquarters is now located in an old church in the center of Fuissé. The domain is run by cousins Jean-Pierre and Michel. Grapes come from vineyards held by various members of the family or from a negociant activity. The major holding is in Pouilly-Fuissé, with another small holding in Mâcon-Solutré. The Pouilly-Fuissé Hors-Classe and the Vieilles Vignes (vines aged around 70 years) are both blends from Solutré and Fuissé. Cuvée Naturelle is an organic wine from Solutré. There are four more cuvées of Pouilly-Fuissé from specific locations or blends. There are also cuvées from St. Véran, Mâcon and Bourgogne. Everything ferments and ages in barriques.

Domaine Carrette

39 Route des Crays, 71960 Vergisson	📞 *+33 6 62 18 61 92*
@ *contact@domaine-carrette.fr*	👤 *Nathalie Carrette*
🌐 *domaine-carrette.fr*	🔘 *Pouilly-Fuissé [map]*
🗓️🏭🍇🍂	*16 ha; 60,000 btl*

The domain is located in an old house with vaulted cellars in the village of Vergisson, just below the cliff, that Henri Carrette bought in 1980 when he acquired the vineyards. His son Jean-Michel expanded the domain to its present size. Jean-Michel's son, Hervé, together with his wife Nathalie, took over in 2019, with Hervé managing the vineyards and Nathalie (a qualified oenologist) making the wine. Henri started bottling wine in the 1970s even before he established the domain, but much wine was sold in bulk until complete estate-bottling started in 2008. There are 8 ha in Pouilly-Fuissé and 3 ha in St. Véran, with other holdings in Mâcon Solutré and Milly-Lamartine. The Pouilly-Fuissé is a blend from Vergisson and Solutré, fermented and aged mostly in oak foudres. Ronchevat comes from 35-65-year-old vines in Vergisson, and Les Crays comes from a 1 ha plot of 35-year-old vines in the premier cru; they ferment and age in barriques with 10-15% new oak. Prés des Gours comes from a small plot just above the village that is half of the *climat*, and ferments and ages in barriques with 20-25% new oak. The St. Vérans age in a mix of oak and stainless steel vats, and the Mâcons age in stainless steel.

Domaine du Chalet Pouilly

Les Gerbeaux, 71960 Solutré-Pouilly	📞 *+33 3 85 35 80 07*
@ *contact@chaletpouilly.com*	👤 *Marie-Eve Léger*
🌐 *www.chaletpouilly.com*	🔘 *Pouilly-Fuissé [map]*
🚫🍶🍇🚜	*9 ha; 50,000 btl*

This family domain dates from 1850. The winery is a small building on a hillside overlooking the village of Pouilly, with the appearance of a chalet. Vineyards are 5 ha in Pouilly-Fuissé, 3 ha in St. Véran, and 0.5 ha planted in 2009 in Mâcon-Solutré at the foot of the famous rock face. Unlike the trend towards splitting up appellations into cuvées from single parcels, there is only one cuvée here from each appellation. The Pouilly-Fuissé ages in used demi-muids for 15-20 months, while the St. Véran and Mâcon-Solutré age in vat.

Clos des Rocs

64, 71000 Chemin de la Colonge, Loché	📞 *+33 3 85 32 97 53*
@ *vin@closdesrocs.fr*	👤 *Olivier Giroux*
🌐 *www.closdesrocs.fr*	🔘 *Pouilly-Loché [map]*
🗓️⛏️🍇🍂	*9 ha; 55,000 btl*

Pouilly-Loché is a small appellation, really an adjunct of Pouilly-Fuissé, and almost a quarter of it belongs to Clos des Rocs, which has 6 ha in the AOP, including 3 ha in the monopole of the Clos des Rocs. Oliver Giroux comes from a winemaking family (where his brother now runs Domaine Sébastien Giroux; see profile), but this is a domain he purchased in 2002 after spending time in the Rhône. The domain was formerly called Domaine Saint Philibert, but Olivier renamed it after its top vineyard. For such a small domain, there is a large number of cuvées. From Pouilly-Loché, Les 4 Saisons comes from clay terroir, Les Barres comes from gravelly soils, Les Mures comes from a 1 ha parcel of clay-limestone, En Chantone comes from 0.65 plot of 70-year-old vines on very poor soils, #2 Monopole comes from the *clos* and ages in stainless steel, while Monopole, the flagship wine of the domain, ages 40% in stainless steel and 60% in barriques, and Révélation comes from the oldest vines, which are on iron-rich soil, with no addition of sulfur, and aged in barriques. There are also a Mâcon Loché and a Pouilly-Fuissé.

Château du Clos

Hameau de Pouilly, 71960 Solutré-Pouilly	📞 *+33 3 85 35 87 40*
@ *chateau-du-clos@orange.fr*	👤 *Frédéric Marc Burrier*
🌐 *www.joseph-burrier.com*	🔘 *Pouilly-Fuissé [map]*
🗓️🍷🍇🍂	*3 ha; 15,000 btl*

This tiny property, a single holding of 3 ha in one block in the heart of Pouilly, has been in the same family since 1782. Jean-François Combier took over in 2006. Since 2012 the vineyards have been rented on a twenty year lease to Frédéric-Marc Burrier of neighboring Château de Beauregard (see profile), but the wines continue to be produced as separate cuvées. In addition to the regular cuvée, Hommage à Léonard Chandon is a separate cuvée coming from the oldest vines, half planted in 1938 and half in 1961. Élevage is the same for both cuvées, with fermentation in barrique followed by aging for 12 months. The wines can be tasted at the Oenothèque Georges Burrier in Fuissé.

Domaine Cordier Père et Fils

Les Molards, 71960 Fuissé	📞 *+33 3 85 35 62 89*
@ *domaine.cordier@wanadoo.fr*	👤 *Christophe Cordier*
🌐 *www.domainecordier.com*	🔘 *Pouilly-Fuissé [map]*
🗓️⛏️🍇🚜	*35 ha; 150,000 btl*

The Cordiers have been growing grapes here since 1945. Roger Cordier established the domain in 1968 with 5 ha; his son Christophe joined in 1987 and expanded it from 12 to 35 ha, with 110 parcels in 8 villages. He started a negociant activity in 2003, which he keeps separate (under his own name) from the domain. Wines for both domain and negociant are made in a new facility built in 2012 with all the latest equipment. Aging is in foudres for 18 months. The range includes multiple cuvées in Mâcon, St. Véran, and Pouilly-Fuissé (22 for the domain and 10 for the negociant); under the negociant label there are some reds from Beaujolais.

Domaine Dominique Cornin

339 rue de Savy le Haut, 71570 Chaintré	📞 *+33 6 09 93 15 33*
@ *dominique@cornin.net*	🧑 *Romain Cornin*
🌐 *www.cornin.net*	🔘 *Pouilly-Fuissé [map]*
🗓️ 🏭 🍇 🥂	*12 ha; 30,000 btl*

The Cornins started growing grapes under métayage (leasing the land and sharing the crop with the landlord). Originally the grapes were harvested by machine and sent to the coop, but after the domain as such was established in 1993, harvesting became manual and Dominique Cornin started to bottle his own wine. His son Romain took over in 2012. Vineyards include a large proportion of old vines, many from two generations ago when Romain's grandfather started planting. The Pouilly-Fuissé is a blend from Chaintré and Fuissé,. aged in stainless steel. There are three single-parcel wines. Les Plesseys comes from clay-rich soil at the top of the slope, and ferments and ages 50% in demi-muids, 50% in barriques for 12 months. Clos Reyssié from vines planted in 1937 on an iron-rich plot, and premier cru Les Chevrières from vines planted in 1963, age in barriques for 12 months. (Romain's grandfather planted the vineyard in Les Chevrières, which is now owned by the Hospices de Beaune, who produce a cuvée from part of it.) Oak-aging is followed by another 12 months in stainless steel. Other cuvées include Mâcon-Chaintré, Mâcon-Fuissé, and St. Véran. Les Serreuxdières in Mâcon-Chaintré includes vines planted in 1936. Mâcons and St. Véran ferment and age in vat.

Domaine de la Denante

Les Gravières, 71960 Davayé	📞 *+33 3 85 35 82 88*
@ *martin.denante@wanadoo.fr*	🧑 *Damien Martin*
🌐 *domaine-de-la-denante.business.site*	🔘 *Pouilly-Fuissé [map]*
🚶 🏭 🍇 🚜	*20 ha*

"My father created the domain in 1975 with 2.5 ha," says Damien Martin. When Damien joined in 2010, the domain had grown to 10 ha, and since then Damien has doubled it. This is a winemaking family: Damien's grandfather established Domaine de la Croix Senaillet (see profile) which is run by Damien's uncle. The domain is named for the Denante stream that runs through Davayé. Damien has extended the range from a single cuvée each from Mâcon, Saint-Véran, and Pouilly-Fuissé to focus on single-vineyard wines. Vinification depends on the cuvée. The largest holding is 8 ha of St. Véran in the village of Davayé. This now makes a St. Véran (blended from several plots that vary with the vintage), and the lieu-dits, Les Maillettes (from a sunny plot next to the winery, aged half in cuve and half in barriques) and Les Cras (the latest cuvée, added in 2017, from a 60-year-old plot of vines, which ages for 10 months in barrique followed by 10 months in cuve). Mâcon-Davayé and Mâcon-Verzé (from a flinty 4 ha plot) are the cuvées in Mâcon Villages. There's also a little Pouilly-Fuissé. Whites make up 80% of production. There are also some Gamay and Pinot Noir for the two reds, Mâcon-Davayé and Bourgogne Rouge.

Domaine Robert-Denogent

Le Plan, 71960 Fuissé	📞 *+33 3 85 35 65 39*
@ *info@robert-denogent.com*	🧑 *Nicolas & Antoine Robert*
🌐 *www.robert-denogent.com*	🔘 *Pouilly-Fuissé [map]*
🗓️ 🏭 🍇 🥂	*13 ha; 65,000 btl*

Claude Denogent bought the property in 1922. It passed to his daughter Andrée Robert in 1971, and then in 1988 her son, Jean-Jacques Robert changed from studying law to take over the 5 ha estate. Jean-Jacques's sons, Nicolas and Antoine, joined the domain in 2007 and 2013. In addition to the 30 parcels of vineyards in Fuissé and Solutré-Pouilly, since 2012 the domaine has been making wine from Jules Chauvet's 6 ha vineyard in Beaujolais, of which they own a small part. Cuvées include Mâcon (Mâcon-Villages, Mâcon-Fuissé, and Mâcon-Solutré), St. Véran, and several cuvées from Pouilly-Fuissé, many from old vines. La Croix comes from 50-year-old vines on schist in Fuissé, Le Clos Reyssié from a 50-year-old parcel of clay and limestone in Chaintré, Les Reisses from 60-year old vines on clay in Fuissé, Claude Denogent from 80-year-old vines on limestone in premier cru Les Cras in Fuissé, and Le Carron from a tiny parcel of 90-year-old vines on limestone in Fuissé. The Beaujolais is the Beaujolais Villages Cuvée Jules Chauvet. The wines age in barrique for 15-18 months.

Domaine Denuziller

Le Bourg, 71960 Solutré-Pouilly	📞 +33 3 85 35 80 77
@ *domaine.denuziller@orange.fr*	👤 *Gilles Denuziller*
🧍🏭🍇🕰️ *14 ha; 30,000 btl*	🔴 *Pouilly-Fuissé [map]*

Located in the village under the rock of Solutré, this family domain dates from 1919 and moved relatively recently from selling its production to estate bottling. It is run today by brothers Gilles and Joël Denuziller. Vineyards are 2 ha in Mâcon-Solutré, 0.5 ha in St. Véran, and 11 ha in Pouilly-Fuissé, where there is a plot in the top site of Le Clos. Mâcon, St. Véran, and Pouilly-Fuissé Cuvée Prestige age in stainless steel, but Le Clos spends 12 months in barriques.

Domaine des Deux Roches

Route De Fuissé, 71960 Davayé	📞 +33 3 85 35 86 51
@ *info@collovrayterrier.com*	👤 *Christian Collovray & Jean-Luc Terrier*
🌐 *www.collovrayterrier.com*	🔴 *Pouilly-Fuissé [map]*
📅🏭🍇🚜	*36 ha; 300,000 btl*

Jean-Luc Terrier and Christian Collovray were childhood friends who married two sisters and created this domain from their wives' family vineyards in 1986. The domain is one of the most important properties in St. Véran, where it has 20 ha; there are another 16 ha in Mâcon (including 1 ha of black grapes), and a tiny plot in Pouilly-Fuissé. In 1997, they expanded by purchasing Château d'Antugnac in Limoux in the Languedoc. Under the title of Tradition there are St. Véran, Viré-Clessé, Mâcon Villages, and Bourgogne Blanc, aged in vat except for Viré-Clessé in demi-muids. Under the title of Coeur de Gamme, there's a more extensive range with 5 cuvées of St. Véran, a red and a white Mâcon, and a Pouilly-Fuissé, aged in a mix of stainless steel and barriques. Under the name of Micro Cuvée, there are single-parcel wines from St. Véran, Mâcon, and Pouilly-Fuissé, aged in oak.

Éric Forest

56 rue du Martelet, 71960 Vergisson	📞 +33 6 22 41 42 55
@ *contact@ericforest.fr*	👤 *Éric Forest*
🌐 *www.ericforest.fr*	🔴 *Pouilly-Fuissé [map]*
📅🏭🍇🕰️	*8 ha; 40,000 btl*

Éric Forest is proud of being the eight generation in a direct line from fathers to sons making wine at Vergisson. After working with Jean-Marie Guffens at Maison Verget for two years, he inherited the estate in 1999 from his grandfather, who planted the vineyards mostly in the 1960s. There are two cuvées from Pouilly-Fuissé: l'Âme Forest is a blend from two terroirs, one clay-limestone, and the other with more clay; Les Crays comes from plots based on limestone on the south side of the Vergisson hill. The Mâcon-Vergisson cuvée, Sur la Roche, comes from the north side of the hill. A St. Véran, Le Paradis, comes from a plot in Davayé. Wines are made in a mixture of barriques and demi-muids, with some new oak.

Domaine Giroux

10 Les Mollards, 71960 Fuissé	☎ +33 6 80 72 28 91
@ contact@domainegiroux.com	👤 Sébastien Giroux
🌐 www.domainegiroux.com	🔴 Pouilly-Fuissé [map]
🅿️ 🏭 🍇 🍷	7 ha; 35,000 btl

Yves Giroux created the domain in 1973 with vines inherited from his father. His son Sébastien took over in 2009 after working at Brett Brothers (the negociant arm of Domaine La Soufrandière; see profile). Sébastien's brother established his own domain, Domaine Olivier Giroux (see profile), in Pouilly-Loché. Sébastien produces four cuvées, all at appellation level: Mâcon-Fuissé (from 0.5 ha in Fuissé), Pouilly-Loché (from 1 ha in Loché), Pouilly-Fuissé (from two *climats* in Fuissé), and Pouilly-Fuissé Vieilles Vignes (from a parcel in Fuissé mostly planted in 1942). Mâcon-Fuissé and Pouilly-Loché age for 11 months in stainless steel, Pouilly-Fuissé half in stainless steel and half in 400-liter barrels, and the Vieilles Vignes completely in 400-liter barrels.

Domaine Guerrin et fils

572 route des Bruyères, 71960 Vergisson	☎ +33 6 16 94 95 59
@ guerrin.maurice@wanadoo.fr	👤 Maurice Guerrin
🌐 www.domaineguerrin.com	🔴 Pouilly-Fuissé [map]
🅰️ 🏭 🍇 🚜	14 ha

The domain has a splendid location above the village of Vergisson with views across to the Roche de Vergisson and the Roche de Solutré. It was founded in 1926 by a marriage between two families of growers, passed to their daughter Georgette who married Henri Guerrin, and in 1984 their son Maurice and his wife Nadine took over. Their son Bastien joined in 2011 in order to extend estate-bottling. Vines are divided into 35 small plots in Mâcon-Vergisson, St. Véran, and Pouilly-Fuissé. Mâcon-Vergisson is a blend from two plots, one rich in limestone, one clay-based; St. Véran comes from a plot on limestone at 200m altitude; both are vinified in stainless steel. Pouilly-Fuissé is a blend from plots on three terroirs, but all with vines aged more than 40 years.; Les Crays premier cru comes from a plot high up the steep slopes of th crue, while La Marechaude premier cru comes from mid slope facing full south. All the Pouilly-Fuissés age in barriques for 10-12 months with 15% new oak.

Domaine Denis Jeandeau

161, rue du Bourg, 71960 Fuissé	☎ +33 3 85 40 97 55
@ contact@denisjeandeau.com	👤 Denis Jeandeau
🌐 www.denisjeandeau.com	🔴 Pouilly-Fuissé [map]
🅿️ 🏭 🍇 🚜	5 ha; 30,000 btl

After qualifying in viticulture, Denis Jeandeau worked at his family domain in Pouilly Fuissé for five years, and then struck out on his own by purchasing a hectare at Viré-Clessé and renting another 4 ha. He now has cellars in the village of Fuissé. The vineyard at Viré-Clessé is organic, with 40-year old vines, and ages two thirds in vat, one third in barriques with a mix of new and 1-2-year. St. Véran comes from 45-year old vines. There are two cuvées from Pouilly-Fuissé. Secret Minéral comes from 45-year old vines and has the same élevage as the St. Véran. The Vieilles Vignes comes from 55-year old vines at Pouilly. The St. Véran and the Pouilly-Fuissé cuvées ages in barriques with up to 15% new oak, the rest being 1-4-years old oak. Denis expanded in 2019 into making a Vin de France cuvée from Jacquère grapes that he purchased from Jérémy Dupraz in Savoie.

Domaine de la Croix Senaillet

71960 Davayé	📞 *+33 3 85 35 82 83*
@ *contact@signaturesmartin.com*	👤 *Richard & Stéphane Martin*
🌐 *www.domainecroixsenaillet.com*	🔵 *Pouilly-Fuissé [map]*
🗓 🏭 🍇 ⚒	*27 ha; 200,000 btl*

The domain takes its name from a cross given to the town of Davayé in 1866 to replace one destroyed in the Revolution. Founded by Maurice Martin in 1969, it had 6 ha when his sons took over in 1992. Stéphane is the vineyard manager and Richard is the winemaker. The brothers extended the domain and increased the range of wines, which has a Mâcon Davayé, 7 cuvées from St. Véran, Pouilly-Vinzelles, and Pouilly-Fuissé. The heart of the domain is 17 ha in St. Véran, from which there is a general blend, 5 cuvées from single vineyards, and a cuvée made entirely without sulfur. They mostly age in cuve, but sur-la-Carrière ages in demi-muids and en Pommards ages partly in barriques. The two Pouilly cuvées come from tiny plots in Vinzelles and Fuissé and age in barriques.

Domaine Lassarat et fils

121, rue du Martelet, 71960 Vergisson	📞 *+33 3 85 35 84 28*
@ *info@roger-lassarat.com*	👤 *Pierre-Henri Lassarat*
🌐 *www.lassaratetfils.com*	🔵 *Pouilly-Fuissé [map]*
🗓 🏭 🍇 ⚒	*11 ha; 60,000 btl*

Roger Lassarat started working in the vineyards when he was only 13, and founded his own domain with 3 ha in 1969 when he was only 20 His son Pierre-Henri also started young and now works with Roger. The focus is on making cuvées from specific parcels, so there is a range of about 13 cuvées, mostly vinified in barriques. From St. Véran, Plaisir ages in stainless steel, Prestige is a blend of five parcels aged 60% in new oak and 40% in stainless steel, and there are two cuvées from parcels of old vines at Les Mûres and Les Cras. The Pouilly-Fuissé range starts with Terroirs de Vergisson, and there are single-parcel cuvées from Clos du Martelet and Clos du France, and Racines from three parcels of 100-year-old vines in Solutré and Vergisson. There's also Mâcon and Mâcon-Vergisson.

Domaine Gilles Morat

Domaine Chataigneraie-Laborier 595 route des Bruyères, 71960 Vergisson	📞 *+33 3 85 35 85 51*
@ *contact@domainemorat.fr*	👤 *Gilles et Pierre Morat*
🌐 *www.domainemorat.fr*	🔵 *Pouilly-Fuissé [map]*
🗓 🏭 🍇 ⚒	*7 ha; 40,000 btl*

The Morat family owned vineyards in Vergisson but sold the grapes to negociants until Gilles Morat changed career after fifteen years in electronics, qualified in oenology, and together with his wife Joëlle, founded the domain in 1997. Their son Pierre spent a year making wine in Oregon and Australia, and then joined the domain in 2020. Gilles expanded the family vineyards, but has kept the domain small, with plots divided between Pouilly-Fuissé and St. Véran. Vineyards are in 19 parcels, mostly on steep slopes facing east around Vergisson, going up from 300m to 450m. There is one cuvée from St. Véran and four from Pouilly-Fuissé. Grapes are pressed as whole clusters, then the St. Véran ferments and ages in stainless steel, and the Pouilly-Fuissé cuvées ferment and age in barriques. Bélemnites comes from the village of Vergisson, Terres du Menhir comes mostly from lieu-dit En Buland, and Aux Vignes Dessus and Sur La Roche are *climats* in Vergisson (Sur la Roche is premier cru from 2020).

Domaine Gilles Noblet

135 rue En Collonge, 71960 Fuissé	📞 +33 3 85 35 63 02
@ gillesnoblet@wanadoo.fr	👤 Mylène Noblet Durand
🌐 www.domaine-gillesnoblet.com	◉ Pouilly-Fuissé [map]
📅 🏭 🍇 🍷	11 ha; 65,000 btl

This family domain is focused on Pouilly-Fuissé, where it produces 4 cuvées from its 9.5 ha; there are also cuvées from smaller holdings in Pouilly Loche, Macon-Fuissé, and St. Véran. Gilles took over in 1977, and started estate bottling in 1979. The present cellar was built in 1990. Pouilly-Fuissé La Collage comes from the major holding, and ages in a mix of foudres and barriques. The other cuvées from Pouilly-Fuissé come from old vines (more than 50-years of age): Les Champs comes from a plot in Fuissé, Maison du Villard from Chaintré, and Prestige is a blend from Fuissé and Chaintré. The St. Véran and Mâcon age in stainless steel.

Château de Pouilly

Rue du Château , 71960 Solutré-Pouilly	📞 +33 3 85 35 89 80
@ chateau@chateaupouilly.fr	👤 Alexa Canal Du Comet
🌐 www.chateaupouilly.fr	◉ Pouilly-Fuissé [map]
📅 🏭 🍇 🚜	7 ha

Unusually for the area, this is a real château, originating in the eleventh century, mostly built in the fifteenth century, overlooking the village of Solutré-Pouilly. It is surrounded by vineyards with a record of the first vintage in 1551. In the nineteenth century the château took several prizes for its wine at various grand expositions. It stayed in the same family, passing to four grandchildren of the owners in 1965, and then in 1981 Guaïta Véronique Canal du Comet bought out the others' shares. The entire crop has been estate-bottled since 2004. There is a single wine, vinified two-thirds in vat and one third in barriques with aging for 12 months.

Château des Quarts

71570 Chaintré	
@ chateaudesquarts@gmail.com	👤 Olivier Merlin
🌐 chateau-des-quarts.com/fr	◉ Pouilly-Fuissé [map]
📅 🏭 🛢 🍇	3 ha; 12,000 btl

This is a collaborative venture between Dominique Lafon of Comtes Lafon (see profile) and Olivier Merlin of Domaine Merlin (see profile), started in 2012 when they purchased the Clos des Quarts vineyard together. Olivier had been buying grapes from the vineyard since 2003, which made his best cuvée. Just over 2 ha, planted in 1937, it has clay-limestone soils, located at the top of the hill of Chaintré, and is surrounded by high stone walls. The wine is made in Olivier's cellar at La Roche Vineuse, and is classic Pouilly-Fuissé with that burst of oak on top of ripe fruits.

Domaine Pascal Renaud

Impasse du Tonnelier, 71960 Solutré-Pouilly	📞 +33 6 65 56 23 11
@ contact@domainepascalrenaud.fr	👤 Pascal Renaud
🌐 domainepascalrenaud.fr	◉ Pouilly-Fuissé
🚶 🏭 🍇 🚜	10 ha

This family estate dates from 1927 and Pascal is the third generation. The Renauds first leased the property under a métayage contract (sharing the production with the owners), and then Pascal and his wife Mireille purchased it in 1998. Their children Guillaume and Amandine have now joined them. There are five cuvées from plots of old vines Pouilly Fuissé, comprising a Vieilles Vignes and four lieu-dits, St. Véran, and two cuvées from villages in Macon. The Mâcon and St. Véran age in vat, Pouilly Fuissé Vieilles Vignes (from 65-year-old vines) in a mix of demi-muids and foudres, Pouilly Fuissé Aux Instarts (55-year-old vines), Aux Chailloux (65-year-old vines), and Vers Cras (75-year-old vines) in 500-liter barrels, and Pouilly Fuissé Aux Bouthières (100-year-old vines) in new 500-liter barrels.

Vins Rijckaert

En Cuette, 71960 Davayé	📞 *+33 3 71 41 00 06*
@ *info@rijckaert.fr*	👤 *Florent Rouve*
🌐 *www.vinsrijckaert.com*	🔴 *Pouilly-Fuissé [map]*
📅 🏭 🍇 🍷	*10 ha; 100,000 btl*

There are really two Domaine Rijckaerts: one in Mâcon and one in the Jura (in Villette-les-Arbois), created by Jean Rijckaert in 1998. There are 4 ha in Mâcon and 5.5 ha in the Jura. The estates were purchased by Florent Rouve (from the Jura) in 2013, and he now divides his time between the two locations. The focus is on Chardonnay, with only a little Savagnin at the Jura estate. Domaine Rijckaert is used for estate grapes from both locations; there is also a negociant activity, with wines labeled as Maison Rijckaert. The range in Burgundy extends from Bourgogne to Puligny Montrachet and Corton Blanc, but the domain is best known for its cuvées of Pouilly-Fuissé. In the Jura, the wines are Arbois or Côtes de Jura.

Domaine Roc des Boutires

Château du Moulin-à-Vent, 4 rue des Thorins, 71570 Romanèche-Thorins	📞 *+33 3 85 35 50 68*
@ *contact@rocdesboutires.com*	👤 *Brice Laffond*
🌐 *www.chateaudumoulinavent.com*	🔴 *Pouilly-Fuissé [map]*
📅 🏭 🍇 🍷	*4 ha; 25,000 btl*

This small domain was originally located in the village of Pouilly-Fuissé. The juice was sold to the Parinet family of Château du Moulin-à-Vent from 2011, and in 2016 the Parinets bought the domain. The wine is made in Romanèche Thorins at Château du Moulin-à-Vent (see profile). Near the Roche de Solutré, the vineyard consists of 14 parcels planted in the 1970s. There's an estate cuvée and two cuvées from single parcels, En Bertilionne (0.57 ha) and Aux Bouthières (0.66 ha), now a premier cru. All harvest is manual, there is a cold soak for 2 days before fermentation, and then the estate wine ages 80% in stainless steel and 20% in barriques, while the single-parcel cuvées age 70% in stainless steel and 30% in barriques. There is also a Macon-Solutré from 0.6 ha outside the Pouilly-Fuissé AOP.

Château des Rontets

814, chemin des Rontés, 71960 Fuissé	📞 *+33 3 85 32 90 18*
@ *base@chateaurontets.com*	👤 *Claire & Fabio Gazeau-Montrasi*
🌐 *www.chateaurontets.com*	🔴 *Pouilly-Fuissé [map]*
📅 🏭 🍇 🍷	*7 ha; 30,000 btl*

Claire et Fabio Gazeau-Montrasi were architects who changed careers in 1995 to make wine at this small domain at the top of Pouilly-Fuissé, which has been in the family since 1850. Almost all the vineyards are in Fuissé: 5.5 ha are in the clos around the winery at Rontets, at an elevation around 350m; 500m to the south the *climat* of Pierrefolle is across a fault line on the facing hillside, and has granitic terroir facing east, protected from the north wind, and so warmer than Rontets; and there is a half hectare of Gamay on the Côte de Besset in Saint Amour. The hamlet of Rontet is not included in the proposed premier crus for Pouilly-Fuissé, but most people feel that these wines are among the very best of the appellation. The soils here are thin, never more than 20 cm, on a base of hard limestone. Clos Varambon comes from various parcels of vines planted since 1945. It ages for 12-18 months in a mix of foudres, 400-liter barrels, and barriques, with no new oak. Pierrefolle comes from the climat, which was planted in the 1970s; it ages in a mix of recent but not new 400-liter barrels and barriques. Les Birbettes is a cuvée from the oldest vines, from two parcels planted in the 1920s and two planted at the end of 1945; it ages in a mix of 400-liter barrels and barriques aged from one to six years.

Domaine Jacques Saumaize

Les Bruyeres, 71960 Vergisson	📞 +33 3 85 35 82 14
@ nathalie.saumaize@wanadoo.fr	👤 Jacques Saumaize
⊕ www.saumaize.com	◎ Pouilly-Fuissé [map]
🗓 ⛰ 🍇 🍂	12 ha; 70,000 btl

Jacques & Nathalie Saumaize created the domain in 1981 with 4 ha when Jacques split the holdings of the family estate (Domaine Léon Saumaize) with his brother Roger (whose domain is Saumaize-Michelin; see profile). Nathalie brought some vineyards from her family, and the domain ended up with 10 ha. Their son Anthony worked in South Africa, but returned home when he was offered 3 ha of vines; subsequently in 2012 he joined his parents, adding his vines to the domaine, which was then renamed as Domaine Jacques Saumaize instead of Domaine Jacques et Nathalie Saumaize. The domain consists of a very large number of parcels, many only a tenth of a hectare or so. Everything is harvested by hand (not so common in the area). There are holdings in St. Véran (vinified in vat), Mâcon (vinified partly in tank and partly in barrels), and Pouilly-Fuissé (mostly vinified in barriques). There are several cuvées from Pouilly-Fuissé, including some single parcels. Single-parcel vines are vinified in barriques with 20% new oak, and so is the cuvée Poncetys from vines planted in 1944 in St. Véran. A Pouilly-Fuissé comes from Vergisson and vinifies in cuve, the Vieilles Vignes from three parcels of vines over 60 years old, and Nuance is a blend of two young parcels. In single parcels, Les Scélés is schist rather than limestone, Les Creuzettes has 50-year-old vines on shallow soil on rock near the Roche de Solutré, Le Maréchaude has deeper soil facing south near the Roche de Vergisson, and on the other side of Vergisson, Les Courtelongs is north-facing, but protected by the Roche so it does not get too cold, and Sur La Roche has 50-year-old vines at high altitude. .

Domaine La Soufrandise

Rouette Du Clos, 71960 Fuissé	📞 +33 3 85 35 64 04
@ la-soufrandise@wanadoo.fr	👤 Françoise & Nicolas Melin
⊕ soufrandise.com	◎ Pouilly-Fuissé [map]
🗓 ⛰ 🍇 🚜	7 ha; 35,000 btl

The Melin family have owned the estate since 1851—they were negociants in wine—but recently it was leased out until 1986. When the lease expired, Nicolas Melin and his wife Françoise took over the domain. The cellars in a house in the village built in 1831 by one of Napoleon's colonels. Nicolas, with a background in engineering and without experience in winemaking, simultaneously studied oenology in Dijon. Vineyards are spread over 20 separate parcels; half include vines more than 45 years old. There are four cuvées. The Mâcon-Fuissé comes from vines outside the Pouilly-Fuissé AOP. The flagship Pouilly-Fuissé Vieilles Vignes comes from the oldest plots (from 40- to 90-years old), and is harvested late to get ripe flavors. Some of the plots are in premier crus Les Ménétrières, Les Perrières and Vers Cras. It ages 70% in stainless steel, 30% in barriques with 50% new oak. Clos Marie comes from 30-50-year old vines in the *clos* next to the cellars. It ages 70% in stainless steel and 30% in used barriques. Levrouté Velours d'Automne is a special cuvé from successive passes through plots based on schist (unusual in Burgundy), for very late harvest of over-mature grapes, including botrytized grapes when conditions allow. (Levrouté is an old term in the region for demi-sec, although this wine is technically dry, albeit close to the limit for residual sugar, since sweet wines are now allowed in the AOP.)

Domaine Pierre Vessigaud Père et Fils

Hameau De Pouilly, Chemin des Concizes, 71960 Solutré-Pouilly	📞 +33 3 85 35 81 18
@ contact@vins-pierrevessigaud.fr	👤 Pierre Vessigaud
🌐 www.vins-pierrevessigaud.fr	🔘 Pouilly-Fuissé [map]
🗓 🏭 🍇 🚜	11 ha; 80,000 btl

Founded in 1839, this family domain is in its fifth generation under Pierre Vessigaud, who took over in 1987. Most of the vineyards are in Fuissé, at elevations of 200-250m, on calcareous terroir facing south-southeast; there are also 3 ha in Mâcon and 1 ha in Saint Amour. There are several single-parcel cuvées from Pouilly-Fuissé: Vers Pouilly (around 2,000 bottles from 0.5 ha of 70-year-old vines in one of the best *climats* in Pouilly-Fuissé, aged in barriques); Les Tâches (a rocky 0.8 ha plot in Fuissé); Vers Agnières (a calcareous 0.6 ha plot in Fuissé); Les Pierres a Canards (an 0.3 ha plot of 60-year-old vines in Fuissé). The Vieilles Vignes cuvée is an assemblage from several plots of vines varying from 40- to 70-years old. All the wines age in barriques for 12 months. There are also three cuvées from Mâcon (aged in foudres) and a single cuvée from St. Amour.

Château Vitallis

106 Rue Adrien Arcelin, 71960 Fuissé	📞 +33 3 85 35 64 42
@ contact@chateauvitallis.com	👤 Maxime Dutron
🌐 www.chateauvitallis.com	🔘 Pouilly-Fuissé [map]
🗓 🏭 🍇 ☘	17 ha; 80,000 btl

The château originated in the fourteenth century, and took its name from an owner at the beginning of the nineteenth century. The Dutron family are his direct descendants. Denis Dutron took over in 1981, and works today with his son Maxine. Vineyards comprise 11 ha in Pouilly, 2 ha in Fuissé, 2 ha in Mâcon-Fuissé, 1 ha in St. Véran, and 0.5 ha in Mâcon-Vinzelles. Cuvées from Mâcon age in vat for 6 months. The St. Véran comes from high up (500m) in the appellation and usually ages in vat. The major cuvée from Pouilly-Fuissé is Les Vignes du Château, a blend from many plots with an average age of 35 years, vinified in a mix of 30% barriques and 70% stainless steel. There are two special cuvées, both fermented and then aged in barriques for 11-12 months. The Vieilles Vignes comes from the oldest vines, up to 85 years of age, and Les Perrières, introduced in 2013, comes from plots in the *climat*, a premier cru as of 2020.

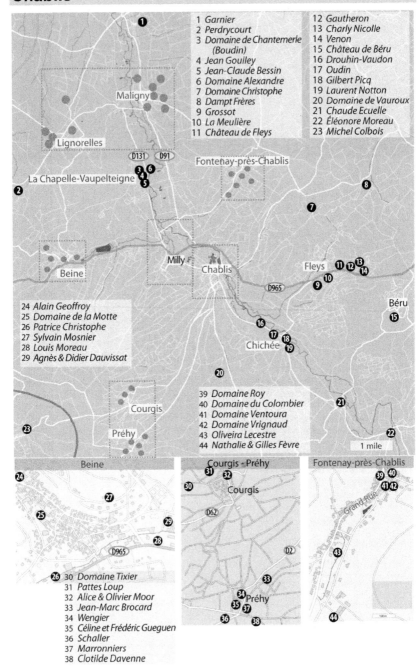

1 Garnier
2 Perdrycourt
3 Domaine de Chantemerle
   (Boudin)
4 Jean Goulley
5 Jean-Claude Bessin
6 Domaine Alexandre
7 Domaine Christophe
8 Dampt Frères
9 Grossot
10 La Meulière
11 Château de Fleys

12 Gautheron
13 Charly Nicolle
14 Venon
15 Château de Béru
16 Drouhin-Vaudon
17 Oudin
18 Gilbert Picq
19 Laurent Notton
20 Domaine de Vauroux
21 Chaude Ecuelle
22 Éléonore Moreau
23 Michel Colbois

Maligny

Lignorelles

D131   D91

La Chapelle-Vaupelteigne

Fontenay-près-Chablis

Milly

Chablis

Fleys

Béru

D965

Chichée

24 Alain Geoffroy
25 Domaine de la Motte
26 Patrice Christophe
27 Sylvain Mosnier
28 Louis Moreau
29 Agnès & Didier Dauvissat

Beine

Courgis

Préhy

39 Domaine Roy
40 Domaine du Colombier
41 Domaine Ventoura
42 Domaine Vrignaud
43 Oliveira Lecestre
44 Nathalie & Gilles Fèvre

1 mile

Beine

Courgis - Préhy

Courgis

D62

D965

30 Domaine Tixier
31 Pattes Loup
32 Alice & Olivier Moor
33 Jean-Marc Brocard
34 Wengier
35 Céline et Frédéric Gueguen
36 Schaller
37 Marronniers
38 Clotilde Davenne

Courgis

D2

Préhy

Fontenay-près-Chablis

Grand Rue

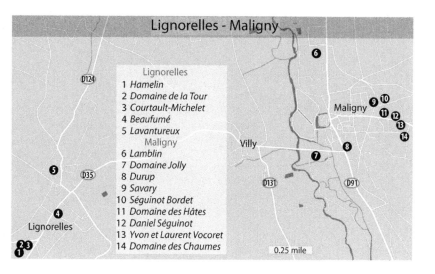

Lignorelles - Maligny

Lignorelles
1 Hamelin
2 Domaine de la Tour
3 Courtault-Michelet
4 Beaufumé
5 Lavantureux

Maligny
6 Lamblin
7 Domaine Jolly
8 Durup
9 Savary
10 Séguinot Bordet
11 Domaine des Hâtes
12 Daniel Séguinot
13 Yvon et Laurent Vocoret
14 Domaine des Chaumes

Maligny

Villy

Lignorelles

0.25 mile

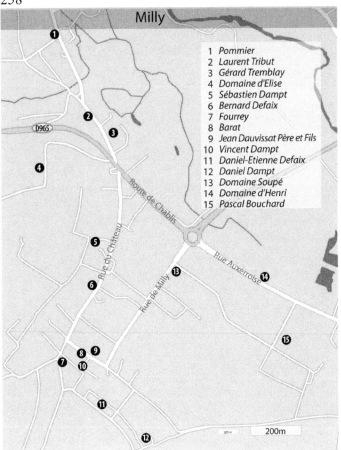

Milly

1 Pommier
2 Laurent Tribut
3 Gérard Tremblay
4 Domaine d'Elise
5 Sébastien Dampt
6 Bernard Defaix
7 Fourrey
8 Barat
9 Jean Dauvissat Père et Fils
10 Vincent Dampt
11 Daniel-Etienne Defaix
12 Daniel Dampt
13 Domaine Soupé
14 Domaine d'Henri
15 Pascal Bouchard

200m

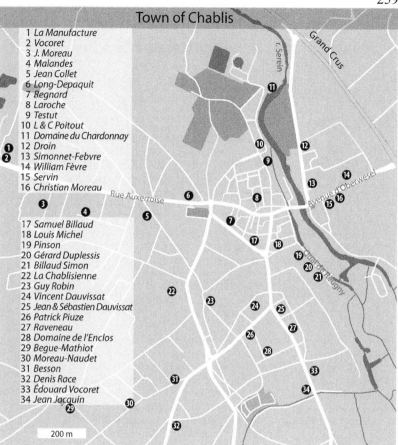

Town of Chablis

1 La Manufacture
2 Vocoret
3 J. Moreau
4 Malandes
5 Jean Collet
6 Long-Depaquit
7 Regnard
8 Laroche
9 Testut
10 L & C Poitout
11 Domaine du Chardonnay
12 Droin
13 Simonnet-Febvre
14 William Fèvre
15 Servin
16 Christian Moreau

17 Samuel Billaud
18 Louis Michel
19 Pinson
20 Gérard Duplessis
21 Billaud Simon
22 La Chablisienne
23 Guy Robin
24 Vincent Dauvissat
25 Jean & Sébastien Dauvissat
26 Patrick Piuze
27 Raveneau
28 Domaine de l'Enclos
29 Begue-Mathiot
30 Moreau-Naudet
31 Besson
32 Denis Race
33 Édouard Vocoret
34 Jean Jacquin

200 m

Profiles of Leading Estates

Domaine Jean-Claude et Romain Bessin   **

Rue des Cours, 89800 La Chapelle Vaupelteigne	📞 +33 3 86 42 46 77
@ dnejcbessin@wanadoo.fr	👤 Evelyne & Jean-Claude Bessin
	🔵 Chablis [map]
📅 🏭 🍇 🍷 12 ha; 40,000 btl	La Forêt

The domain is hidden away in the village of La Chapelle a few miles outside Chablis. Jean-Claude took over in 1992; his wife represents the sixth generation since the estate started in 1825. Estate bottling started with Jean-Claude. "My father-in-law sold all the juice to negociants. When I took over, I found it frustrating to work on the vines and vinification and sell the juice."

Most of the wine is exported. "When I started I didn't have many clients and as things developed the demand came from export, with Berry Bros in London. We just never had time to develop agents and a commercial network in France, so most is exported. I'm an artisan that's why I've never wanted to expand the domain."

Almost half the holdings are in AOP Chablis around La Chapelle: the rest are in premier and grand crus. "We don't look to increase production, we have the luck to have some vieilles vignes," Jean-Claude says. There is mixed use of wood and cuve, depending on the cuvée, and élevage lasts a year. Chablis AOP is kept in cuve with only a small proportion of barriques. Premier and grand crus are handled the same way with about 60% in barriques, using only old wood.

The style here is to bring out the minerality of the fruits. Going up the hierarchy, there is more precision, more reserve or even austerity, but increasing finesse. The single cuvée of Chablis has more character than usual for the AOP, because it comes only from old (about 60-year) vines. The Montmains has more intensity, and then La Forêt (part of Montmains, and matured only in foudre) has increased precision and minerality. Fourchaume shows more open generosity of fruits (usually there are two cuvées, one from vines of 35-45 years, the other from vines over 60 years). Valmur is relatively austere and needs more time to open out.

Domaine Samuel Billaud   **

8 Boulevard du Dr Tacussel, 89800 Chablis	📞 +33 3 86 51 00 07
@ samuel.billaud@orange.fr	👤 Samuel Billaud
🌐 samuel-billaud.com	🔵 Chablis [map]
📅 🏭 🍇 🛢 🍷 4 ha; 60,000 btl	Mont de Milieu

"I worked for a long time at Domaine Billaud-Simon, and left in 2014 when they decided to sell the domain. I bought these premises from Moreau-Naudet in 2015," says Samuel Billaud. His new domain is set up right under the ramparts of Chablis in a group of medieval buildings around a courtyard. The buildings have been stylishly modernized inside, and there's a chic tasting room. The cuverie is full of stainless steel tanks, with many small sizes to allow vinification by parcel. In spite of the youth of the domain, there is a wide range of cuvées, including five premier crus and three grand crus.

Petit Chablis comes from an area above Les Clos. Chablis is a blend from three plots. There's also a Bourgogne to expand production. The Bourgogne and Chablis share bright lemony fruits supported by lively acidity (The Bourgogne is a blend of a third from Chablis with two thirds from Mâcon. It sells at around the same price as the Petit Chablis). Petit Chablis, Chablis, and premier crus Vaillons and Séchet are handled in stainless steel. Élevage is twelve months, a bit longer for grand cru. The house style of bright fruits with fresh acidity continues from Chablis to the Vaillons, coming out to full effect in a cooler year like 2016, and more rounded in a warmer year like 2015. In a typical year, these will be vins de garde that will benefit from a few years aging. "Séchet is the most mineral and tense of the left bank premier crus," Samuel says.

Mont de Milieu is more concentrated than Vaillons, but the full effect of the right bank shows with Montée de Tonnerre, where there is more weight to balance those bright fruits. Mont de Milieu and Montée de Tonnerre have partial aging in oak (20% in tonneaux), and the grand crus age in tonneaux (500 liters). Mont de Milieu may offer the most classic representation of Chablis. Montée de Tonnerre is very close to grand cru in quality. Bougros is a continuation from the right bank premier crus, with more subtle impressions of texture, Vaudésir is deeper, and Les Preuses shows its pedigree in great finesse. Some wood spice impressions show on the grand crus on release. There is a clear consistency of style from left bank premier crus to right bank premier crus to grand crus, with increasingly fine texture and more subtle flavor impressions. Obviously the proof will come in a few years time, but all the signs are that the premier and grand crus have great aging potential.

Domaine Billaud Simon   **

1, Quai De Reugny, BP 46, 89800 Chablis	📞 +33 3 86 42 10 33
@ contact@billaud-simon.com	👤 *Catherine Lesueur*
🌐 www.billaud-simon.com	📷 Chablis [map]
◒ 🏷 🍇 ⌚ 17 ha; 150,000 btl	Montée de Tonnerre

The domain originated in a marriage between Jean Billaud and Renée Simon before the second world war, bringing together the vineyards from two viticultural families, and their son Bernard Billaud ran the domain until it was sold to Faiveley in 2014. Samuel Billaud had been the winemaker until he left to form his own domain (he obtained some of the vineyards when the domain was sold in 2014). Faiveley effectively obtained two thirds of the vineyards and the winery. Behind the gracious old house where tastings are held is a large cuverie, constructed in 1991. Holdings are divided into about forty separate plots, with only six larger than a hectare, but more than half are in premier or grand crus.

In winemaking, there are two Billaud Simons. Going round the cuverie, there are lots of stainless steel tanks, and a rather small barrel room with a mix of barriques and demi-muids. The larger group of wines, about 80% of production, comprises Cuvées Haute Tradition; these are vinified exclusively in stainless steel, and range from Petit Chablis to grand crus. The smaller group of Cuvées Prestige has at least some oak maturation, 20% for Chablis Tête d'Or (which comes from a special plot just below Montée de Tonnerre), 10% for Fourchaume, 60% for Mont de Milieu, and 100% for Blanchots. Vaudésir was switched from stainless steel to 100% oak as an experiment in 2011, because it was always too closed previously. I have the feeling that Bernard's heart lay with the stainless steel cuvées, "All oak is old, new oak would be too marked,"? he said. Freshness is the quality that is most emphasized in tasting, and is marked in the Haute Tradition series, which shows traditional zesty character. Under Faiveley's ownership, the policy seems to be to use oak cautiously.

Jean-Marc Brocard   *

3, Route de Chablis, 89800 Préhy	📞 +33 3 86 41 49 00
@ info@brocard.fr	👤 Sebastien Guy
🌐 www.brocard.fr	🗺 Chablis [map]
😊 🏭 🐿 🍷 ⭕ 180 ha; 1,400,000 btl	Chablis, Sainte Claire

Jean-Marc created the domain in 1973 without any vineyards. The first vineyards were a couple of hectares inherited by his wife, just next to the fifteenth century church that is adjacent to the present winery. The domain occupies a rather splendid and vast modern building dating from 1984 in the middle of the vineyards just outside the village of Préhy. The building has a salle de vinification full of large foudres and some concrete eggs. Just below and partly out of sight is a more industrial-looking group of buildings (built in 2001) where the cuveries with stainless steel tanks are located. Jean-Marc has now retired and the domain is run by his son Julien and other members of the family. Today this is the largest family owned domain in Chablis. Production is split more or less equally between estate and purchased grapes.

Brocard is organic, but Julien is an enthusiast for biodynamics, and makes a separate range of wines under his own label from biodynamic vineyards. They are vinified and aged exclusively in old foudres; they include three cuvées from Chablis AOP, two grand cru, and Les Preuses. They are presented in a special bottle with a wax seal, and are just a little more expensive than the J. M. Brocard wines, which have a more extensive range with Petit Chablis, four cuvées of Chablis, five premier crus, and five grand crus. The J.M. Brocard range is extended by Bourgogne Blanc and Rouge, and local wines from the Auxerrois. Vinification varies for the J.M. Brocard wines, from stainless steel for Chablis, to a mixture of stainless steel and oak for premier crus, to all oak for grand crus. All the oak is old: "No new oak, that's not our style, it's just not for us," says Sébastien Guy, Julien's brother-in-law, who is charge of exports and mans the tasting room.

The Brocard house style tends to elegance, with fruits showing as light citrus against balanced acidity, never anything to excess. The same style runs through the whole range, with finesse on the palate, intensity increasing along the range, with more subtle flavor variety. The Julien Brocard wines follow the same stylistic imperatives, but tend to have more presence on the palate due to an extremely fine granular texture; perhaps this comes from the aging in foudres.

For both J.M. Brocard and Julien Brocard, the Vaudevey premier cru is just a tad deeper than the Chablis, and the real impression of premier crus comes with Montmains for J.M. Brocard, where the characteristic delicacy of the house style really shows, and Côte de Léchet for Julien Brocard. J.M. Brocard's Fourchaume, matured in foudres, is quite forceful for the house, but retains elegance. Comparing Les Preuses from J.M. Brocard with Julien Brocard is interesting because both are aged in foudres: both show the characteristic delicacy of this grand cru, but Julien's has more presence on the palate due to its exceptionally fine structure. Also matured in foudres, J.M. Brocard's Vaudésir has a little more weight, and Les Clos has the most presence on the palate of any of the crus, although showing its usual austerity.

La Chablisienne *

8, Boulevard Pasteur, 89800 Chablis	📞 *+33 3 86 42 89 98*
@ *caveau@chablisienne.fr*	👤 *Le Caveau*
🌐 *www.chablisienne.com*	📍 *Chablis [map]*
😊 🏭 ▬ 🚜 *1300 ha; 8,000,000 btl*	*Fourchaume*

This important cooperative started in 1923 as a means for individual growers to sell their wines, blending and selling in bulk to negociants. In the 1950s, La Chablisienne made a transition to taking musts, and producing wine for direct sale. It has a splendid modern facility with a constant stream of visitors to its spacious tasting room. Representing 300 growers, today it accounts for around a quarter of all production in Chablis, including cuvées from 12 premier crus and 4 grand crus.

Vinification varies with the level of appellation: Petit Chablis and Chablis are vinified in steel, premier crus in 25% oak, and grand crus in 50% oak. There are three cuvées of Chablis: Finage comes from young vines, Sereine has some old vines, and Venerable comes from vines over 40 years old.

The cooperative actually purchased the estate of Château Grenouilles in 2003, which gave it ownership of most of the grand cru of Grenouilles. There are two cuvées: Fiefs de Grenouilles comes from young vines, and Château Grenouilles comes from the old vines, and is the top wine from La Chablisienne, even a little more powerful and aromatic than Les Clos. The differences between the various premier and grand crus stand out—in fact tasting the range offers an unusual opportunity because few producers have so many different crus—and there is good representation of vintage character. The wines are reliable with good typicity.

Domaine de Chantemerle *

3, Place Des Côtats, 89800 La Chapelle Vaupelteigne	📞 *+33 3 86 42 18 95*
@ *dom.chantemerle@orange.fr*	👤 *Francis & Angélique Boudin*
🌐 *www.chablis-boudin-vins.fr*	📍 *Chablis [map]*
🧍 🏭 🍇 ☙ *19 ha; 120,000 btl*	*Fourchaume*

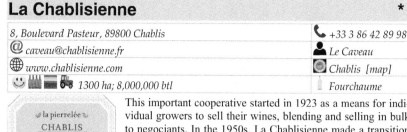

Domaine de Chantemerle has various names. It is also is known as Domaine Adhémar & Francis Boudin, or alternatively as Boudin Père & Fils. Adhémar Boudin was the son of a cooper, who created the domain the 1960s, but reacted to the family background by refusing to use any wood in his wines. His son, Francis, continues the tradition of avoiding all wood. "This is to avoid masking the aromas of Chardonnay or hardening or drying out the wine." All vinification is in cement. (The artisanal nature of the operation is indicated by a note of protest when I asked whether stainless steel was used.) Winemaking is natural, with whole bunch pressing followed by fermentation with indigenous yeasts.

The domain occupies a large square where most of the surrounding buildings seem to be part of the Boudin operation. Madame comes down from the family residence to open the tasting room, but tasting is a bit restricted as most of the wines have been sold out. Madame points to a few crates and says, "That's all that's left!" The range is smaller than most producers of similar size: Chablis (12 ha), Fourchaume (5 ha), and l'Homme Mort (a very small production from only 22 areas that is not exported). They are bottled under labels of either Boudin or Chantemerle, but the wine is the same. The style is clean and fruity, with citrus flavors predominating.

Jean Collet et Fils *

15, Avenue De La Liberté, 89800 Chablis	📞 +33 3 86 42 11 93
@ collet.chablis@wanadoo.fr	👤 Romain Collet
🌐 www.domaine-collet.fr	💿 Chablis [map]
😊 🏭 🍇 🖐 40 ha; 200,000 btl	La Forêt

The domain is housed in a modern facility on the outskirts of Chablis. Tastings take place in the large cave underneath. The domain was created by Jean Collet in 1952, although the family had already been in wine for a long time. The domain started with less than a hectare. Jean's son, Gilles, took over in 1989, and his son, Romain, started in 2009. Grapes come only from the estate, except for some Crémant. There are 2 ha of Petit Chablis, half of the vineyards are Chablis AOP (including a Vieilles Vignes), and the rest are premier and grand cru. Vaillons is the largest holding at 9 ha; "it is an assemblage of plots that truly reflects Vaillons," says Romain. Altogether there are 10 cuvées in Chablis.

Everything is fermented in stainless steel, but aging depends on the wine. Petit Chablis, Chablis, and some premier crus are handled only in stainless steel. Some premier crus are partly or wholly aged in oak, usually old (but with small proportions of new wood for some cuvées), using a range of sizes from barriques or demi-muids to large (3,000 liter) vats.

"You find our style in tension and minerality, according to the vintage," Romain says. "My father used to go for late maturity, but I harvest a bit sooner to keep acidity." The varying use of oak makes it difficult to define a single style. The Chablis conveys that sense of lively acidity and minerality, strengthened in Montmains, which is matured in stainless steel. Butteaux and La Forêt, which are within Montmains, are aged in wood: Butteaux has more tension and Forêt has greater richness. Vaillons has a classic balance between minerality and fruits. The right bank premier crus, Mont de Milieu and Montée de Tonnerre (aged in barriques), show as richer than the left bank premier crus. Although the grand crus, Valmur and Les Clos, see only a small amount of new oak, they show some spiciness. The unifying character is that sense of balancing the fruits against lively acidity.

Jean Collet also produces wines in collaboration with American importer Kermit Lynch under the separate label of Domaine Henri Costal. They include premier crus Mont de Mileu, Les Truffières, and Vaillons, and age in demi-muids.

Domaine Daniel Dampt et fils *

1, chemin des Violettes Milly, 89800 Chablis	📞 +33 3 86 42 47 23
@ domaine.dampt.defaix@wanadoo.fr	👤 Daniel, Vincent, & Sébastien Dampt
🌐 www.chablis-dampt.com	💿 Chablis [map]
📅 🏭 🍇 ⏱ 23 ha; 180,000 btl	Beauroy

It is a bit tricky to keep track of all the Dampt domains. Domaine Daniel Dampt was formed when Daniel Dampt joined his vineyards with those of his father-in-law, Jean

Defaix. Daniel has now been joined by his two sons, Vincent and Sébastien. The domain has 21 ha, including five premier crus, but because they do not own any grand crus, in 2008 they formed Maison Dampt to extend the range with a negociant activity. This allows the Dampts to add Bougros, Valmur, and Les Clos to the portfolio. In addition, Vincent and Sébastien each have 7 ha in their own name, including Chablis and some premier crus, which are vinified under the names of Domaine Vincent Dampt and Domaine Sébastien Dampt. "The aim of forming the family group and working all together was to bottle all our production," explains Vincent. All the wines are produced at the modern cellars in Milly, built in 1989 on the outskirts of the town. A new tasting room has been added next to the stockage facility, with splendid views across the vineyards over the town of Chablis to the grand crus.

Everything is vinified and matured in stainless steel, except for some oak used for the grand crus. "Stainless steel allows us to keep all the typicity of Chablis, with freshness and fruitiness, we like to make delicate wines without too much weight," Vincent says. Grand crus are vinified in old barriques. The barriques are at least three years old, but Vincent thinks even that would be too much for the premier crus. There is no battonage or racking. "The problem with battonage is that you can get richness but lose a lot of fruit, and we prefer to preserve the minerality in the wines. Sometimes using oak barrels hides the identity of the terroir," Vincent believes.

The Chablis is delicate, even a little aromatic, and then the impressions of minerality start with the premier crus. The left bank wines are more mineral than the right bank wines. Vaillons has a powerful expression of minerality. The Dampts have three different climats in Vaillons, and Les Lys is a special bottling from old vines—"it's probably the only north-facing vineyard in Chablis," says Vincent—which is a more concentrated and intense version of Vaillons. Côte de Léchet shows the most overt acidity of the premier crus, enhancing the sense of minerality, with salinity coming in at the end. "It always ages well, with increasing minerality," Vincent says. Beauroy is quite rounded, Fourchaume is in the same style but deeper. Les Clos is quite rich. Vincent recommends that the premier crus should be started about five years after the vintage.

Jean et Sébastien Dauvissat   *

3, Rue De Chichée, 89800 Chablis	☎ +33 3 86 42 14 62
@ jean.dauvissat@wanadoo.fr	👤 Evelyne & Sébastien Dauvissat
🌐 www.jeanetsebastien-dauvissat.fr	🍷 Chablis [map]
📅 🏭 🍇 ⌚ 11 ha; 45,000 btl	Vaillons

The name reflects the last two generations who have been charge of this domain, which has been in the family since 1899. It is one of several domains lining the street out of Chablis to Chichée, and you would never suspect that behind the front door lies a charming courtyard in front of the family house, which dates from the seventeenth century. Just to one side are stairs leading down to the caves underneath. Jean Dauvissat started bottling in the seventies, and slowly increased until all production was estate bottled. Since his death in an accident, the domain has been run by his wife Evelyne and son Sébastien. This is a small estate with three premier crus and one grand cru.

The wines have quite a full style. Montmains and Vaillons show stone and citrus fruits with an edge of minerality. In addition to the Vaillons tout court, there are two cuvées from climats within Vaillons. The Vieilles Vignes cuvée comes from 82-year-old vines in the Chatains climat. This is one of the two exceptions to the rule that the wines are vinified and aged in stainless steel "to keep freshness." Matured half in stainless steel and half in barriques—"but no new wood," Evelyne emphasizes—the wine is kept for two years before assemblage and bottling. Everything is intensified: it is simultaneously richer, rounder, and more mineral. The other climat in Vaillons is Séchet. "After the old vines, we will taste the Séchet, it is completely different," says Evelyne. This has more overt acidity, and a greater sense of salinity. Ever conscious of terroir, explaining the differences between the cuvées, Evelyne says that, "Montmains has clay, Vaillons is more calcareous, and Séchet is really calcareous." The grand cru, Les Preuses, is matured like the Vaillons Vieilles Vignes in cuve and barrique. Depending on the year, the wines tend to peak about five years after the vintage. The domain still offers older wines because is the policy is that, "We try to sell wines to our clients that are ready to drink."

Domaine Vincent Dauvissat   ★★★★

8, Rue Emile Zola, 89800 Chablis	📞 *+33 3 86 42 11 58*
@ *dauvissat.vincent@wanadoo.fr*	👤 *Vincent Dauvissat*
	🌐 *Chablis [map]*
🚫 ⚗ 🍇 📋 *13 ha; 70,000 btl*	*La Forêt*

Dauvissat's approach was epitomized for me the first time I visited, when I asked Vincent how he decided on the length of élevage. Slightly startled at the naivety of the question, he shrugged, and said simply, "The wine tells me." Today his children Etiennette Dauvissat and Ghislain, are taking over.

Without question, this is one of Chablis's top domains, making wines with rare intensity. Fermentation is mostly in cuve, but élevage is in old barriques (the average age of the barriques is ten years). "The fact that the wine matures in a container that breathes brings out the terroir for me," Vincent says, "but new oak loses the subtlety of terroir, the delicacy on the finish, I don't like that." Are there any differences in viticulture and vinification between the cuvées? "No, no, it's the same work in the vineyards and the cave. The only difference in élevage is the Petit Chablis, which has only 9 months, everything else is a year." So the differences are all due to terroir.

Half of the vineyards are in premier crus and a quarter in grand crus; average vine age is around 50 years. La Forêt and Vaillons are mineral, Preuses the most delicate, and Les Clos verges on austere until it develops that classic edge of anise. Is Les Clos always best? "Well each cru has its style. Clos is always the most powerful, but Preuses has its own distinct aromatic spectrum." Viticulture is biodynamic, but, "I'm a peasant, and need to be practical and efficient, so holding to the phases of the moon is tempered by the weather."

There is nothing less than exceptional here: on a visit in 2014, we were discussing the aging of Les Clos, when Vincent said, "Of course it ages well, but the Petit Chablis also ages, the 2012 will last twenty years." He proved his point by bringing out a 1996 Petit Chablis, which was mature but still lively. Some wines are bottled under the alternative label of Dauvissat-Camus.

Domaine Jean-Paul et Benoît Droin   ★★

14 Bis, Rue Jean Jaurés, 89800 Chablis	📞 *+33 3 86 42 16 78*

@ benoit@jeanpaulbenoit-droin.fr	🏃 Benoît Droin
⊕ www.jeanpaul-droin.fr	◉ Chablis [map]
⊘ ▨ 🍇 ℃ 26 ha; 185,000 btl	Montée de Tonnerre

This family domain has been passed from father to son for fourteen generations. Benoît has been in charge since the end of the 1990s. A new cuverie was built in 1999 on the road at the foot of the grand crus, but the elegant tasting room remains in the cave under the old family house in town. The domain has grown from 8 ha under Benoît's grandfather to its present size, with a range extending from Petit Chablis to nine premier and five grand crus. Only a few hectares are actually owned by the domain; most are owned by various members of the family, but worked by the domain.

Two generations ago the wines had no oak exposure, but oak was introduced in the 1980s, and the domain is now one of the leading producers of oaked premier and grand crus. Petit Chablis (from a single plot on Portlandian soil just above the grand crus) and Chablis (from several plots totaling 9 ha on the other side of the river) are produced in stainless steel. After fermentation in stainless steel, premier and grand crus are matured in a mix of cuves and oak barriques for about 10 months until assemblage just prior to bottling. Oak usage for the crus at first was up to 100%, but "has been reduced from 15 years ago to bring out terroir and elegance," explains Benoit. Today the premier crus (9 ha total) see from 20-40% oak, and the grand crus (4 ha total) from 40-50%.

Accentuated by recent vintages, the style is on the fuller side for Chablis, sometimes quite Burgundian, more fruit-driven than savory, with Montée de Tonnerre usually beating out Montmains as the best premier cru, Grenouilles showing as the fullest grand cru, and Les Clos more austere. "The premier crus you can drink when very young, with the freshness for 2 or 3 years, after that wait until 7-10 years. It's a real pity when people say, I don't want to drink it young, I'll wait 3 years. That puts them right into the closed period, when they lose freshness but haven't gained complexity," Benoît says. In effect the message is, drink them young or drink them old.

Domaine Drouhin-Vaudon   *

Chemin du Moulin, 89800 Chablis	📞 +33 3 80 24 68 88
@ maisondrouhin@drouhin.com	🏃 Famille Drouhin
⊕ www.drouhin-vaudon-chablis.com	◉ Chablis [map]
⊘ ▨ 🍇 🛢 🥄 38 ha; 250,000 btl	Montmains

The wines here used to be labeled as Joseph Drouhin—the Chablis AOP was described as Domaine de Vaudon Chablis, which caused some confusion—but since 2008 have been described as Drouhin-Vaudon to emphasize its separate identity. The domain takes its name from the old water mill, the Moulin de Vaudon, which was built in the eighteenth century. The Drouhins come from Chablis, and although most of their vineyards are now on the Côte d'Or, they have always had vineyards here. Hidden away at the entrance to the village, the property is located in an extensive park, and as an old water mill, the building straddles the river.

The vineyards in Chablis amount to almost half of the Drouhin's total vineyard holdings in Burgundy. They include seven premier crus and four grand crus. There is only a press room at the property, and the must is transferred immediately by tanker to Beaune, where vinification and aging take place. There are plans to build a winery in Chablis, but these were delayed when the Drouhins made a further acquisition in Oregon; they have become a far-flung company.

Wines come from both estate and purchased grapes; the balance varies widely, depending on the year. Wines made from estate grapes are labeled Propriétés de la Famille Drouhin. Chablis and premier crus are handled exclusively in stainless steel; grand crus are aged in demi-muids (600 liter). The style tends to freshness; indeed, Drouhin seems to have retained the typicity of Chablis better than many in its 2015s, with freshness dominating the palate, more tightly wound for the left bank, more obviously softened by some fat on the right bank. Perhaps the most classic representation of Chablis is the tightly wound Séchet premier cru; Montmains is a little rounder. On the right bank, Mont de Milieu is classic, with just a touch of that right bank fat, while Vaudésir is deeper and spicier, and Les Clos shows its austerity.

Domaine Nathalie et Gilles Fèvre   *

Route de Chablis, 89800 Fontenay-près-Chablis	📞 +33 3 86 18 94 47
@ domaine@nathalieetgillesfevre.com	👤 Gilles Fèvre
🌐 www.nathalieetgillesfevre.com	Chablis [map]
📅 🏭 🍇 🍂 50 ha; 120,000 btl	Fourchaume

"We are an old family of Chablis, related to William Fèvre. My branch of the family has always been in Fontenay, my grandfather founded the La Chablisienne coop, and my father was President for many years. Nathalie was cellarmaster at the coop for ten years. In 2003 we decided to form our own domain, so we left La Chablisienne. We had 12-13 ha, and we built a small winery. In 2003 our parents retired and gave us their vineyards, so now we have 50 ha, including a range of 15 appellations from Petit Chablis to grand cru. All our vines are around the village, basically between here and the grand crus," says Gilles Fèvre. The largest holdings are in premier cru Fourchaume and grand cru Les Preuses. The Fèvres have not entirely deserted the coop, as they sell about a third of their grapes to La Chablisienne. The wines are sometimes labeled as Marcel et Blanche Fèvre by way of tribute to Gilles' grandparents.

The style here tends to freshness, often with attractive herbal notes and a sense of fragrancy, running through the range. but intensifying from Petit Chablis, to Chablis, to premier cru, and to grand cru. Vinification focuses on stainless steel, but some wood is used for Vaulorent and Les Preuses. "We want to keep the freshness and minerality. We think 30% wood is enough," Nathalie says. "Chablis should be tense and mineral." As the premier crus come from the right bank, they tend to have that sense of greater roundness to soften the minerality, but Fourchaume retains the light, almost fragrant, impression that typifies the domain. Coming from a plot with more clay in Fourchaume, Vaulorent is richer, certainly the roundest of the cuvées, with a glycerinic sheen in warm years. That same sheen shows on grand cru Les Preuses. "Vaulorent is the cuvée with most character, it is perhaps less serious than Preuses, but it is the reference of the domain," Nathalie says. Gilles thinks the premier crus should be enjoyed at about 4-5 years; approaching ten years, they tend to show some tertiary development.

Domaine William Fèvre   **

10, Rue Jules Rathier, 89800 Chablis	📞 +33 3 86 18 14 37

@ caveau@williamfevre.com	👤 Alain Marcuello
🌐 www.williamfevre.fr	🟢 Chablis [map]
😊 🏭 🍇 🛢 78 ha; 500,000 btl	Vaulurent

The domain owes its present position to William Fèvre, the tenth generation in his family, who built it up to its present size from 7 ha after he took over in 1957. Half of the 90 individual parcels are in premier or grand crus. William was a significant figure in Chablis, trying to maintain quality, and arguing against the expansion of the seventies. With no one to succeed him, he sold to Champagne Henriot in 1998, and Didier Seguier came from Bouchard to run the domain.

A large winery at the edge of town has a splendid view of the slope of grand crus, and there's a spacious tasting room and bistro in the town center. The domain produces wines separately from estate and purchased grapes: estate wines state "Domain" discreetly on the label. Overall about half the grapes are purchased, but they go mostly into Petit Chablis and Chablis.

The style has changed significantly since the takeover: Fèvre used to show new oak, but now there is none. Didier vinifies Petit Chablis in cuve, and uses only 5-10% oak for Chablis. Premier and grand crus have around 40-60% oak, but "nothing gets more than 70% oak, and nothing spends more than six months in oak," he says. After six months in barriques, assemblage is followed by six months more in cuve.

The style continues to be on the ripe and powerful side for Chablis, and oak sometimes remains noticeable in young wines (although less so in recent vintages). The impressive range includes six grand crus and eight grand crus, but William would surely have cringed at the latest cuvée, "hipster" Chablis in a bottle that glows in the dark.

Domaine Garnier et Fils   *

Chemin De Méré, 89144 Ligny-Le-Chatel	📞 +33 3 86 47 42 12
@ info@chablis-garnier.com	👤 Xavier & Jérôme Garnier
🌐 www.chablis-garnier.com	🟢 Chablis [map]
🚫 ⚒ 🍇 🛢 🌿 25 ha; 200,000 btl	Montmains

"We are very happy with out short history, it has allowed us to show our own style," says winemaker Jérôme Garnier, who established the domain together with his brother Xavier, who manages the vineyards. "We are not like other growers, we make round and fat wines, from grapes with good maturity, we are not in the acidic line." Located in the northernmost village of the Chablis appellation, the domain has vineyards of Petit Chablis and Chablis located on Portlandian soil. "It's less chalky and we have more clay, we want to express the fruit in the wine."

"Our father was a farmer, and I and my brother decided to plant vineyards. We also buy grapes from premier crus and grand crus to complement the range, as well as some red grapes. We try to give the same expression to the wine from the grapes we buy, generally our style is rich with a powerful body. Most growers want to start harvest earlier because they want to keep freshness, but we want exactly the opposite—ripe and rich." The first vintage was 1999.

Petit Chablis comes from Lignorelles and ages 6 months in stainless steel. It's quite full on the palate, and nutty in the background. Chablis is the major part of production; a blend from all the estate plots, it ages 10-12 months in stainless steel. It's fuller on the palate, with a glossy sheen, more inclined to stone fruits than citrus. Grains Dorées comes from specific estate plots, with two years aging, starting with 60% in wood and 40% in cuve, and is round, rich, and soft. "I think when this cuvée is bottled, it's at maturity," Jérôme says.

Premier and Grand Crus age for 16-18 months in a mix of demi-muids and foudres, with no new oak except when it's necessary to replace a barrel. "All the oak comes from Austria because it doesn't give a wood impression to the wine." Mont de Milieu has a sense of reserve, Côte de Jouan moves farther in a spicy direction, Montmains is full and soft with a spicy texture, and a sense of density moving towards grand cru, while Fourchaume is something of a break with the style, moving more towards the traditional freshness of Chablis. Grand Crus Vaudésir ages for two years in demi-muids, and has a textured, spicy impression, dense but not immediately so opulent as Montmains because of greater structure. In some years there is also a cuvée from Les Clos.

Domaine Guilhem & Jean-Hugues Goisot   *

30, Rue Bienvenu Martin, 89530 Saint-Bris-Le-Vineux	📞 *+33 3 86 53 35 15*
@ *domaine.jhg@goisot.com*	👤 *Guilhem Goisot*
🌐 *www.goisot.com*	*Chablis*
📅 🏭 🍇 *30 ha; 160,000 btl*	*Sauvignon St. Bris, Exogyra virgula*

This family domain, whose name refers to father and son, occupies a pretty winery building in the center of St. Bris. "We've been in the village since the fifteenth or sixteenth century; members of the family have been innkeepers or tonneliers, but there's always been at least one vigneron each generation," says Guilhem Goisot. "I'm the seventh direct generation to run this domain. My great grandfather planted most of it." The domain includes Bourgogne Aligoté, Irancy, Bourgogne Côtes d'Auxerrois, and Sauvignon de St. Bris. The cuvées represent different soils or altitudes: most of the terroirs are Kimmeridgian, with varying extents of clay, but exposures and altitudes vary. Pinot Noir or Chardonnay are planted on south-facing sites, Sauvignon Blanc is planted elsewhere. There are three different cuvées from St. Bris and five from the Côtes d'Auxerrois. "All the names of the cuvées represent places—we don't use people's names etc." The names are a better indication of sources than the appellation, as Coys de Garde (for example) is Côtes d'Auxerre for Pinot Noir or Chardonnay, but St. Bris for Sauvignon. Vinification is the same for all wines, and the fascinating thing is that the same style of rounded citrus fruits supported by crisp acidity, some more mineral than others, transcends cépage and runs through the Auxerrois and the St. Bris. This makes for a very Burgundian take on the Sauvignon Blanc variety, and as a result, I find the St. Bris cuvées to be the most interesting.

Domaine Corinne et Jean Pierre Grossot   *

4, Route Mont De Milieu, 89800 Fleys	📞 *+33 3 86 42 44 64*
@ *info@chablis-grossot.com*	👤 *Corinne, Jean-Pierre & Eve Grossot*
🌐 *www.chablis-grossot.com*	*Chablis [map]*
📅 🏭 🍇 🍂 *17 ha; 80,000 btl*	*Vaucoupin*

Located in the village of Fleys a little to the east of the town of Chablis, the domain was created by Jean-Pierre Grossot in 1980; previously his parents and grandparents sold grapes to the coop. Today Jean-Pierre works with his daughter Eve, who is taking over winemaking. The vineyards were converted to organic in 2012 (previously viticulture had been lutte raison-née); in fact, Jean-Pierre was in the vineyards with an organic inspector when I arrived. Organic viticulture was interrupted by bad conditions in 2016 but then resumed. The major part of the vineyards (13 ha) is in appellation Chablis, giving a cuvée that is about half of all production. A small (1.5 ha) parcel just near the domain, with extremely calcareous soil, is the basis for a separate cuvée, La Part des Anges. There are five premier crus, occupying 5 ha altogether. Almost everything is vinified and then matured on the lees in stainless steel, but Mont de Milieu and Les Fourneaux see a quarter to a third élevage in old oak. The cellar has a mix of tonneaux and barriques. After six months there is assemblage, and then a further eight months in cuve. The style offers fairly direct fruits for the Chablis and the La Part des Anges cuvée, a sense of more complexity with the little-known premier cru Côte de Troemes, and then savory, herbal impressions strengthen going up the hierarchy to Vaucoupin and Fourchaume. At the premier cru level, house style is typified by a fine impression with precision of fruits. Wines are made for enjoyment in the years immediately after release.

Domaine Laroche   **

L'Obediencerie, 89800 22 rue Louis Bro, Chablis	📞 +33 3 86 42 89 00
@ info@larochewines.com	👤 Thierry Bellicaud
⊕ www.larochewines.com	Chablis [map]
🗓 🏭 🍇 🛢 🥄 90 ha; 5,000,000 btl	Montmains

One of the largest producers in Chablis, Domaine Laroche has expanded enormously since Michel Laroche made his first crop from 6 ha in 1967. There is a tasting room in the center of Chablis, and the winery is nearby, behind an old monastery dating from the ninth century. Today the estate includes 62 ha of Chablis AOP and another 21 ha of premier crus, making it one of the larger producers in Chablis.

The Chablis St. Martin cuvée under Domaine Laroche comes from the best lots of estate vineyards (roughly 70% of total); the other 30% is blended with purchased grapes and is the simple Chablis cuvée, just labeled Laroche. You have to look carefully at the label to see a difference. Chablis is vinified exclusively in stainless steel; oak is used for premier and grand crus, varying from 15-25% for the premier crus, and around 30% for grand crus.

The style tends to be relatively fruity, but of course varies with the cru. "Beauroy is south facing and warmer, Vaudevey on the other side of the hill is more north facing. Like a red wine, the south exposure favors phenolic development; Beauroy is rounder than Vaudevey, which is straighter and more mineral. We do the same work in the vines but the wines are completely different. Vaillons is another warm spot, if we let the vines ripen as much as they would like, you would lose the terroir," says vineyard manager Gilles Madelin. In grand crus, as the largest proprietor of Blanchots, Laroche makes a special cuvée, La Réserve de l'Obédience, based on selecting the best lots by blind tasting: here oak has varied from 30% to 100% over the past few years.

Laroche is a modernist not only in style, but in moving to screwcaps. "Michel Laroche was dark red when he saw cork manufacturers because he was fed up with quality," explains Sandrine Audegond at the domain. From 2006, premier and grand crus were available with either screwcap or cork, so the buyer could choose, but in 2016 there was a move back to cork. Laroche expanded beyond Chablis, first in southern France and then in Chile and South Africa, before merging with JeanJean to form the Advini wine group in 2010. Laroche also owns Mas La Chevalière in Languedoc. Michel and his children have gone on to start a new, smaller producer, called Domaine d'Henri (see profile).

Domaine Long-Depaquit *

45, Rue Auxerroise, 89800 Chablis	📞 +33 3 86 42 11 13
@ chateau-long-depaquit@albert-bichot.com	👤 Angélique Sévrain
🌐 www.albert-bichot.com	Chablis [map]
😊 🏭 🍇 🍷 65 ha; 400,000 btl	Vaillons

"The styles are really different here. The common features of Chablis are freshness and minerality, but Bichot's style is to produce wine with fruity character. We work on the picking date, we don't want to lose the acidity, but we want the wine to show fruit, it needs to speak quickly," said winemaker Matthieu Mangenot, who made the wine for eleven years before handing over to Cécilia Trimaille in 2016. Founded at the time of the French Revolution, Long-Depaquit was purchased by Beaune negociant Albert Bichot in 1968; Bichot built it up from 10 ha to its present position as one of the major estates in Chablis. The splendid château dates from the eighteenth century; a new winery was constructed in 1991 and has been renovated and extended.

The Chablis is split into two parts: the best selection goes to Long Depaquit Chablis, the rest is labeled as Bichot. Everything is vinified in small tanks of stainless steel; the Chablis and some premier crus remain in cuve. Since the 1990s, the more important premier crus have seen 10-25% oak, and grand crus range from 25% to 100%; oak exposure lasts 6-8 months, after which assemblage is followed by another 9-12 months in cuve. The style is distinctly fruity, and you have to go halfway through the premier cru range really to see minerality. No extremes might be the motto of the house. The house style does have a lovely, smooth, silky balance, with extremely judicious use of oak. Grand crus show their terroir, especially Les Clos and the flagship La Moutonne, a monopole that is essentially part of Vaudésir. The style is similar at the much smaller Château de Viviers, which is also owned by Bichot.

Domaine des Malandes *

11 route d'Auxerre, 89800 Chablis	📞 +33 3 86 42 41 37
@ contact@domainedesmalandes.com	👤 Richard Rottiers
🌐 www.domainedesmalandes.com	Chablis [map]
📅 🏭 🍇 🍷 28 ha; 180,000 btl	Chablis, Tour du Roy

"The domain in Chablis was founded in 1972, but before that my father and grandfather were in La Chapelle—all my ancestors are in the cemetery there—they were farmers because it was impossible to make a living from the vineyard. So it is not exactly true if I tell you I come from a very old family of winemakers,"? said Lyne Marchive. "If global warming continues we may have to go back to growing crops and keeping animals.'"? Lynn managed the domain for forty years before handing over in 2018 to her son and daughter. Richard already had his own domain in Beaujolais, and manages the vineyards, while Amandine took over sales. Guénolé Breteaudeau (from Muscadet) has made the wine since 2006.

The building is a rather commercial-looking warehouse just off the main road into Chablis (extended in 2014). The tasting is down in the cave, and has the one decorative feature of the building, a mural representing the vineyards of Chablis. There is a fair-sized range here, as there are plots all over the appellation, including five premier crus and two grand crus. Screwcaps are used for the Petit Chablis and Chablis. Petit Chablis and Chablis are produced only in steel, but the general procedure is to vinify partially (for the premier crus) or wholly (for the grand crus) in oak, and then to age only in steel. What is the advantage? "It's difficult to vinify in oak, it's much easier in tank. But when you vinify in oak, it's completely different, there is exchange, because of the bubbles released during fermentation, between wine and the oak. But after vinification, the oak has done its work in Chablis. To conserve the delicacy and freshness it's best to age in tank, you can lose it by aging in oak," Lyne explains.

The style is elegant and delicate, almost perfumed, and you really see the difference between the left bank, where minerality and salinity are more obvious, and the right bank, which is more rounded; but the balance is always subtle. The sense of fragrancy increases from Petit Chablis to Chablis, with a big step up to the Chablis Tour du Ray, which comes from a single vineyard of 62-year-old vines. The minerality with faint overtones of herbs and salinity of both Vaudevey and Montmains is true to Chablis's tradition. Moving to the right bank, "Fourchaume always has a more seductive style. You can find Fourchaume that is richer than ours, but we are always the first to harvest because I want to showcase elegance." It is quite delicate for Fourchaume, with that understated sense of minerality typifying the house style. In the grand crus, Vaudésir (from a plot on the side of the shadow) is more feminine, while Les Clos (from a full south-facing plot) is typically is more masculine, with more sense of austerity. You can see where Lyne's heart is from a comment about vintages. "The 2016 vintage for me is purely Chablis. It is not very charming, but it is really for the people who love Chablis. 2015 is very charming."

La Manufacture   *

40, Route d'Auxerre, 89800 Chablis	📞 +33 3 86 32 19 50
@ contact@lamanufacture-vins.fr	👤 Benjamin Laroche
🌐 www.lamanufacture-vins.fr	🔵 Chablis [map]
🚫🍷🛢🍇 25 ha; 80,000 btl	Vaillons

Founded in 2012, this negociant is a project of Benjamin Laroche, a nephew of Michel Laroche (see profile). Benjamin spent ten years working at Laroche before starting his own enterprise. The name is a play on the origins of the word "manufacture," meaning made by hand. "We have a new model of micro-trading," says Benjamin's partner, Vanessa Gicquel. Basically the growers make the wine to Benjamin's specifications, then it is aged at La Manufacture's facility, which is effectively an aging cellar (located behind Vocoret's winery on the route d'Auxerre leading into Chablis).

"We have a dozen producers who make wine for us, we have our own vats there, etc," Virginia explains. "We can have more variety of sources this way, but we maintain a style. Some of the producers make wine for themselves also, some mostly sell grapes or wine to the negociants or cooperative. Our winemakers are young, they know how to make a great wine from certain plots, if they sell it to others it's lost because it's blended out. Benjamin had to explain that we would value their work more, although it will be less productive."

Chablis and premier crus ferment in stainless steel, and grand crus ferment in barriques. Aging follows a traditional model in which more oak is used going up the hierarchy. "We use a lot of demi-muids, 1-2-year old but not new, because they don't hide the wine," Virginia says. Typically Chablis sees 25% demi-muids, premier cru Beauroy uses 30%, premier cru Vaillons uses 100%.

There are 16 cuvées in Chablis, including Petit Chablis, Chablis, premier crus, and six of the seven grand crus. Each cuvée comes from a single grower. The style tends towards fruity, tinged with minerality, intensifying from Petit Chablis to Chablis, and becoming more forceful with Beauroy. "This is always the most exuberant of our crus," Virginia says. The Vaillons Vieilles Vignes (from 45-year-old vines) makes a more subtle impression, with the fruits more subdued by the sense of minerality. Grand Cru Blanchots is smooth and weightier, with hints of spice. For me, Vaillons gives the most intense sense of the typicity of Chablis.

Other wines include red and white Bourgogne, and a Sauvignon St. Bris, which is quite exuberant. The Atelier range consists of red wines from the Côte d'Or, produced on a conventional negociant model.

Domaine Louis Michel ★★★

9, Boulevard De Ferrières, 89800 Chablis	📞 +33 3 86 42 88 55
@ contact@louismicheletfils.com	👤 Guillaume Michel
🌐 www.louismicheletfils.com	Chablis [map]
😊 🍷 🍇 🖐 25 ha; 150,000 btl	Montée de Tonnerre

"Our policy is simply to make wines that represent the terroir of Chablis: fresh, pure and mineral," says Guillaume Michel. This translates to élevage in stainless steel. There has been no oak since 1969, and Louis Michel is now the pre-eminent domain for the unoaked style of Chablis. "My grandfather didn't like the taste of oak, and he didn't have a lot of time to maintain barrels in the cellar," Guillaume explains.

The domain stretches out along a street running down to the river. The old barrel cellars below have been renovated into a chic tasting room. The major difference between cuvées is the length of time in cuve before bottling: 6 months for Petit Chablis and Chablis, on average 12 months for premier crus, and 18 months for grand crus. While lees-aging in steel is common in Chablis, few others achieve the complexity of Louis Michel. Slow fermentation leads to rich extraction. After that, "premier and grand crus wines may be matured on lees but it's not systematic as we want to focus on purity and precision and avoid wines that would be too heavy. It would depend on the vintage. As far as Petit and Chablis is concerned, we do not mature on lees."

The balance of fruity to savory notes changes with each premier cru, but all share a delicious textured background, which often leads to confusion with oak aging. The emphasis is on bringing out terroir. "We have vineyards in all three parts of Montmains (including climats Butteaux and Forêt); my grandfather used to blend but I prefer to make separate cuvées. Montmains has more clay, Forêt has more limestone, Butteaux has more clay with larger lumps of Kimmeridgian limestone. Clay brings flesh and roundness, limestone brings minerality. Butteaux is an interesting intermediate. There are only a few 100 meters between the vineyards."

In the grand crus, Vaudésir is rich and savory. "There are two sides to Vaudésir. We are on the back, not the side that faces south. So this is not our ripest grand cru, but it is the only one of the grand crus that is expressive when young." Grenouilles is even fuller bodied, and Les Clos shows its usual austerity. These are wines that often can be drunk early, but this misses the complexity that develops later, after say 6 years for premier crus and 10 years for grand crus. Guillaume has a view: "I would say a premier cru needs at least 4-5 years, and depending on the vintage can last for 20 years. When you bottle the wine, for the first few months you can drink it, but then depending on the vintage it closes down."

Domaine Christian Moreau Père et Fils ★★

26, Avenue d'Oberwesel, 89800 Chablis	📞 +33 3 86 42 86 34
@ contact@domainechristianmoreau.com	👤 Fabien Moreau
🌐 www.domainechristianmoreau.com	Chablis [map]
🗺 🍇 🛢 🥄 12 ha; 150,000 btl	Vaillons, Cuvée Guy Moreau

This is nominally a new domain, but Christian Moreau is the sixth generation of winemakers in his family. Christian had been at the family estate of J. Moreau for thirty years when the company was sold to Boisset, but he kept the family vineyards, although grapes continued to be supplied to J. Moreau under contract until 2002, when the new domain started. The domain is housed in a utilitarian warehouse just across the bridge from the town center. "Our goal was to produce top quality Chablis," says Fabien Moreau, who has been involved in the domain with his father since the beginning. "The domain is basically me and my father, with a small vineyard crew. I'm the only person in the cellar."

Some grapes are purchased to increase volume for the Chablis, but the premier and grand crus come only from estate vineyards. "I don't like to say there's a Christian Moreau style, I want to respect each terroir," is how Fabien describes stylistic objectives. Oak is used for premier and grand crus, varying from 30-50% depending on the cru and the vintage. The Chablis and the Vaillons focus directly on fruit, but the Guy Moreau cuvée from a plot of old vines in Vaillons begins the move towards a more structured character, which accentuates through the grand crus. The flagship wine is Clos des Hospices, from a plot in Les Clos, which the Moreau family bought in 1904 from the Hospices; this has always been a big wine for Chablis.

Domaine Louis Moreau ★

10, Grande Rue, 89800 Beine	📞 +33 3 86 42 87 20
@ contact@louismoreau.com	👤 Frédérique Chamoy
🌐 www.louismoreau.com	Chablis [map]
😊 🍇 🌿 45 ha; 250,000 btl	Vaillons

The Moreaus are an old family in Chablis, going back to 1814. Louis is the six generation. He holds three domains, two inherited and one that he established. Domaine de Biéville, created in 1965 by Louis's father, Jean-Jacques, produces Chablis AOP from a single holding of 45 ha (very rare in the area). Jean-Jacques also established Domaine du Cèdre Doré, another 5 ha, also producing Chablis AOP. Louis worked in California for ten years, and when he returned in 1992, he wanted to make his own wine. He created his own domain, which includes half of the vineyards that used to be leased to the family firm, J. Moreau (created by Jean-Jacques in the 1970s, but no longer in the family). Domaine Louis Moreau extends from Chablis AOP to grand crus, and represents just under a third of the production from all three domains. Wine is made at the domain headquarters, right on the road through Beine. Behind the ordinary front, there is a large warehouse-like facility for winemaking. A huge new facility for stockage has been built just round the corner, and next to it is a dedicated tasting room.

The attitude to winemaking is summarized by an offhand comment: "People are coming back, they are looking for real Chablis, without any oak." From Petit Chablis to grand cru, vinification is the same, in steel; then the wine is left on the fine lees. Blanchots and Valmur are exceptions that age in barrique. Petit Chablis and Chablis spend 4-5 months aging, premier crus take 8-10 months, and grand crus spend 12-18 months. Up to premier cru, bottling is Diam (agglomerated cork) or screwcap, depending on market, but grand crus stay under cork.

Louis Moreau says that, "The wines are upright and linear with good tension," which is a fair description. There is always a sense of minerality, often with a delicious saline catch on the finish. Chablis AOP and premier crus are textbook examples of the unoaked style. Les Clos tends to austerity, and Valmur has greater breadth, enhanced by its vinification and aging in oak.

Domaine Pattes Loup   *

2, 89800 Grande-Rue Nicolas Droin, Courgis	📞 +33 3 86 41 46 38
@ *thomas.pico@pattes-loup.com*	👤 *Thomas Pico*
🌐 *www.pattes-loup.com*	◉ *Chablis [map]*
😊 🏭 🍇 🍷 *23 ha*	🍷 *Chablis, Vente d'Ange*

Domaine de Bois d'Yver was the family domain, where Georges Pico planted most of the vines, but Thomas Pico wanted to work organically, so separated to found his own domain, which he called Pattes Loup. He started with 2.5 ha that his father gave him in 2007, and now makes wine from 25 ha, including Chablis and four premier crus. Georges Pico has now retired, but Thomas still makes wines for Domaine de Bois d'Yver from 10 ha. The domains are located in a building right at the end of the village, which was renovated in 2014. Operating on three levels, everything is gravity-fed.

Vinification takes place in stainless steel tanks and in concrete eggs. Chablis ages mostly in cuve, and the premier crus age in old oak. There are lots of very old barriques and some demi-muids (600 liter). Wines tasted from cuve have a forceful style that owes something to long élevage; in 2017 I tasted 2015s (including Chablis AOP) that would not be bottled until 2018. "The premier crus have will 30 months élevage this year, although usually it's 18 months." The wine calms down and becomes more integrated once in bottle, but still has a very lively style of lemony citrus flavors supported by bright acidity.

The Chablis Vent d'Ange has some weight, and the two estate premier crus, Côte de Jouan and Beauregard, both come from the vicinity of Courgis. Vaillons and Butteaux come from purchased grapes.

Usually the domain confines itself to Chablis, but low production forced a change. "Last year because of hail I bought some grapes and made a Vin de France Chardonnay," Thomas explains. The attitude here is committed artisanal. During the tasting, my companion remarked, "Now wine is more scientific." "No it isn't," Thomas shot back.

Domaine Gilbert Picq et Fils　　　*

3, Route De Chablis, 89800 Chichée	📞 *+33 3 86 42 18 30*
@ *domaine.picq-gilbert@wanadoo.fr*	👤 *Didier & Pascal Picq*
	🔘 *Chablis* [map]
🚫 🎽 🍇 🐌 *14 ha; 90,000 btl*	*Chablis, Vieilles Vignes*

This tiny property is right in the center of Chichée, occupying a cluster of buildings on either side of the main road. The tasting room is in a very old but charming cave underneath. This is very much a family domain focused on the neighborhood: Didier Picq is the sixth generation, and works with his brother. "The Picqs have always produced their own wine," Didier says. A little reticent at first, Didier opens up with enthusiasm to describe the wines. Vinification is the same for all the wines: all in stainless steel, no wood. Only estate grapes are used. "If Vincent Dauvissat wanted to sell me grapes, I'd buy, but I haven't found any source I like."

There are two left bank premier crus, but four different cuvées from Chablis AOP, which represents more than half the domain. The style tends to be nicely rounded with herbal impressions on the palate. La Vaudécorse is a 1 ha single vineyard parcel, presenting more subtle herbal notes and finer texture than the Chablis tout court. The domain is well known for its Vieilles Vignes, which comes from 60-70-year old vines and has that extra density of old vines, together with a kick of richness at the end. Dessus La Carrière is a very stony 2 ha parcel giving wines with increased intensity. The 0.5 ha plot of premier cru Vaucoupin has a more mineral impression than the Chablis cuvées, with great purity of fruits. It shows the same style as the Chablis, but with greater subtlety of expression and more flavor variety on the palate. The 1.5 ha plot of Vosgros makes a restrained mineral impression, not quite austere, but with great potential for aging.

Most of the production is exported, with the U.S. as the major market, focused on New York. In France you are more likely to find the wines in a restaurant than in a shop.

Domaine Pinson Frères　　　*

5, Quai Voltaire, 89800 Chablis	📞 *+33 3 86 42 10 26*
@ *pinson@domaine-pinson.com*	👤 *Laurent & Charlène Pinson*
🌐 *www.domaine-pinson.com*	🔘 *Chablis* [map]
📅 🏭 🍇 🐌 *14 ha; 75,000 btl*	*Mont de Milieu*

The Pinsons have been making wine in Chablis since the seventeenth century, but the domain was really created in its present form by Louis Pinson in the 1940s when he focused on producing and bottling his own Chablis. The name changed after his grandsons Laurent (winemaker) and Christophe (viticulturalist) came into the domain in the early 1980s and increased its size from an initial 4 ha. Laurent's daughter Charlene has been making wine since 2008. Because the crop was reduced by a series of climate problems, since 2014 there has also been a small range called Charlène et Laurent Pinson from grapes from other vineyards. About half the estate vineyards are premier cru, and another quarter are in the grand cru Les Clos. Located at the edge of town on the Serein river, a new cuverie was built in 2004 with stainless steel fermentation cuves.

The domain is one of the arch exponents of the oaked style: after fermentation wines are transferred to barriques, using nine months élevage in 1- to 3-year-oak for premier crus, and a year for Les Clos, which includes 10% new oak. There's a special cuvée from Les Clos, Authentique, from older vines, which spends the first 6 months in entirely new oak, followed by 18 months in older oak. The same style at Pinson runs through the Chablis, premier crus, and grand crus. There's a faint note of apples on top of a tendency towards the savory, giving almost a piquant impression. Minerality is in the background. Pinson's premier and grand crus tend to be delicious when released, then after two or three years they close up: do not panic, but it's better not to touch them for the best part of a decade, until they open out again into a full, creamy style that brings a more subtle representation of the oak regime.

Patrick Piuze *

25 rue Emile Zola, 89800 Chablis	📞 *+33 3 86 18 85 73*
@ *contact@patrickpiuze.com*	👤 *Patrick Piuze*
🌐 *www.patrickpiuze.com*	◉ *Chablis [map]*
🚫🏭🍷🚜 *0 ha; 150,000 btl*	*Montée de Tonnerre*

VENDANGES 2009

CHABLIS PREMIER CRU
LES FORÊTS

Patrick Piuze

As a micro-negociant, Patrick Piuze makes an unusually wide range of cuvées. His winery in the heart of Chablis is an old building bought from Vocoret, larger than it appears at first, as it's connected by a tunnel under the road to caves on the other side. "This was constructed in the period when a Vocoret was the mayor of Chablis, it probably wouldn't be possible today," Patrick explains. What is the driving force to be a negociant in Chablis? "I wasn't born here, I came from Montreal. The only way to express a lot of terroirs is to be a negociant. We buy grapes we like from special sites, before we worry about having a specific appellation."

Production is 65% Petit Chablis or Chablis; 35% is premier and grand cru. Patrick harvests with his own team. "Choosing harvest date is one of the most important things. We are an early picker. A wine can have only one backbone. 90% of white wines in the world have an alcohol backbone, but we have an acid backbone. Our wines are never more than 12.3%." Petit Chablis is matured in cuve, Chablis in a mixture of cuve and barriques, and premier and grand crus are entirely in barrique. The style gets to full ripeness without excess, with a silky sheen to the fruits, a sense of stone fruits adding to the citrus and minerality of Chablis; yet always with that wonderfully moderate alcohol.

A sense of tension counterpoised against elegant fruits runs through the range from premier crus to the more overtly full grand crus. Vaillons Les Minots is something of a flagship in premier crus, always one of the most complex, and Montee de Tonnerre has the fullness of the grand crus, sometimes with an exotic edge of lime to the citrus fruits. In grand crus, Bougros can be almost as reserved as Les Clos. They develop slowly: allow at least 5-6 years for premier and grand crus. Even after opening, the wine may take some time to come out fully.

L & C Poitout *

3 Rue Laffitte, 89800 Chablis	📞 *+33 9 79 61 62 16*
@ *contact@lc-poitout.fr*	👤 *Catherine & Louis Poitout*
🌐 *lc-poitout.fr*	◉ *Chablis [map]*

| | Chablis, Les Vénérés |
| 26 ha; 50,000 btl | Vin de France, l'Inextinct |

Both from families involved with winemaking in Chablis, Catherine and Louis Poitout formed their own domain in 2011. "We started with many small parcels," explains Louis, "but they weren't all the true taste of Chablis, so we sold many in 2012 and bought others." Vinification is not fully organic, but no insecticides are used in the vineyards, which are ploughed using a horse. The domain is located in a charming old house on the banks of the Serein, with a modern tasting room.

The Petit Chablis comes from a plot overlooking Valmur, the Chablis Bienommé comes from the north, and keeps freshness, while Chablis Les Vénérées comes from old vines planted in 1946 and 1960. There are two premier crus: Les Fourneaux faces pure south, and Vaucoupin faces west. "The difference is enormous," says Louis.

So what is the true taste of Chablis? "The true taste of Chablis is mineral with the most simple vinification. We do exactly the same vinification for all cuvées. There is never any wood. Everything is kept as simple as possible," Louis explains. The Petit Chablis is a textbook example: simple, direct, and fruity. Chablis Bienommé is more restrained with the first impression of minerality; then Les Vénérées moves in a herbal direction, with a real sense of texture to the palate that makes you think of wood, "but there is none." Vaucoupin really brings out minerality, and Les Fourneaux is fuller and richer. "It's hot and in full sun, you lose minerality but gain roundness."

The most unusual wine comes from a tiny plot of 55 ares of old, ungrafted vines in the area of Petit Chablis. "In 2012 we were looking for parcels, and we found one that was in very bad condition. The vines had been cut at the base and everyone thought they would die, because they'd been cut at the graft, but they grew," Louis recalls. They turned out to be ungrafted. "The wine is labeled as Vin de France because it doesn't fit our idea of Petit Chablis," Louis says. Called L'Inextinct to reflect its origins, it shows great purity of fruits, richness on the palate, yet retains the lively acidity of Chablis. It's a rare experience.

Domaine Denis Race   *

15 rue de la Croix Duché, 89800 Chablis	☎ +33 3 86 42 45 87
@ domaine@chablisrace.com	👤 Claire & Marine Race
🌐 www.chablisrace.com	📍 Chablis [map]
😊 🏭 🍇 🦌 18 ha; 90,000 btl	Mont de Milieu

The entrance to the original premises looks like a quiet shop front in a residential street, but underneath is a large cave that has been completely modernized. There's a dedicated tasting room at the front of the cave, and it's a mark of the hands-on nature of the operation that when visitors descend to the tasting room, the lady running the bottling line in the next room stops bottling and comes to manage a tasting. Now the domain has moved from the center of town to more spacious premises on the outskirts. The estate was founded in the 1930s; Denis Race is the grandson of the founder, and the fourth generation, in the form of his daughter Claire, has now joined.

The domain has moved to mechanical harvesting—Denis has not quite retired and still drives the tractor—then the grapes are pressed immediately in pneumatic presses. The domain is committed to stainless steel, and wines mature in cuve for 9-10 months before bottling and release. "It's true that wood adds something to the wine, but it's not what we are looking for. What we are after is something more natural," Clare says. Marine is a fan of barrels, so there's an experiment with wood in the form of three barriques, but this remains confined to a very small cuvée.

There are three premier crus, of which Montmains is the most important with a total of 5 ha in several different parcels. One plot of 60-year-old vines is bottled separately as the Vieilles Vignes; the others are blended into the Montmains cuvée. The Chablis is relatively soft and a little aromatic, Montmains is broader and more restrained, Vaillons is more linear and more delicate, tilting in the direction of minerality, and Mont de Milieu broadens the herbal impressions with a typical touch of fat from the right bank. The Vieilles Vignes shows a real increase in concentration from the Montmains tout court.

Domaine François Raveneau ★★★★

9, Rue de Chichée, Bp 13, 89800 Chablis	☎ *+33 3 86 42 17 46*
📠 *+33 3 86 42 45 55*	👤 *Isabelle et Maxime Raveneau*
	🌐 *Chablis [map]*
🚫🏷🍇🕯 *10 ha; 45,000 btl*	*Chapelot*

This very discrete domain is identified only by a metal sign above the door. Created in 1948 by François Raveneau from vineyards owned by his and his wife's families, it's the flagship for oak-aged Chablis. Since 1995 the domain has been run by brothers Bernard and Jean-Marie, and now their children, Isabelle and Maxime, are taking over. Most of the plots are very small, less than a hectare each. "My father started with only 3 ha," says Bernard Raveneau, and looking at his daughter Isabelle, adds, "We grow only slowly."

Élevage is the same for everything from Chablis to grand cru, with fermentation followed by aging for a year in old oak. A horizontal tasting at Raveneau is an education in the terroirs of Chablis. Consistency of style shows all the way from Chablis AOP (produced since 2007) to the grand cru Les Clos: fruits give an impression of being more textured than simply dense, with a savory overlay that turns in the direction of anise with time.

The Chablis is the most openly fruity; it is very good but the special character of Raveneau really starts with the premier crus. La Fôret (part of Montmains) isn't so much more intense as just shifting the balance a bit from fruity to savory, Butteaux (another part of Montmains) adds more mineral notes as do the Montmains and Vaillons. Butteaux is the most reserved, but I usually find Forêt and Montmains to be more complex than Vaillons, and more subtle than Montée de Tonnerre on the right bank, but we are talking about differences between superlatives here. If I were forced to pick my favorite premier cru from Raveneau, it would probably be Montmains.

Chapelot (part of Montée de Tonnerre) is usually more steely and less powerful than the Montée de Tonnerre cuvée, which shows intimations of the power of the grand crus. Montée de Tonnerre is the largest cuvée, about a third of all production. Among the grand crus, Blanchots is usually broad, Valmur is more precise, Clos is always the most austere and backward.

What's the secret, I asked, what gives Raveneau Chablis its unique quality? "It's the origin, travail attentif in the vines. A chef would say that if the ingredients are top quality, there is no need for artifice: it's exactly the same with wine. There is no secret (except that) we never go to extremes here. Many people today say they do something special, such as biodynamics."

The steely minerality of the young wines begins to open out after about 5-6 years for premier crus and 8-10 years for grand crus. (Don't even think of opening Les Clos until it is close to 10 years old: it would be sheer vinicide.) Raveneau Chablis is virtually unique; unfortunately this is now also true of the price.

Domaine Servin   *

20, Avenue d'Oberwesel, 89800 Chablis	📞 +33 3 86 18 90 00
@ contact@servin.fr	👤 François Servin
🌐 www.servin.fr	📷 Chablis [map]
😊 🏭 🍇 🛢 36 ha; 250,000 btl	Vaillons

The Servin family have owned vines in Chablis since the seventeenth century. Located in old buildings just across the river from the town center, the domain is run today by the seventh generation, François Servin, together with his brother-in-law. Vineyard holdings include an impressive range of six top premier crus as well as four grand crus. The emphasis here is on a fairly straightforward style, with vinification and maturation largely in stainless steel for Petit Chablis, Chablis, and premier crus, and oak used only for grand crus: Les Preuses is vinified in stainless steel but partly matured in oak, and only Les Clos is both vinified and matured in barrique.

The wines are attractive and ready for drinking on release, with a citrus fruit spectrum balanced by occasional savory hints and a nice sense of texture to the palate. Servin's general style favors minerality or delicacy over power. In addition to the AOP Chablis, there is a cuvée of Vieilles Vignes from a plot of 50-year old vines in Pargues (at one time considered on a level with the premier crus Montmains and Vaillons, but abandoned during the first world war). The premier crus have more intensity than the AOP Chablis, but I do not see as much distinction between them as I would like, and although there is more intensity at the grand cru level, the only wine that strikes me as having serious aging potential is Les Clos. François also makes wines for a label under his father's name, Marcel Servin.

Maison Simonnet-Febvre   *

9, Avenue d'Oberwesel, 89800 Chablis	📞 +33 3 86 98 99 00
@ caveau@simonnet-febvre.com	👤 Paul Espitalié
🌐 www.simonnet-febvre.com	📷 Chablis [map]
😊 🏭 🍇 🛢 ⚙ 20 ha; 800,000 btl	Montmains

CHABLIS
PREMIER CRU
VAILLONS
MILLÉSIME
2010
SIMONNET-FEBVRE
À CHABLIS

"We are a bit different, because Chablis is 50%, and the rest is sparkling wine (25%) and regional wines (25%)," says Jean-Philippe Archambaud, who came to run the house after Louis Latour bought it in 2003. Simonnet-Febvre is an old house, founded in 1840, and originally concentrating on sparkling wine. Today sparkling wine is made at the old cellars just across the river from the Chablis town center, and the still wines are made in a new cellar at Chitry, a few miles away. Estate vineyards are only a small part of the supply for this large house. With 42 cuvées in all, there's a wide range of vintage and nonvintage Crémants, red and white wines from the Auxerrois, and Chablis extending from Petit Chablis to grand cru.

"Almost all our wines are made in the same way," Jean-Philippe explains: "whole bunch pressing, vinification in stainless steel, and then aging in steel on fine lees, no wood. I think most Chablis need 10-12 months aging. When we leave them on the lees we don't do racking or battonage, we just leave them alone. The Simonnet style is very much no oak, except for two grand crus, Blanchots and Les Clos, which have 15% aged in 2-year-old barriques. I'm not a fan of new oak, I don't use any even for the premier crus. The nutty impressions come from lees not oak." Petit Chablis has slightly shorter élevage at 10 months, Chablis and premier crus have 12 months, the grand crus have 17-18 months.

The Petit Chablis is fruity and workmanlike, the Chablis begins to move in a mineral direction, but there is a big jump in intensity going to the Montmains premier cru. This is the real typicity of Chablis. Vaillons is more backward, Mont de Milieu is close to grand cru intensity, and Fourchaume is richer. "Whenever I want to explain what Chablis is, I think Montmains is a good example. Our Vaillons is always a little austere, a bit flinty. Mont de Milieu is fascinating because it can be a cool year or a warm year, but you always get this exotic character, Fourchaume is lovely wine but can be richer," says Jean-Philippe. In grand crus, Preuses is tightly wound, and Les Clos has more depth but is equally backward.

Domaine Laurent Tribut ★★★

15 Rue de Poinchy, 89800 Chablis	☎ +33 3 86 42 46 22
🖷 +33 3 86 42 48 23	👤 Laurent Tribut
	🌐 Chablis [map]
📅 🚜 🍇 ♨ 7 ha; 31,000 btl	🍷 Beauroy

Laurent Tribut is married to Vincent Dauvissat's sister, Marie Clotilde, and there is a family relationship to the style of the wines. The vineyards are part of Marie Clotilde's inheritance from René Dauvissat. For the first ten years, Laurent made his wines in the Dauvissat cellars, but then he moved to his own premises in Poinchy just outside the town of Chablis. Fermentation is in stainless steel, then everything is matured in old barriques. "Everything stays six months in barrique, longer than that they would show the wood, and I don't like that," Laurent says. This small domain is a very hands-on operation—there was some difficulty in arranging an appointment because Laurent thought he might need to be in the vineyards—and the wine is made in a tiny cramped cellar stuffed with barriques.

All the wines here start out full flavored, with that distinct hint of savory character. Moving from Chablis to Lechet there is more sense of extract and greater intensity. "Léchet is Léchet," says Laurent, "it is always a bit more aggressive." Then Beauroy is a touch rounder and deeper. Montmains has the greatest intensity of the premier crus, very much the savory style with wider flavor variety, and a grip on the palate. The wines are masterful representations of their appellations.

Domaine Vrignaud ★

10, Rue De Beauvoir, 89800 Fontenay-près-Chablis	📞 *+33 3 86 42 15 69*
@ *guillaume@domaine-vrignaud.com*	👤 *Guillaume Vrignaud*
🌐 *www.domaine-vrignaud.com*	🔲 *Chablis [map]*
📅 🏭 🍇 🍂 *28 ha*	*Mont de Milieu*

Michel and Joëlle Vrignaud abandoned general agriculture and focused on viticulture, starting estate bottling on a small scale in 1991; a new winery was built in 2000 and extended in 2008. The domain is still in the process of making the move to bottling all its own wines, and today half of production is bottled at the domain, which is run by Michel's son, Guillaume. The domain is located in a series of buildings around a courtyard at the back of Fontenay-près-Chablis. It's a very hands-on operation, as Guillaume Vrignaud was on his tractor in the vineyards and (to the exasperation of his mother) was difficult to reach when we arrived.

The range extends from Petit Chablis and Chablis to two right bank premier crus, Fourchaume and Mont de Milieu. "We don't have any grand crus but we vinify a bit from a colleague," Joëlle Vrignaud explains. Most of the wines are vinified and aged in stainless steel, and the style shows a citric purity that develops increasing minerality and salinity moving from Petit Chablis to Chablis to Mont de Milieu.

Fourchaume is divided into three cuvées: Fourchaume tout court, Vaupulans. which comes from a specific plot of less than a hectare in the premier cru, and Côte de Fontenay, which comes from a hectare of older vines, more than 50 years of age. Fourchaume is sometimes aged in oak: the rich 2015 was aged in cuve, but the more acid 2014 was broadened by vinifying in wood. The old vines cuvée was vinified in cuve—"it was complex enough, it did not need oak." Fourchaume is the richest of the cuvées, and is further intensified by the concentration of the old vines.

Profiles of Important Estates

Domaine Alexandre

36 rue du Serein, 89800 La Chapelle-Vaupelteigne	📞 *+33 3 86 42 44 57*
@ *info@chablis-alexandre.com*	👤 *Olivier Alexandre*
🌐 *www.chablis-alexandre.com*	🔲 *Chablis [map]*
🧍 🏭 🍇 🍷	*13 ha; 33,000 btl*

This family domain is in its third generation and Olivier has taken over from his father Guy. Vineyards are in four communes in the northwest quadrant of the appellation: Beines, La Chapelle Vaupelteigne, Lignorelles, and Villy. The bulk of production is Petit Chablis and Chablis, but there are two special cuvées. The Vieilles Vignes Chablis comes from 60-year-old vines, "planted by my grandfather," Olivier says. The top wine is premier cru Fourchaume. No oak is used in aging.

Domaine Jérémy Arnaud

8, rue de Derrière les Fossés, 89700 Viviers	📞 *+33 6 95 95 09 33*
@ *domaine.jeremy.arnaud@gmail.com*	👤 *Jérémy Arnaud*
🌐 *www.domainejeremyarnaud.com*	🔲 *Chablis*
📅 🏭 🍇 🍷	*3 ha; 14,000 btl*

Located at the northeast corner of the appellation, halfway to Tonnerre, this new domain must be the smallest in Chablis, but the wines have been winning acclaim since their release. Jérémy has been assembling the domain, plot by plot, since he graduated in oenology in 2016 and gained experience working at various domains in Chablis and elsewhere in Burgundy. The range starts with a tiny plot of Petit Chablis planted 40 years ago (so small it produces only 600 bottles, but Jérémy says it will be reclassified as Vau de Vey). The range goes straight to the main holding, 0.5 ha of Vau de Vey, planted at the same time as the Petit Chablis. The main holding, if you can use that term about such a small plot, gives about 2,800 bottles. It ages half in stainless steel and half in barriques, including 10% of new oak. La Grande Chaume comes from single parcel in Vau de Vey, on a very steep slope on Kimmeridgian terroir, aged for two years in barrique: production is only 900 bottles.

Domaine Barat

6, Rue De Lechet, 89800 Milly	📞 +33 3 86 42 40 07
@ domaine.barat.angele@orange.fr	👤 Angèle & Ludovic Barat
🌐 www.domaine-barat.fr	🌀 Chablis [map]
🗓️ 🏭 🍇 🚜	22 ha; 100,000 btl

In its sixth generation under Angèle & Ludovic Barat since the estate was founded in 1795, this family domain has half its vineyards in AOP Chablis, with small plots in Petit Chablis and four premier crus, Côte de Léchet, Vaillons, Fourneaux, and Mont de Milieu. Michel Barat retired in 2003 and handed over winemaking to his son Angèle, while his other son, Ludovic, manages the vineyards. Harvesting is mechanical. Wines age for six months in stainless steel. There is one cuvée in each category, except for Côte de Léchet, where there is a second cuvée from 40-year-old vines, l'Umami, which spends 18 months aging in cuve, and is the top wine.

Domaine Beaufumé

5 Rue des Vignes, 89800 Lignorelles	📞 +33 3 86 47 56 32
@ scevdomainebeaufume@orange.fr	👤 Valérie Beaufumé
🌐 www.chablis-beaufume.com	🌀 Chablis [map]
🍇 🌱	18 ha

Three generations have grown grapes at the domain. Since Bernard Beaufumé took over in 1989, he has doubled the size, and then estate-bottling started in 2014, building a winery, with Bernard's wife Valérie as the winemaker, starting on a small basis with 6,000 bottles. Vineyards in Lignorelles and Villy are a mix of Petit Chablis and Chablis, in 25 separate parcels. Wines age on the lees in stainless steel for 6-12 months depending on the vintage.

Domaine Begue-Mathiot

Les Epinottes, 89800 Chablis	📞 +33 3 86 42 16 65
@ contact@chablis-begue-mathiot.com	👤 Guylhaine Begue
🌐 www.chablis-begue-mathiot.com	🌀 Chablis [map]
🗓️ 🏭 🍇 🚜	17 ha

While working at a large producer, Joël Begue acquired 3 ha of his own of AOP Chablis, and in 1985 began to produce his own wine. Joël died in 2008, and his wife Maryse, with her daughter Guylhaine, continue to run the domain. In addition to the Chablis AOP, there are several premier crus: Vosgros, Vaucoupin, Vaillons (the largest production from 40-year old vines), Fourchaume, and the Fourchaume Vieilles Vignes (from vines planted in 1949). All the wines age in cuve for 10 months.

Château de Béru

32, Grande Rue, 89700 Béru	📞 *+33 3 86 75 90 43*
@ *athenaisdeberu@gmail.com*	👤 *Athénais de Béru*
🌐 *www.chateaudeberu.com*	🔵 *Chablis [map]*
🗓️ 🏭 🏠 🍇 🍾 ◯	*15 ha; 65,000 btl*

The Béru family has owned the property for 400 years, but grapes went to the cooperative until Athénais de Béru took over the family property in 2006 after a career in finance. "I worked at UBS, but I knew where ma vocation would lead," she says. Château de Béru produces three cuvées of AOP Chablis from different plots in the vicinity, and the premier cru Vaucoupin, but the top wine, the Clos de Béru, comes from a 5 ha clos at the property. Long aging (around 18 months) takes place in a mixture of large wood casks, barriques, and amphora. The style is distinctive and can be quite herbal and saline. Negociant wines are produced under the Athénais label and include Sauvignon St. Bris and Bourgogne Rouge as well as Chablis.

Domaine Besson

8 chemin de la Vallée de Valvan, 89800 Chablis	📞 *+33 3 86 42 40 88*
@ *contact@domaine-besson.com*	👤 *Camille Besson*
🌐 *www.domainebesson.com*	🔵 *Chablis [map]*
🗓️ 🏭 🍇 🌿	*21 ha; 100,000 btl*

This family domain is just south of the town of Chablis, next to premier cru Montmains. Eugène Besson founded the domain with some small plots in 1902. His son Félix expanded it, and Félix's son Alain formed his own domain with some small plots in 1980. In 1985, Félix and Alain joined their domains together into what is now Domaine Besson, constructed a new cuverie in 1997, and expanded the vineyards further. Alain bottled about 10% of production under the domain name, selling the rest off in bulk to negociants. His children Adrien and Camille took over in 2013, with Adrien managing the vineyards and Camille making the wine. Now the domain bottles all its production. The range runs from Petit Chablis and Chablis through premier crus Vaillons, Montmains, and Mont de Milieu to grand crus Vaudésir and Les Clos. The largest holding is 5 ha in Montmains; the smallest 0.15 ha in Les Clos, amounting to just five rows of vines. Vines have an average age of 35 years. All the wines are vinified principally in stainless steel with a small proportion, varying from 3-8%, vinified in barriques, except for Les Clos, which is only stainless steel (with a production of only 800 bottles, there isn't enough wine to make a small proportion in a barrique).

Domaine du Chardonnay

Rue Lafitte, 89800 Chablis	📞 *+33 3 86 42 48 03*
@ *info@domaine-du-chardonnay.fr*	👤 *Arnaud Nahan & Thomas Labille*
🌐 *www.domaine-du-chardonnay.fr*	🔵 *Chablis [map]*
🚶 🏭 🍇 🌿	*35 ha; 266,000 btl*

As you might guess from its name, the Domaine du Chardonnay is not an old domain, but was created when three associates joined their holdings together in 1987. They started in polyculture with 11 ha of vines and 80 ha of cereals. They moved immediately into viticulture, doubling the vineyard area in the first year, and by 1992 they stopped producing cereals altogether. Located in an old water mill, the Moulin du Pâtis, on the Serein at the edge of the town, the winery was completed in 1993. The three founders retired in 2019. The domain is heavy on Petit Chablis (10 ha) and Chablis (19 ha), which together make 85% of production, and has smaller plots in five premier crus, Vaillons, Montmains, Vosgros, Mont de Milieu, and Montée de Tonnerre. A small amount of oak is used in aging some of the premier crus.

Domaine de Chaude Ecuelle

35, Grande Rue, 89800 Chemilly-Sur-Serein	📞 *+33 3 86 42 40 44*
@ *chaudeecuelle@wanadoo.fr*	👤 *Claire & Gérald Vilain*
🌐 *www.chaudeecuelle.com*	🔴 *Chablis [map]*
📅 🏭 🍇 🚚	*60 ha; 100,000 btl*

The domain started under the great-great grandfather of the present generation, who grew grapes and bottled wine for the family. Gérald and Claire Vilain established the domain in its present form in the 1990s; their children, Guillaume, Marie-France and Marianne Vilain, are now involved. Harvesting is mechanical for Petit Chablis and Chablis, but manual for the premier crus and a plot of 60-year-old vines. The estate bottles about a third of the harvest and sells the rest. Production was all in stainless steel, until barriques started to be used for premier crus in 2016. Élevage lasts 10 months for Chablis and Petit Chablis,18 months for the Chablis Vieilles Vignes, Cuvée Clovis, and the premier crus, Vaillons, Montmains, and Montée de Tonnerre (which also has some very old vines). Production is mostly Chablis AOP, with quite small amounts of the other cuvées.

Domaine des Chaumes

6 rue du Temple, 89800 Maligny	📞 *+33 3 86 98 21 83*
@ *domainedeschaumes@wanadoo.fr*	👤 *Céline & Romain Poullet*
🌐 *www.chablis-domainedeschaumes.com*	🔴 *Chablis [map]*
📅 🏭 🍇 🌿	*11 ha*

Fresh from his studies in oenology at Beaune, Romain Poullet started his own domain at Maligny in 2000, while helping his parents at their Domaine des Chaumes. Then in 2014 he took over the family domain. Production from the estate vineyards has been supplemented by a small negociant activity since 2011. Petit Chablis, Chablis, and the Chablis Vieilles Vignes (which comes from vines up to 10—years old) age in stainless steel, and there is also a Chablis Elévé en Fût de Chêne, which ages in barriques. The single premier cru is Vaillons. There are also red wines from Irancy and Bourgogne, a Crémant, and some liqueurs.

Domaine Michel Colbois

69 Grande Rue, 89530 Chitry le Fort	📞 *+33 3 86 41 43 48*
@ *contact@colbois-chitry.com*	👤 *Benjamin Colbois*
🌐 *www.colbois-chitry.com*	🔴 *Chablis [map]*
🚶 🏭 🍇 🚜	*20 ha; 100,000 btl*

The Colbois family were vignerons growing grapes from the start of the twentieth century and making small amounts of wine. Michel worked with his parents until l1970, when he started to work independently with 2 ha. The operation grew and became Domaine Michel Colbois in 1009. His son Benjamin joined in 2009, and today runs the domain. About 7 ha are in Chablis, 8 ha in Bourgogne Chitry (divided between white and red), and another 4 ha in Bourgogne Aligoté. The Chablis AOP is vinified exclusively in stainless steel. The Vieilles Vignes Chablis (from 50-year-old vines) is partly aged in barriques, with 5% new oak. Premier cru Côte de Jouan ages in stainless steel. The Chablis AOP is the largest production, about three quarters of the 60,000 bottles from Chablis.

Domaine du Colombier

42, Grand Rue, 89800 Fontenay-près-Chablis	📞 *+33 3 86 42 15 04*
@ *domaine@chabliscolombier.com*	👤 *Thierry Mothe*
🌐 *www.chabliscolombier.com*	🔴 *Chablis [map]*
📅 🏭 🍇 🌿	*55 ha; 400,000 btl*

The family has been growing grapes since 1887, but the estate also includes other crops and cattle. Guy Mothe took over in 1957, starting with a very small holding, and expanded the domain by buying additional plots as opportunities arose. He made the move into estate-bottling in the 1980s. Today his three sons, Jean-Louis, Thierry (the winemaker), and Vincent run the domain. The approach is workmanlike, using machine harvesting, with fermentation and aging in stainless steel in a modern winery. The range has Petit Chablis, Chablis, Chablis Vieilles Vignes, and premier crus Vaucoupin and Fourchaume. The only wine to see any oak is grand cru Bougros, which is aged 20% in barriques.

Domaines Courtault & Michelet

1, Route de Montfort, 89800 Lignorelles	📞 *+33 3 86 47 50 59*
@ *contact@chablis-courtault-michelet.com*	👤 *Stéphanie & Vincent Michelet*
🌐 *www.chablis-courtault-michelet.com*	🔵 *Chablis [map]*
🚶 ⛏ 🍇 🛢 ❦	*29 ha; 120,000 btl*

Jean-Claude Courtault came from Touraine to become vineyard manager at Domaine de l'Orme in Lignorelles in 1974. Ten years later he bought 1.5 ha of old vines and rented some land in Chablis AOP which he planted. He produced his first wine under the name of the estate in 1987, while continuing at Domaine de l'Orme, and by 1995 the estate had grown to 12 ha of Petit Chablis and Chablis, and he was able to work at it full time. His daughter Stéphanie, and her husband Vincent Michelet, created their own estate in 2008, now with 6 ha of Petit Chablis and a hectare of Chablis. Stéphanie and Vincent took over Domaine JC Courtault in 2019, so now the two domains run under the rubric of Domaines Courtault & Michelet. Together the two domains have about half their holdings in Petit Chablis and half in Chablis. The main difference between them is the source, coming from parcels around Lignorelles for JC Courtault, which produces fruitier wines, and mostly around Fyé and Beines for Michelet, which produces more mineral wines. The Petit Chablis and Chablis for both domains age in stainless steel. Under JC Courtault there is also a Chablis Élevée in Fût de Chêne, which ages in demi-muids. Premier crus Mont de Milieu and Beauroy come from purchased grapes; Beauroy ages partly in small steel tanks and partly in 3-year barriques. Grand cru Valmur, from purchased must, ages 80% in demi-muids and 20% in new barriques. There's also some negociant Chablis, which may use either label.

Vignoble Dampt Frères

1 rue de Fleys, 89700 Collan	📞 *+33 3 86 55 29 55*
@ *vignoble@dampt.com*	👤 *Emmanuel & Eric Dampt*
🌐 *www.dampt.com*	🔵 *Chablis [map]*
🚶 ⛏ 🍇 🛢 🚜	*135 ha; 900,000 btl*

Bernard Dampt bought his first plots in 1980 and extended the domain as his sons, Eric and Emmanuel joined, and each had his own plots. When Bernard retired in 1993, his third son, Hervé, took over his plots. The domain changed its name as others joined, bringing more vineyards, and in 2009 the brothers created Vignoble Dampt Frères, which today has vineyards in Chablis, Tonnerre, and Irancy. Much of the expansion has been in Tonnerre, restoring vineyards that had been abandoned after phylloxera, where land is cheaper, but the domain produces Petit Chablis, 4 cuvées of Chablis, 8 premier crus, and 2 grand crus. From Chablis, cuvées Tradition and Vieilles Vignes (from 30-year-old vines) age in stainless steel, a cuvée from lieu-dit Bréchain ages 70% in stainless steel and 30% in oak, and the blend Lisa-Blanche ages for 10 months in barrels, which range in size from the standard 228 liter to 350 liter. Premier crus variously age with 10-25% in barrel, and the two grand crus, Bougros and Preuses, age with 20-30% in oak depending on the vintage. Wines from Bourgogne, Bourgogne Epineuil, Bourgogne Tonnerre, Irancy, and Saint Bris bring the total range to 30 cuvées.

Domaine Sébastien Dampt

23c Rue du Château, Milly 89800 Chablis	📞 *+33 3 86 18 96 50*
@ *seb.dampt@wanadoo.fr*	👤 *Sébastien Dampt*
🌐 *www.sebastien-dampt.com*	🔘 *Chablis [map]*
🗓 🏭 🍇 ⌂	*9 ha; 60,000 btl*

Domaine Daniel Dampt is the family domain, run by Daniel with his sons Vincent and Sébastien, but Vincent and Sébastien both also make wines under their own names. Sébastien started with 7 ha from the family holdings, and has purchased some further small plots. All the wines are made at the family winery in Milly (see profile of Daniel Dampt). Vinification is similar for all three domains, using stainless steel for Chablis and premier crus, although Sébastien now makes one cuvée, Les Beugnons, in a concrete egg. The style is lively and tends to minerality whichever label is used.

Domaine Agnès et Didier Dauvissat

1 Voie Gain, 89800 Beine	📞 *+33 3 86 42 46 40*
@ *agnes-didier.dauvissat@wanadoo.fr*	👤 *Florent Dauvissat*
🌐 *domaine-dauvissat-agnes-et-didier.business.site*	🔘 *Chablis [map]*
🚶 🏭 🍇 ⌂	*13 ha; 45,000 btl*

This is the most recent of the three Dauvissat domains in Chablis, created in 1987. "There were no vines in the family, so my parents had to start from scratch," says Florent Dauvissat, who came into the domain in 2011. They were able to buy some uncultivated land and plant vineyards. Today the domain has 3.5 ha in Petit Chablis, 4.5 ha of Chablis, and 2 ha of premier cru Beauroy, in the climat Côte de Savant, close to the winery. Initially the crop was sold to negociants; today half is estate-bottled, and the proportion is increasing. All the wines are vinified in stainless steel, except for a micro-cuvée of Beauroy, which ages in oak.

Domaine Jean Dauvissat Père et Fils

11 et 13 rue de Léchet, 89800 Milly	📞 *+33 3 86 42 12 23*
@ *fabien@jeandauvissat.com*	👤 *Fabien Dauvissat*
🌐 *www.chablis-dauvissat.com*	🔘 *Chablis [map]*
🗓 🏭 🍇 🍂	*22 ha; 70,000 btl*

There are two domains Jean Dauvissat in AOP Chablis: Jean Dauvissat Père et Fils (in Milly) and Jean et Sébastien Dauvissat (in the town of Chablis). When Fabien Dauvissat took over Père et Fils in 2009, he changed the policy from his father (the eponymous Jean), who had sold the grapes to negociants, and moved to estate-bottling. Today Fabien bottles about half the total production. Vineyards fall into 53 different plots (averaging only 0.5 ha each), with 17 ha in Chablis AOP, and smaller overall holdings in premier crus Côte de Lechet (the largest), Vaillons, Montmains, and Fourchaume, including a parcel in l'Homme Mort. Harvesting is mechanical. Fermentation and aging are in stainless steel, except for l'Homme Mort which gets part in 500- and 600-liter barrels. The Héritage Chablis cuvée from the oldest vines (planted in the 1940s) and the premier crus get extended aging, 18-20 months.

Clotilde Davenne

3, Rue Chantemerle, 89800 Préhy	📞 *+33 3 86 41 46 05*
@ *serviceclient@clotildedavenne.fr*	👤 *Clotilde Davenne*
🌐 *www.clotildedavenne.fr*	🔘 *Chablis [map]*
🗓 🏭 🗄 🍇 🛢 ⌂	*30 ha; 250,000 btl*

Clotilde Davenne comes from a farming family, but became an oenologist. While she was working at Jean-Marc Brocard, she purchased a house in Préhy (the most southern point of the Chablis appellation) and planted some vines, selling off the grapes to help pay for the house. By 2005 she was making wine from her own domain, focused on Sauvignon Blanc from St. Bris, but with holdings in Bourgogne Blanc as well as Chablis. The estate holdings are extended by purchasing grapes from premier and grand crus. The domaine was called Les Temps Perdus, but today the wines are simply labeled as Clotilde Davenne. The style focuses on freshness, with all cuvées vinified and aged exclusively in stainless steel.

Domaine Bernard Defaix

17 Rue du Château, Milly, 89800 Chablis	📞 +33 3 86 42 40 75
@ didier@bernard-defaix.com	👤 Didier Defaix
🌐 www.bernard-defaix.com	⬤ Chablis [map]
📅 🏚 🍇 🛢 🍷	27 ha; 300,000 btl

This is very much a left bank domain, started by Bernard Defaix in 1959 with only 2 ha, and run since the 1990s by his sons Sylvain (winemaker) and Didier (viticulture). The estate focuses on premier crus, which comprise about half the vineyard holdings, and its top wines are Vaillons, Les Lys (which used to be included in Vaillons but is now vinified separately), and Côte de Léchet, in which Defaix is the largest landholder. Wines are mostly aged in stainless steel. The top wine is the Reserve from old vines planted in Léchet in 1955, which is aged half in steel and half in used barriques. The range is extended into the right bank premier and grand crus by a negociant activity, labeled simply as Bernard Defaix.

Domaine Daniel-Etienne Defaix

23 Rue de Champlain, 89800 Chablis (winery)	📞 +33 3 86 42 14 44
14 Rue Auxerroise, 89800 Chablis (shop)	
@ caveau@chablisdefaix.com	👤 Daniel Defaix
🌐 www.chablisdefaix.com	⬤ Chablis [map]
🚶 🏚 ✖ 📇 🍇 🍂	28 ha; 180,000 btl

The domain claims to be the oldest in Chablis, now in its fourteenth generation under Daniel-Etienne (known as Danny), who took over from his father in 1978, and Danny's son, Paul-Etienne. Vineyards are mostly around Milly, on the left bank just west of the town of Chablis, half in Chablis and half in premier crus, and a tiny parcel in grand cru Blanchot. An unusual feature in winemaking here is the extended aging, on the lees in cuve, with battonage each month. Chablis Vieilles Vignes ages for two years, and the premier crus age for four years, sometimes longer. Some premier crus from 2005 were not released until 2018. Danny Defaix says that this used to be common practice; "I'm the last of the Mohicans," he says. Three of the top wines are Vaillon (the label is singular rather than the more usual Vaillons, reflecting the fact that the Defaix plot is in the original area before the premier cru was extended), Côte de Lechet (this was considered a grand cru in the middle ages, Danny says), and Les Lys (pure Kimmeridgian terroir). Defaix has expanded into oenotourism, with a hotel and restaurant (Aux Lys de Chablis) in the center of Chablis.

Domaine Christophe et fils

Ferme Des Carrières Fyé, 89800 Fyé	📞 +33 3 86 55 23 10
@ domaine.christophe@wanadoo.fr	👤 Sébastien Christophe
🛇 🖊 🍇 🛢 🍂 30 ha; 180,000 btl	⬤ Chablis [map]

Sébastien Christophe started to make wine with a half hectare of Petit Chablis he got from his grandfather in 1999. He has since been able to add some more Petit Chablis and Chablis AOP, and also rents some parcels. A Vieilles Vignes Chablis is a blend from two 50-year old parcels, one above Fourchaume and the other above Les Clos. He has three premier crus on the right bank, Fourchaume, Mont de Milieu and Montée de Tonnerre. The domain is located on the Fyé plateau, above the slope of grand crus. Harvesting is mechanical except for some old vines and the premier crus. Petit Chablis and Chablis age in stainless steel, and some used barriques are used for the Vieilles Vignes (10%) and the premier crus (20%). Production is expanded by a negociant activity which purchases both grapes and musts.

Domaine Gérard Duplessis

5, Quai De Reugny, 89800 Chablis	📞 +33 3 86 42 10 35
@ chablis-duplessis@bbox.fr	👤 Lilian Duplessis
⊕ www.chablis-duplessis.com	🌐 Chablis [map]
📅 🏭 🍇 🍂	10 ha; 25,000 btl

Founded in 1895, the domain has been handed from father to son for five generations. Located in the heart of the town, the domain has holdings in top premier crus, with Montée de Tonnerre at the forefront. Gérard planted most of the domain, and his son Lilian Duplessis worked in Burgundy, rather than gaining experience elsewhere—"because I wanted to learn how to make Chardonnay"—before taking over in 2007. Chablis and the premier cru Vaugiraut (which has the youngest vines of the premier crus) age in stainless steel; the other premier crus age first in stainless steel followed by a further six months in old barriques. Les Clos is the only holding in the grand crus, and is fermented as well as aged in barrique. The wines can be a little tight in the first few years.

Domaine Jean Durup Père et Fils

4, Grande Rue, 89800 Maligny	📞 +33 3 86 47 44 49
@ contact@domainesdurup.com	👤 Jean-Paul Durup
⊕ www.durup-chablis.com	🌐 Chablis [map]
🧍 🏭 🍇 🍂	205 ha; 1,500,000 btl

One of the largest producers in Chablis, Jean Durup is considered a modernist, with wines on the lighter side. The family has been producing wine for a long time, but grew to its present size after 1968, when Jean Durup took over with only 2 ha. As well as expanding his own domain, Jean was involved in extending the appellation in the 1970s; today his son Jean-Paul, who claims to be the fourteenth generation, runs the domain, which includes 35 ha of premier crus but no grand crus. Wines are bottled under the names Domaine de l'Eglantière and Château de Maligny (an estate that Jean bought in 1978), but the cuvées are the same. There was no oak until Romain Menissier came as winemaker in 2011 and introduced a little. The wines are well made but sometimes lack character. The top wine is the Fourchaume premier cru, at 18 ha the largest holding among the premier crus. There are also Montée de Tonnerre, Montmains, L'Homme Mort, and Vaudevay (although half the holding in Vaudevay was sold).

Domaine d'Elise

Milly, 89800 Chablis	📞 +33 3 86 42 40 82
@ frederic.prain@wanadoo.fr	👤 Frédéric Prain
📅 🏭 🍇 🍂 13 ha; 80,000 btl	🌐 Chablis [map]

The vineyards are in a single block in Milly, above and on the Côte de Léchet, with a quarter in the premier cru, and then going up the slope, the rest are classified successively as Chablis and Petit Chablis. The domain was founded in 1970, and was taken over in 1982 by Frédéric Prain, who changed career from a civil engineer in Paris to a wine producer. Access is not easy as the winery is located right at the top of the hill. Production was reduced while some of the plots were replanted starting in 2005. Frédéric is known for harvesting late to get very ripe grapes. Petit Chablis and Chablis age in stainless steel for six months. The Galilée cuvée of

Chablis gets longer aging. The Côte de Léchet ages in 1-5-year barriques. Some of the production is sold off to negociants.

Domaine de l'Enclos

1 Rue du Puits, 89800 Chablis	☎ +33 3 86 48 29 17
@ *romain@domainedelenclos.fr*	👤 *Romain & Damien Bouchard*
🌐 *www.domainedelenclos.fr*	◉ *Chablis [map]*
🗓 🏭 🍇 🥄	*29 ha; 120,000 btl*

Romain and Damien Bouchard got their start as independent winemakers when they bought the 3 ha of Domaine de la Grande Chaume and started making wine in 2005 in borrowed space in Maison Pascal Bouchard, their father's large winery (which produced 400,000 bottles per year). When Maison Bouchard was sold to Albert Bichot in 2015, the brothers lost their space but gained the family vineyards. They purchased a building in the center of Chablis and constructed a gravity-feed winery in the garden, and converted the vineyards to organic viticulture. Domaine de l'Enclos has a range from Petit Chablis to Grand Cru. The largest parcels are 2-3 ha each in premier crus Vau de Vey and Beauroy. The oldest vines are the 0.67 ha in Les Clos, planted by their grandfather. Other old parcels going back to grandfather's time are in Montmains and Fourchaume. Wines age on the lees for a year mostly in stainless steel, but some barriques are used for the top cuvées. "Our first vintage was very hard from the perspective of wood, because we like 5 year-old barrels, but in this vintage we started from nothing," Damien says. The domain got off to a slow start because problems with frost reduced production in 2016 and 2017 to not much over 20,000 bottles each year (with one barrique each of Les Clos and Blanchots in 2016); 2018 was the first year at full spate.

Domaine du Château de Fleys

2, rue des Fourneaux, 89800 Fleys	☎ +33 3 86 42 47 70
@ *philippon.beatrice@orange.fr*	👤 *Béatrice Philippon*
🌐 *www.chablis-philippon.com*	◉ *Chablis [map]*
🗓 🏭 🍇 ☍	*24 ha; 40,000 btl*

The domain was founded in 1868 by Julien Philippon, who acquired most of the vineyards that make up the estate today. His grandson André bought the "château" (an old hunting lodge which came with a 1 ha clos of vines) in 1988. André's children Béatrice and Benoît built the new cuverie, where the wine is now made, in 2006. The small level of production relative to the vineyard area reflects the fact that much of the crop is sold off. Vinification is mostly in stainless steel, but some old barriques are used also, depending on the cuvée. The top wine is the premier cru Mont de Milieu, where there is a plot of very old vines, planted in 1936.

Domaine Alain et Cyril Gautheron

18, Rue Des Prégirots, 89800 Fleys	☎ +33 3 86 42 44 34
@ *vins@chablis-gautheron.com*	👤 *Alain Gautheron*
🌐 *www.chablis-gautheron.com*	◉ *Chablis [map]*
🚶 🏭 🍇 🚜	*25 ha; 150,000 btl*

This family estate started in 1809 and is now in its sixth generation. When Alain Gautheron took over from his father in 1991, the domain was half its present size. Alain extended the vineyards and constructed a new cuverie in 2004, and in due course handed winemaking over to his son Cyril. In addition to Petit Chablis and Chablis, the domain has holdings in premier crus Vaucoupin, Montmains, Mont de Milieu, Fourneaux (immediately across from the winery), and L'Homme Mort. Vinification is in stainless steel (except for the Chablis Vieilles vignes and the Montmains Vieilles Vignes, which see some oak), and wine stays on the lees for 9 months. The style is rich, giving the impression, for example with Vaillons, that there has been oak exposure. In addition to the regular cuvées, there is an organic cuvée, Emeraude Chablis, which comes from two tiny parcels.

Domaine Alain Geoffroy

4, rue de l'Equerre, 89800 Beine	📞 *+33 3 86 42 43 76*
@ *info@chablis-geoffroy.com*	👤 *Nathalie Geoffroy*
🌐 *www.chablis-geoffroy.com*	🔘 *Chablis [map]*
📅 🏭 🍇 🍷	*50 ha; 420,000 btl*

This family domain dates from 1850. Wines are vinified in steel or oak depending on the cuvée. Petit Chablis (from 10-year-old vines) and Chablis (from 20-40-year-old vines) are vinified in cuves of stainless steel, but the Chablis Vieilles Vignes (from 45-70-year-old vines) in oak. Premier crus, Beauroy, Vau Ligneau, and Fourchaume, are vinified in stainless steel, but the Beauroy Vieilles Vignes, and Les Clos (the sole grand cru, which comes from purchased grapes) are matured in oak. Alain has built a museum of corkscrews at the winery, with more than 5.000 examples.

Domaine Jean Goulley et Fils

11 Bis, Vallée Des Rosiers, 89800 La Chapelle Vaupelteigne	📞 *+33 3 86 42 40 85*
@ *phil.goulley@wanadoo.fr*	👤 *Philippe Goulley*
🌐 *www.goulley.fr*	🔘 *Chablis [map]*
📅 🏭 🍇 🍷	*14 ha*

Jean Goulley and his son Philippe make wine under three labels: Jean Goulley et fils, Philippe Goulley, and Simone Tremblay. Philippe joined his father in 1986, when the domain had only 6 ha. The Philippe Goulley label started in 1991; and Philippe's daughter Maud joined in 2013. Petit Chablis is about a third of the plots, then there is Chablis, a sizeable area in premier cru Montmains, and a small parcel in premier cru Fourchaume. All these appear under both Jean Goulley and Philippe Goulley. Under Jean Goulley there is also a Mont de Milieu premier cru. Jean's wife, Simone, inherited a plot in the center of Fourchaume, and this is labeled as Domaine Simone Tremblay. All the wines under the Jean Goulley label age in stainless steel; under Philippe Goulley, the premier crus age in used barriques. Élevage of the premier crus lasts 18 months.

Domaine Céline et Frédéric Gueguen

31 grande rue de Chablis, 89800 Préhy	📞 *+33 6 08 74 63 85*
@ *contact@chablis-gueguen.fr*	👤 *Céline & Frédéric Gueguen*
🌐 *www.chablis-gueguen.fr*	🔘 *Chablis [map]*
🚶 🏭 🍇 🍷	*25 ha; 200,000 btl*

Céline is Jean-Marc Brocard's daughter and Frédéric comes from the family domain of Domaine des Chenevières, where they worked until they set up their own domain in 2013, with vineyards spread across Chablis, Saint Bris, Irancy, and Bourgogne. They were able to find space a stone's thrown from Brocard. There are 8 ha in Chablis, with 1.3 ha in Petit Chablis, 6 ha in Chablis (including a plot of old vines that is the source for the 1975 cuvée), and small plots (less than 0.5 ha each) in premier crus Vosgros and Vaucoupin (with 40-year-old vines), and grand cru Bougros. Wines age in stainless steel.

Domaine Hamelin

6 route de Bleigny, 89800 Lignorelles	📞 *+33 3 86 47 54 60*
@ *domaine.hamelin@wanadoo.fr*	👤 *Thierry Hamelin*
🌐 *www.domaine-hamelin.fr*	🔘 *Chablis [map]*
🚶 🏭 🍇 🍷	*37 ha; 270,000 btl*

Gustave Hamelin started with 2 ha of vines in 1840. With a new gravity-feed winery constructed at Lignorelles in the northwest quadrant of Chablis, Thierry Hamelin (the seventh generation in succession), together with his son Charles (who qualified in oenology and worked in New Zealand before joining his father), is now producing 10 ha of Petit Chablis, 20 ha of Chablis and Chablis Vieilles Vignes, and 4 ha each of premier crus Beauroy and Vauligneau. Vinification is mostly in steel, but a few barrels, mostly 500-liter, are used for the premier crus. The new winery has brought increased precision.

Domaine des Hâtes

5 chemin des Hâtes, 89800 Maligny	📞 +33 3 86 18 03 23
@ contact@domainedeshates.fr	👤 Pierrick Laroche
🗓 🏭 🍇 🛢 ℃ 28 ha; 100,000 btl	⊙ Chablis [map]

The estate was established by Pierrick Laroche's father in the 1970s, and sent its grapes to the cooperative until a change of generations when Pierrick took over. A qualified oenologist, he worked in New Zealand before returning home to take over the domain in 2009. Most of the estate vineyards are in Petit Chablis, with 12 ha in Chablis AOP, and 1 ha in the l'Homme Mort part of the Fourchaume premier cru. In 2019, Pierrick inherited 3 ha from his father-in-law, including a tiny plot in the Butteaux part of Montée de Tonnerre. The oldest plot of vines is Les Châtillons, which effectively makes a Vieilles Vignes cuvée. Pierrick added a negociant activity in 2016 to buy grapes to make premier crus Beauroy, Beauregard, and Vau de Vey, and grand cru Bougros (these are labeled as Maison des Hâtes). Harvest is relatively early to keep freshness, the wines have long aging on the lees in cuve, and oak is used only for a small part of premier or grand cru, usually tonneaux rather than barriques.

Domaine d'Henri

Route d'Auxerre, 89800 Chablis	📞 +33 6 74 21 18 72
@ margaux@ledomainedhenri.fr	👤 Margaux Laroche
🌐 ledomainedhenri.fr	⊙ Chablis [map]
🗓 🏭 🍇 🍴	28 ha; 160,000 btl

Michel Laroche is a legendary figure in Chablis. After selling Domaine Laroche to Advini in 2010, he created Domaine d'Henri in 2012. Holdings are mostly on the right bank, running through the premier and grand crus, with plots of Chablis or Petit Chablis beyond them. The domain is based on 20 ha of old family plots that Michel kept when Domaine Laroche was sold, but has since been expanded a bit. All those plots were originally the property of his father, Henri, for whom the domain is named. The largest holding is in Fourchaume, historically the strength of Domaine Laroche, where there are three cuvées, Fourchaume, l'Homme-Mort, and Héritage (from a plot of vines planted in 1937). (At Domaine Laroche, the three parts were all blended into the single Fourchaume cuvée.) Wines under the Domaine d'Henri label are fermented and aged partly in barriques and partly in stainless steel. A second line, Les Allées do Domaine, is used for young vines. "We use it as the Bordeaux chateaux do with the second label," Michel says. Michel runs Domaine d'Henri with his two daughters, Cécile and Margaux. "It's completely different. It's not like Laroche that was producing millions of bottles. Now I can visit the vineyards every week."

Domaine Jean Jacquin et fils

32 Rue de Chichée, 89800 Chablis	📞 +33 3 86 42 16 32
@ contact@domainejacquin.com	👤 Maryse & Jean-Michel Jacquin
🌐 domainejacquin.com	⊙ Chablis [map]
🚶 🏭 🍇 🚜	8 ha

294

Jean Jacquin created the domain with a quarter hectares of vines in 1978. From 1995 he expanded the holdings until he retired in 2007; his wife Maryse and son Jean-Michel took over, started estate-bottling, and expanded the domain further to its present size. There are now almost 3 ha in premier crus (Montée de Tonnerre and Vaillons), 4 ha in Chablis, and less than a hectare of Petit Chablis. Wines age in cuve.

Domaine Jolly et fils

2, Rue Auxerroise, 89800 Maligny	📞 +33 3 86 47 42 31
@ dom-jolly-fils@wanadoo.fr	👤 Denis Jolly
⊕ www.domainejolly.com	🔲 Chablis [map]
🏃🏭🍷🍇🚜	18 ha

Dennis Jolly is the third generation at this family domain, and took over from his father in 1998. The domain is mostly Petit Chablis (5 ha) and Chablis (13 ha), with less than a hectare of premier cru L'Homme Mort (part of Fourchaume). Harvesting is manual, grapes ferment for 7 days in stainless steel, and then age on the lees for 7-8 months.

Domaine Lamblin et Fils

Rue Marguerite de Bourgogne, 89800 Maligny	📞 +33 3 86 98 22 00
@ infovin@lamblin.com	👤 Clément Lamblin
⊕ www.lamblin.com	🔲 Chablis [map]
🏃🏭🍇🍷🚜	7 ha; 1,000,000 btl

The Lamblin family has been in the area for 300 years, and started producing wine under Henri Lamblin. His son Jacques developed a negociant business. Since 1987, Jacques's sons, Michel (management) and Didier (winemaking) have been in charge, joined after 2003 by their sons Clément and Alexandre. The negociant activity is well at the forefront, with wines mostly made from purchased juice. Chablis is about half of production; there are also wines from the Auxerrois, Burgundy, Beaujolais, and various IGPs. Chablis includes cuvées vinified in cuve and in new oak—the cuvée "Elevé en fût" was a project of the new generation—a Vieilles Vignes, five premier crus, and grand crus Vaudésir and Les Clos. The style is quite weighty.

Domaine Roland Lavantureux

4 Rue Saint-Martin, 89800 Lignorelles	📞 +33 3 86 47 53 75
@ domaine.lavantureux@gmail.com	👤 David & Arnaud Lavantureux
⊕ chablis-lavantureux.fr	🔲 Chablis [map]
📱🏭🍇🍷🍃	21 ha; 70,000 btl

The domain started by selling wine in casks in Auxerre and Paris; after Roland took over in 1979, he started bottling the wine, gave his name to the domain, and expanded the vineyards. He sons Arnaud (winemaker) and David (manager) took over in 2010. The Petit Chablis and Chablis come from around the property in Lignorelles; the Vieilles Vignes Chablis comes from some parcels of 60-year old vines planted by their grandfather near the domain, and Chablis Vauprin comes from a single parcel at the tope of the slope in Lignorelles (one of the highest parcels in Chablis) that the brothers consider to be the flagship of the domain. (They usually place it after premier cru Fourchaume in tastings because it's more powerful.) Premier Cru Vau de Vey comes from a 1 ha plot that is the most recent addition to the vineyards, and in grand crus there are Bougros and Vaudésir (from purchased grapes). Aging uses a mix of stainless steel and old barriques, with 20% barriques for the basic Chablis, 40% for the Vieilles Vignes and Vauprin, and moving to 100% for the grand crus, including some new oak. The domain has been white wine only, but the brothers are now also making wine from 4 ha of Bourgogne Epineuil that came from their grandparents.

Domaine des Marronniers

3, Grande Rue de Chablis, 89800 Préhy	📞 +33 3 86 41 42 70
@ *contact@chablismarronniers.com*	👤 *Laurent Ternynck*
🌐 *www.mauperthuis.fr*	⊙ *Chablis [map]*
🚶 🏭 🍇 🥄	*19 ha; 135,000 btl*

Laurent et Marie-Noëlle Ternynck purchased this domain in 2013 when previous owner Bernard Legland retired. They also make wine from the Domaine de Mauperthuis, where they started in 1995 (where the range includes Bourgogne, Petit Chablis, and Chablis.) At Marronniers, Chablis and premier cru Montmains age in stainless steel; grand cru Valmur and the Valmur Vieilles Vignes (from vines planted in 1976) age in large oak casks. The Chablis can show something of the herbaceous character of their Sauvignon St. Bris.

Domaine Alain Mathias

Route De Troyes, 89700 Épineuil	📞 +33 3 86 54 43 90
@ *mail@domainealainmathias.com*	👤 *Carole & Bastien Mathias*
🌐 *www.domainealainmathias.com*	⊙ *Chablis*
🚶 🏭 🍇 🛢 🥄	*13 ha; 60,000 btl*

Originally a surveyor, Alain Mathias became a winegrower in 1982. In 2015 his son Bastien and daughter-in-law Carole, both qualified as oenologues, took over. Located just north of Tonnerre, production is split between Bourgogne Tonnerre, Bourgogne Épineuil, and Chablis, where there are four cuvées: Petit Chablis, Chablis, and premier crus Côte de Jouan and Vau de Vey (added in 2017). Petit Chablis and Chablis age in stainless steel; the premier crus age in a mix of stainless steel and neutral oak (50% for Côte de Jouan and 70% for Vau de Vey). The domain itself is organic, but some cuvées come from purchased grapes that are not organic.

Domaine de la Meulière

18, Route de Mont de Milieu, 89800 Fleys	📞 +33 3 86 42 13 56
@ *contact@chablis-meuliere.com*	👤 *Vincent Laroche*
🌐 *www.chablis-meuliere.com*	⊙ *Chablis [map]*
🚶 🏭 🍇 🥄	*25 ha; 180,000 btl*

Created by Claude Laroche in 1984, this domain comes from a branch of the Laroche family that has been involved in wine since the eighteenth century (but is not connected with the Laroche domain in Chablis). Claude's sons, Nicolas (winemaker) and Vincent, are now running the domain. There's an old cellar, used for events and tastings, but the wines are made in a newer cuverie. As a rough rule, Chablis and premier crus without further description are vinified in stainless steel, while premier crus with fanciful names come from old vines and are matured in barriques or 500-liter casks, but oak maturation accounts for only about 5% of production.

Domaine Millet

Ferme De Marcault, Route De Viviers, 89700 Tonnerre	📞 +33 3 86 75 92 56
@ *intensement@chablis-millet.com*	👤 *Baudouin Millet*
🌐 *www.chablis-millet.com*	⊙ *Chablis*
🚶 🏭 🍇 ♻	*14 ha*

The domain was created in the 1980s when Philippe Millet replanted land that had been growing cereals with vines to make Petit Chablis. The original 9 ha of Petit Chablis still provide the major part of production, but since then the estate has added 4 ha of Chablis and 1 ha of premier cru Vaucoupin. Philippe's sons Paterne and Baudouin run the estate today. There are two cuvées of Petit Chablis: La Perle spends longer on the lees. The Chablis Vieilles Vignes comes from 60-year-old vines. Production has been expanded by a negociant activity under the name of Baudouin Millet, adding premier cru Vosgros and grand cru Vaudésir. Wines age in stainless steel.

Domaine Olivier et Alice De Moor

4 & 17 Rue Jacques Ferrand, 89800 Courgis	☎ *+33 3 86 41 47 94*
@ *aodemoor@aliceadsl.fr*	👤 *Alice De Moor*
⊕ *www.aetodemoor.fr*	◉ *Chablis [map]*
🗓🖊🍇🥄	*11 ha; 45,000 btl*

Olivier and Alice de Moor planted this small domain in 1989 while they were working at other estates. They have worked full time at the domain since the first vintage in 1994. They built a small gravity-feed winery in 2007 in some nineteenth century cellars. They produce Aligoté and Sauvignon St. Bris as well as several cuvées of Chablis coming from different parcels, and some premier crus. Their Burgundian origins show in the use of barrel fermentation and long aging in barriques for all wines. There's also a negociant activity called Le Vendangeur Masqué, which includes wines from other regions. Olivier argues that low-yielding, ripe Chardonnay should have a buttery, nutty character, and he views his wines as made in a sufficiently different way from the rest of Chablis that he caused something of a stir by refusing to allow them to be included in tastings from the appellation.

Maison J. Moreau et Fils

Route d'Auxerre, 89800 Chablis	☎ *+33 3 86 42 88 00*
@ *depuydt.l@jmoreau-fils.com*	👤 *Lucie Depuydt*
⊕ *www.jmoreau-fils.com*	◉ *Chablis [map]*
🚫🖊🛢🚜	*120 ha; 5,000,000 btl*

Moreau is an old negociant and grower in Chablis, and had some important vineyard holdings, but in 1997 the negociant was sold to Boisset of Burgundy, while the vineyards became the domains of Christian Moreau and Louis Moreau (see profiles). Wines are vinified in stainless style to give a mainstream style. The range includes five premier crus and three grand crus; in addition to Chablis, there are other AOPs from Burgundy and the Loire, IGPs, and Vins de France, made in a very large modern facility on the main road out of Chablis. The Maison is the largest producer of Chablis after the La Chablisienne cooperative.

Éléonore Moreau

1 Route de Lichères, 89310 Poilly-sur-Serein	☎ *+33 3 86 75 94 29*
@ *eleonoremoreau.chablis@gmail.com*	👤 *Éléonore Moreau*
⊕ *www.chablis-eleonoremoreau.fr*	◉ *Chablis [map]*
🗓🏭🍇🥄	*14 ha; 20,000 btl*

Domaine Moreau et Fille was originally viticultural, then turned to growing other crops and producing milk, and returned to viticulture in 1982 when Laurent Moreau replanted the vineyards. He constructed a winery in 1995. His daughter Éléonore joined him in 2011 and took over in 2016, subsequently changing to bottling under her own name. (She is not related to any of the other Moreau producers in Chablis.) Vineyards are at the southwest border of the appellation, facing south for Chablis, with less favorable orientation for Petit Chablis. Pérégrinations is a special cuvée from a selection of Petit Chablis. All wines age on the lees in stainless steel for about 9 months.

Domaine Moreau-Naudet

4, Chemin de la Vallée de Valvan, 89800 Chablis	📞 *+33 3 86 42 14 83*
@ *moreau.naudet@wanadoo.fr*	👤 *Virginie Moreau*
🚫 💅 🍇 ⚓ *25 ha; 100,000 btl*	🌐 *Chablis [map]*

Stéphane Moreau-Naudet and his father created the domain in 1993; setting up their winery in a house on the edge of the town. Previously they sold the grapes to negociant Regnard, and they continued to sell some grapes as they expanded the domain. Widely regarded as a very talented winemaker, Stéphane Moreau sadly died young in 2016, just after the domain moved from its headquarters in the town to new premises near Vaillons, but his wife Virginie has taken over. The policy has been to harvest late, press very slowly, and age in a mix of steel and wood, using both oval demi-muids and barriques for the wood, with a little new oak. Premier crus get about a third aged in oak. The style tends to tautness. The range includes premier crus Forêts, Vaillons, and Montmains, and grand cru Valmur.

Domaine Mosnier

36, Route Nationale, 89800 Beine	📞 *+33 6 66 13 11 81*
@ *contact@chablis-mosnier.com*	👤 *Stéphanie Mosnier*
🌐 *www.chablis-mosnier.com*	🌐 *Chablis [map]*
📋 🏭 🍇 ☙	*19 ha; 55,000 btl*

The family has long been involved in producing and selling wine, and Sylvain Mosnier created the domain in 1978 when his father-in-law retired and gave him 2 ha of vines. His daughter Stéphanie gave up her career in logistics and took over when Sylvain retired in 2007. The range includes Petit Chablis, Chablis and a Vieilles Vignes, and premier crus Beauroy and Côte de Léchet, at very reasonable prices. The Vieilles Vignes Chablis is considered the flagship of the domain. Oak is used only in the Vieilles Vignes and Beauroy.

Domaine de la Motte

35, Grand Rue, 89800 Beine (shop)	📞 *+33 3 86 42 43 71*
35, rue du Ruisseau, 89800 Beine (cellars)	
@ *caveau@chablis-michaut.fr*	👤 *Bernard Michaut*
🌐 *www.chablis-michaut.fr*	🌐 *Chablis [map]*
🚶 🏭 🍇 🚜	*28 ha; 250,000 btl*

The Michaut family has been growing vines in Beine since 1950, and the domaine was created in 2011 when they left the cooperative. Actually, the family has two domains: since 2011 they have effectively bottled all the production from Domaine de la Motte; and they sell most of the production of the other domain, the 20 ha Michaut Frères, in bulk. Today the domains are run by Bertrand (a former chef) and his son Adrien and nephew Guillaume. Vineyards are all local, and include Petit Chablis, Chablis, a Vieilles Vignes from 40-year old vines, and premier crus Vauligneau and Beauroy. Grapes are harvested by machine, and chaptalization is used. Petit Chablis, Chablis, and Val-Ligneau are aged in stainless steel; and only Beauroy sees oak.

Domaine Charly Nicolle

17 Rue des Pregirots, 89800 Fleys	📞 *+33 6 63 56 56 13*
@ *contact@chablis-charlynicolle.com*	👤 *Charly Nicolle*
🌐 *www.chablis-charlynicolle.com*	🌐 *Chablis [map]*
📋 🏭 🍇 🍾 ☙	*28 ha; 200,000 btl*

"I am a vigneron," says Charly Nicolle. He's a seventh generation winemaker who joined his father, Robert Nicolle, at the family's domain, variously known as Domaine Paul Nicolle or Domaine de la Mandelière, where he made the wine from 1999. Since 2013 he has been producing wine under his own name in parallel. Most of the grapes come from the estate, but are augmented by 10% of purchased grapes. The Chablis is about half of production. The Chablis cuvee from older (30-year) vines in plots on the right bank started out as the Ancestrum cuvée and then changed its name to Per Aspera. There are also premier crus Les Fourneaux (from 40-year-old vines) and Mont de Mileu (50-60-year-old vines), and a small amount of grand cru Bougros (50-year-old vines). The premier and grand crus age in a mix of stainless steel and demi-muids (400- or 500 liter barrels). The style is relatively forward.

Laurent et Céline Notton

4 Impasse Saint Paul à Chichée, 89800 Chichée	📞 +33 3 86 42 10 04
@ *domaine.notton@gmail.com*	👤 *Laurent Notton*
🌐 *chablis-notton.com*	⬤ *Chablis [map]*
📅 ⚒ 🍇 🍷	*17 ha*

Both coming from families of growers, Laurent and Céline Notton started to make wine in Chichée in 2005 with 2.5 ha. The domain was formally created in 2012, and in 2016 they built a new cuverie. The range includes Chablis and Bourgogne Chitry. The Chablis comes from Chichée and Courgis, and there is a Vieilles Vignes cuvée from Courgis. The two premier crus are Vaucoupin and Vaugiraut (part of Vogros).

Domaine De Oliveira Lecestre

11, rue des Chénevières, 89800 Fontenay-près-Chablis	📞 +33 3 86 42 40 78
@ *gaecdeoliveira@wanadoo.fr*	👤 *Benjamin Quevreux*
🌐 *www.deoliveira-chablis.com*	⬤ *Chablis [map]*
🚶 ⚒ 🍷 🛢	*48 ha; 35,000 btl*

Lucien de Oliveira created the domain in 1955, while he was working at William Fèvre. In 1965, when it was only 7 ha, it became a full-time occupation when he partnered with his brother-in-law, adding Lecestra to the name. Lucien's daughter and her husband Benjamin Quevreux took over in 1997, and were in turn joined by their daughter in 2004. Vineyards are 8 ha in Petit Chablis, 35 ha in Chablis, 4 ha in premier crus Fourchaume and Côte de Fontenay, and a tiny plot (less than 1 ha) in grand cru Les Clos. The Petit Chablis is notable as it comes from plots very close to Les Clos. Wines age exclusively in stainless steel.

Domaine Oudin

5, rue du Pont, 89800 Chichée	📞 +33 6 42 40 71 90
@ *domaine.oudin@wanadoo.fr*	👤 *Nathalie Oudin*
📅 ⚒ 🍇 🍷 *10 ha; 50,000 btl*	⬤ *Chablis [map]*

Jean-Claude Oudin and his wife Christiane returned from Paris to reclaim a couple of hectares of her family's land in 1988. Her parents reclaimed some family land in 1988. By the time their daughter Nathalie Oudin joined in 2007, the domain had grown to its present size. Nathalie's sister Isabelle joined her soon after, and the two officially took the reins in 2014. Vineyards are on the slopes around Chichée, facing south or southwest. In addition to the Chablis, the Les Serres cuvée comes from a single plot. The top wines are Vaucoupin and Vaugiraut premier crus from vines dating from the 1950s. Wines age in stainless steel.

Domaine Christophe Patrice

52 route Nationale, 89800 Beine	📞 +33 6 60 23 37 52
@ *christophe.patrice@orange.fr*	👤 *Christophe Patrice*

🌐 www.christophe-patrice.fr	◉ Chablis [map]
🚶 🏭 🍇 🥂	21 ha; 150,000 btl

It would be hard to miss Christophe Patrice's winery in Beine: a large extension in front of the building has Chablis in huge letters on one side, and Christophe Patrice on the other. Christophe worked with his father and uncle at the family domain until 2006, when he set up on his own with 5 ha. In 2011, he purchased the much larger Domaine Daniel Roblot, bringing his domain to its present size. The wines are sometimes labeled as Domaine Gendraud-Patrice (his wife is Aurélie Gendraud). One unusual feature of the vineyards is plantings at rather low density for the area, only 5,800 vines/ha. Cuvées include Petit Chablis, Chablis, and plots of under a hectare each in premier crus Beauroy, Beauregards, and Montmains. Wines age in stainless steel.

Domaine de Perdrycourt

9, Voie Romaine, 89230 Montigny-La-Resle (winery)	📞 +33 3 86 41 82 07
1 rue du four 89800 Chablis (boutique)	
@ domainecourty@orange.fr	👤 Rémi Courty
🌐 www.perdrycourt.fr	◉ Chablis [map]
🚶 🏭 🍇 🛢 🥂	15 ha; 60,000 btl

Arlette and Roger Courty started their domain in 1986 with only 0.5 ha of vines, and produced their first vintage in 1989. Their son Rémi has now taken over winemaking. The winery is just outside the Chablis AOP, but the vines are in Beines. The estate vineyards are all Petit Chablis and Chablis, plus a small plot of Vaudevey that was added recently. Grapes are purchased for the primer crus Fourchaume and Montée de Tonnerre, and grand cru Les Clos. All these are found in Classique range, plus the Chablis Cuvée Elégance which comes from 60-year-old vines. They age exclusively in stainless steel, with élevage lasting 6-8 months. Under the title of the Collection range, Chablis from the old vines is aged for 24 months in new barriques. The label changes its color each year.

Domaine Isabelle et Denis Pommier

31, Rue de Poinchy, 89800 Poinchy	📞 +33 3 86 42 83 04
@ isabelle@denis-pommier.com	👤 Isabelle Pommier
🌐 www.denis-pommier.com	◉ Chablis [map]
📦 🏭 🍇 🍇	23 ha; 130,000 btl

Starting with 2 ha of vines in Poinchy in 1990 (with estate-bottling starting in 1994), the domain has grown slowly to its present size, the latest acquisition being in premier crus Fourchaume and Beauroy in 2012. There are two cuvées each of Petit Chablis (Hauterivien is rich for the AOP) and Chablis, and four premier crus. The start of the range is aged in steel, but Chablis Croix aux Moines and the premier crus are fermented and aged one third in used barriques for 18 months. Bourgogne Pinot Noir comes from the Yonne. Because of the loss of grapes due to climatic conditions, the Grain de Survie cuvées of Bourgogne Blanc and Rouge were added from purchased grapes.

Maison Regnard

28, Boulevard du Dr Tacussel, 89800 Chablis	📞 +33 3 86 18 95 08
@ regnard.chablis@regnard-chablis.fr	👤 Philippe Rossignol
🌐 regnard-chablis.deladoucette.fr	◉ Chablis [map]
📦 🏭 🍇 🛢 🚜	10 ha; 500,000 btl

Dating from 1860, this negociant takes its name from founder Zéphir Regnard. It absorbed another negociant, Maison Albert Pic, in 1957, and in 1984 was purchased by the Ladoucette domain of Pouilly Fumé. The focus remains on Chablis, with all production in stainless steel. The major production is the Grand Regnard Chablis, followed by the prestige cuvée, Pic 1er, a blend of the best premier crus, only made in top years. Individual premier crus include Fourchaume and Montée de Tonnerre. All seven grand crus are produced. Regnard is regarded as one of the best local negociants, and also produces wines from elsewhere in Burgundy.

Domaine Guy Robin et Fils

13, Rue Berthelot, 89800 Chablis	📞 *+33 3 86 42 12 63*
@ *info@domaineguyrobin.com*	👤 *Marie-Ange Robin*
🌐 *www.domaineguyrobin.com*	🔴 *Chablis [map]*
🚶 🏭 🍇 🍷	*20 ha; 10,000 btl*

The domain goes back four generations, but made its reputation in the 1960s when Guy Robin acquired holdings of old vines, some going back to the era of phylloxera. By the turn of the century it had fallen off the charts, however, but was then revived when his daughter Marie-Ange gave up her career as a fine art dealer in Paris and returned to run the domain. The Chablis comes from 30-year old vines, while the premier and grand crus have an average age over 40 years. Chablis ages in steel, the premier crus are a roll-call of top sites, including Montée de Tonnerre, Mont de Milieu, Montmains, and Vaillons, and age in old barriques, and the top cuvees (including five of the seven grand crus) age in barriques including some new oak.

Domaine Roy

71 Grande Rue, 89800 Fontenay-près-Chablis	📞 *+33 6 29 48 81 17*
@ *domaine.roy@orange.fr*	👤 *Claude Roy*
🌐 *www.domaine-roy.com*	🔴 *Chablis [map]*
🚶 🏭 🍇 🚜	*18 ha; 35,000 btl*

The Roy family have been vignerons at least since 1810, and Fernand Roy bought the first vineyards in 1936, which today are the heart of the domain. Today it is in the hands of the third and fourth generations, Claude Roy and his daughter Karine and nephew David . They have moved towards bottling an increasing proportion of the crop at the estate. Vineyards are all on the right bank of the Serein, with Petit Chablis, Chablis, premier crus Fourchaume and Vaulorent, and grand crus Bougros and Preuses. All wines age in stainless steel, Petit Chablis and Chablis for a few months, but premier and grand crus for two years or more.

Famille Savary

4 Chemin des Hâtes, 89800 Maligny	📞 *+33 3 86 47 42 09*
@ *contact@chablis-savary.com*	👤 *Mathieu & Maxime Savary*
🌐 *www.chablis-savary.com*	🔴 *Chablis [map]*
📅 🏭 🍇 🛢 🍷	*20 ha; 200,000 btl*

Olivier Savary comes from a winemaking family, but his parents did not go into wine (his father was in finance and made wine on the side from 1 ha). After attending oenology school in Dijon, he started out with his wife Francine in 1984 by renting vineyards in Petit Chablis and Chablis, and selling off most of the production to negociants. In 1986 they built a cellar, and by 1990 the Savarys were bottling under their own label. By 1999, they were bottling wine from 8 ha. In 2015, their sons Maxime and Mathieu joined the domain. The range starts with Petit Chablis and Chablis, then the Chablis Vieilles Vignes comes from 40-year-old vines. Premier crus are Fourchaume and Vaillons. All the wines age in tank except for grand cru Bougros, which ages in barriques. There is also a red produced as Bourgogne Epineuil.

Camille et Laurent Schaller

20 Grande Rue de Chablis, 89800 Préhy	📞 *+33 6 81 85 07 95*
@ *domaine@chablis-schaller.com*	👤 *Camille Schaller*
🌐 *www.chablis-schaller.com*	🔵 *Chablis [map]*
🔲 🏭 📷 🍇 🌿	*18 ha; 40,000 btl*

Laurent Schaller started by raising cattle and grain, and then turned to growing grapes in 1980, but sent them to the cooperative until his son Camille joined him in 2015, when they built a winery, and started estate-bottling. They bottle wine from about half of their production. The distinction here is between Petit Chablis or Chablis and the premier crus: the former are machine-harvested, but premier crus are picked manually. Wines age on the lees for 8-10 months, in stainless steel for Petit Chablis and Chablis, 30% in barriques for Chablis Vieilles Vignes, and 20% in barriques for premier crus Vau de Vey and Vaucoupin (which comes from only 0.25 ha). Petit Chablis and Chablis come from 20-30-year old vines, and the Vieilles Vignes from 40-year-old vines.

Domaine Séguinot Bordet

8 Chemin des Hâtes, 89800 Maligny	📞 *+33 3 86 47 44 42*
@ *contact@seguinot-bordet.com*	👤 *Jean-François Bordet*
🌐 *seguinot-bordet.com*	🔵 *Chablis [map]*
🚶 🖌 🍇 🛢 🚜	*19 ha; 130,000 btl*

The Bordets are one of the oldest winemaking families in Chablis—Jean-François, who took over from his grandfather in 1998, says he is the thirteenth generation. Most of the domain's vineyards are Petit Chablis or Chablis from plots on the right bank; the Vieilles Vignes cuvée comes from really old (80-100-year) vines. The largest production premier cru is Fourchaume, from 45-60-year-old vines. There are smaller amounts of Vaillons. Grand cru Vaudésir comes from vines of the same age. Fermentation and aging take place in a new cellar in horizontal stainless steel tanks that maximize lees contact; the wines age for 3-5 months. The style is contemporary and fruity.

Domaine Daniel Séguinot

3 Route De Tonnerre, 89800 Maligny	📞 *+33 3 86 47 51 40*
@ *domaine.danielseguinot@wanadoo.fr*	👤 *Emilie Seguinot*
🌐 *chablis-daniel-seguinot.com*	🔵 *Chablis [map]*
🔲 🏭 🍇 🚜	*20 ha; 50,000 btl*

Daniel Séguinot created the domain in 1971, starting with 2 ha of his father's vineyards in Chablis, followed by 3 ha of his grandfather's holdings in premier cru Fourchaume, including part in l'Homme Mort, in 1975. "We have always worked in the vines, as far back as we can trace the family," Daniel says. He has since considerably expanded the holdings, and his daughters, Emilie and Laurence, joined the domain in 2003 and 2008, and took over when Daniel retired in 2012. Most of the holdings are in Chablis AOP, including 2.5 ha of 40-year-old vines that make the Vieilles Vignes cuvée. The Chablis Demoizelle is a selection from plots facing south. The wines age on the lees in stainless steel.

Domaine Vincent Wengier

45 Grande Rue de Chablis, 89800 Préhy (cellars)	📞 *+33 6 51 22 77 39*
@ *dwengier@orange.fr*	👤 *Vincent Wengier*
🌐 *www.chablis-wengier.fr*	🔵 *Chablis [map]*
🔲 🏭 🍇 🏭	*26 ha; 10,000 btl*

Vincent and Sophie Wengier took over the family domain in 1998. They started estate-bottling in 2018. Their holdings are in Chablis, Petit Chablis, and Bourgogne (both Chardonnay and Aligoté). The vines for the Chablis AOP or over 30 years old. All the wines ferment in stainless steel, then go into malolactic fermentation, and age in the vat.

Domaine Soupé

Za des Violettes, 1 rue de la Paix, 89800 Chablis	📞 *+33 3 86 52 79 50*
@ *contact@domainesoupe.com*	👤 *Frédéric & Jean-Michel Soupé*
🌐 *www.domainesoupe.com*	🔵 *Chablis [map]*
📅 ⛏ 🍇 ⌘	*15 ha; 15,000 btl*

With its vineyards fragmented and distributed over several miles, the domain produces Petit Chablis, two cuvées of Chablis, three premier crus, and one grand cru. The domain dates from the 1920s, and Frédéric and Jean-Michel Soupé are the fourth generation. Grapes were sent to the cooperative until they took over in 2018. The Chablis AOP cuvée comes from 25-year-old vines, while the cuvée Les Doyennes comes from a hectare of 40-year-old vines. Montée de Tonnerre is the largest premier cru, with almost 3 ha, while Vaillons and Mont de Milieu are much smaller; all have vines aged over 60 years. Grand cru Les Preuses is the smallest holding, only a tenth of a hectare. All wines have the same élevage, with aging in stainless steel for 6 months.

Domaine Testut

38, Rue des Moulins, 89800 Chablis	📞 *+33 3 86 42 45 00*
@ *marie@domaine-testut.fr*	👤 *Cyril Testut*
🌐 *www.domaine-testut.fr*	🔵 *Chablis [map]*
📅 ⛏ 🍇 ⌘	*13 ha; 90,000 btl*

Philippe Testut started making Chablis in 1967, and bought vineyards, but due to family difficulties many were later sold off. Philippe went off to Châteauneuf-du-Pape, but came back to help when his son Cyril took over in 1998 and resumed estate bottling. Chablis Rive Droite is a blend exclusively from the right bank (a large part comes from the Côte de Bréchain next to Montée de Tonnerre), and there are three top premier crus, Fôrets, Vaillons, and Montée de Tonnerre, and grand cru Grenouilles (a rarity that owes its inclusion to the fact that Philippe Testut came from Grenouilles). Grenouilles is the only cuvée to see any oak, but only 15-20%. Vines are over 40-years-old for Chablis, and over 50-years-old for the crus.

Domaine Tixier

7, Chemin Des Sanguinots, 89800 Courgis	📞 *+33 3 86 41 47 62*
@ *domaine-tixier@orange.fr*	👤 *Thomas Tixier*
🌐 *chablis-tixier.com*	🔵 *Chablis [map]*
📅 ⛏ 🍇 ⌘	*7 ha; 10,000 btl*

Martine Tixier started the domain with less than half a hectare in 1986. By 1998 it had reached its present size. Grapes were sold to negociants and the cooperative until 2003, when estate-bottling started. The next generation, Thomas Tixier, started in 2007. Vineyards are mostly around the village of Courgis. The cuvées are Chablis, Chablis Grosse-Terre from old vines, and premier cru Montmains (from a tiny plot of 37 areas). Harvesting is mechanical for Chablis, manual for Montmains. Vinification is in stainless steel.

Domaine de La Tour

3, Route de Monfort, 89800 Lignorelles, Chablis	📞 *+33 3 86 47 55 68*
@ *contact@ledomainedelatour.info*	👤 *Vincent Fabrici*

🌐 *www.ledomainedelatour.eu*	🔵 *Chablis [map]*
📅 🏚 🍇 🥂	*15 ha; 25,000 btl*

The Domaine de la Tour acquired its present name when Jacques Chalmeau (whose family had been making wine in the area for two hundred years) handed over in 1992 to his son-in-law, Renato Fabrici (who was Italian by origin). This remains a small family domain, and Renato's son, Vincent, is now in charge. Petit Chablis, Chablis, and two less-known premier crus, are vinified in cuve; premier cru Montmains is aged in a mix of vats and oak. The Chablis and Montmains are the majority of production. There are also Bourgogne Blanc and Aligoté.

Domaine Gérard Tremblay

12, Rue de Poinchy, 89800 Chablis	📞 *+33 3 86 42 40 98*
@ *contact@chablis-tremblay.com*	👤 *Vincent & Eleonore Tremblay*
🌐 *www.chablis-tremblay.com*	🔵 *Chablis [map]*
🚶 🏚 🍇 🥂	*37 ha; 250,000 btl*

Now led by the fifth generation, the domain has tripled in size since Gérard took over in 1970 and started estate-bottling. At first wine was sold only at the cellar door; now it is exported worldwide. A gravity-feed winery was constructed in 1990. A third of the estate is in premier or grand cru. Gérard's son Vincent worked in Australia, and has been at the domain since 1999. In addition to Petit Chablis and Chablis (aged in cuve), there are two cuvées of Vieilles Vignes from 40-year old vines. One is aged in steel; Cuvée Hélène comes from the same juice, but is aged in new oak. Premier cru Fourchaume (the only right bank cru of the domain) is aged in steel, but the other premier crus, and grand cru Vaudésir, are aged in a mix of steel and old barriques.

Domaine de Vauroux

Ferme De Vauroux, Route d'Avallon, 89800 Chablis	📞 *+33 3 86 42 10 37*
@ *maison.tricon@gmail.com*	👤 *Olivier Tricon*
🌐 *www.maison-tricon.com*	🔵 *Chablis [map]*
🚶 🍇 🚜	*46 ha*

Brothers Jean-Pierre and Claude Tricon returned from Sudan in 1956 bought a 13 ha plot on the Pargues hillside just south of the town of Chablis. In 1972 they planted vines and started making wine. Jean-Pierre's son, Olivier, worked at the domain and also established his own negociant business. In 1998, he took over Domaine du Vauroux, which has expanded beyond Chablis AOP into premier crus Montée de Tonnerre and Montmains, and grand cru Bougros. Other premier and grand crus are produced by the negociant activity under the label of Olivier Tricon. The wines are made in stainless steel, but have extended aging on the lees.

Venon et Fils

10, rue des Prégirots, 89800 Fleys	📞 *+33 6 60 38 87 08*
@ *celine.jeremy@wanadoo.fr*	👤 *Jérémy Venon*
🌐 *jeremyvenon.com*	🔵 *Chablis [map]*
📅 🏚 🍇 🚜	*4 ha*

Jérémy Venon created the domain from scratch in 2014. He worked as a courtier in wine for eleven years, until he was able to buy a tiny plot in his home village of Fleys, only a quarter hectare. The wine from this plot is still made as a separate cuvée, called l'Inattendue. It's vinified mostly in stainless steel, but with a small part in barrique. Petit Chablis and Chablis l'Expression are vinified exclusively in stainless steel. There is also a small production of premier cru Les Fourneaux, which sees a little oak. There is a red Bourgogne.

Domaine Ventoura

3 rue du Puits, 89800 Fontenay-près-Chablis	📞 +33 6 08 92 40 00
@ contact@domaine-ventoura.com	👤 Thomas Ventoura
🌐 www.chablis-ventoura.com	🟢 Chablis [map]
🔳 🏭 🍇 🦢	11 ha; 40,000 btl

The domain started when Auguste Ventoura started growing Chardonnay on his farm just outside Chablis in 1953. His son Claude expanded the estate to its current size, continuing to send grapes to the coop. Claude's son Thomas joined the domaine in 2009, and started estate bottling in 2013. Holdings are in Petit Chablis (from the plateau above Maligny), Chablis, and Fourchaume and Mont de Milieu premier crus. Thomas is not committed specifically to either stainless steel or wood, but uses both, depending on the cuvée and vintage.

Domaine Vocoret et Fils

40, Route d'Auxerre, 89800 Chablis	📞 +33 3 86 42 12 53
@ contact@domainevocoret.com	👤 Patrice & Jérôme Vocoret
🌐 www.domaine-vocoret.com	🟢 Chablis [map]
🚹 🏭 🍇 🚜	50 ha; 300,000 btl

Founded by Edouard Vocoret in 1870, this is one of the larger domains in Chablis, now managed by Patrice (winemaker) and his nephew Jérôme (viticulturalist). The domain has been bottling its own wines since 1930. The village wine is aged in steel, but Vocoret is known for its forceful style, running through an impressive range of the best premier crus (Montmains, including Forêt, and Vaillons, Côte de Léchet, and Montée de Tonnerre) and four grand crus (Blanchots, Vaudésir, Valmur, and Les Clos), all matured in old oak (50 hl) foudres; close to half the vineyards are premier or grand cru. Some of the top wines get greater oak exposure in the form of demi-muids.

Domaine Eleni et Édouard Vocoret

19, rue de Chichée, 89800 Chablis	📞 +33 9 53 21 66 20
@ info@vocoret.fr	👤 Eleni & Édouard Vocoret
🌐 www.vocoret.fr	🟢 Chablis [map]
🚫 🎨 🍇 🦢	5 ha

Edouard's family owns Domaine Vocoret, and he founded this small domain in 2012 together with his wife Eléni, whom he met while working the harvest in New Zealand. The first vintage was 2013, made in Edouard's grandfather's garage. They are now located in Chichée, at the southern border of the appellation. The vineyards came from the family holdings. There are four wines, three Chablis AOP and one premier cru: "one parcel, one cuvée, is the principle," Edouard says. Bas le Chapelot is the major holding (3 ha), just below Montée de Tonnerre (classified as Chablis AOP and not premier cru because it has darker soil than in the Chapelot part of Montée de Tonnerre). The other two holdings in Chablis are on the left bank of the Serein, En Boucheran and Les Pargues, near premier crus Montmains and Vaillons. The premier cru Les Butteaux comes from a tiny parcel in Montmains. The wines ferment and go through malolactic in stainless steel, and then age in old barriques (the youngest is five years old), 9 months for the village wines, and 12 months for the premier cru.

Domaine Yvon et Laurent Vocoret

9, Chemin De Beaune, 89800 Maligny	📞 *+33 3 86 47 51 60*
@ *domaine.yvon.vocoret@wanadoo.fr*	👤 *Yvon Vocoret*
🌐 *www.yvon-laurent-vocoret.com*	🔵 *Chablis [map]*
🧍 🏭 🍇 🚜	*10 ha; 25,000 btl*

The family has been making wine since 1707. Laurent Vocoret is the sixth generation; his father Laurent started estate-bottling. (The family is not related to the Vocorets of Chablis.) Vineyards include Petit Chablis, Chablis, premier cru Fourchaume, and l'Homme Mort (within Fourchaume). Esquisse is a special cuvée of Fourchaume from vines planted in 1979.Harvesting is mechanical, except for 10% of the domain that consists of old vines in Chablis AOP, which is harvested manually for the Chablis Renaissance cuvée, and which ages in 500-liter barrels; everything else ages in stainless steel for 9 months.

Glossary of French Wine Terms

Classification

There are three levels of classification, but their names have changed:

- *AOP* (Appellation d'Origine Protégée, formerly AOC or Appellation d'Origine Contrôlée) is the highest level of classification. AOPs are tightly regulated for which grape varieties can be planted and for various aspects of viticulture and vinification.

- *IGP* (Indication Géographique Protegée, formerly Vin de Pays) covers broader areas with more flexibility for planting grape varieties, and few or no restrictions on viticulture and vinification.

- *Vin de France* (formerly Vin de Table) is the lowest level of classification and allows complete freedom with regards to varieties, viticulture, and vinification.

- *INAO* is the regulatory authority for AOP and IGP wines.

Producers

- *Château* in Bordeaux means a producer who makes wine from estate grapes; purchased grapes cannot be used.

- There is no word for winemaker in French. The closest would be *oenologue*, meaning a specialist in vinification; larger estates may have consulting oenologues.

- A *régisseur* is the estate manager at a larger property, and may encompass anything from general management to taking charge of viticulture or (commonly) vinification.

Viticulture

- There are three types of viticulture where use of conventional treatments (herbicides, insecticides, fertilizers, etc.) is restricted:

- *Bio* is organic viticulture; certification is by AB France (Agriculture Biologique).

- *Biodynamique* is biodynamic viticulture, certified by Demeter.

- *Lutte raisonnée* means sustainable viticulture (using treatments only when necessary). HVE (Haute Valeur Environnementale) is the best known certification.

- *Selection Massale* means that cuttings are taken from the best vines in a vineyard and then grafted on to rootstocks for replanting the vineyard.

- *Clonal selection* uses (commercially available) clones for replanting.

- *Vendange Vert* (green pruning) removes some berries during the season to reduce the yield.

Winemaking

- *Vendange entière* means that grapes are fermented as whole clusters.

- *Destemming* means that the grapes are taken off the stems and individual berries are put into the fermentation vat.

- *Vinification intégrale* for black grapes means the wine ferments in a barrique standing up open without an end piece. After fermentation, the end is inserted and the wine ages in the same barrique in which it was fermented.

- During fermentation of red wine, grape skins are pushed up to the surface to form a cap. There are three ways of dealing with it:
  - *Pigeage* (*Punch-down*) means using a plunger to push the cap into the fermenting wine.
  - *Remontage* (pump-over) means pumping up the fermenting wine from the bottom of the vat to spray over the cap.
  - *Délestage* (rack-and-return) means running the juice completely out of the tank, and then pouring it over the cap (which has fallen to the bottom of the vat)

- *Chaptalization* is the addition of sugar before or during fermentation. The sugar is converted into alcohol, so the result is to strengthen the alcoholic level of the wine, not to sweeten it.

- A *cuve* is a large vat of neutral material—old wood, concrete, or stainless steel.

- *Cuvaison* is the period a wine spends in contact with the grape skins.

- *Battonage* describes stirring up the wine when it is aging (usually) in cask.

- *Soutirage* (racking) transfers the wine (without the lees) from one barrique to another.

- *Élevage* is the aging of wine after fermentation has been completed.

- *Malo* is an abbreviation for malolactic fermentation, performed after the alcoholic fermentation. It reduces acidity, and is almost always done with red wines, and often for non-aromatic white wines.

- A *vin de garde* is a wine intended for long aging.

Aging in oak

- A *fût* (*de chêne*) is an oak barrel of unspecified size.

- A *barrique* (in Bordeaux or elsewhere) has 225 liters or 228 liters (called a *pièce* in Burgundy).

- *Tonneau* is an old term for a 900 liter container, sometimes used colloquially for containers larger than barriques, most often 500 or 600 liter.

- A *demi-muid* is a 600 liter barrel.

- A *foudre* is a large oak cask, round or oval, from 20-100 hl.

Index of Estates by Rating

Jean Collet et Fils
Domaine Comte Senard
Domaine Daniel Dampt et fils
Jean et Sébastien Dauvissat
Domaine Drouhin-Vaudon
Domaine David Duband
Domaine Nathalie et Gilles Fèvre
Domaine Jean Fournier
Domaine Jean-Noël Gagnard
Maison Alex Gambal
Domaine Garnier et Fils
Domaine Henri Germain et fils
Domaine Guilhem & Jean-Hugues Goisot
Domaine Corinne et Jean Pierre Grossot
Domaine Hoffmann-Jayer
Maison P. et M. Jacqueson
Domaine Joblot
Domaine Michel Juillot
Domaine Michel Lafarge
Domaine Héritiers du Comte Lafon
Domaine Hubert Lamy
Maison Louis Latour
Domaine Philippe Leclerc
Domaine Leflaive
Maison Olivier Leflaive Frères
Maison Benjamin Leroux
Domaine Long-Depaquit
Domaine Bruno Lorenzon
Domaine François Lumpp

Domaine Michel Magnien
Domaine des Malandes
La Manufacture
Marchand-Tawse
Domaine Louis Moreau
Domaine Sylvain Pataille
Domaine Pattes Loup
Domaine Gilbert Picq et Fils
Domaine Jean-Marc Pillot
Domaine Pinson Frères
Patrick Piuze
L & C Poitout
Domaine de La Pousse d'Or
Domaine Jacques Prieur
Domaine Denis Race
Domaine Rapet Père et Fils
Domaine François Raquillet
Remoissenet Père et Fils
Domaine Servin
Maison Simonnet-Febvre
Domaine La Soufrandière
Domaine de la Bongran-Gillet
Domaine Thibert Père et Fils
Domaine Tollot-Beaut et Fils
Domaine des Vignes du Maynes
Domaine Aubert et Pamela De Villaine
Domaine Anne-Marie et Jean-Marc Vincent
Domaine de La Vougeraie
Domaine Vrignaud

Index of Organic and Biodynamic Estates

Domaine Thibault Liger-Belair
Domaine Hubert Lignier
Domaine Bruno Lorenzon
Bertrand & Axelle Machard de Gramont
Domaine Michel Magnien
Domaine des Malandes
La Manufacture
Marchand-Tawse
Domaine Alain Mathias
Château de Messey
Domaine Louis Michel
Domaine François Mikulski
Château de Monthelie
Domaine Hubert de Montille
Domaine Olivier et Alice De Moor
Domaine Gilles Morat
Domaine Christian Moreau Père et Fils
Éléonore Moreau
Domaine Moreau-Naudet
Domaine Morey-Coffinet
Domaine Pierre Morey
Domaine Thomas Morey
Domaine Nicolas Maillet
Domaine Ninot
Domaine Parent
Domaine Pattes Loup
Domaine Henri Perrot-Minot
Château de Pommard
Domaine Isabelle et Denis Pommier
Domaine de La Pousse d'Or
Domaine Jacques Prieur
Domaine Prieuré-Roch
Château des Quarts
Domaine Henri Rebourseau
Domaine Michèle et Patrice Rion
Domaine Roblet-Monnot
Domaine de La Romanée-Conti
Château des Rontets
Domaine Rossignol-Trapet
Domaine Guy Roulot
Domaine Sainte Barbe
Domaine du Clos Salomon
Domaine de la Sarazinière
Domaine Jacques Saumaize
Domaine Saumaize-Michelin

Domaine Étienne Sauzet
Domaine Seguin-Manuel
Domaine La Soufrandière
Domaine du Clos de Tart
Domaine Taupenot-Merme
Domaine de Thalie
Domaine de la Bongran-Gillet
Domaine du Château de la Tour
Domaine Trapet Père et Fils
Domaine Cécile Tremblay
Maison Céline et Laurent Tripoz
Domaine des Vignes du Maynes
Domaine Vigot Fabrice
Domaine Aubert et Pamela De Villaine
Domaine Thierry Violot-Guillemard
Domaine de La Vougeraie
Domaine Vrignaud

Producers Making Natural Wines or Wines With No Sulfur

Domaine Simon Bize
Domaine Christophe Buisson
Domaine Henri et Gilles Buisson
Domaine du Chardonnay
Domaine de Chassorney
Clos des Rocs
Domaine des Croix
Domaine Fourrier
Domaine Céline et Frédéric Gueguen
Domaine Guillemot-Michel
Domaine d'Henri
Domaine de la Croix Senaillet
Marchand-Tawse
Domaine Olivier et Alice De Moor
Domaine Thomas Morey
Philippe Pacalet
Domaine Ponsot
Domaine Prieuré-Roch
Domaine des Vignes du Maynes
Domaine Anne-Marie et Jean-Marc Vincent

Index of Estates by Appellation

Aloxe Corton
Domaine Chapuis
Domaine Comte Senard
Domaine Follin-Arbelet
Maison Louis Latour

Beaune
Domaine de Bellene
Olivier Bernstein
Maison Albert Bichot
Maison Bouchard Aîné et Fils
Domaine Bouchard Père et Fils
Maison Camille Giroud
Maison Champy
Chanson Père Et Fils
Domaine des Croix
Maison Joseph Drouhin
Maison Alex Gambal
Maison Louis Jadot
Lucien Le Moine
Maison Benjamin Leroux
Domaine Newman
Philippe Pacalet
Remoissenet Père et Fils
Domaine Seguin-Manuel

Bouzeron
Maison Chanzy
Domaine Aubert et Pamela De Villaine

Chablis
Domaine Alexandre
Domaine Jérémy Arnaud
Domaine Barat
Domaine Beaufumé
Domaine Begue-Mathiot
Château de Béru
Domaine Jean-Claude et Romain Bessin
Domaine Besson
Domaine Samuel Billaud
Domaine Billaud Simon
Jean-Marc Brocard
La Chablisienne
Domaine de Chantemerle
Domaine du Chardonnay
Domaine de Chaude Ecuelle
Domaine des Chaumes
Domaine Michel Colbois
Jean Collet et Fils
Domaine du Colombier
Domaines Courtault & Michelet
Domaine Daniel Dampt et fils
Vignoble Dampt Frères
Domaine Sébastien Dampt
Domaine Agnès et Didier Dauvissat
Domaine Jean Dauvissat Père et Fils

Jean et Sébastien Dauvissat
Domaine Vincent Dauvissat
Clotilde Davenne
Domaine Bernard Defaix
Domaine Daniel-Etienne Defaix
Domaine Christophe et fils
Domaine Jean-Paul et Benoît Droin
Domaine Drouhin-Vaudon
Domaine Gérard Duplessis
Domaine Jean Durup Père et Fils
Domaine d'Elise
Domaine de l'Enclos
Domaine Nathalie et Gilles Fèvre
Domaine William Fèvre
Domaine du Château de Fleys
Domaine Garnier et Fils
Domaine Alain et Cyril Gautheron
Domaine Alain Geoffroy
Domaine Guilhem & Jean-Hugues Goisot
Domaine Jean Goulley et Fils
Domaine Corinne et Jean Pierre Grossot
Domaine Céline et Frédéric Gueguen
Domaine Hamelin
Domaine des Hâtes
Domaine d'Henri
Domaine Jean Jacquin et fils
Domaine Jolly et fils
Domaine Lamblin et Fils
Domaine Laroche
Domaine Roland Lavantureux
Domaine Long-Depaquit
Domaine des Malandes
La Manufacture
Domaine des Marronniers
Domaine Alain Mathias
Domaine de la Meulière
Domaine Louis Michel
Domaine Millet
Domaine Olivier et Alice De Moor
Maison J. Moreau et Fils
Domaine Christian Moreau Père et Fils
Éléonore Moreau
Domaine Louis Moreau
Domaine Moreau-Naudet
Domaine Mosnier
Domaine de la Motte
Domaine Charly Nicolle
Laurent et Céline Notton
Domaine De Oliveira Lecestre
Domaine Oudin
Domaine Christophe Patrice
Domaine Pattes Loup
Domaine de Perdrycourt

Domaine Gilbert Picq et Fils
Domaine Pinson Frères
Patrick Piuze
L & C Poitout
Domaine Isabelle et Denis Pommier
Domaine Denis Race
Domaine François Raveneau
Maison Regnard
Domaine Guy Robin et Fils
Domaine Roy
. Famille Savary
Camille et Laurent Schaller
Domaine Séguinot Bordet
Domaine Daniel Séguinot
Domaine Servin
Maison Simonnet-Febvre
Domaine Soupé
Domaine Testut
Domaine Tixier
Domaine de La Tour
Domaine Gérard Tremblay
Domaine Laurent Tribut
Domaine de Vauroux
Venon et Fils
Domaine Ventoura
Maison Verget
Domaine Vocoret et Fils
Domaine Eleni et Édouard Vocoret
Domaine Yvon et Laurent Vocoret
Domaine Vrignaud
Domaine Vincent Wengier

Chambolle Musigny
Domaine Amiot-Servelle
Domaine Ghislaine Barthod
Domaine Louis Boillot et Fils
Domaine Hudelot-Noëllat
Domaine Jacques Frédéric Mugnier
Domaine Georges Roumier
Domaine Anne et Hervé Sigaut
Domaine Comte Georges de Vogüé

Chassagne Montrachet
Domaine Guy Amiot et Fils
Domaine Vincent Bachelet
Domaine Jean-Marc Blain Gagnard
Domaine Bruno Colin
Domaine Colin-Deléger
Domaine Pierre-Yves Colin-Morey
Domaine Philippe Colin
Domaine Vincent Dancer
Domaine Fontaine-Gagnard
Domaine Gagnard-Delagrange
Domaine Jean-Noël Gagnard
Domaine Heitz-Lochardet
Domaine Château de la Maltroye
Domaine Bernard Moreau et Fils

Domaine Morey-Coffinet
Domaine Thomas Morey
Domaine Vincent and Sophie Morey
Domaine Michel Niellon
Domaine Paul Pillot
Domaine Fernand et Laurent Pillot
Domaine Jean-Marc Pillot
Domaine Ramonet

Chorey-lès-Beaune
Maillard Père et Fils
Domaine Tollot-Beaut et Fils

Fixin
Domaine Berthaut-Gerbet
Domaine Pierre Gelin
Domaine Joliet Père et Fils
Domaine Philippe Naddef

Flagey-Echézeaux
Domaine Emmanuel Rouget

Gevrey Chambertin
Domaine Bachelet
Pierre Bourée Fils
Domaine René Bouvier
Domaine Alain Burguet
Domaine Camus Père et Fils
Domaine Philippe Charlopin-Parizot
Domaine des Chézeaux
Domaine Pierre Damoy
Domaine Drouhin-Laroze
Domaine Claude Dugat
Domaine Bernard Dugat-Py
Domaine Dupont-Tisserandot
Domaine Gilles Duroché
Domaine Sylvie Esmonin
Domaine Fourrier
Domaine Jérôme Galeyrand
Domaine Geantet-Pansiot
Domaine Le Guellec-Ducouet
Domaine Harmand-Geoffroy
Domaine Heresztyn-Mazzini
Domaine Humbert Frères
Domaine Philippe Leclerc
Domaine Philippe Livera
Domaine Denis Mortet
Domaine Henri Rebourseau
René Leclerc
Domaine Philippe Rossignol
Domaine Rossignol-Trapet
Domaine Joseph Roty
Domaine Armand Rousseau
Domaine Sérafin Père et Fils
Domaine Trapet Père et Fils
Domaine des Varoilles

Givry
Domaine Besson
Domaine du Cellier aux Moines

Domaine Chofflet-Valdenaire
Domaine Joblot
Domaine François Lumpp
Domaine Vincent Lumpp
Domaine Laurent Mouton
Domaine Ragot
Domaine du Clos Salomon
Domaine Michel Sarrazin et Fils
Domaine Baron Thénard

Hautes Côtes de Nuits
Domaine Hoffmann-Jayer

Ladoix-Serrigny
Edmond Cornu et Fils
Domaine Michel Mallard et Fils
Domaine Nudant

Mâcon
Domaine Guillot-Broux
Domaine Héritiers du Comte Lafon
Château de Messey
Domaine de Thalie
Maison Verget
Domaine des Vignes du Maynes

Mâcon Charnay les Mâcon
Domaine Jean Manciat
Maison Trénel et Fils

Mâcon Igé
Domaine Fichet

Mâcon La Roche Vineuse
Domaine Merlin
Domaine Sylvaine & Alain Normand

Mâcon Loché
Maison Céline et Laurent Tripoz

Mâcon Pierreclos
Domaine Frantz Chagnoleau
Domaine Marc Jambon et Fils

Mâcon Uchizy
Domaine Gérald Talmard

Mâcon Verzé
Domaine Leflaive
Domaine Nicolas Maillet

Mâcon Villages
Domaine David Bienfait
Domaine de la Sarazinière

Maranges
Domaine Bachelet Monnot
Domaine Chevrot et Fils

Marsannay-la-Côte
Domaine Bart
Domaine Bruno Clair
Domaine Jean Fournier
Domaine Huguenot Père et fils
Domaine du Château de Marsannay
Domaine Sylvain Pataille

Mercurey
Château de Chamilly
Château de Chamirey
Domaine de l'Évêché
Domaine la Ferté
Domaine Gouffier
Domaine Jeannin-Naltet
Domaine Michel Juillot
Domaine Bruno Lorenzon
Domaine du Meix Foulot
Domaine François Raquillet
Maison Antonin Rodet
Château de Santenay
Domaine de Suremain
Domaine Theulot-Juillot
Domaine Tupinier-Bautista

Meursault
Domaine Robert Ampeau et Fils
Domaine D'Auvenay
Domaine Ballot-Millot & Fils
Domaine Bernard Boisson-Vadot
Domaine Bouzereau-Gruère et Filles
Domaine Michel Bouzereau et Fils
Domaine Yves Boyer-Martenot
Domaine Buisson-Charles
Domaine Jean-François Coche Dury
Domaine Arnaud Ente
Domaine Jean-Philippe Fichet
Domaine Jean-Michel Gaunoux
Domaine Génot Boulanger
Domaine Henri Germain et fils
Maison Vincent Girardin
Domaine Albert Grivault
Domaine Huber-Verdereau
Domaine Patrick Javillier
Domaine Antoine Jobard
Domaine Rémi Jobard
Domaine Comtes Lafon
Domaine Latour-Giraud
Domaine Matrot
Domaine du Château de Meursault
Domaine François Mikulski
Domaine Bernard Millot
Domaine Xavier Monnot
Domaine Pierre Morey
Domaine Jacques Prieur
Domaine Guy Roulot

Montagny
Domaine Stéphane Aladame
Domaine Berthenet
Cave des Vignerons de Buxy
Domaine Laurent Cognard
Domaine Feuillat-Juillot
Domaine Masse Père et Fils

Monthélie
Domaine Darviot Perrin

Domaine Dujardin
Château de Monthelie

Morey St. Denis

Domaine Arlaud
Domaine Castagnier
Domaine Dujac
Domaine Robert Groffier Père Et Fils
Domaine des Lambrays
Domaine Georges Lignier et Fils
Domaine Hubert Lignier
Domaine Michel Magnien
Domaine Henri Perrot-Minot
Domaine Ponsot
Domaine Chantal Rémy
Domaine du Clos de Tart
Domaine Taupenot-Merme
Domaine Cécile Tremblay

Nuits St. Georges

Domaine d'Ardhuy
Domaine de l'Arlot
Maison Jean-Claude Boisset
Domaine Jérôme Chezeaux
Domaine Georges Chicotot
Domaine Jean-Jacques Confuron
Domaine David Duband
Domaine Guy & Yvan Dufouleur
Domaine Faiveley
Domaine Didier Fornerol
Domaine Henri Gouges
Domaine Jean Chauvenet
Maison Dominique Laurent
Domaine Philippe et Vincent Lécheneaut
Domaine Chantal Lescure
Domaine Thibault Liger-Belair
Maison Lupé-Cholet
Bertrand & Axelle Machard de Gramont
Domaine Machard de Gramont
Marchand-Tawse
Maison Louis Max
Domaine Alain Michelot
Domaine des Perdrix
Laurent Ponsot
Domaine Prieuré-Roch
Domaine Daniel Rion et Fils
Domaine Michèle et Patrice Rion
Domaine Robert Chevillon
Domaine de La Vougeraie

Pernand Vergelesses

Domaine Aurélie Berthod
Domaine Bonneau du Martray
Domaine Rapet Père et Fils

Pommard

Domaine Jean-Marc Boillot
Domaine Comte Armand
Domaine de Courcel

Domaine Michel Gaunoux
Domaine Aleth Girardin
Domaine A. F Gros
Domaine Lejeune
Domaine Parent
Château de Pommard
Domaine Thierry Violot-Guillemard

Pouilly-Fuissé

Maison Auvigue
Domaine Daniel et Martine Barraud
Château de Beauregard
Domaine Carrette
Domaine du Chalet Pouilly
Château du Clos
Domaine Cordier Père et Fils
Domaine Dominique Cornin
Domaine de la Denante
Domaine Robert-Denogent
Domaine Denuziller
Domaine des Deux Roches
Domaine J.-A. Ferret
Éric Forest
Château-Fuissé
Domaine Giroux
Domaine Guerrin et fils
Domaine Denis Jeandeau
Domaine de la Croix Senaillet
Domaine Lassarat et fils
Domaine Gilles Morat
Domaine Gilles Noblet
Château de Pouilly
Château des Quarts
Domaine Pascal Renaud
Vins Rijckaert
Domaine Roc des Boutires
Château des Rontets
Domaine Jacques Saumaize
Domaine Saumaize-Michelin
Domaine La Soufrandise
Domaine Thibert Père et Fils
Domaine Pierre Vessigaud Père et Fils
Château Vitallis

Pouilly-Loche

Clos des Rocs

Pouilly-Vinzelles

Domaine La Soufrandière

Puligny Montrachet

Domaine Henri Boillot
Domaine François Carillon
Domaine Jacques Carillon
Domaine Jean Chartron
Maison Chartron et Trébuchet
Domaine Alain Chavy
Domaine Comtesse de Chérisey
Domaine Benoît Ente

Domaine Leflaive
Maison Olivier Leflaive Frères
Domaine Paul Pernot
Domaine Étienne Sauzet

Rully

Domaine Michel Briday
Domaine Vincent Dureuil-Janthial
Domaine de la Folie
Maison P. et M. Jacqueson
Maison André Delorme
Domaine Ninot
Domaine Jean Baptiste Ponsot
Domaine Rois Mages

Saint-Aubin

Domaine Marc Colin et Fils
Domaine Hubert Lamy
Sylvain Langoureau
Domaine Henri Prudhon et Fils
Domaine Gérard Thomas et Filles

Saint-Romain

Domaine Christophe Buisson
Domaine Henri et Gilles Buisson
Domaine de Chassorney
Domaine Alain Gras

Santenay

Domaine Françoise et Denis Clair
Domaine Jessiaume
Domaine Louis Lequin
Domaine Lucien Muzard et Fils
Domaine Anne-Marie et Jean-Marc Vincent

Savigny-lès-Beaune

Domaine Simon Bize
Domaine Chandon de Briailles
Domaine Clos de la Chapelle
Domaine Louis Chenu et Filles
Domaine Cruchandeau
Domaine Antonin Guyon
Domaine Jean-Marc & Hugues Pavelot
Maison Henri de Villamont

Viré-Clessé

Domaine André Bonhomme
Domaine Guillemot-Michel

Domaine Robert et Marielle Marin
Domaine Michel
Domaine Jean-Pierre Michel
Domaine Sainte Barbe
Domaine de la Bongran-Gillet

Volnay

Domaine Marquis d'Angerville
Domaine Bitouzet-Prieur
Domaine Jean-Marc Bouley
Domaine Pascal Bouley
Domaine Yvon Clerget
Domaine Georges Glantenay et fils
Domaine Michel Lafarge
Domaine Hubert de Montille
Domaine de La Pousse d'Or
Domaine Roblet-Monnot
Nicolas Rossignol
Domaine Christophe & Pierre Vaudoisey
Domaine Joseph Voillot

Vosne Romanée

Domaine Arnoux-Lachaux
Domaine Sylvain Cathiard
Domaine Bruno Clavelier
Domaine J. Confuron-Cotetidot
Domaine d'Eugénie
Domaine Forey Père et Fils
Domaine Jean Grivot
Domaine Anne Gros
Domaine François Lamarche
Domaine Leroy
Domaine du Comte Liger-Belair
Domaine Méo-Camuzet
Domaine Mongeard-Mugneret
Domaine Georges Mugneret-Gibourg
Vignoble Georges Noëllat
Domaine Michel Noëllat
Domaine de La Romanée-Conti
Domaine Vigot Fabrice

Vougeot

Domaine Bertagna
Domaine du Château de la Tour

Index of Estates by Name

Printed in Great Britain
by Amazon